The Definitive Guide to Plone

ANDY MCKAY

The Definitive Guide to Plone
Copyright © 2004 by Andy McKay

ISBN (pbk): 1-59059-329-4

Printed and bound in the United States of America 9 8 7 6 5 4 3 2 1

Trademarked names may appear in this book. Rather than use a trademark symbol with every occurrence of a trademarked name, we use the names only in an editorial fashion and to the benefit of the trademark owner, with no intention of infringement of the trademark.

Lead Editor: Dominic Shakeshaft

Technical Reviewer: Michel Pelletier

Editorial Board: Steve Anglin, Dan Appleman, Ewan Buckingham, Gary Cornell, Tony Davis, John Franklin, Jason Gilmore, Chris Mills, Steve Rycroft, Dominic Shakeshaft, Jim Sumser, Karen Watterson, Gavin Wray, John Zukowski

Project Manager: Beth Christmas

Copy Edit Manager: Nicole LeClerc

Copy Editor: Kim Wimpsett

Production Manager: Kari Brooks

Production Editor: Janet Vail

Compositor: Susan Glinert

Proofreader: Christy Wagner

Indexer: Valerie Robbins

Artist: Kinetic Publishing Services, LLC

Cover Designer: Kurt Krames

Manufacturing Manager: Tom Debolski

Distributed to the book trade in the United States by Springer-Verlag New York, Inc., 175 Fifth Avenue, New York, NY 10010 and outside the United States by Springer-Verlag GmbH & Co. KG, Tiergartenstr. 17, 69112 Heidelberg, Germany.

In the United States: phone 1-800-SPRINGER, e-mail orders@springer-ny.com, or visit http://www.springer-ny.com. Outside the United States: fax +49 6221 345229, e-mail orders@springer.de, or visit http://www.springer.de.

For information on translations, please contact Apress directly at 2560 Ninth Street, Suite 219, Berkeley, CA 94710. Phone 510-549-5930, fax 510-549-5939, e-mail info@apress.com, or visit http://www.apress.com.

The source code for this book is available to readers at http://www.apress.com in the Downloads section.

Contents at a Glance

Contents

Foreword

MAY 2004—I'm on a flight to Las Vegas, Nevada, to announce at CA World 2004 the formation of the nonprofit Plone Foundation. Whilst on the plane, I'm also writing this foreword for the book—something I'm excited to see released as open source. Both are pieces in the bigger jigsaw puzzle of Plone, and I'm thrilled to see the holes in the puzzle being filled.

Over the past two weeks, the focus of the Plone community has moved from purely technical to much more unfamiliar territory: marketing. The Las Vegas trip will end with Computer Associates announcing that it's sponsoring the Plone Foundation. All of this will happen about three years after Alexander Limi and I first released what would become Plone. As Bill Hicks once said, "Who woulda thunk it?"

In May 2001, the startup company that I was the second employee at grew from 3 people to 160 people and then submerged under top heaviness, in both the development cycle (J2EE on every project) and the increasingly large management. I saw the handwriting on the wall. During the death throes, I practiced Python. I had been using Zope on our intranet and was fascinated by the software for several years (since International Python Conference 8). I thought Python was the only way I could accomplish the projects I was going to take on in my new life as a consultant.

As we were doing inventory during the day to sell off the company, at night I was writing Python code and lollygagging in the #zope channel. I met Alex in IRC (on #zope), and during our exchanges we decided that nothing in the world of Zope was near presentable to a customer. There was no polish. Alex—being in tune with usability and interface design—loathed the existing out-of-the-box Zope projects. I had a miserable time trying to sell developers on Zope because of the lack of pizzazz. We vowed we would make a user interface for Zope that would attract the world to the wonderful infrastructure it provided.

This is where I think Plone's pace and success was formed. Any sort of project requires momentum from the participants to keep rolling. Vidar Anderson created a mock-up of the proposed user interface, Alexander tweaked it and turned it into HTML, and I integrated the HTML into the code. This all occurred in about a 72-hour period. We went back and forth with the code for about two months. Different parts naturally fell into place. We had no master plan—it just consisted of fun and peer review. I think this productive/creative cycle of interaction between Alex and me provided enough feedback and stimuli to keep our involvement. When Alex disappeared for a month, I kept at it. When I dropped out of sight for a few weeks, he kept the project moving. We always kept the momentum of the project and understood that any long cessation would most likely spiral the project into abandonment or neglect.

We got our first contributor within three months of releasing some software. Now we have approximately 60 contributors. The mailing lists have so much traffic on them that it's impossible for me to keep up and do my regular job. We now have more than 35 translations of the user interface in different languages. We now have *sprints* (a term coined by Tres Seaver from Zope Corporation) all over the world where developers work on projects related to Plone and Zope, which moves Plone forward. We now have a foundation to ensure the longevity of the project. And, finally, we have corporate sponsorship, both large and small, to ensure that the foundation's vision can be realized.

The second Plone Conference will take place in September 2004 in Vienna, Austria. Wow.

Many people have helped paddle the Plone boat down the stream. But the momentum now has been transferred from developers to end users and business development. Only with documentation such as *The Definitive Guide to Plone* can the software be adopted on a larger scale. It isn't the existing audience of Plone we must serve—it's tomorrow's audience and newbies who must be more easily bootstrapped into being productive users and customizers of Plone. I think that with the current state of the project and supporting efforts such as this book, by the end of 2004 we'll be a unique project in the open-source landscape that focuses on business and user adoption and lets development fill in the cracks to ease the next generations of converts.

Alan Runyan
Plone Cofounder

About the Author

Andy McKay has been building Web sites for more than six years and developing in Python for the past three years. Andy has a degree in economics from Bath University and has taken postgraduate courses at the British Columbia Institute of Technology. He started his career at ActiveState, where he got lured into the world of Zope and Python.

As a Plone developer and Zope contributor, he has made many key offerings to the projects. For the past three years, he has gone by the alias of *zopista* on his Weblog at http://www.zopezen.org. When not kayaking rivers, he can be found walking his dog.

About the Technical Reviewer

Michel Pelletier is a Zope, Python, and Java programmer and the coauthor of the Zope Book and several magazine articles about Zope and Python. Michel lives and works in Portland, Oregon, where he does consulting, technical writing, and volunteer work in his spare time.

Acknowledgments

As with all good open-source projects, this book has a cast of thousands. The list could be long; you have my apologies if I've left out anyone. Those titans of the open-source CMS world, Alexander Limi and Alan Runyan, provided us with a product and a community, and they supported me throughout the book. Laura Trippi got me into Plone, so she will always take some blame for that.

Other contributors include Paul Everitt, Ben Saller, Kapil Thangavelu, Chris McDonough, Geoff Davis, Joel Burton, Jim Roepcke, the Victoria sprint gang, Jodok and the Austria sprint gang, Philipp Auersperg, the NASA Maestro team, Alma Ong, Michael Zeltner, Joe Geldart, Tom Croucher, Brad Bollenbach, Sidnei da Silva, Fabiano Wiemar dos Santos, Andreas Jung, and many more. Thanks also to David Ascher, Paul Prescod, and Scott Robertson, who put me on the straight and narrow about the publishing business.

The Apress gang of Beth Christmas, Kim Wimpsett, and Janet Vail got me through the production stage and kept the deadlines happening. Dominic Shakeshaft provided the help, guidance, and support I needed to make sense of all this and get the book out the door. Michel Pelletier did the technical review and did a great job of it, too. Joel Burton helped out a lot—but unfortunately not enough!

Of course, none of this would have been possible without the eternal support, patience, and devotion from my wife Danae. Near the end of writing this book, we were delivered the greatest present ever—our daughter, Emily Constance. It will be a while until this will be more than a doorstop for you, Emily, but this book is dedicated to you.

Introducing Plone

A COMPANY WITHOUT a Web site is unthinkable—and most companies and organizations have more than one site. Whether it's an external site for communicating with clients, an intranet for employees to use, or a site for direct client communication and feedback, all Web sites have a common problem—how to manage the content on them. This is a challenge that can often cost organizations large amounts of time and effort. Producing a powerful yet flexible system for these sites that meets ever-changing requirements while growing to meet your company's emerging needs isn't easy.

No matter what the requirements for your Web site are or the amount of content or users, Plone is a user-friendly, powerful solution that lets you easily add and edit any type of content through the Web, produce navigation and searches for that content, and apply security and workflow to that content.

Plone enables you to put together almost any Web site and easily update it. This lets you build content-rich sites quickly so you can gain a competitive advantage. Finally, probably the best things about this system are that it's free and it's open source. With its large and impressive feature set, it's comparable to, if not better than, many closed-source content management systems that cost hundreds of thousands of dollars.

Mike Sugarbaker says the following when reporting on the Open Source Content Management Conference (OSCOM) in 2002 for the Mindjack site (http://www.mindjack.com/events/oscom.html):

> I won't do the complete rundown of all the "competing" open-source content management frameworks. I'll cut to the chase: The winner is Plone. This "productized" take on the six-year-old web application framework Zope was the package with the most tools, the most professionalism, the most traction, and, above all, the most buzz.

You can find the Plone Web site at http://www.plone.org, as shown in Figure 1-1. To try Plone easily, a demonstration site is available at http://demo.plone.org. There you can quickly and easily add and edit content through the Web. Specifically, you can add events, upload pictures, add documents, and process them all through the framework that Plone provides.

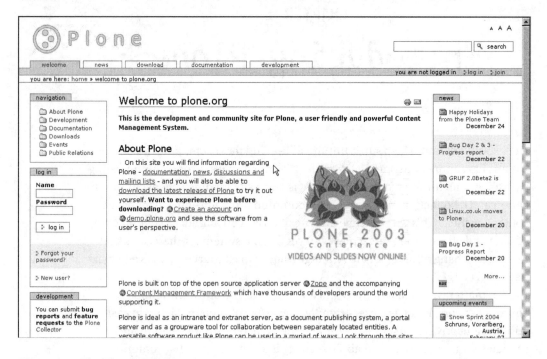

Figure 1-1. The Plone Web site

What Is a Content Management System?

One simple definition for a Content Management System (CMS) is that it's a system for managing content. This is a rather unhelpful definition, so I'll break it down into smaller parts for a fuller explanation. I'll start with a broad definition of *content*: Content is a unit of data with some extra information attached to it. That piece of data could be a Web page, information about an upcoming event, a Microsoft Word document, an image, a movie clip, or any piece of data that has meaning to the organization deploying the system.

All these items are called *content*, and they all share similar attributes, such as the need to be added or edited by certain users and be published in various ways. A system called *workflow* controls these attributes. Workflow is logic defined by the organization's business rules, and it describes a system for managing the content.

Historically there has been a difference between document management systems and CMSs, but mostly these two systems have converged. The essential difference is the items being managed; it's often considered that *content* is any unit of information, and a *document* refers to something that's created and edited by humans using software such as Microsoft Office. Take, for example, a book: A book contains many units of data and may require management slightly different from that required by content. However, in most cases, this is a small difference, and products such as Plone are able to manage the small units of a larger piece of content and reassemble them.

With the ubiquitousness of the Web, many CMSs are now classified as Web CMSs, either because they have a Web-based interface or because they focus on a Web-based delivery system over the Internet or an intranet. Plone provides a Web management interface and Web-based delivery system.

The following is one definition of a CMS (`http://www.contentmanager.eu.com/history.htm`):

> *A CMS is a tool that enables a variety of (centralized) technical and (decentralized) nontechnical staff to create, edit, manage, and finally publish a variety of content (such as text, graphics, video, and so on) whilst being constrained by a centralized set of rules, process, and workflows that ensure a coherent, validated Web site appearance.*

Do You Want a Content Management System?

Although not the only advantage of a CMS, the most obvious benefit of a CMS is coordinating a Web site easily. Take a situation where one person, a *Webmaster*, coordinates a Web site, either an intranet or an external site. Content comes from users in a variety of formats, and the Webmaster turns these into usable Web pages by converting them to Hypertext Markup Language (HTML). If a user has to change those pages, then the user sends the changes to the Webmaster, who changes the pages, and so on.

This presents many problems for the organization, the biggest being that all content is flowing through one person—an obvious bottleneck. That one person can do only so much work, and if that person is sick or leaves the company, a great deal of productivity is lost in finding a replacement. The publishing process can be quite frustrating as e-mails fly between the Webmaster and the user trying to get content published.

What's needed is a system that does the following:

Separates the content of a page from the presentation: If the actual content is separate from the presentation method, then the content author doesn't need to know any HTML or how the page is delivered. In fact, one piece of content could have many different templates applied to it, including formats other than HTML, such as Portable Document Format (PDF) or Scalable Vector Graphics (SVG). When you want to change the look and feel of the site, you have to change only that one template rather than all the content.

Allows certain users to add and edit content: If specified users can add and edit content easily, then there's no need to send content to the Webmaster or Web team. Instead, the user who wants to create a page can do so and edit it as much as necessary.

Applies rules to whom can publish what and when: Your business rules might not want just anybody publishing content on your Web site; for example, people in marketing would be able to publish to the press release part of the site and not to the engineering section.

Can apply business rules to content: If a person from marketing creates a press release, somebody in legal might need to review that document. In this case, the document will be passed through a review process that ensures it won't go live until these reviews are done.

Can search and index information intelligently: Since the CMS can keep track of structured information about the content (such as author's name, publication date, modification dates, categories, and so on), it can produce listings of content by author, recent content, and so on. It can also provide searching capabilities that are much smarter and more useful than just a simple textual search.

Although this example portrays paybacks that are more significant for large organizations, organizations of all levels benefit from this approach. In fact, typically small organizations that don't employ a full-time Webmaster can be one of the key beneficiaries of such a system. By installing a CMS, you can resolve all these issues and more.

The key factor of any CMS is that it provides a clear separation of the key elements in it: security, workflow, templates, and so on. For example, the templates presenting an item are separate from the content. This allows you to easily modify the presentation.

Introducing Plone's Features

Plone is open source, licensed under the General Public License (GPL), which is a common open-source license that allows anyone to use the source for free. For more information about the GPL, go to the Free Software Foundation Web site at http://ww.gnu.org. You can examine any aspect of Plone's code and alter it to fit your application. There are no licensing fees to pay, there's no license that will expire, and all the code is visible. This open-source philosophy means that Plone already has a large user base and legion of developers, usability experts, translators, technical writers, and graphic designers who are able to work *on* Plone. By choosing Plone, you're not locked into one company; rather, nearly a dozen companies offer different Plone services.

Packaging

Plone maintains easy installers for Windows, Linux, and Mac. Other third-party products and add-ons also come with the installers. Maintaining quality releases of these products makes installation and management easy. Also, each new release maintains migration paths and updates so that your Plone site will keep working and stay up to date.

Internationalization

The whole Plone user interface is translated into more than 20 languages, including Korean, Japanese, French, Spanish, and German. Inserting your own translation is easy (see Chapter 4).

Usability

Plone offers an excellent user experience that provides high levels of usability and accessibility. This isn't just a matter of presenting pretty HTML but instead goes to the core of Plone. Plone provides an interface that's compatible with the industry and government standard WAI-AAA and U.S. Section 508. This allows sites built with Plone to be used by people with vision disabilities. In addition, this provides the unexpected but related benefit that your page may index better in search engines such as Google.

Skinnable

Plone separates the content from the actual templates used to present the content, often called *skins*. The skins are written in the excellent HTML templating system, Zope Page Templates, and a large amount of Cascading Style Sheets (CSS). With little knowledge of Plone, you can apply multiple skins, achieve multiple looks, and totally customize your Web site's appearance.

Registration and Personalization

Plone features a complete user registration system. Users register with a Plone site using their own username, password, and any other information you might want to add about the user. You can then personalize the whole user interface for that user. In addition, with add-ons, you can use information you already have

5

about users, coming from many places, such as relational databases, Lightweight Directory Access Protocol (LDAP), Active Directory, and more. Chapter 8 covers how to register and configure users.

Workflow and Security

Workflow controls the logic of processing content through the site. You can configure this logic through the Web using graphical tools. Site administrators can make sites as complex or as simple as they'd like; for example, you can add notification tools such as sending e-mails or instant messages to users. Chapter 8 covers workflow in great detail.

For every item of content in a Plone site, you can set up access control lists to decide who has access to that item and how they'll be able to interact with it. Will they be able to edit it, view it, or comment on it? All this is configurable through the Web (see Chapter 9).

Extensible

Since Plone is open source, it can be easily altered. You can change and configure almost any aspect of Plone to suit your needs. Countless packages and tools for Plone provide a wide array of options for smaller sites and for large-scale enterprises. Repositories of free add-ons for Plone are available at http://www.plone.org. With development tools such as Archetypes (covered in Chapter 13), you can generate and alter Plone code easily through the Web or using Unified Modeling Language (UML) tools. Chapter 10 covers integration of Plone with enterprise solutions such as LDAP, Apache, Microsoft Internet Information Services (IIS), Macromedia Dreamweaver, and so on.

Content Customization

Users of a Plone site can add all manner of content, but the data added isn't limited or constrained. Plone developers can create their own content types so that almost any type of content can be managed; the only limit is your own imagination. In Chapters 11 and 12, I'll discuss how to customize the content types. Chapter 13 will introduce Archetypes, which is a very powerful system for generating content types that don't require programming; for instance, you can generate new types of content from UML tools.

Documentation

The Plone project maintains documentation, including this book, which is published under the Creative Commons license. The best starting place for the community documentation is at http://www.plone.org/documentation.

Community

One of the best things about Plone is the community of developers and companies that supports and develops Plone. With more than 60 developers involved to some degree in the project around the world, it's almost always possible to find a Plone developer online who is willing and able to help you. Alan Runyan, Alexander Limi, and Vidar Andersen started Plone; however, it quickly grew into a thriving open-source project as more developers became involved. The contributions from these developers form the Plone product that's now available.

Example Plone Sites

Many Plone sites exist; some are obvious because of their looks, and some aren't. The following is just a small sample of the more diverse sites:

- **Plone** (http://www.plone.org): The definitive Plone site that provides all you'll ever want to know about Plone, including documentation and downloads.

- **Plone Demo Site** (http://demo.plone.org): A demo site that comes with a large collection of products.

- **Zope.org** (http://www.zope.org): The definitive Zope community site run by Zope Corporation. It provides lots of information about Zope. This is probably one of the largest community Plone sites.

- **Liquidnet** (http://www.liquidnet.com): An investment company site featuring Flash.

- **Design Science Toys** (http://www.dstoys.com): A site that sells toys and utilizes an open-source e-commerce product for Plone: CMFCommerce.

- **Give Kids the World** (http://www.gktw.org): A site for raising funds for children; it's written in Plone and uses a lot of Flash.

- **Propane** (http://www.usepropane.com): A heavy-volume consumer site with a sophisticated search, all managed by Plone.

- **Maestro Headquarters** (http://mars.telascience.org): A NASA site for providing information about the Mars rovers. Its user interface is covered as a case study in Chapter 7.

More Plone sites are available at http://www.plone.org/about/sites, including sites that provide a quite different user interface. Without knowing about the development of these sites, it would in fact be hard to tell that these sites use Plone.

Getting Involved in Plone's Development

Although Plone has an impressive list of features, its list of "wants" is even more impressive. For this reason, the project is always on the lookout for new people willing to contribute time for the project.

Fortunately, because Plone is focused on the end user, there's a need for a very broad spectrum of disciplines. Volunteers in a range of areas, rather than just coders or Web developers, are welcomed. Plone needs user interface developers, usability experts, graphic designers, translators, writers, and testers. You can find the current development status on the Plone Web site at http://plone.org/development, and the best way to get involved is to join the mailing lists or join the developers on an Internet Relay Chat (IRC) channel.

What Is Zope and the CMF?

Plone is built on top of Zope and the Content Management Framework (CMF). To understand Plone, you have to understand Zope and the CMF as the underlying architecture. For this reason, I'll explain these two items and how they integrate with Plone in this section.

Zope is a powerful and flexible open-source Web application server developed by Zope Corporation (http://www.zope.org). Originally, Zope was developed as a stand-alone CMS, but over time it didn't satisfy the needs of its users. Then Zope Corporation developed the CMF an open-source project. The CMF provides developers with the tools necessary to create complex CMSs; it enables workflow, provides site skinning, and offers other functions.

The CMF is a framework for a system; in other words, it provides the tools for developers to build a product, rather than just providing an out-of-the-box system that users can use immediately. Plone takes this and many other features and improves upon them to provide the user with a high-quality product. Plone is a layer on top of the CMF, which is an application running on top of Zope. Understanding the CMF is key to understanding Plone. Most administration functions require the use of Zope's administration interface, and developing Plone requires an understanding of Zope and its objects.

This book doesn't go into depth about Zope; rather, it gives you enough information to complete tasks in Plone. Just reading this book will give you enough information to customize and modify almost anything you want in Plone. For more information on Zope, I recommend *The Zope Book*. Originally published by New Riders, it has since been placed online and is updated by community members. It's available free online at `http://www.zope.org/Documentation/Books/ZopeBook/` `2_6Edition`.

Both Zope and the CMF are key technologies that Plone needs; without them, Plone wouldn't exist. The Plone team owes a great deal of thanks to everyone at Zope Corporation for having the vision to create and then offer both Zope and the CMF as open source. The list of people I'd like to thank there and in the CMF communities is long. Thank you, everyone involved.

What Is Python?

Zope is written in Python, a powerful object-oriented, open-source programming language comparable to Perl or Tcl. Knowledge of Python isn't required to use Plone or even to do some basic administration; however, customizing products and scripting Plone does require some Python.

Tommy Burnette, a senior technical director at Industrial Light & Magic, says this about Python (`http://www.python.org/Quotes.html`):

> *Python plays a key role in our production pipeline. Without it a project the size of* Star Wars: Episode II *would have been very difficult to pull off. From crowd rendering to batch processing to compositing, Python binds all things together.*

If you plan to do anything sophisticated with Plone, take a day or two to learn the basics of Python. Not only will this allow you to customize Plone substantially, but it'll also familiarize you with objects and how they interact in the Plone environment. Teaching you Python is outside the scope of this book; instead, I assume you have a basic knowledge of Python. That fundamental knowledge of Python will be enough to get you through this book and allow you to customize the Plone installation easily.

Fortunately, Python is an easy programming language to learn; on average, it takes an experienced programmer a day to become productive in it. New programmers take a little longer. If you're installing Plone using the Windows or Mac installers, then the correct version of Python will be included. To download Python as separate product, for almost any operating system, go to `http://www.python.org`.

The best way to master Python is to try it from the command Python interpreter. If you have a Windows installation of Plone, there's a link for the PythonWin, a Python Integrated Development Environment (IDE) already in the Start menu; go to Start ➤ Programs ➤ Plone ➤ PythonWin (see Figure 1-2).

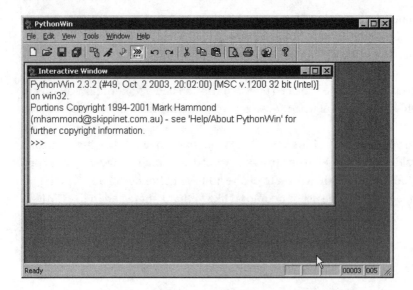

Figure 1-2. The Python prompt on Windows

On Linux and Mac OS X, usually typing **python** will start the Python interpreter:

```
$ python
Pyython 2.3.2 (#1, Oct  6 2003, 10:07:16)
[GCC 3.2.2 20030222 (Red Hat Linux 3.2.2-5)] on linux2
Type "help", "copyright", "credits" or "license" for more information.
>>>
```

Since Python is an interpreted language, instead of the whole Python script being compiled and run, you can just send lines of code to the interpreter as you write them. This makes the interpreter an amazingly useful place for testing and debugging code. In the interpreter, each line waiting for input is prefixed with >>>.

For example, the simplest "Hello, World" program is as follows:

```
>>> print "Hello, world!"
Hello, world!
>>>
```

To exit the interpreter, press Ctrl+D (press the D key while holding down Ctrl) on Linux or press Ctrl+Z on Windows. (You'll also use this later for more advanced Zope and Plone interaction.) You can execute normal Python scripts by passing them to the interpreter; for example, given the following script called hello.py:

```
print "Hello, world!"
```

you can run this using the following command:

```
$ python hello.py
Hello, world!
```

The Python Web site at `http://www.python.org` has excellent documentation, especially the tutorial. Also, the following books provide a good overview of Python:

- *Dive Into Python* (**Apress, 2004**): Based on Mark Pilgrim's popular Web-based tutorial, this books treats readers to a fast-paced introduction to the Python language. This is a great book geared toward experienced programmers.

- *Learning Python*, **Second Edition (O'Reilly, 2003)**: This book covers version 2.3 of Python and provides a good overview of Python and all the new features. This is good for relatively new programmers.

- *Practical Python* (**Apress, 2002**): This highly practical introduction to Python offers insight into the language's array of features. The reader can immediately put this knowledge into practice, following along with the creation of ten interesting projects, including a Web-based bulletin board and a Graphical User Interface–based file-sharing application.

- *Python Essential Reference*, **Second Edition (Sams, 2001)**: A reference book that provides a great overview of all the key libraries and functions. This is an excellent book for experienced programmers.

About This Book

This book uses the following conventions:

- **Italics:** New terms are *italicized*. (Appendix C contains an extensive glossary that defines all acronyms.) Also, links that appear in the user interface are italicized.

- **Bold:** If there are instructions within the text that include something you should type on your keyboard, these words are in **bold**.

- **Code font:** A `monospaced font` indicates filenames, folder paths, code, variables, and Uniform Resource Locators (URLs).

This book contains lots of screen shots of Zope, Python, and Plone. Since Plone is a rapidly developing product, the screen shots might vary slightly from the version of software you're using; these changes should be minor and shouldn't affect your understanding of the system.

Software Used

For this book, the following versions of software are used; although this book is specifically written with these versions in mind, all the software should work on these and later versions for some time to come.

Plone 2.0 was the most recently released version of Plone at the time of writing. This is the second major release of the software, and it provides many new features over 1.0, including group user management, a new interface, and an improved Zope distribution. It's strongly suggested you start any new projects in 2.0 or later, rather than using the earlier versions of Plone.

Version 2.0 of Plone has the following dependencies: Zope 2.7, CMF 1.4.2, and Python 2.3.3. All of the code examples in this book have been specifically designed not to be dependent upon these versions or a particular operating system. However, there may be situations where this isn't the case; I apologize for any inconvenience.

Book License

Originally, a group of Plone users keen to produce quality documentation came up with the idea of this book. We released the first version of that book on the Plone Web site as an open-source documentation project. All the content added to the Plone Web site was under the open publication license.

Growing interest in Plone made a commercial book more feasible, and in the summer of 2003, Apress and I started this book. I used some of the material from the old book with the original owners' permissions. With the change to Plone 2, I added a large amount of new material. This book is now published under the Creative Commons license, which allows for the reuse of this work as long as the original author is attributed. However, you may not use this work for commercial purposes. For more information, see the license online at http://creativecommons.org/licenses/by-nc-sa/1.0/.

CHAPTER 2

Installing Plone

THIS CHAPTER EXPLAINS how to install Plone on a variety of platforms and set the basic configuration options for Plone. If you want to try Plone really quickly, then your best bet is to go to the live demonstration site at http://demo.plone.org; you can try adding and editing content immediately without installing anything.

Unlike the other chapters, reading this chapter from one end to the other may not make the most sense. Instead, I've broken this chapter down by operating system, so you can read only the sections you need to in order to install Plone. Plone will install on any of the platforms that Zope supports: Windows, Mac OS X, Linux, most Unix platforms, and Solaris.

For a Plone server, a high-performance computer will obviously make Plone perform better. Plone is a complicated system that requires processing power and memory. In general, it's recommended you don't go into production with a machine slower than 2GHz with less than 1GB of Random Access Memory (RAM) if you're serving a large Web site. It works fine with setups as low as 500MHz and 64MB of memory for more modest sites, however. For advanced information about the performance, caching, and acceleration of Plone, see Chapter 14. For a base installation of Plone, you'll need about 50MB of hard drive space. If you already have installations of Zope or Python, then this will be a great deal less; you'll need about 2MB. You must also account for the Plone object database, which can grow to almost any size depending upon the amount of data you store.

To use Plone, you need a Web browser that can access the server. If users want to log into your site, then they must have cookies enabled. JavaScript isn't required but will provide a richer user experience. Because of the large amount of Cascading Style Sheets (CSS) in Plone, modern browsers will see the correct Plone interface in a richer, more attractive way; however, it should be quite functional in any reasonable browser.

I recommend any of the following browsers:

- Microsoft Internet Explorer 5.5 and later

- Netscape 7.0 and later

- Mozilla 1.0 and later

- Opera 7.0 and later

- Konqueror 3.0 and later

- Safari 1.0 and later

Plone also is fully functional in the following browsers but may look different from the original Plone:

- Netscape 4. *x*

- Microsoft Internet Explorer 5.0

- Microsoft Internet Explorer 4.0

- Konqueror 2. *x*

- Lynx (text-based)

- w3m (text-based)

- AWeb

- Links (text-based, with optional graphics)

- Any browser that handles a basic set of Hypertext Markup Language (HTML) and form input cookies, including most mobile/Personal Digital Assistant (PDA) browsers

Installing Plone on Windows

By far the easiest way to install Plone is to use the Plone Windows installer, which automates the installation of Plone on Windows. The installation includes extra packages and options, a Hypertext Transfer Protocol (HTTP)-loaded database, the setup of services, and Python for Windows packages. You can download this installer from http://www.plone.org/download.

Using the Installer

The installer has been tested on Windows 9*x*, ME, NT 3.51+, 2000, and XP, but it should also work on other Windows versions. It's recommended you have administrator access on the computer you want to install on since the installer will try to set up as a service and install settings into the Windows Registry. If you already have Zope or Python installed, you may want to install the source separately to save hard drive space.

Before installing Plone, you should make note of any current Web servers you have running. For example, later versions of Windows automatically install and start Microsoft Internet Information Services (IIS), which listens to port 80. The installer starts Plone on ports 80 and 8080. To test if something is using port 80 already, the easiest way to test is by opening a browser to http://127.0.0.1/ and seeing if it finds a page. You can either disable that Web server or change the ports for Plone; see "Configuring the Web Server" later in this chapter. If you want to run Plone behind IIS or run both Plone and IIS on the same server at the same time, then see Chapter 14 for more information. At the moment, however, it's easiest to just disable that Web server.

Once you've downloaded the installer, double-click the installer to begin (see Figure 2-1).

Figure 2-1. The start of the Plone installer

The installer goes through the usual steps for installing software; click Next to continue the setup or Cancel to exit. The Plone installer lets you choose a location to install the software; the default is c:\Program Files\Plone 2 (see Figure 2-2).

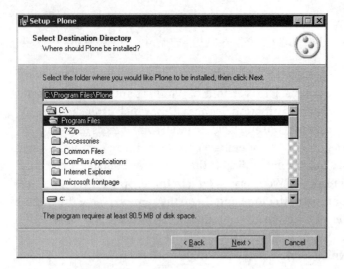

Figure 2-2. Selecting a directory

When you get to the password screen, as shown in Figure 2-3, you must enter a username and a password. This will create a user for you, and this will make the Plone site in that user's name. Often people create one user called *admin* or similar for this role. You'll need this username and password later, so remember it; however, if you do lose this password, you can enter a new one later.

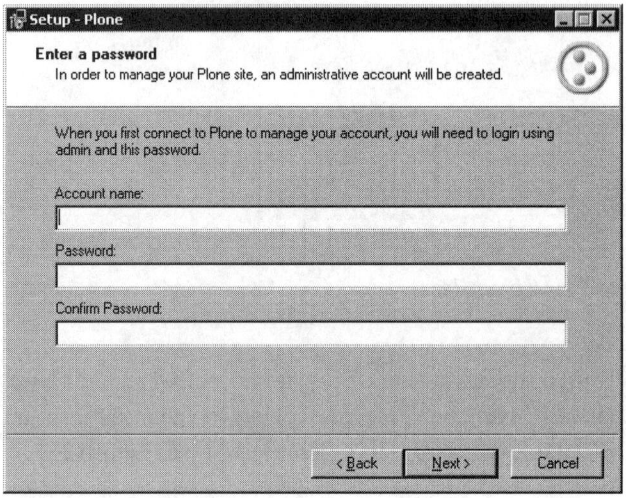

Figure 2-3. Entering a username and password

The installation takes about five minutes, depending upon the speed of your computer. The installation performs a few tasks at the end of the installation, such as compiling all the Python files and setting up the database. When the installation has finished, a message displays to let you know that it's done (see Figure 2-4).

Figure 2-4. Final setup screen

To start Plone, access the Plone controller by going to Start ➤ Programs ➤ Plone ➤ Plone. The controller is an application that provides a nice user interface for starting and stopping Plone. It begins with the Status page, which lets you easily start or stop your Plone installation (see Figure 2-5).

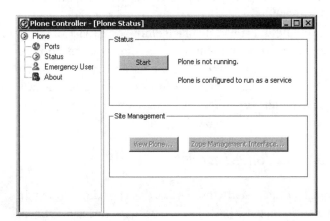

Figure 2-5. Plone isn't running.

As shown in Figure 2-5, the screen displays the status of your Plone installation. Plone doesn't start automatically; you'll have to click Start to start Plone. Once you've clicked this, you may have to wait a minute as it completes the startup process (see Figure 2-6).

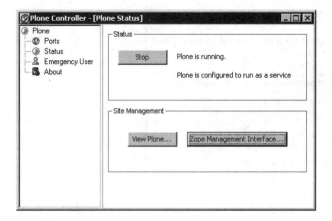

Figure 2-6. Plone is now running.

When Plone has started, you can access the Plone site by clicking the View Plone button. This starts a browser and accesses the Plone site; you should then see the Plone welcome page. Note that the address in the browser is `http://localhost/`; this is the address to access your Plone site. Clicking the Zope Management Interface button starts a browser and accesses the management interface; the address in the browser for this is `http://localhost::8080/manage`, which gives you access to the underlying application server. When you click the Manage button and access Plone, it'll ask you for your username and password. This is the username and password you added in the installer.

The controller will know whether you've installed Plone as a service or not as a service. If Plone has been installed as a Windows service, then you can stop and start Plone using the standard service management screens and commands. If it hasn't been installed as Windows service, you'll see a little icon appear in the task bar. At this point if you want to edit content, move on to Chapter 3.

Configuring the Server on Windows

The configuration for Plone is contained in a text file that you can edit to configure your Plone instance. You can change the ports Plone listens to, the log files used, and a whole host of options. On Windows some of the key features are available through the controller and the Graphical User Interface (GUI). If you want to alter some of the other configuration options, refer to Appendix A for a full list of configuration options. To access the controller, select Start ➤ Programs ➤ Plone ➤ Plone; this will start the controller.

As discussed earlier, the first page you'll see is the Status page, which allows you to stop or start Plone. On the left of the controller are a few other screens that I'll now discuss.

Changing the Ports

The Ports choice, as shown in Figure 2-7, allows you to specify the ports that Plone listens to for incoming connections such as HTTP, File Transfer Protocol (FTP), and Web-based Distributed Authoring and Versioning (WebDAV).

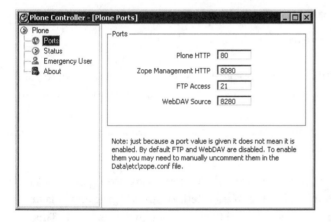

Figure 2-7. The Ports page displays the ports on which Plone is running.

As mentioned when installing Plone, you'll want to ensure that no other server is listening to the same port as Plone—servers such as IIS, Apache, and Personal Web Server (PWS) could be listening to port 80. At the time of writing, only the Plone HTTP and Zope Management HTTP ports are enabled; to enable them, you have to go into a text file to configure them. The following are the four fields on the Ports page:

Plone HTTP: This field specifies the port to access Plone for the user. The default is port 80, the standard default for a Web server. Although this port isn't required, without it you won't be able to access Plone with a Web browser. If this port is enabled and Plone is running, the View Plone button is enabled on the Status page.

Zope Management HTTP: This field specifies the port to access Plone as the manager. The default is port 8080. This port gives you access to Zope Management Interface (ZMI) for the root of Zope. You can still get to this through the HTTP port; however, it's easier and more convenient to have a separate port. If this port is enabled and Plone is running, the Manage Plone button is enabled on the Status page.

FTP Access: This field specifies the port to access Plone via FTP. The default is blank, meaning that this isn't enabled; if you want to enable this, the usual port is 21. You can use FTP to transfer large files to and from Plone.

WebDAV Source: This field specifies the port to access Plone via WebDAV. The default is blank, meaning that this isn't enabled; if you want to enable this, the usual port is 8081. (WebDAV is a protocol for remotely authoring content in Plone. With WebDAV, you're able to perform tasks such as mapping your Plone server to a Windows drive letter.)

Using the Emergency User Page

Chapter 9 covers the Emergency User page, but, put briefly, it allows you to get emergency access to your system should you forget your username or password.

Starting Plone in Debug Mode

Up to this point, you've started and stopped Plone in production mode. This is the fastest way to run Plone and is recommended. For developing add-ons in Plone or debugging problems, you'll need to start Plone in debug mode. This mode is the recommended way of running Plone when you're developing products and skins, as you'll do in later chapters. This method isn't the default because you'll note that Plone is about ten times slower than normal.

To start Plone in debug mode, select Start ➤ Programs ➤ Plone ➤ Plone (Debug Mode), and a command prompt will appear; all the log information will be printed to this window (see Figure 2-8).

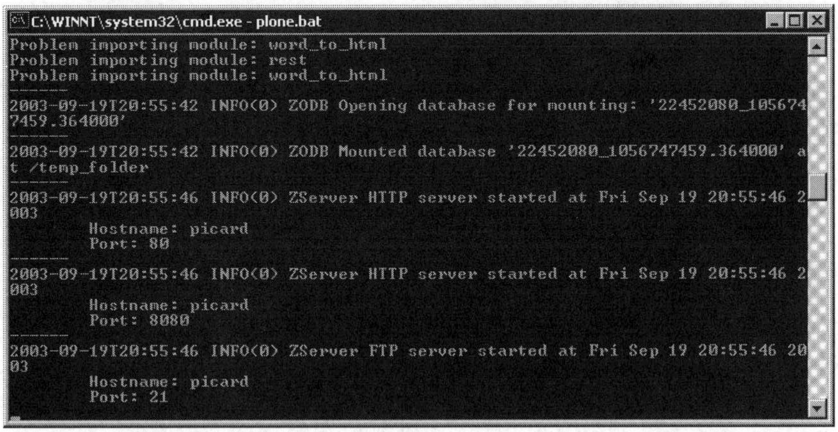

Figure 2-8. Running Plone from the command line

To test that Plone is running, start a browser and go to http://localhost/; if Plone is installed successfully, you'll see the Plone welcome screen.

Installing Plone on Mac OS X, Unix, and Linux

The installations for Mac OS X, Unix, and Linux are different, but the configurations are similar. Specific packages exist for different operating systems, including Mac OS X, Debian, Gentoo, FreeBSD, OpenBSD, and RPM Package Managers (RPMs) for Red Hat, SuSE, and Mandrake. In the following sections, I'll cover some of the more popular: Mac OS X, Red Hat, and Debian. For information about your specific operating system, consult the installation instructions for the specific installation system.

Installing on Mac OS X

The installer automates the installation of Plone on Mac OS X and has been tested on version 10.2.3 and later. You'll need administrator access on the computer on which you want to install. You can download this installer from http://ww.plone.org/download. Once you've downloaded the installer, double-click the installer to decompress the archive, and double-click the resulting installer package to begin the install. You should see the screen shown in Figure 2-9.

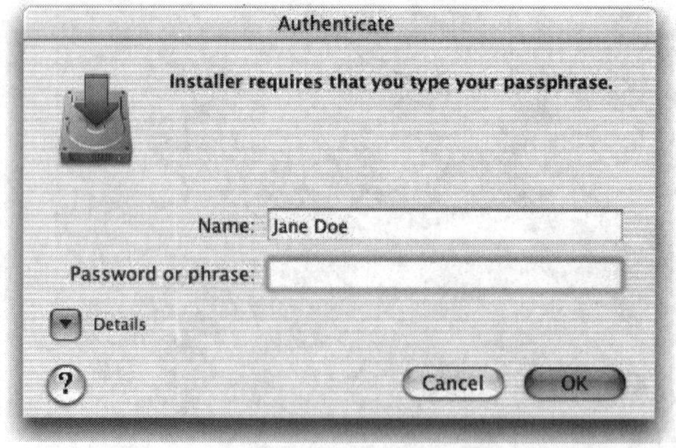

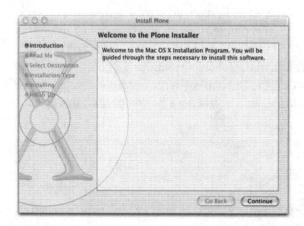

Figure 2-9. Authorizing the installation using your Mac OS X password

Enter your Mac OS X account password to authorize the installation; your account must have administrator privileges to do this. If your account doesn't have administrator privileges, log out and log back in as someone who does and then relaunch the installer. You may want to move the installer package to /Users/Shared before you log out so you can access it from the other account. Once the installation is authorized, you'll see the screen shown in Figure 2-10.

Figure 2-10. Welcome to the installer.

The installer goes through the usual steps for installing software. Click the Continue and Go Back buttons at the bottom as necessary; most of the steps are self-explanatory. However, when presented with the choice of volumes to install Plone on, you must choose the partition on which Mac OS X is installed (see Figure 2-11).

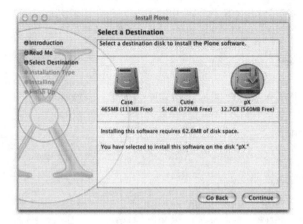

Figure 2-11. Choosing the boot volume

The installation takes about five minutes, depending upon the speed of your computer. When the installation has finished, Plone isn't started by default. The ReadMe.html file in /Applications/Plone2 contains a lot of useful information about running and managing your Plone installation, including how to start Plone. For example, running the following command will start Plone:

```
/Applications/Plone2/Tools/start Default
```

To test whether Plone has worked, use a browser to go to http:// localhost:8200/; you should see the Plone welcome page. In the file /Applications/Plone2/Sites/Default/admin-password.txt you'll find the default username and password that Plone has set up for you to access the server.

Installing Using an RPM

RPMs are available for the Red Hat, Mandrake, and SuSE distributions. You can download the latest packages from http://www.plone.org/download. The RPM requires that Python 2.3 is installed. To find out which version of Python you have, run the following command in a shell:

```
$ python -V
Python 2.3.2
```

In this case, Python 2.3.2 is installed; if you don't have this, RPMs for Python are available from the Python Web site at http://www.python.org. After downloading the files, install using the standard rpm command; fortunately, the Plone installation prints some really useful information. For example:

```
[root@lappi i386]# rpm -ivh Plone2-2.0.0rh-2.i386.rpm
Preparing...                   ##########################################
[100%]
Making group plone (not altered if already exists).
Making user plone.
~   1:Plone2                    ##########################################
[100%]
Creating initial 'main' instance...
Instance created. Listening on 127.0.0.1:8080, initial user: 'plone'
with password: 'plone'.
Setup of initial database in 'main' instance...
/usr/lib/plone2/lib/python/AccessControl/Owned.py:79:
DeprecationWarning: Owned.getOwner(1) is deprecated; please use
getOwnerTuple() instead.
~  DeprecationWarning)
Created initial database content.
look at /etc/plone2/main/zope.conf.
Run then "/etc/rc.d/init.d/plone2 start" to start Plone2.
you may create new Plone instances with mkploneinstance.
```

As shown in the previous output, to start Plone, run the following:

```
/etc/rc.d/init.d/plone2 start
```

To test that Plone is working, use a browser to go to http://localhost:8080/; you should see the Plone welcome page. The username plone and the password plone have been created for you.

Installing on Debian Linux

Plone is a standard package in Debian and moves through the standard release process, so you'll want to either get the stable or get the unstable version of Plone, depending upon how your Debian installation is configured. To install Plone, simply use Debian's apt system to get the package. This is an example installation:

```
agmweb:/home/andy# apt-get install plone
Reading Package Lists... Done
Building Dependency Tree... Done
The following extra packages will be installed:
  zope zope-cmf zope-cmfcalendar zope-cmfcore zope-cmfdefault
zope-cmfplone zope-cmftopic zope-cmfworkflow
  zope-formulator zopectl
```

```
Suggested packages:
  zope-cmfwiki python-unit zope-devguide zope-book
Recommended packages:
  zope-cmfforum zope-localizer
The following NEW packages will be installed:
  plone zope zope-cmf zope-cmfcalendar zope-cmfcore zope-cmfdefault
zope-cmfplone zope-cmftopic zope-cmfworkflow
  zope-formulator zopectl
0 upgraded, 11 newly installed, 0 to remove and 49 not upgraded.
Need to get 4743kB of archives.
After unpacking 24.9MB of additional disk space will be used.
Do you want to continue? [Y/n]
```

Press Y to continue and install all the required packages. To start and stop Zope, an install script has been created in the init.d directory, called zope. To start Plone, run the following:

```
/etc/init.d/zope start
```

The Debian installer starts Zope on the nonstandard port 9673. Since the Debian installer is quite unusual, it's recommended that you read the documentation for the packages at /usr/share/doc/zope and /usr/share/doc/zope-cmfplone.

Installing from Source

As an alternative to using an installer or package, you can install from the source tarball. If you're familiar with installing from source, it's actually rather simple but does require familiarity with basic tools such as tar. The following sections demonstrate how to install it on Linux.

This installation assumes you're familiar with basic operations such as "untarring" files and moving files. This requires a working Zope installation.

 NOTE   To install Zope, see the Zope installation instructions in the doc/INSTALL.txt file of your Zope download. For more information, see http://zope.org/Documentation/Books/ZopeBook/2_6Edition/InstallingZope.stx).

Follow these steps to install Plone:

1. Download Plone 2 from `http://www.plone.org/download`, and select the tarball file.

2. Unzip the archive using the following:

   ```
   tar xzf CMFPlone2.0.tar.gz
   ```

3. You'll find that a directory has been created called `CMFPlone-xxx`, where *xxx* is the version (for example, `CMFPlone-2.0`).

4. Move the contents of that directory into your Zope installation's `Product` directory. For example, if the Zope `Products` directory is in `/var/zope`, then do this:

   ```
   mv CMFPlone2.0/* /var/zope/Products
   ```

After completing this installation, restart Zope. Once Zope has restarted, access Zope by opening a browser and going to `http://localhost:8080/manage`. You'll need a username and password for this (for example, the username and password you gave during the Zope installation).

In the ZMI, there's a drop-down list of products you can add located in the top-right corner. Ensure that Plone Site is one of the options. If so, your installation is complete (see Figure 2-12).

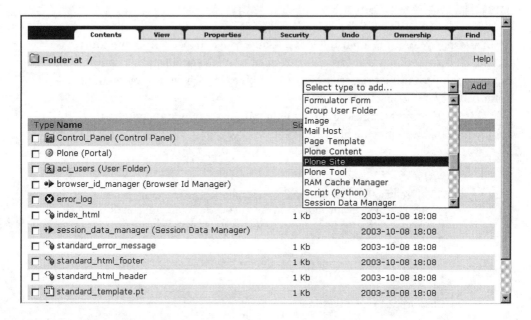

Figure 2-12. Plone Site in the drop-down list

Installing from CVS

Concurrent Versioning System (CVS) access is recommended only for experienced users and developers. You can find current CVS access information at http://ww.plone.org/development/cvs. The current CVS checkout command is as follows:

```
cvs -d:pserver:anonymous@cvs.sf.net:/cvsroot/plone login
cvs -d:pserver:anonymous@cvs.sf.net:/cvsroot/plone co CMFPlone
```

Plone 2 has a whole host of other dependencies (such as DCWorkflow, Formulator, Group User Folder, and so on) that aren't in Plone CVS, meaning users will have to go and find all these dependencies. When you start Plone, it'll print any errors regarding packages not found. For example:

```
2003-11-21T12:23:11 ERROR(200) Plone Dependency
CMFActionIcons not found.  Please download it from http://cvs.zope.org/Products/
```

Adding a Plone Site

Once you've installed Plone from source, you need to create an instance of Plone. To do this, you'll need to log into the ZMI and add a Plone site. You can access this by going to the Uniform Resource Locator (URL) for the management interface, which is normally http://localhost:8080/manage (this port will change depending upon your installation). You'll need a manager's username and password for access to the ZMI; this password is created during the Zope installation.

NOTE   If you've forgotten the password for Plone that was created in the installation, don't panic. You can create a new one; see Chapter 9 for more information.

You add all objects via the drop-down list in the top-right corner, as shown in Figure 2-12. Scroll down the list until you find Plone Site, and click Add.

After selecting the option Plone Site, a form will display that prompts for some more information (see Figure 2-13):

- **Id**: This is the unique ID of the Plone site (for example, enter **Plone** or **Site**).

- **Title**: This is the title of the Plone site (for example, enter **My Portal**).

- **Membership source:** For the moment, leave this as the default option, Create a New User Folder in the Portal. This allows you to have user authentication somewhere other than the portal (see Chapter 9 for more information).

- **Description:** This is a description of the portal that members will see in e-mails (for example, enter **A site all about the exciting new widget technology**). Don't worry too much about this; you can always change this later in the portal's properties.

```
Add Plone Site

Enter an ID and click the button below to create a new Plone site.
Id
┌────────────────────────────────────────┐
│ Plone                          I        │
└────────────────────────────────────────┘
Title
┌────────────────────────────────────────┐
│ Plone demo site                         │
└────────────────────────────────────────┘
Membership source
┌──────────────────────────────────────┬──┐
│ Create a new user folder in the portal │ ▾ │
└──────────────────────────────────────┴──┘
Description
┌──────────────────────────────────────────┐
│ This is a demonstration site for Plone│    │
│                                            │
│                                            │
│                                            │
│                                            │
│                                            │
└──────────────────────────────────────────┘
┌──────────────────────┐
│    Add Plone Site     │
└──────────────────────┘
```

Figure 2-13. Adding a Plone site

After clicking Add Plone Site, a Plone site will be created. This may take a minute or two on slower machines because a great deal of processing occurs. The screen will then redirect you to the Plone welcome page.

Configuring the Web Server

Once Plone has been installed, you may want to configure the Plone site so that it runs on a different port, has FTP capabilities, logs to a different file, and so on. This section covers these basic setup issues. Note that you aren't configuring the Plone sites themselves; you're altering the configuration of the underlying Web server.

NOTE If you've installed on Windows using the Windows installer, then most of this configuration is provided through a nice user interface program; see "Configuring the Server on Windows" earlier in this chapter.

NOTE If you've installed using Mac OS X or the Windows installer, then you'll find one extra file (plone.conf), which contains port definitions used in the main Zope configuration file.

Zope 2.7 creates a configuration file inside each instance installed. All the configuration for the server is located in that one file. A full list of the configuration options is available in Appendix A. To find the configuration file, look for a file called zope.conf located in the etc folder of your Plone installation. Some installers (Windows and Mac OS X, for example) create a second configuration file called plone.conf that contains Plone-specific configuration options. If your installation contains a plone.conf file, then use that configuration file to make changes; they'll be included in the main configuration file.

The configuration file is extremely verbose and contains a great deal of useful comments and examples. If you're familiar with Unix configuration files such as Apache, then you'll find the Zope configuration file familiar. To alter Zope configuration, open the configuration in a text editor, and change the lines as needed; after altering the configuration, you'll need to restart Zope.

It's possible to run Plone 2.0 with a version of Zope prior to 2.7; however, Zope 2.7 offers increased stability and new features, including easier configuration. If you're using a version of Zope prior to 2.7, you'll need to read the documentation on how to change the configuration.

Changing the Ports

To change a port, add the address lines for that port. For example, to run Plone on port 80 instead of the default, change the following bold line in zope.conf:

```
<http-server>
  # valid keys are "address" and "force-connection-close"
  address 8080
  # force-connection-close on
</http-server>
```

to the following:

```
<http-server>
  # valid keys are "address" and "force-connection-close"
  address 80
  # force-connection-close on
</http-server>
```

If you used the Windows or Mac OS X installer, then you'll find these port definitions in `plone.conf`. These values are then imported into the main configuration file. So, on a Mac to change the port, you'll edit `plone.conf` from this:

```
## PLONE_WEBSERVER_PORT
## --------------------
## This is the port you will access your Plone site from.  Set this to a port
## number above 1024 not used for any other server on your computer.
%define PLONE_WEBSERVER_PORT 8080
```

to the following:

```
%define PLONE_WEBSERVER_PORT 80
```

Using the Debug Mode

By default in Zope 2.7 debug mode is enabled. Note that Plone runs significantly slower in debug mode, approximately 10-20 times slower. To turn this off, add the following line to the configuration file:

```
debug-mode off
```

To make the out-of-the-box experience more impressive for Windows users (debug mode slows Plone down on Windows even more than on Linux), it ships with debug mode off already. If you have a Plone site running and want to know if debug mode is running, go to `portal_migration` in the ZMI and look at the variables listed there; this will tell you if debug mode is enabled.

Using Logs

By default there are two logs in Plone: an access log that you can produce site statistics from and an event log that contains debug information about Plone products. The event log is the place to find errors and messages in Plone. The default configuration looks like the following:

```
<eventlog>
  level all
  <logfile>
    path $INSTANCE/log/event.log
    level INFO
  </logfile>
</eventlog>

<logger access>
  level WARN
  <logfile>
    path $INSTANCE/log/Z2.log
    format %(message)s
  </logfile>
</logger>
```

This is where you can change the path to the file by defining a new file. The values that are logged are based upon a level sent with error messages; more serious messages are sent with higher levels. By default, only information and the previous message are sent to the log, but that value could be one of the following: CRITICAL, ERROR, WARN, INFO, DEBUG, and ALL. If you wanted to log only errors, then you'd change level INFO to level ERROR.

## CHAPTER 3

Adding and Editing Content

ADDING AND EDITING content is a simplification of the sheer power that Plone has available to leverage. Creating content-rich and feature-rich Web pages with Plone is an absolute breeze. If you have Plone installed locally, then this chapter shows you how Plone works straight out of the box. However, if you don't have Plone installed, then don't worry; you can try Plone online by going to http://demo.plone.org.

Before you can alter or edit a Plone site, you need to log into a Plone site. If you installed Plone, you should have the username and password that came with the installation. This user has the role of an administrator user, which allows you to log in and alter any content. Most users of a Plone site will join the site and log in through the login process described in the "Joining a Site" section. Users can, of course, view a Plone site without logging in, but they won't be able to add or edit content.

In this chapter, I'll go through the steps a user takes to create content on a Plone site. First, I'll cover how to join the site and log in. Once you've accomplished this, I'll cover how to create and then edit a document. Finally, I'll show how you can search and publish this content. In short, this chapter covers how to use Plone.

Joining a Site

When you join a Plone site, you create an account on the server. That account gives you the right as a member to add content such as images, documents, and so forth. To join a site, click the *join* link in the top-right corner of the Web site (see Figure 3-1).

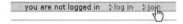

Figure 3-1. Clicking the join *link in the top-right corner of the page*

This will take you to a registration form that you'll have to complete (see Figure 3-2). Because this is the first Plone form you've encountered, take note of the following:

- Some fields are required; a little re d box next to the text indicates the required fields.

- For most fields, some grayed-out he lp text beneath the field name indicates what you should enter.

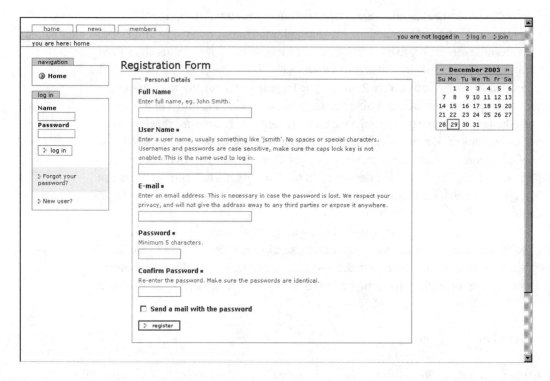

Figure 3-2. The registration page

NOTE   Because many of the Plone pages are quite large, the figures in this book have been cropped to show only the key parts (in this case, the form) and not the Plone logo or the footer. These elements are still there, but they're superfluous.

To complete the form, complete the fields that are reasonably obvious. The values of the fields are as follows:

Full Name: Enter your full name. This field is optional.

User Name: Enter the username you want to use. Most people choose an alphanumeric value without spaces, such as *bob* or *jane97*. This username will be used throughout the Web site to refer to you. This field is required.

E-mail: A valid e-mail address is required. This will allow the site administrator to contact you and to send a password to you. You can change this e-mail address later by editing your member preferences. This field is required.

Password and Confirm Password: This is the password you want to use; it must be more than four characters and can contain letters, numbers, and the underscore (_) character. Passwords are case sensitive (in other words, SomePassword isn't the same as somepassword). These fields are required.

Send a mail with the password: Check this box if you'd like your password sent to the e-mail address you provided. This field is optional.

Once you've completed this form, click Register to submit your information. If you've made any errors on this form, then you'll see a message at the top and the key fields that have an error highlighted. In Figure 3-3, I entered a password but didn't enter a value for the Confirm Password field. Again, this is the standard way that Plone forms will show errors to you.

If you've completed the form correctly, then you'll be given the option of logging in immediately. Click the Log In button to log in. You'll see the page shown in Figure 3-4.

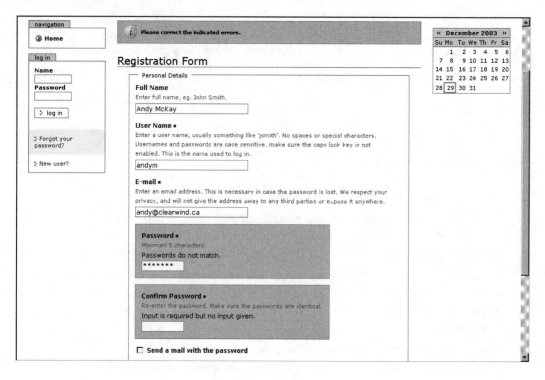

Figure 3-3. Errors on a form

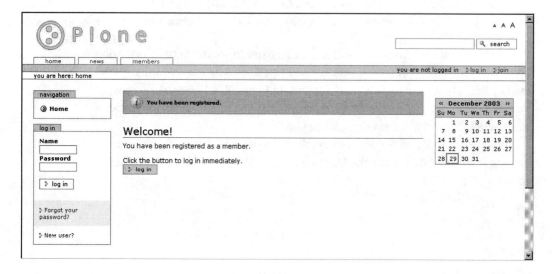

Figure 3-4. After registering

If you already have a username and password or are returning to a site you've previously joined, then you can enter your name and password in the boxes in the left column of the site and click the Log In button.

Enabling Cookies

To log into a Plone site, you must have cookies enabled. If you access a Plone site and try to log in with cookies disabled, you'll get a friendly message telling you that cookies must be enabled with a link to more information. To enable cookies, perform the following steps, depending on your browser.

Internet Explorer 6.x

If you're using Internet Explorer 6.*x*, then follow these steps:

1. Select Tools ➤ Internet Options.
2. Click the Privacy tab at the top of the screen.
3. Move the slider to Medium, and click OK.

Internet Explorer 5.x

If you're using Internet Explorer 5.*x*, then follow these steps:

1. Select Tools ➤ Internet Options.
2. Click the Security tab at the top of the screen.
3. Click Custom Level, and scroll down to the Cookies section.
4. Set Allow Per-Session Cookies to Enable, and click OK.

Internet Explorer 4.x

If you're using Internet Explorer 4.*x*, then follow these steps:

1. Select View ➤ Internet Options.
2. Click the Security tab at the top of the screen.
3. Click Custom Level, and scroll down to the Cookies section.
4. Select Always Accept Cookies or Prompt Before Accepting Cookies, and click OK.

Mozilla 1.x

If you're using Mozilla 1.*x*, then follow these steps:

1. Select Edit ➤ Preferences.

2. Find Privacy & Security in the menu on the left. If there's a plus sign (+) to the left of Privacy & Security, click it.

3. Select Cookies under Advanced.

4. Select Enable Cookies for the Originating Web Site Only or Enable All Cookies, and click OK.

Opera

If you're using Opera, then follow these steps:

1. Press F12.

2. Click Enable Cookies.

Netscape Navigator 6.x

If you're using Netscape Navigator 6.*x*, then follow these steps:

1. Select Edit ➤ Preferences.

2. Find Privacy & Security in the menu on the left. If there's a triangle pointing to the right next to Privacy & Security, click it.

3. Select Cookies under Privacy & Security.

4. Select Enable Cookies for the Originating Web Site Only or Enable All Cookies, and click OK.

If you forget your password at some point, you can get it sent to the e-mail address you provided when you registered with the Plone site. To have your password mailed to you, click the *Forgot your password?* link located in the left column of the Web site. This will bring up the forgotten password form, as shown in Figure 3-5; enter your login name, and a password will be e-mailed to you.

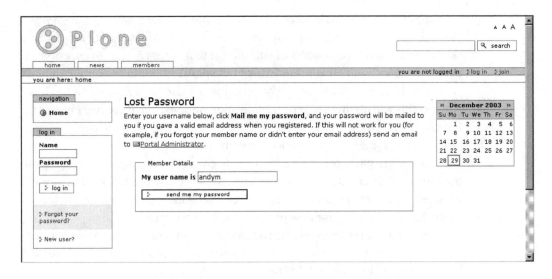

Figure 3-5. Getting a forgotten password

Unfortunately, if you have no longer access to that e-mail account, or you can't even remember the username, you'll have to contact a site administrator. Using the techniques discussed in Chapter 9, the administrator can change your e-mail and find your user account. Once logged in to the Plone site, you'll see a *log out* link in the upper-right corner. When your work is finished, it's good practice to log out of Plone site, especially if you're accessing it from a computer that's likely to be used by other people.

Setting Up Your Folder and Preferences

After you've logged in, the member bar in the top-right corner will change to represent the options available to you as a member of the site (see Figure 3-6).

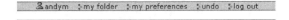

Figure 3-6. Your personal choices in the top-right corner have changed.

One of these options is that each member has a folder created for them when they join a site. This folder is set up with particular security so only that member (and administrators) can add and edit the content in that folder. To access your personal folder, click the *my folder* link in the personal bar in the upper-right corner of the site. In the upper-right corner you'll also see a *my preferences* link; clicking this will open a list of personalization options. You'll see two choices at the moment; you can change your password, or you can go to the personal preferences and change key preferences in your site.

The change password form allows you to change your password. To complete the form, give your current password and the new password twice. After you've changed your password, the change will be immediate. You don't have to log in again; just remember your new password when you return.

The personal preferences form allows you to set a number of preferences that change how you see the site. These preferences are stored on the server so they're retained between uses of the site (see Figure 3-7).

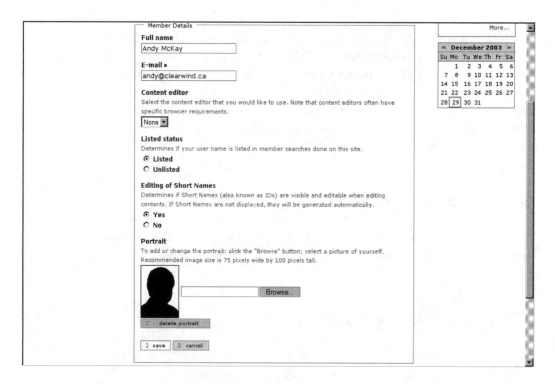

Figure 3-7. Changing preferences

The options are as follows:

Full name: This is the full name you gave when you registered with the site.

E-mail: This is the e-mail address associated with your membership and is used a number of places in a Plone site. Most important, if you lose or forget your password, this is the address to which the system will send it.

Content editor: When editing complex content, you may want the help of an editor. If your site administrator has made one available, you can select it here. It will then be used when you click the edit tab of an object. If you're unsure, leave this as the default.

Listed status: This property specifies whether your profile will show up on the members tab and when someone searches the members listing.

Editing of Short Names: Objects have an ID or Short Name property that's used for the internal representation of the content object. This also shows up in the item's Web address and the item's Uniform Resource Locator (URL). By default these look something like `News_Item.2002-11-16.4102`, but you could make it much simpler, such as `november_news`, by changing the Short Name value.

NOTE   When you change an object's name value, anything that references the older name will no longer be valid and will result in the page not being found. It's best not to change the name value after you submit an object for review or link to it from elsewhere. For this reason, I recommend setting this option to No.

Portrait: In larger organizations and in community Web sites, it's useful to see pictures of other members. The Portrait field allows you to upload a picture of yourself. The picture should be 75x100 pixels.

Once you've made the desired changes, click the Save button to commit the changes. Now that you've logged in, it's time to start adding and editing content.

Adding and Editing Documents

As mentioned, now that you're a site member, a folder has been created for you where you can store content. Of course, you can add content to any folder that the site administrator has given you the right to do so, but by default every user can add content to their member folder.

Each type of content you can add is distinct, and you can edit and view it in different ways. For this reason, Plone references each type of content differently; for example, you can add images, links, documents, and so on. Out of the box, Plone provides the following content types:

- **Document**: This is an item that presents some static information to the user. This is the most common type of content added and most closely represents a typical Web page.

- **News item**: This is a document that's to be shown under the news tab (for example, a press release).

- **Link**: This is a link to another item, which may be internal or external to another Web site.

- **Image**: This is an image, such as a `.gif` or `.jpeg` file.

- **Event**: This is an upcoming meeting, conference, or other event.

- **Folder**: This is like a folder on a hard drive; this is a folder for putting content into so that it's easy to find later.

- **Topic**: This is a grouping of other content. This is essentially a saved search criteria that you can reuse later. Only privileged site users can add topics.

- **File**: This is another piece of content such as a movie, sound clip, text file, spreadsheet, compressed file, or anything else you'd like to upload.

I'll go through each of these items using the document as an example, showing in detail how to add and edit documents easily and quickly. Using these basic content types, I'll show you how to build a dynamic site through a browser, without doing any programming.

Actually, you have many ways of adding and editing content in a Plone site than just through a Web browser. Access via File Transfer Protocol (FTP), via Web-based Distributed Authoring and Versioning (WebDAV), or via scripts is all possible. I'll discuss how to set these up in Chapter 10 and just deal with the Web browser interface for now. In Chapters 11 to 13 of this book, I'll discuss how to make new custom content types that you can tailor to a particular site's needs.

Understanding the Document Content Types

Rather than detailing how to add and edit all the different types of content available, I'll cover adding one type of content, a document, in detail. After adding and editing a few of these documents, the approach to adding content should be second nature, and editing other content will be easy.

A *document* is a page of content, usually a self-contained piece of text. Although all items added to Plone are accessible as Web pages, if there's one content type you could think of as a Web page, this is it. The default home page for a Plone site that you've seen already—the now-famous Welcome to Plone page—is one example of a document (see Figure 3-8).

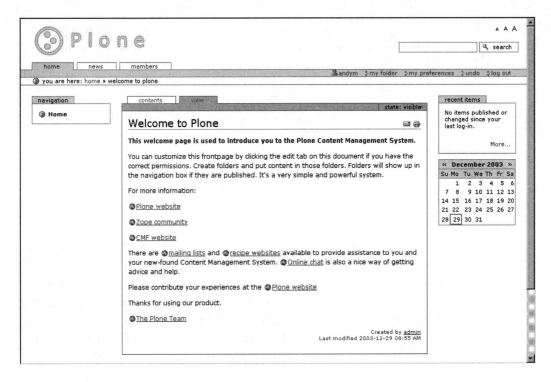

Figure 3-8. Welcome to Plone, a simple document

Adding a Document

You have two ways to add any piece of content using a Web browser. First, ensure you're logged in, because only logged-in users can add content. Second, select the *my folder* link from the top-right navigation bar. This will take you to your home folder, an area that you control. If you're able to add content to a folder, then the folder will show up with the green border around the top (see Figure 3-9).

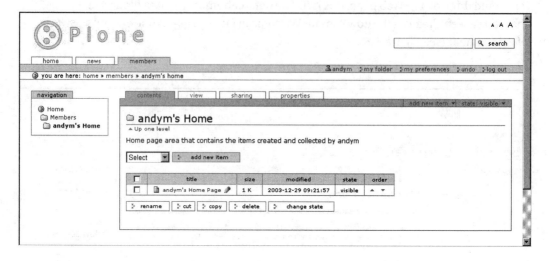

Figure 3-9. My content

If the green border doesn't appear, then you won't be able to add content; this border contains the actions you can perform in the current location. In Figure 3-9, you can see that the page shows the contents of the folder, because that's the highlighted tab. Other tabs appear such as view, sharing, and properties for more advanced options. In the top-right corner of the green border, you'll see an Add New Item drop-down menu and a State drop-down menu. Click the Add New Item menu to open a drop-down list of items to add (see Figure 3-10).

Figure 3-10. Adding a document from the green drop-down menu

To add a new document, select Document. Alternatively, if you look in the body of the page, you can see another Add New Item drop-down box. Again, click the down arrow to open a list of items that can be added and then select the item you'd like to add (see Figure 3-11).

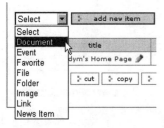

Figure 3-11. Adding a document from the main folder's content menu

Using the Add New Item list from the green border is a handy menu since it's available most of the time.

NOTE If you're familiar with Zope, you should never, never, never add content from the Zope Management Interface (ZMI). Depending upon how you've installed Plone, you may have already seen the ZMI and used it for customizing and developing Plone through the Web. However, adding content through the ZMI will create content items that are incomplete and don't work properly.

Understanding Where to Add Content

The easiest place to add content at the beginning is in the user's member folder, accessible by clicking the *my folder* link. Although this is useful, it's probably not the best approach for a long-term solution. Most noticeably it creates long URLs (for example, /Members/andy/Docum...). It also means your content isn't accurately reflected in the navigation tree.

As you'll see later, a few solutions exist for this; the most common solution is to make a folder and give certain users the right to access it. For example, that folder may be Help or News. The "Using Folders" section later in this chapter discusses adding folders, and Chapter 9 discusses using group workspaces and security.

Editing a Document

Once you've clicked to add a document, you'll be taken directly to the edit page with a message telling you that the document has been created. If this doesn't happen, you can click a document and then click the edit tab. Again, you'll see that the edit tab becomes highlighted in green (see Figure 3-12).

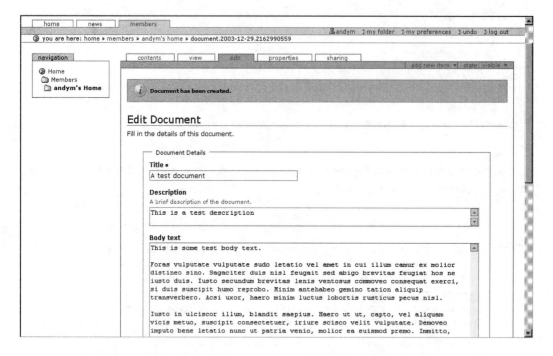

Figure 3-12. Editing a document

Now you can edit the document in your Web browser, using the form provided. If you look at the URL in the address bar of your browser, you'll note that a short name for the object has been created for you, something such as `Document.2003-12-29.43787`. The following is a list of the fields and their meanings:

Short name: The short name will become part of the document's URL, so keep the name short and descriptive, preferably without spaces. Keeping to these rules will make URLs easier to read. For example, use something such as `audit-report-2003`. If you don't provide a name, Plone will create one for you.

NOTE   This field won't appear if you selected No for the short names in your preferences page.

Title: This is the title for the item, and it'll be shown throughout the site (for example, at the top of the page, in the search interface, in the title of the browser, and so on). This field is required.

Description: This is a short lead-in to the document, usually about 20 words to introduce the document and provide a teaser for the remainder of the document. This is useful for pages that show summaries of documents, such as search results and folder contents.

Body text: This contains the body of the document. The format for the content is set using the Format field (described next).

Format: You have three choices for the format of body content: Structured Text, HTML, and Plain Text. These types of text are discussed in the "Choosing a Text Format" sidebar; if you're unsure, leave this field alone and type the body text as usual.

Upload document: If you do have your document as a file on your computer, you can upload it instead of typing the content into the Body Text field. Use the Upload button at the bottom of the page to select a file. The contents of an uploaded file will *replace* any content in the Body Text field.

Once you've finished editing your document, click the Save button to commit your changes. You'll be returned to the view tab where you can see how the document will be shown to users (see Figure 3-13); to edit it again, click the edit tab.

If you don't provide the correct input on the edit form, when you save the document you'll be returned to the edit page, and your errors will be highlighted. At this point your changes haven't been applied—you must correct the mistakes and click Save again before the changes will be committed. The view tab shown in Figure 3-13 shows the document you've created. You'll see that the title, description, and content are all shown in slightly different styles. At the bottom of the page is a byline that contains information about the author of the document, including the date the page was created.

You'll note that if you go back to folder contents after saving your changes, you'll see two documents in your folder: the existing one that's created for you and the new one you've just added. You can edit either of these documents by clicking them to open the view tab, which allows you to select the edit tab.

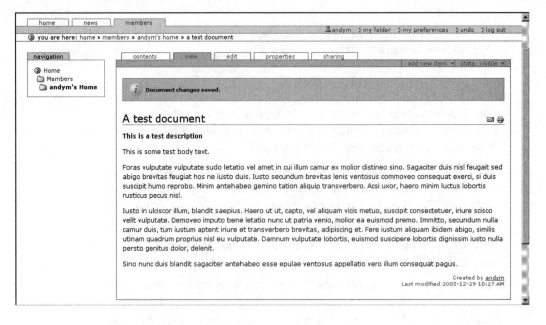

Figure 3-13. Saving the content will take you to the view tab.

Choosing a Text Format

As mentioned previously, you can edit the document content in at least three formats: structured text, HTML, and plain text. This rather confusing state of affairs is brought about by trying to produce easy systems for users to write rich marked-up content in plain text without having to use fancy editors.

Unfortunately, in most cases, this really doesn't work; training is required to understand the formatting. Structured text requires quite a bit of understanding in itself because it has a frustrating syntax and doesn't internationalize well. If I had to pick one format that I'd recommend over all the others, I'd pick HTML because it's widely understood, and you can use What You See Is What You Get (WYSIWYG) editors such as Epoz to produce it.

HTML

HTML is the most standard format; if a document is entered as HTML, it will be rendered in the same format. This HTML shouldn't be a complete page but rather a snippet. For example:

```
<p>Here is a sample in <i>HTML</i> for a demonstration.</p>
```

Ideally the HTML should also be valid Extensible HTML (XHTML) to comply with the rest of the Plone system; if it's not, your pages don't comply with Web standards. Entering text as XHTML isn't for the faint of heart, so in Chapter 9, you'll see how into integrate rich-editing tools into Plone that allow users to easily write content in XHTML. The following screen shot shows Plone using Epoz so users don't have to understand HTML.

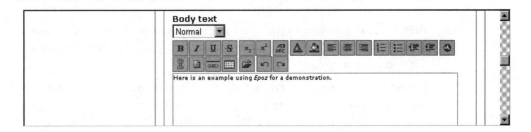

Plain Text

Plain text is simple. It does no major conversion or manipulation of the text entered; it's just plain text. The only modification made is that new lines are converted into HTML when rendered so that new lines appear in the Web browser. No other altering happens. For example:

```
Here is a sample in plain text for a demonstration
```

Structured Text

Structured text is a system for writing plain-text documents in a particular format, which can then be interpreted in different ways. For example, if a piece of text needs to be highlighted, then it can written as *italics*; this will then be shown as *italics*. This series of rules means that a user can write a page that contains formatting information easily. For a full list of structured text rules and examples, please see Appendix A. The following is a sample of structured text:

```
Here is a sample in *structured text* for a demonstration
```

Setting Document Metadata

Any piece of content can have any number of properties assigned to it. These properties are known as *metadata* and provide information such as keywords, copyrights, and contributors of an item.

This entire set of properties is optional and is usually used only if there are special requirements for this piece of content, especially since this information isn't normally shown to the person viewing the content. So the main reason for entering this data is to add information for tasks such as searching or categorizing the content.

You can access properties on an object by selecting the green properties tab. This properties form has the following fields, which are common to all content types:

Allow Discussion: This lets this document be discussed by users who have the right to do so. If the value is left as default, it'll use the sitewide policy for that content type.

Keywords: Each item can have keywords assigned to it to enable grouping and sorting of the items. For example, an article about recent events in politics may have the keywords *politics* and *prime minister*. Keywords are flexible, and you can use any keyword from the given list. By default there are no keywords in the Plone system; site administrators may add new keywords so that other users can select them.

Effective Date: The effective date is the first day a piece of content should be available. You can specify this date by entering the values in the form or clicking the little calendar icon, which opens a calendar, and picking a date (see Figure 3-14).

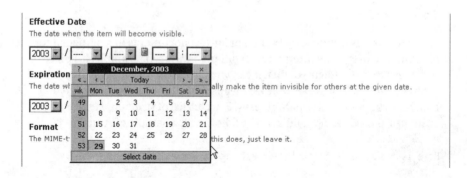

Figure 3-14. Entering an effective date

Expiration Date: The expiration date is the last day a piece of content should be available. Usually the Effective Date and Expiration Date fields are left blank.

Format: This is the Multipurpose Internet Mail Extensions (MIME) type of the item. The term *MIME type* refers to a computer definition of the type of content (for example, application/msword or image/jpeg). This is set at a default value; if you're unsure about this field, just ignore it.

Language: This is the language in which the document is written; the default is English.

Copyright: This is the copyright information for the content, which is usually blank.

Contributors: This includes the names of the people outside the Plone system who contributed to the object. Each person's name should be on its own line.

After completing the values for this form, click Save to commit the changes. As stated, usually you won't need to edit the values on this tab. Editing the contents of this tab is usually based upon the requirements for your site and the type of site you're building.

What Are Effective and Expiration Dates?

Any item in the Plone system can have effective and expiration dates if the person editing the content wants. Both of these are optional, and leaving the fields blank will ensure that these values aren't set.

One example of an item that may have an effective date is a press release. In the ideal world, the news item is crafted, prepared, and reviewed in Plone. However, suppose the news item has to go live on the Web site at midnight, but that's exactly when you plan to be sleeping. Not a problem—give the press release an effective date and a time of midnight. Up until the effective date, it won't be visible in the calendar, in navigation, in searches, or in pages that use a search as the listing under the news tab. However, anybody who knows about the press release will be able to access the page directly. Once the effective date has passed, the item will appear in all the aforementioned places and be live to the world.

The effect is similar with expiration dates. If you have a special offer that stops being effective on a particular day, then you could set an expiration date of that day. After that, date it wouldn't appear in calendar, navigation, searches, and so on.

The effective and expiration dates don't actually change the state of the item in workflow (see Chapter 7 for more information on workflow); rather, they just change where it displays. You can also set effective and expiration dates on the state tab, which you'll learn about in the next section.

Publishing Your Document

When a document is created, it's given an initial state, called *visible*. By default, content isn't automatically published and available to the world; instead, others can view your content, but it doesn't show up in searches or the navigation tree.

This is a useful state because you can point other users to this content, but because it won't show up in navigation or searches, it's not visible unless users know about it.

At any point in time, each item of content in your Plone site is in a particular state. This state describes its permissions and roles within the Plone site. By having items in different states, it's possible to apply different security to each item of content. For example, sometimes an item may take a week or two to prepare and involve multiple revisions. Eventually you'll want to publish the content so that it's visible for all users and shows up in the navigation and search.

You can publish the content using the State drop-down menu located at the top right of the main navigation (see Figure 3-15).

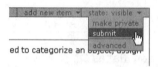

Figure 3-15. State drop-down menu

To publish an object, select Submit from the drop-down menu. By default you can't directly publish content, but you can submit it for review. When an item is submitted for review, it moves into the review state. This is an intermediary state between visible and published. It allows for the review of content by users of your site with the reviewer role, before it goes live for the entire world to see. After you've submitted the content, you'll notice that the content is now in the review state by looking at the box in the top-right corner. You'll also notice that in Figure 3-16, there's no longer an edit tab.

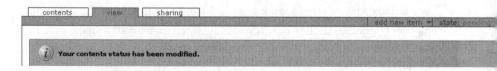

Figure 3-16. The content has been submitted for review, the state has changed to pending, and the edit tab is no longer an option.

 NOTE   If you're logged in as a manager, then you'll note there will be one extra option in the drop-down publishing list called Publish. This lets you put content straight into the published state with no intermediate step.

In the workflow drop-down list in the top-right corner, there's also an option for Advanced, which opens the state form for changing the status of an object. This form is the same as clicking the state tab. It has the following fields:

Effective Date: This is the same as the Effective Date field in the properties (see the "Setting Document Metadata" section).

Expiration Date: This is the same as the Expiration Date field in the properties (see the "Setting Document Metadata" section).

Comments: This includes any comments you want to make for this change in state that will be recorded in history. For example, you could enter **First draft; Bob, please see second paragraph.**

Change State: These mirror the choices available in the drop-down menu. For example, the options are Publish, Submit, and so on. One further option, No Change, is available if no change is necessary.

Select the change of state you'd like to occur, and click Save to commit the changes.

What Are the Workflow States?

At this point you may be asking yourself what this *workflow* thing is and what the states mean. Workflow, as discussed in Chapter 7, is the ability to apply different states to the content. The following are the default states:

Visible: Content is created in the visible state. All users can find visible content through the search function and can access it directly by visiting the object URL. Visible content doesn't show up in the navigation tree. Visible content is editable by their owners and site managers.

Pending: Pending content includes items that have been submitted for publishing by site members. From a user standpoint, pending content behaves like content in the visible state. The difference between the two types is that pending items are flagged for review; site reviewers are prompted to publish or reject pending items. Pending items are editable only by managers and reviewers.

Published: Published items are visible to all site visitors. They appear in search results and the navigation tree. They may also appear in other areas specific to that type (news items, for example, also appear when you click the news tab). Published items are editable only by managers, but owners can retract them for editing (retracting reverts an item to the public draft state).

Private: Items in the private state are visible and editable only by their owners and others with manager access to the folder in which they exist. They won't appear in search results or on the navigation tree for other users. Private items are editable by managers.

How Does Content Get Reviewed?

If you're a reviewer, then in the right column of the home page you'll see a new review list when you first log in. This is a list of the items that have been submitted for review and need reviewing by you or another reviewer (see Figure 3-17).

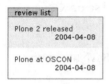

Figure 3-17. The review list

The review list will appear on the right when you log in as a user with the review role and there are items to review. In my case, I logged in as admin, which was the user created during my install process. You can tell you're logged in because your name will appear in the member bar. The review list gives a list of items to review—in this case, you need to review the test document. Click the document to open the item. At this point you essentially have the following choices for this item:

Reject it: Reject it by selecting Reject from the drop-down choices. This will move the content back into the visible state and assumes that as a reviewer you're unhappy with it. Usually you may want to click the Advanced option to open the comments form and add some comments stating why you're rejecting it.

Approve it: Approve it by selecting Publish; this will change the content into the published state. This will make the content publicly available.

Do nothing: Leave it by doing nothing. This leaves the content in limbo but sometimes happens when you need to check information or talk to others. Eventually you should return to do something with this content because it'll continue to show up in your list of items until you make one of the previous actions.

Edit it: Edit it, and then perform one of the previous actions. As the reviewer, you can make any change you'd like to do, so feel free to change the content by using the edit tab.

Once you've moved content *out* of the review state by publishing or retracting it, it will no longer show up in the review list. Of course, this assumes you do have someone as a reviewer for your site; this usually (although not necessarily) is also the user who created the Plone site as an administrator. In Chapter 8, I'll discuss how to add and edit users and give some users the review role.

How Do You Edit a Published Document?

Once a document has been published, it must be *retracted* to be edited. To do this, select Retract from the workflow drop-down menu, which will move the item back into the visible state. Once it has returned to the visible state, you can reedit it and place it back into the review queue.

This step, although a little annoying, is necessary to ensure that all content goes through a review step. For example, you have to ensure that any edits made to a page are appropriate by reviewing the content. Users with the manager role can edit the content at any time, so they can quickly go in and fix a typo without having to go through the review step. It's assumed that users with a manager role are trustworthy! If you're a manager, as defined in Chapter 9, you can go to any piece of content and will see the edit tab. At that point, click Edit to alter the document and make your changes.

Sharing Your Document

This allows you to assign more rights to other users or groups of users of the system to your document. This is an advanced feature and is covered in more detail in Chapter 9.

Adding and Editing Other Types of Content

I've just covered how to add and edit documents in detail. All the other content types are similar. They all have the same or similar actions to edit; it's just the forms and the data in them that change. In the following sections, I'll cover some of these other types of content. All the following types of content use the same workflow process, so they need to be published in the same manner as documents.

Adding and Editing Images

Images are graphical pieces of content; you add them by selecting Image from the drop-down list. When you add an image, the name of the content changes to the file of the image. So, if you upload an image called photo.gif, it'll be accessible in Plone as photo.gif. When adding or uploading a new image, you can select the image from your hard drive by clicking the Browse button and selecting the file (see Figure 3-18).

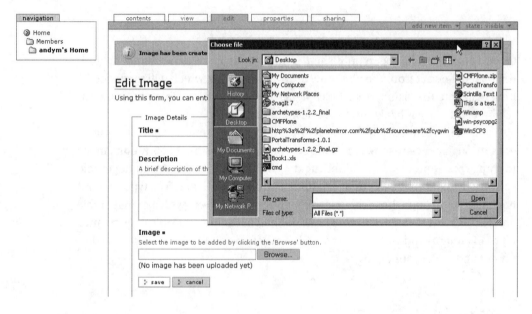

Figure 3-18. Uploading an image

It's common for image filenames to end with an extension such as .gif, .jpg, .jpeg, .png, or .pict. You can display images inside Plone on a Web page without having to download them to the local computer if the type of the image uploaded is viewable in the user's Web browser. The most common image types are .gif, .jpg, and .png, which are visible on almost computer system. Figure 3-19 shows an image of the Plone logo.

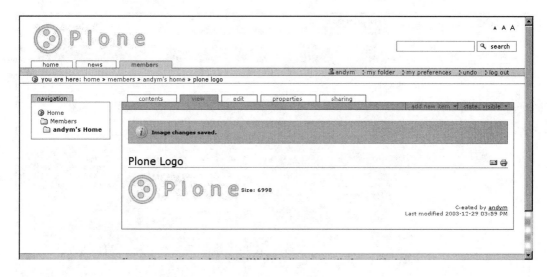

Figure 3-19. Viewing the image

You can't edit images directly; instead, you can edit the image on your hard drive using any program, such as Adobe Photoshop or GNU Image Manipulation Program (GIMP). Once complete, clicking the edit tab allows you upload your new image into Plone. If you do a lot of image manipulation, you can refer to Chapter 10, which covers External Editor, a tool that lets you edit images using a program without having to upload and download them.

Adding and Editing Files

A file is any arbitrary file that can be uploaded from your hard drive. To add a file, select File from the drop-down list. On the edit tab, you'll see an Upload button that lets you pick the file from your hard drive. This could be any sort of item, including a plain-text file, a Microsoft Word document, a Microsoft Excel spreadsheet, an executable program, an Adobe Acrobat document, and so on. When you add a file, the name of the item in Plone changes to the name of the file uploaded. So, if you upload a file called book.pdf, it'll be accessible in Plone as book.pdf. Figure 3-20 shows a plain-text file.

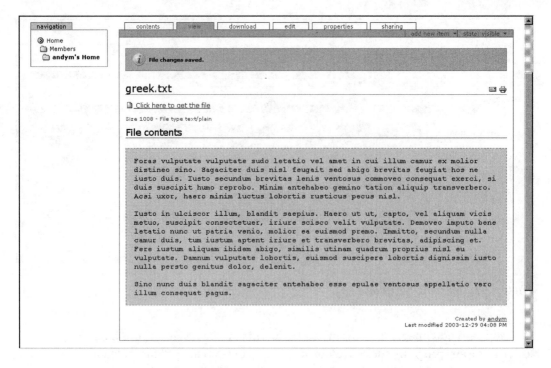

Figure 3-20. Adding a plain-text file

If the file is recognized as being text, then the contents of the file are shown in the Web page and are editable through the edit tab. Otherwise, the file is downloadable, and users must download it to their local hard drive and edit it there. Afterward they can upload it to the system. You'll note that a file object also has an extra download tab that lets you directly download the file.

Adding and Editing Events

An event can be something that will happen in the future or something that happened in past. You can add events to Plone, and they show up on the calendar. To add an event, select Event from the drop-down list. An event has more information than most Plone objects; however, most of it is self-explanatory (see Figure 3-21).

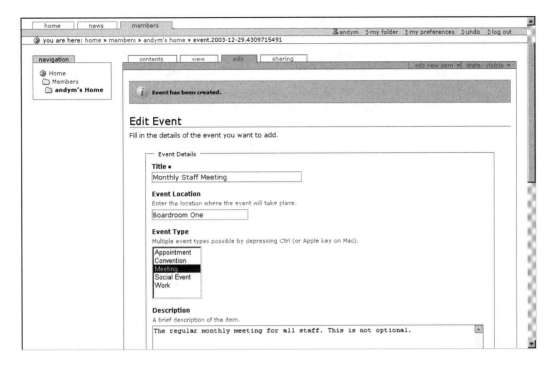

Figure 3-21. Adding an event

As usual, the only required field is Title; however, if you want the event to show up in the calendar, then you must provide a start and end time. Events can span multiple days or be in the past—as long as the start date is before the end date. To enter a date, select the appropriate dates from the drop-down menu, or click the little date icon to open a graphical date picker.

Once the event is published, it'll show up in the calendar. Moving a mouse over the item in the calendar will show the start and end dates for the event, as well as the event's title (see Figure 3-22).

Figure 3-22. Viewing events in the calendar

Adding and Editing Links

Link content types are the primary way for users to share links. These URLs can be resources on the Internet or an intranet, an internal resource, or anything to which the users have access. To add a link, select Link from the drop-down menu.

If you're going to link to an Internet resource, you should preface your link with the suitable protocol (for example, http://). For instance, if I was visiting an interesting page on the BBC's Web site and wanted to share this, I could add a link. The value of the URL will be the text in the address bar (for example, http://news.bbc.co.uk), as shown in Figure 3-23.

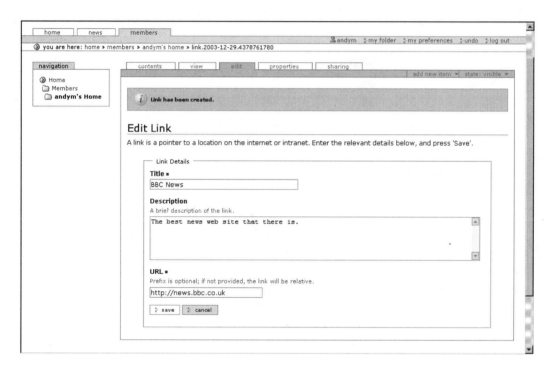

Figure 3-23. Adding a link

Adding and News Items

News items are commonly used in Web sites to display news that's of interest to the reader. Actually, a news item contains the same information as a document. The only real difference is that a news item will show up when a visitor clicks the news tab (once the item is published), as shown in Figure 3-24.

Figure 3-24. A list of news items

If I wanted to write a Web page that was going to be relevant for a long period of time, such as directions to my company's office, I'd use a document. If I wanted a page that detailed my exciting new product and drew attention to it, I'd use a news item. That news item would be visible under the news tab, and as new things happened, it'd slowly move down the page.

Organizing Content

So far you've seen how to add and edit content in a Plone site, but without clear organization, this can become a mess quite quickly. You have two main ways of organizing content: folders and topics. A *folder* is the simplest and most powerful mechanism for organizing content and works just like a folder or a directory on a computer's hard drive. A folder can contain any item of content; content can be copied and pasted between folders, and of course folders can contain other folders.

To organize content that's spread all over a site, a more sophisticated and less-used tool called a *topic* is available. A topic searches your Plone site and finds all objects that match a certain criteria, allowing you to group lots of disparate content.

Using Folders

A folder is just like a folder or a directory on a hard drive, except that the folder and its contents exist inside Plone. You use a folder the same way; when you need to categorize content or make things a little clearer, you can group items and place them in a folder. To add a folder to your site, select Folder from the drop-down list. This will add a folder and take you to the edit properties page for that form. A folder has just three rather simple attributes that a user can edit: Name, Title, and Description. I've discussed all these attributes for documents, and nothing is different for folders.

Folders have two green tabs that represent slightly different views: contents and view. Actually, you may have already noticed that there's a contents tab accessible from any piece of content that you've added to the site; for example, when you were editing a document, the contents tab was there. That contents tab will always take you to the contents for that folder.

Viewing the Contents of a Folder

The folder has the concept of a default page, which is a page that will be shown to the user when they view a folder. It's a concept taken from Web sites where viewing a folder on a Web site shows a default page if one is present; often that default page's name is index.htm or index.html. If a folder has a default page, then clicking the view tab will show that default page. If the folder doesn't have a default page, then it'll show a folder listing of all the content in that folder. When looking for a default page to display, Plone looks through the folder for content with a certain name and shows this item. The page name is usually index.html or index_html; however, the site administrator can add or alter these names.

This contents view of a folder allows a user to perform a variety of tasks, such as move content, rename it, delete it, publish it, and change the order it's listed. As shown in Figure 3-25, you'll also see a simple table of the folder contents. Each row of the table shows the title of the content (plus an icon), the type, its size, when it was last modified, its current workflow status, and order selectors. On the left is a checkbox to select the items you want to change and a series of options across the bottom: Rename, Cut, Copy, Delete, and Change Status. These functions are all pretty self-explanatory, and you can apply them to multiple objects at once by clicking several checkboxes.

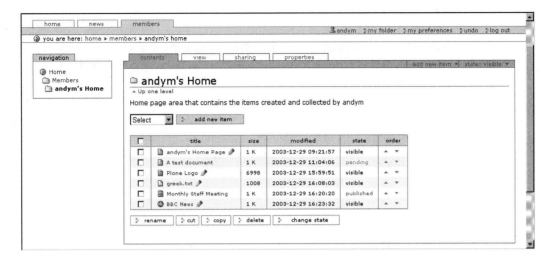

Figure 3-25. *Contents of a folder after I've added some of the content types described in this chapter*

For example, to quickly rename a piece of content, click that item's checkbox and then click Rename. This will open the rename form and allow you to rename the title of each item in that list. Click Save to have the changes take effect. The Cut and Copy buttons allow you to copy or move content between different folders. The Delete button allows you to delete the item from Plone. Just like on your hard drive, if you copy, move, or delete a folder, all the contents of the folder will also be moved, copied, or deleted.

A new feature in Plone 2 is the ability to change the default order of items in a folder. By default, items in a folder will display in the order the items were added. If one item is more important and needs to be moved to the top, use the arrows on the right side of the table to move the item. The following features will appear in the folder contents only when certain things happen:

- If the content has an expiration date set and it has expired, you'll see the word *expired* appear in red next to the item.

- If the server has External Editor installe d, you can click the pencil to edit in External Editor (this is covered in Chapter 10).

- If the content is locked, you'll see a lock icon appear next to the content.

Publishing a Folder

Folders have a much simpler workflow than documents. Earlier in this chapter you saw how to publish content to make it publicly visible because this allows users to create and edit content as much as possible before pushing it live. However, folders are a little different because they contain content but don't have any content of their own. For this reason, folders have no review state. Anyone can directly publish or make private folders, so there are three states: private, visible, and published.

After adding a folder, select Publish from the drop-down list. Then it'll show up in the navigation. As per the earlier rules for workflow, if you don't publish a folder, it won't show up in the navigation.

Using Topics

A topic allows you to collect content from disparate places throughout a Plone site and provide it in one location. Topics work by creating a criterion that's common to all the objects you'd like to gather. This criterion could be all images or all news items with *Plone* in the text. Because topics are a rather complicated type of content, only managers can add them initially. If you can't see Topic in the list of items to add, then you don't have the permission to do so.

To add a topic, select Topic from the drop-down list. After adding the topic, you can create key criteria on the criteria tab. The list of criteria and types is available in the drop-down box at the bottom of the page. This is a rather confusing list; I won't try to discuss it here. Unfortunately, what those terms are and what they mean is based heavily on the underlying technology, such as catalog indexes and object attributes. For this reason, Chapter 11 covers this in detail.

For example, to create a topic that shows all the images, you need to add a criterion that searches for content based on portal_type. For this, select a field name of portal_type, select String Criterion, and then click Add. These criteria will be added to the top of the page; in the field to the right of portal_type, enter **Image**, and then click Save. You now have criteria for your topic that will show all content that's an image. Returning to the view tab, you can now see all the images on a site.

As stated, topics are quite complicated, have a rather unfriendly interface, and are recommended for only advanced users. Many people have found topics useful, which is why they're still available in Plone; however, a more user-friendly system will be developed in the future.

Discussing and Finding Content

Adding and editing content in Plone is much more useful if people can find and then discuss the content. The primary ways users find content is through searching and navigation. Fortunately, Plone automatically sets up searching and navigation for the users, so it's easy to find the content you've added.

Adding Comments to Content

Feedback from users is a vital part of any Web site. By allowing users to add comments, you ensure that users can give feedback, correct typographical errors, or otherwise discuss the content. You can discuss almost any piece of content in Plone; folders and topics are the only exceptions.

You can enable discussions in one of two ways. First, the owner of the content (otherwise known as the person who created it) turns on the discussion feature by clicking the properties tab of the object and selecting Enabled under the Allow Discussion on This Item header, as shown in Figure 3-26. Second, the default option applies the policy for that type of content as defined by the site administrator; setting this option is described for the administrator in Chapter 10.

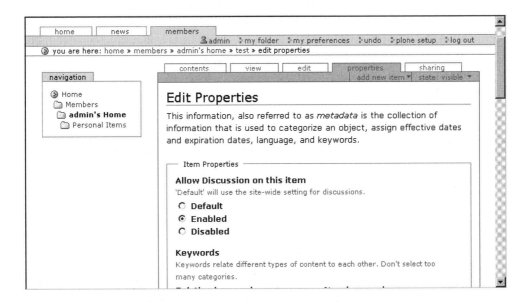

Figure 3-26. Enabling discussions

Once discussions are enabled, click the Add Comment button to discuss the content, which opens a form for adding the comment (see Figure 3-27).

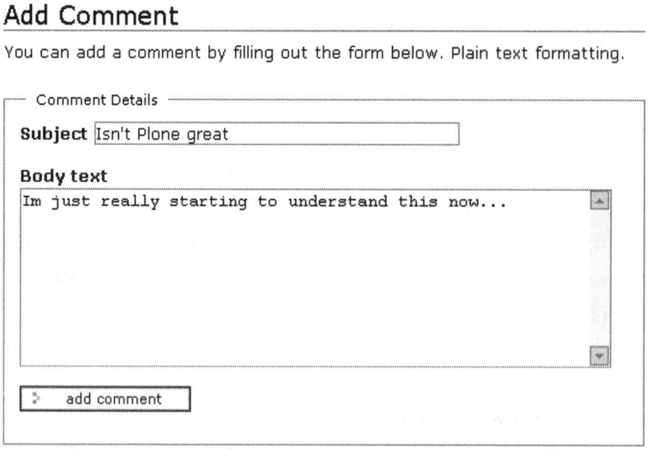

Add Comment

You can add a comment by filling out the form below. Plain text formatting.

Comment Details

Subject Isn't Plone great

Body text

Im just really starting to understand this now...

add comment

Figure 3-27. Adding a comment to a piece of content

Enter the subject of the comment and the text of the comment. The text is entered as plain text, so just type away as usual. Comments don't go through any workflow, so comments show up as soon as they've been added. Once a comment has been entered, it can be replied to, forming a threaded list of comments on an item. Further, comments will be entered in the catalog so they can be searched.

NOTE Administrators logged in as managers can remove any replies or entire threads. Disabling replies doesn't remove the comments; it just stops them being shown, so reenabling comments will show the existing comments again.

Searching for Content

Plone contains a powerful search engine system based on Zope's ZCatalog. This search engine allows content to be cataloged in multiple ways and to be queried efficiently and quickly. Chapter 10 covers the internals of how this works and how it can be queried.

When you're searching for content, the content will be shown to a user if it's one of the two states: published or visible. At the top of your Plone site a search box provides an easy way to do simple textual searches in the same way as a search engine (see Figure 3-28). For example, enter **Tuesday** to find all content that contains the word *Tuesday*. A result of all matching content will display; click the title to get to the content.

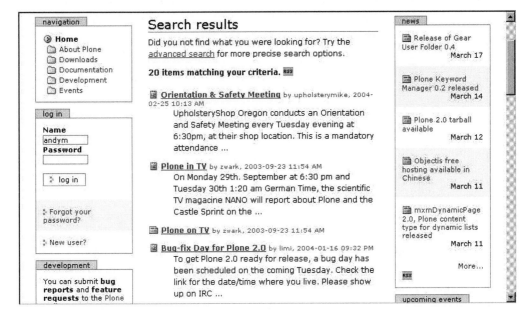

Figure 3-28. A search for Tuesday *on Plone.org*

The search provides a quite sophisticated search, with features similar to most search engines. You can make this simple query quite complex. For example, you can use the following options:

Globbing: You can use an asterisk to signify any letters. For example, entering **Tues*** matches *Tuesday* and *Tuesdays*. You can't use the asterisk at the beginning of a word, though.

Single wildcards: You can use a question mark anywhere to signify one letter. For example, entering **ro?e** matches *rope*, *rote*, *role*, and so on. You can't use the question mark at the beginning of a word, though.

And: You can use the word *and* to signify that both terms on either side of the *and* must exist. For example, entering **Rome and Tuesday** will return a result of when both those words are in the content.

Or: You can use the word *or* to signify that either term can exist. For example, entering **Rome or Tuesday** will return a result of when either of those words are in the content.

Not: You can use the word *not* to return results where the word isn't present; a prefix of *and* is required. For example, entering **welcome and not page** would return matches for pages that contained *welcome*, but not *page*.

Phrases: Phrases are grouped with double quotes (" ") and signify several words one after the other. For example, entering **"welcome page"** matches *This welcome page is used to introduce you to the Plone Content Management System*, but not *Welcome to the front page of my Web site*.

Not *phrase:* You can specify a phrase with a minus (-) prefix. For example, entering **welcome -"welcome page"** matches all pages with *welcome* in them, but not ones that match the phrase *welcome page*.

 NOTE All searches are case insensitive.

Large sites may have a lot of results, so only 20 results display at a time. To page through the results, navigation bars will appear at the top and the bottom of the search result pages. The values on an object used in a search are its title, description, and body text (if the content type has any—for example, news items and documents).

Performing an Advanced Search

You can narrow down the search results by using an advanced search, which is accessible via the search results of a standard search. In old Plone sites, a search tab brought users to this page; you can reenable this tab if you want, as covered in Chapter 4. The advanced search form enables a user to query content using a number of attributes, including title, keywords, description, review state, creation date, content type, and even author, as well as the search text (as used in the quick search available from the top-right corner), as shown in Figure 3-29.

Although the search text field searches both the title and description, you may want to search the description or title only. For that reason, these fields are presented on the advanced search form. You can't search the title and description using the wildcards, globbing, or any of the advanced search options. Any search result will match the input (if given) of all the fields; the results will be an intersection of all the terms.

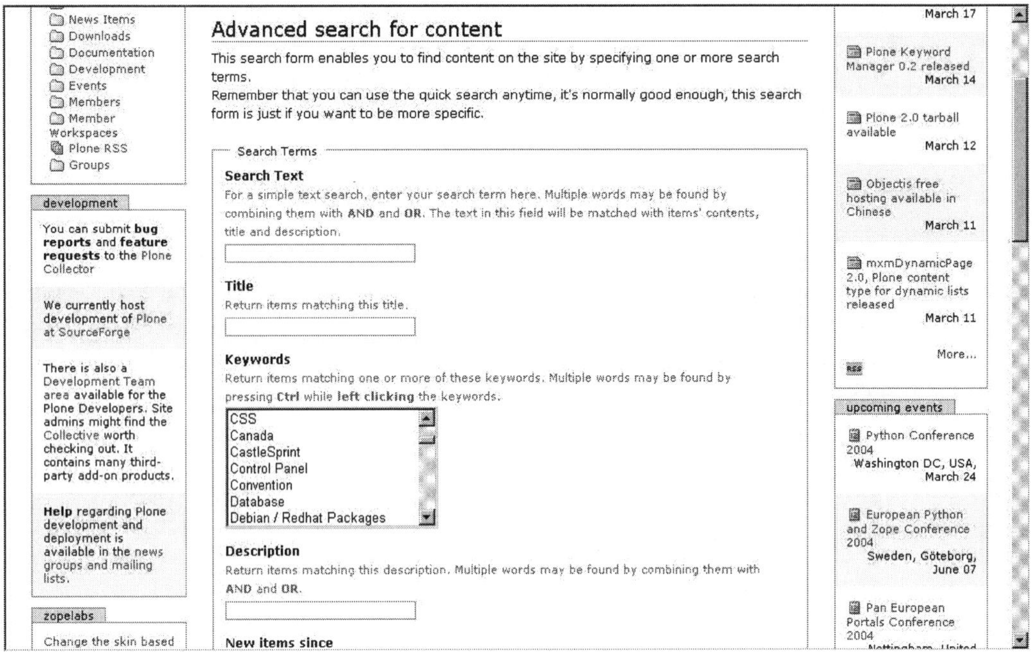

Figure 3-29. Advanced search

Example: Creating the Plone Book Web Site

To give an example Plone site and provide a series of examples, I set up a Web site for this book. This is a Plone site with a few minor modifications. As I go through the book, I'll make references to the site and add new features as they're covered in the book, including new templates, skins, and so on. The Web site for this book is at http://plone-book.agmweb.ca; initially I set this site up on Windows server, as described in Chapter 2. However, I later transferred it to Linux.

The site serves the following purposes:

- It gives people a place to get info rmation about the book and buy it.

- It allows easy access to the software used in the book.

- It gives code examples and allows users to interact with samples in the book.

- It contains any errata or issues found after publication.

Once I set up a Plone site, I created the following basic folder and page structure:

```
Home
 |_ Software
 |_ Chapters
     |_ Chapter 1
     |_ Chapter 2
     ...
```

To do this, I logged in as the user who was created with the installer—in my case, the admin user. After logging in, I went to the home page, clicked the edit tab, and wrote some text for the home page. I created links to the Chapters and Software folders. Then I clicked the contents tab and added two folders, as shown in Figure 3-30.

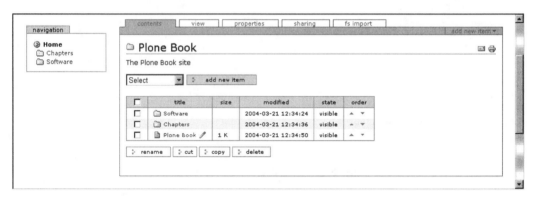

Figure 3-30. The folder contents with my home page and the new folders

Next, I went to the Chapters folder and started adding a folder for each chapter. Because I haven't made a default page, Plone will happily create a listing of all the chapters. The description for each chapter is the name of the chapter (for example, *Introducing to Plone and This Book*), and the short name is the chapter number— this will keep my URLs nice and short (for example, /Chapters/3). I've left everything in the visible state, so after this, it's just a matter of adding content.

CHAPTER 4

Making Simple Customizations

AFTER YOU'VE FIGURED OUT how to add and edit content, you'll want to start customizing your site. This chapter explains how to perform simple customizations in Plone using the options available to administrators. Performing the customizations in this chapter requires a user to be logged in with the manager role, as discussed in Chapter 2.

These customizations are all configuration options you can make through the Web. Rather than explain all these parts in detail, this chapter gives an overview of many subjects and explains how to accomplish certain tasks while showing some of the under-the-hood machinery. These topics are then expanded and explained in later chapters throughout the book.

The first and most useful place to look is the Plone control panel, which offers a variety of options for the site administrator. All the parts of a Plone site are designed to be easily changed and customized; the blue tabs you can see across the top of the page are easy to add and remove. Other examples are the boxes in the left and right columns, which are called *portlets*. Plone comes with several portlets, and you can easily choose where to display certain portlets.

Finally, this chapter shows how to customize Cascading Style Sheets (CSS) and images in Plone. CSS affects everything in a Plone site. In fact, as you'll see in this chapter, CSS determines all the colors, all the positioning, and a lot of the images you see. If you have the ability to change the CSS code, then you can change almost the entire look and feel of your Plone site. All the options covered in this chapter show you the large degree of control you have over your Plone site.

Administering Sites

The first place site administrators should visit is the Plone control panel. This is the way to access some of the administration functions of a site, including the name and description of your Plone site, user and group administration, and any errors that occur within your site.

The term *control panel* is common, so don't confuse it with the Zope Management Interface (ZMI) control panel that shows the low-level ZMI options. The Plone control panel is an ongoing attempt to provide a more user-friendly interface for the functions provided in the ZMI. Since the project is ongoing, it's hard to predict what functionality will be available in the future. Instead, I recommend you go to the control panel and see what functions are currently available; if you can't complete your task there, then you'll have to go to the ZMI.

To access the control panel, log into Plone as a user with the manager role. If you don't have a user with that role and are an administrator of the site, see Chapter 9 for more information on how to do this. If you aren't the administrator of a site and want this level of access, ask your site administrator. To access the control panel, click *plone setup* at the top of the page (see Figure 4-1).

Figure 4-1. Accessing the control panel

This opens the control panel (see Figure 4-2).

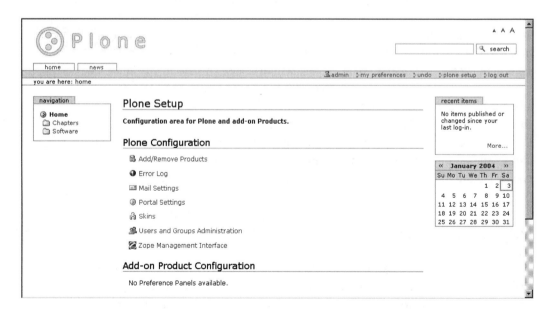

Figure 4-2. Plone control panel

The following functions are available in the control panel:

- **Add/Remove Products**: Clicking this link allows you to automate the installation products (covered in detail in Chapter 10).

- **Error Log**: Clicking this link accesses the log of errors that have occurred in the Plone site.

- **Mail Settings**: Clicking this link allows you to alter the Simple Mail Transfer Protocol (SMTP) server Plone uses to send e-mail.

- **Portal Settings**: Clicking this link allows you to alter portal settings (discussed in the "Changing the Title, Description, and E-Mail Addresses" section of this chapter).

- **Skins**: Clicking this link allows you to set the current skin (discussed in Chapter 7).

- **Users and Groups Administration**: Clicking this link allows you to alter users and groups (discussed in Chapter 8).

- **Zope Management Interface**: Clicking this link takes you to the ZMI.

Throughout the rest of the book, I reference the Plone control panel if the current feature is accessible from there; however, the remainder of book uses the ZMI for altering properties.

Using the ZMI

The ZMI is the basic interface that gives you access to Plone's underlying Zope interface. Before Plone existed, the ZMI was the main way to access, edit, and manage a Zope site and its content. This was originally the Web interface for the content management system. Of course, nowadays Zope isn't really an out-of-the-box content management system but instead is an application that sits under a system such as Plone. After quickly playing with the ZMI, you'll see why it isn't suited as an interface to a content management system.

One thing the ZMI does provide is a simple interface to the underlying Plone and Zope infrastructure. You can find many of the basic features mentioned in this chapter through Plone, but you'll need to use the ZMI eventually. If you haven't gone to the ZMI before, then you'll find that there are a few simple ways to get there; the easiest way is to log in as a user with the manager role, click *plone setup*, and then click *Zope Management Interface*. You'll note that the address of the ZMI is the uniform resource locator (URL) of your Plone site with /manage on the end of it. The ZMI for your Plone site should look like this:

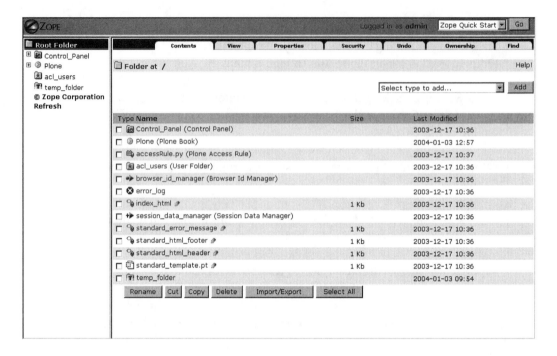

You may have a problem with virtual hosting, which occurs with the Windows and Mac installers. Virtual hosting is the ability to have the Plone site as the root object rather than the root of your Zope instance. For more information on virtual hosting, see Chapter 10. So, to get to the root, you need to access the manage port. On Windows, select Start ➤ Plone ➤ Plone ➤ Manage Root. You'll note that this sets the address to http://localhost:8080/manage. For information on virtual hosting with your installation, see the specific documentation.

You'll need to get to the root of your Zope installation for two reasons. First, you'll need to get to the Zope control panel. Second, you'll need to get to the root of your Plone site to make, rename, and copy Plone sites. The Zope control panel gives you database information and access to products and other add-ons (you'll need access to this for Chapter 10), as shown here:

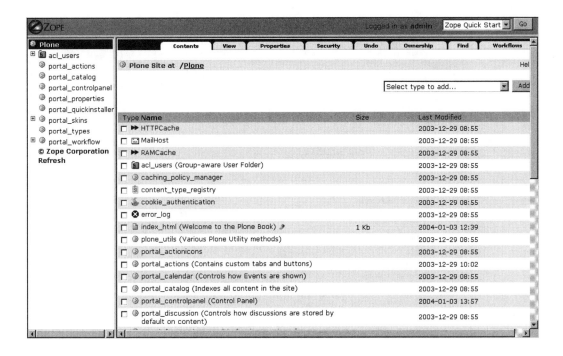

TIP When dealing with the ZMI, I find having two different browsers open helpful. For example, I use Mozilla and Firefox. Besides, as a site administrator, it's always a good idea to have two different browsers to test that your changes work in more than one browser.

Changing the Title, Description, and E-Mail Addresses

The title, description, and e-mail addresses are stored in a Plone site as properties on an object inside Plone. You can access these fields by clicking the *Portal Settings* link in the Plone control panel (see Figure 4-3).

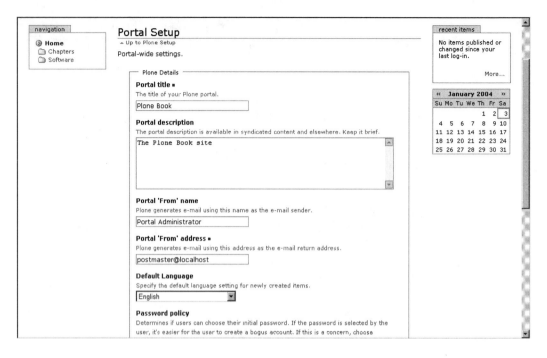

Figure 4-3. Portal options

The portal settings are as follows:

- **Portal title:** This is the title of the site that will appear in the title for browsers, breadcrumbs, navigation, e-mails, and so on. The default is Portal.

- **Portal description:** This is the description for the portal, which is currently used only in syndication.

- **Portal 'From' name:** This field is related to various functions, such as a lost password or the "send-to-a-friend" function. Plone sends the e-mail messages with this name attached. The default is Portal Administrator.

- **Portal 'From' address:** This is the address used for the e-mails that Plone sends. The default is postmaster@localhost.

- **Default Language:** This is the default language that's given in the properties of an object.

- **Password policy:** New users have two options; they can either enter a password or enter a password that's then e-mailed to them. Although in both cases they have to enter an e-mail address, the latter choice ensures that the e-mail address they enter is valid.

- **Enable External Editor Feature:** This will turn on External Editor, which is an advanced editing tool. It requires that External Editor be installed on the user's computer. Chapter 10 covers this in more detail.

After selecting the options you want, click Save to commit the changes. All the changes on this form will occur immediately.

Setting Up a Mail Server

Plone will send e-mail using the `MailHost` object, which provides an interface to an SMTP server and allows the developer to write forms and tools that send e-mails. The "send-to-a-friend" function and the mailing of a forgotten password use the settings configured here.

The default configuration is for a mail server on the localhost at port 25. If the SMTP server is located elsewhere in the network, then you can access the form by clicking *plone setup* and then clicking *Mail Settings*. Then change the mail server and the port to suit your configuration. On my network, the mail server is at `monty.clearwind.ca` on port 1025, so I set the server as shown in Figure 4-4; however, in most cases, you won't need to change this.

 NOTE   The `MailHost` object is a Zope object accessible in the ZMI. This object doesn't currently allow for authentication with the server. If this is needed, change the settings on the server.

Figure 4-4. Setting up the mail server

Logging Errors

The error log catches errors that may occur in a Plone site; these are features such as Page Not Found (404) errors, unauthorized errors, and so on. This isn't designed to trap errors from forms. For instance, if somebody doesn't enter a required field in a form, then this won't be reported; this isn't an error since it's captured by the validation framework. This error log is designed to catch internal server errors that may occur.

From the Plone interface, click *plone setup* and then click *Error Log* to see the errors reported by the Plone site. Click the exception in the list (if there's one reported) to see the error. Figure 4-5 shows an error that occurred when incorrectly filling out the mail settings form. It's a long page that includes a complete Python traceback and the incoming request.

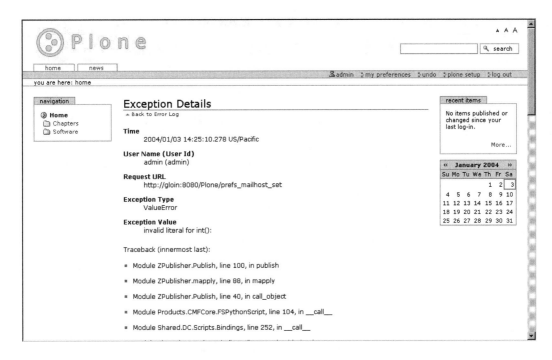

Figure 4-5. An example error

On the error log form you'll see the following settings:

- **Number of exceptions to keep**: These are the exceptions to keep in the active log on the screen. The default is 20.

- **Copy exceptions to the event log**: This copies each exception to the file-based log file. Not doing this means that no permanent record will be kept for exceptions. The default is that this is selected.

- **Ignored exception types**: This is a list (one per line) of exception types to ignore. The default is Unauthorized, NotFound, and Redirect.

You can log each exception and view it on the screen. This means if a user is visiting your site and an error occurs, then you can go to the error log and see what occurred. The three components of an error are the error type (which is the type of the error), the error value (which is a string explaining when an error occurs), and the traceback. These first two items are shown to a user on a standard error page (see Figure 4-6).

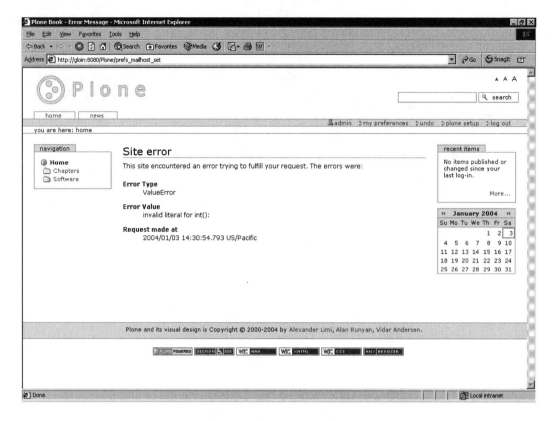

Figure 4-6. An example error message

So, when a user reports an error, the report will often include a message with the error name and a value in it. If user isn't allowed to do something and an Unauthorized error is raised or a Page Not Found (404) is triggered, then you'll get a custom error page rather than the standard page shown in Figure 4-6. The following standard error types occur:

- **Unauthorized**: This occurs when a user doesn't have the right to perform a function.

- **NotFound**: This occurs when the item a user is trying to access doesn't exist.

- **Redirect**: This is an error that can raise a Hypertext Transfer Protocol (HTTP) redirect.

- **AttributeError**: When an object doesn't have this attribute, this error is raised.

- **ValueError**: This occurs when a value given is incorrect and isn't caught correctly by the validation or other framework.

Customizing Plone's Look and Feel

The following sections describe the other customizations you can make to a site; almost of all these require access to the ZMI.

Understanding Portlets

On a Plone site, you'll see three columns to a page by default: the left, middle, and right columns. The middle column contains the content for the object being currently viewed. This is where most of the user functionality is for adding and editing content, completing forms, and so on. The left and right columns contain a series of boxes that display information. Each of these boxes is called a *portlet*. A variable determines which portlets display at a particular point in time. The best way to understand these portlets is to look at the default portlets that ship with a Plone site. You can find the parameters for the portlets in the portal object. To access this, go to the ZMI, ensure you're on the root Plone site, and click the properties tab. This opens a list of properties, including `left_slots`, `right_slots`, and `document_action_slots` (see Figure 4-7).

NOTE   In earlier versions of Plone, the portlets were called *slots*. This is a common term that conflicts with the page template term *slot*, so it was changed to *portlets* for version 2. In certain places in the code and in the text, you may see the term *slot* used. In these contexts, the words *slot* and *portlet* are synonymous.

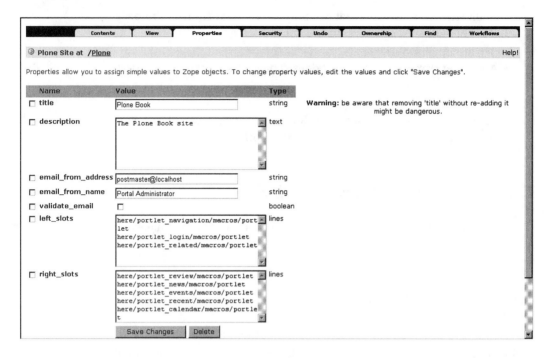

Figure 4-7. The default portlet properties

The left_slots properties refer to portlets shown on the left of the page, and the right_slots properties list the portlets shown on the right of the page. The portlets are shown in the order, from top to bottom, that they're listed in the properties; notice that each portlet is on a new line. However, most portlets have some code to ensure that the portlet displays only if it makes sense. For example, a login portlet is pointless to show if the user is already logged in. In this case, the login portlet is included in the list of portlets but will show up only when needed.

Each portlet value is actually a special value called a Template Attribute Languages Expression Syntax (TALES) path expression (Chapter 5 covers this in detail). Site developers can add their own portlets to a site by creating simple macros and page templates. The default portlets are as follows:

left_slots: This includes the navigation, login, and related portlets.

right_slots: This includes the review, news, events, recently published, and calendar portlets. All the available portlets aren't configured in Plone by default. The following sections describe portlet slot in Plone. Each section describes the portlet and shows what it looks like. Then I give the path expression that you need to add to the slots property so it'll show up in your Plone site.

For example, to show the calendar portlet on left side, enter **here/portlet_calendar/macros/portlet** in the `left_slots` property, and click Save Changes. If you want to remove it from the `right_slots` property, then you could remove the same line from the `right_slots` property and click Save Changes.

Calendar

The calendar portlet is one of the default portlets that displays the calendar on the right of the Plone page. This portlet shows published events for that month in a little calendar. The calendar portlet will appear regardless if there are events to show in the calendar. You can further configure the calendar using the `portal_calendar` tool in the ZMI (see Figure 4-8).

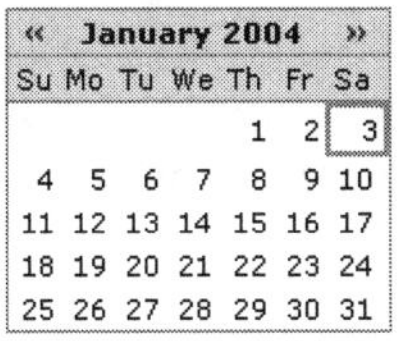
« January 2004 »
Su Mo Tu We Th Fr Sa
1 2 3
4 5 6 7 8 9 10
11 12 13 14 15 16 17
18 19 20 21 22 23 24
25 26 27 28 29 30 31

Figure 4-8. Calendar portlet

The expression to add is `here/portlet_calendar/macros/portlet`.

Events

The events portlet displays a list of the upcoming published events. If you have this item in the portlet list, it won't show up unless there are some published events to display (see Figure 4-9).

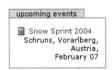

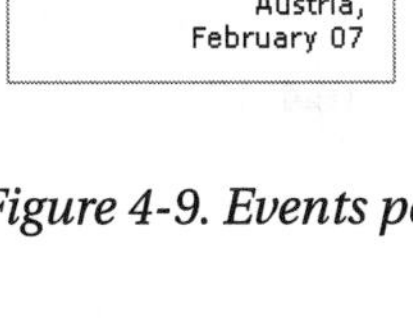
upcoming events
Snow Sprint 2004
Schruns, Vorarlberg,
Austria,
February 07

Figure 4-9. Events portlet

The expression to add is `here/portlet_events/macros/portlet`.

Favorites

In the top-right corner of a Plone document, you'll see a Plone icon. A user can click this logo to add a favorite. A *favorite* is similar to the concept of a bookmark or link to the page to which you want to return; however, this favorite is stored on the Plone site. Figure 4-10 shows the icon to add a favorite.

Figure 4-10. The icon to add a favorite

The favorites are added to the user's home folder, and they display in the favorites portlet along with a link to organize them (see Figure 4-11). The favorites that are shown are particular to the favorites that user has saved, so even if you have this item in the portlet list, it won't show up unless the user has some favorites.

Figure 4-11. Favorites portlet

The expression to add is here/portlet_favorites/macros/portlet.

Login

The login portlet displays the login form so a user can log in using their username and password. If they've forgotten their password, they have an option to get their password e-mailed to them. Even if you have this item in the portlet list, however, it won't show if the user is already logged in (see Figure 4-12).

Figure 4-12. Login portlet

The expression to add is `here/portlet_login/macros/portlet`.

Navigation

The navigation portlet shows a simple tree of the folders in the current position in the form of a tree. It provides a powerful and simple navigation tool. The navigation portlet is extremely customizable; you can alter it by clicking *portal_properties* and then clicking *navtree_properties* inside the ZMI, which is covered in the "Altering the Navigation Portlet" section (see Figure 4-13).

Figure 4-13. Navigation portlet

The expression to add is `here/portlet_navigation/macros/portlet`.

News

The news portlet lists all the recent news items, with links to them (see Figure 4-14). Even if you have this item in the portlet list, it won't show up unless there are some news items published. The news items on a site are also available by clicking the news tab.

Figure 4-14. News portlet

The expression to add is here/portlet_news/macros/portlet.

Recent

The recent portlet lists the recently published items on the site since the last time you logged in (see Figure 4-15). If there are no such items, it'll still display.

Figure 4-15. Related portlet

The expression to add is here/portlet_recent/macros/portlet.

Related

The related portlet shows a list of items that are related to the item you're currently viewing, as determined by the keywords on that item. If a related item is a link to another Web site, then it'll show up in a separate list of external resources. Even if you have this item in the list of portlets, it won't display unless there are some related items (see Figure 4-16).

Figure 4-16. Related portlet

The expression to add is `here/portlet_news/macros/portlet`.

Review

The review portlet displays a list of items that are in the review state and are waiting to be reviewed. This is shown only if the user logged in has the reviewer role and there are items awaiting review (see Figure 4-17).

Figure 4-17. Review portlet

The expression to add is `here/portlet_review/macros/portlet`.

Book Web Site: Altering Slots

For the Plone book site, most of the slots on the right side made no sense. This book has no events, so the calendar and event slots weren't needed. I expect new things to be added to the site, but really they'll be minimal once the site is complete. So I decided to remove all the right slots for my site. I did this by going to the portal root object in the ZMI and clicking the Properties object. Then I deleted right slots. The navigation, login, and related portlets, which normally occur on the left side, are all useful to me, so I kept those.

Here's how the portlet properties for the Plone book site look at this point:

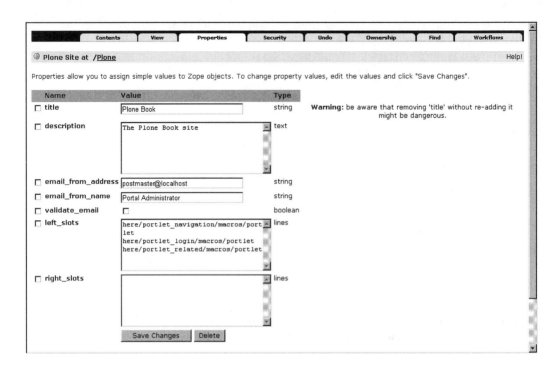

Having Different Portlets in Different Parts of Your Site

The underlying Zope database of Plone provides a feature called *acquisition*. In its simplest form, this means when looking up an item, such as right_slots, Plone finds the closest object that contains the property. So, when looking for what portlets to show in the right column, normally Plone finds the root object and lists those.

That's why you can change the properties in the root portal object to change the whole site. You may notice that if you click the *my folder* link and go to your personal folder, there's no calendar. If you click *Members* and then click *Properties* in the ZMI, you'll see that there's an entry for right_slots. The entry for that folder is an empty list. When the Plone site goes looking for a value to show for the right column's portlets, it moves up the folder hierarchy until it reaches the Members folder. There it finds the right_slots value and uses that. Since the value of right_slot in the Members folder is empty whenever you're viewing content located in Members, the right slot will be empty.

By adding and removing properties from folders through the ZMI, site administrators can customize exactly what portlets appear on their sites. The properties tab is fortunately reasonably straightforward. You just select the item in the ZMI and then click *Properties*. To add a left or right slots property, use the add form at the bottom of the form and ensure that the property type is list.

Altering the Navigation Portlet

Of all the portlets covered, probably the most useful and the most asked about is the navigation portlet. Specifically, how can you alter the navigation portlet and the way that it's displayed? The navigation portlet is list of current folders and documents in the navigation slot. You can alter the navigation slot by changing the code; however, you can make many changes through the ZMI. The biggest thing to remember is that only published objects will be shown in the navigation tree to members and anonymous users. To alter the navigation tree properties, click *portal_properties* and then click *navtree_properties* in the ZMI.

The following is an abridged list of the options available:

- **showMyUserFolderOnly**: This displays only the user folder of the user logged in. So when the Members folder is being shown in the navigation, it won't show every Members folder. This is selected by default.

- **showFolderishSiblingsOnly**: Only folders in parent folders will display if this is selected; otherwise, it will show all content. This is selected by default.

- **showFolderishChildrenOnly**: When this is enabled on a folder, it shows only folders in the same folder rather than all the other types of content. Selecting this option effectively shows you all the contents of the folder currently viewed. This is selected by default.

- **roleSeeUnpublishedContent**: As mentioned, content is shown only if published to members and anonymous users. Add more roles to this list, with each role on a new line, to have nonpublished content display. This is undesirable if the user doesn't actually have access anyway.

- **croppingLength**: This determines how many characters of the names to show in the navigation tree. The default is 256.

- **idsnotToList**: This is the item IDs not to show. Place each ID on a separate line. The default is None.

Make any changes to that form, and then click Save Changes. The order of the items in the navigation tree is determined by the order of the items in the folder contents form. As shown in Chapter 3, using the up and down arrows, users can change this order to suit their own needs.

Book Web Site: Altering the Navigation Tree

For most Web sites I prefer a fuller navigation tree than the one provided by default. So, I went to the navigation tree options and deselected showFolderishChildrenOnly and showFolderishSiblingsOnly. This made the contents show up nicely; for example, here's the software folder with just a few items selected:

Altering the Date Formats

Throughout the portlets and the whole site, Plone presents dates in a consistent format that are editable using formats set internally. Whenever a date is shown in Plone, it calls one of two formats. You can find these formats by accessing the ZMI, clicking *portal_properties*, and clicking *site_properties*. These are the formats:

- **localTimeFormat:** This is the time format to use for dates that should appear in a short format in Plone.

- **localLongTimeFormat:** This is the time format to use for dates that should appear in a long format in Plone, showing seconds.

The format for the date is based on Python's time format module. The reference for the formats are at http://www.python.org/doc/current/lib/module-time.html. For the short date, the default value is %Y-%m-%d, which means *year-month-day* as decimal numbers (for example, *2003-10-26*). For long date, the default value is %Y-%m-%d %I:%M %p, which means *year-month-day hours:minutes am/pm* (for example, *2003-10-26 07:32 PM*).

The following is a quick summary of the options available:

- **%a:** Locale's abbreviated weekday name (for example, *Mon*)

- **%A:** Locale's full weekday name (for example, *Monday*)

- **%b**: Locale's abbreviated month name (for example, *Jan*)

- **%B**: Locale's full month name (for example, *January*)

- **%d**: Day of the month as a decimal number

- **%H**: Hour (24-hour clock) as a decimal number

- **%I**: Hour (12-hour clock) as a decimal number

- **%m**: Month as a decimal number

- **%M**: Minute as a decimal number

- **%S**: Second as a decimal number

- **%y**: Year without century as a decimal number

- **%Y**: Year with century as a decimal number

If you want to include the day name in the short date, it's a simple matter of changing the short date format to read `%A, %b. %d, %y`. This produces *Thursday, Oct. 24, 02*. These dates are used in the boxes on the left and right of the screen, in the search results, in the content byline, and so on.

Adding Keywords and Event Types

One of the tools in Plone, `portal_metadata`, allows the site administrator to define some of the metadata elements. Plone uses the metadata defined in the `portal_metadata` tool in several places.

For example, when you add an event, you're given a list of possible types of events. You can add to this list by clicking *portal_metadata*, clicking *elements*, and then clicking *subject* in the ZMI. You'll see a vocabulary for events that lists the subjects for that content type. It's a simple matter of adding or editing that list, one item per line, to have the relevant event types. These event types will then appear in the forms for adding and editing events.

Another use of `portal_metadata` is the selection of keywords available on a site. On the form at `portal_metadata/elements/subject`, you'll also see a vocabulary form for a content type of `<default>`. If you add items to the Vocabulary field of that page and click Update, you'll add these to the list of available keywords for *every* content type.

If you want keywords to appear for, say, only documents, then use the add form at the bottom of the page. Select a content type, and add some vocabulary, one value for each line. These will then become keywords that users can select for that piece of content only.

If you're logged in as a user with the manager or reviewer role, clicking the properties tab of an object in the Plone interface will display a New Keywords box for the addition of ad-hoc keywords. These keywords won't appear in the portal_metadata vocabulary but will appear on all types of content for other users to enter.

Changing the Default Page

As discussed in Chapter 3, when a user is viewing a folder, the default page for that folder is shown if present. In the old versions of Zope and Plone, the name for that default page was index_html. You'll see these a lot in Plone sites, where Web site addresses often have index_html on the end. If you made this filename an extension that's more commonly recognized as index.html, then it'd be easier to edit using editing programs and Web site tools.

In Plone you can define a list of pages that will be looked up to be rendered as the default page (see Figure 4-18). The default pages are index_html, index.html, index.htm, and FrontPage. You set the list of pages in site_properties/ portal_properties/default_page property, one name per line. When the default page is looked for, Plone will look for each page in that list, starting with the first until it finds one that matches. Further, if you'd like to change the value for a folder only, you can access the folder through the ZMI, click the properties tab, and then add a new list property called default_page.

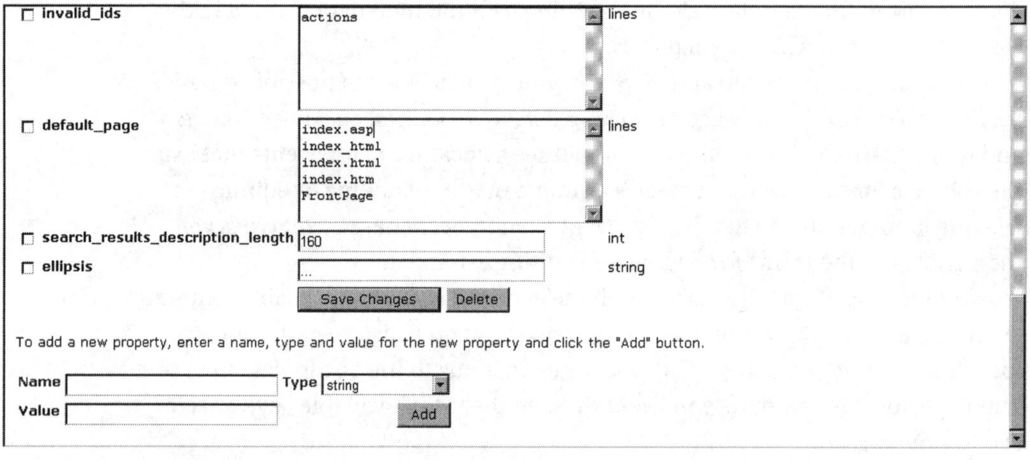

Figure 4-18. Making index.asp *the first default page*

How Can You Make the News Items List the Default Page?

Exactly how this works involves knowing the underlying machinery a little too much. For now, go to your portal root and click *Properties*. Then you need to go to the bottom of the page, complete the add new property form with the following information, and then click the Add button:

1. For the Name field, enter **default_page**.

2. For the Value field, enter **news**.

3. For the Type field, enter **list**.

Now return to your Plone site. Instead of the standard home page, you'll see the news page. The news tab will still show you the news, as well, but in the following sections I'll show how to remove that.

Altering the Site Tabs

In a Plone site various tabs refer to different sections or parts of a site. Using tabs is a familiar concept in Web site design and is common in sites such as Amazon, MSN, and Plone sites.

Two main types of tabs exist: portal tabs and content tabs. The portal tabs are blue and appear at the top of the Plone site. The default ones are home, news, and members. The following sections show how to customize these. The content tabs are green and appear when an item can be edited. The content tabs, as the name suggests, are related to content. Chapter 11 covers how to alter these tabs. The tabs you see in a Plone site are formed by a collection of actions, so to understand how to modify these tabs, you'll take a quick look at actions in general.

Introducing Actions

In Plone certain people can perform certain tasks at different times in different parts of the site. These various tasks are called *actions*. Plone translates them into tabs, links, and other elements. They're a highly configurable way of providing navigational elements for a site.

Each action has the following properties that can be configured in the ZMI. Exactly where you configure them depends upon where the action is stored. The following is a list of the properties for a default action:

Name: This is a user-friendly name for the action. This name is often used in the user interface. For example, when the action is used as a tab, this value is the text in the tab.

Id: This is a unique ID for the action.

Actions: This is the action that's to be performed. For example, when the action is used as a tab, this action is used as the link. This field is a TALES expression (see Chapter 5 for more information).

Condition: This is a condition that has to occur in order for the action to be used. For example, when used as tab, if this condition is met, the tab will appear. This field is a TALES expression (see Chapter 5 for more information).

Permission: This is the permission the user has to have in order to have this action. This permission has to be met in order for the action to be used (see Chapter 9 for more information on security).

Category: This categorizes the actions. In Plone this distinguishes the actions so they're used in different sections of the user interface. For portal tabs, the category value is portal_tabs.

Visible: This indicates if the category is active. Since actions usually relate to visual elements, the term *visible* is used.

Introducing the Top Tabs

In the following sections, you'll alter the portal tabs in two different ways as an example. You'll change the home tab to say *welcome*, and you'll move the members tab to the left of the news tab. The actions for the portal tabs are stored in the portal_actions tool, so to alter these, click *portal_actions* in the ZMI. As shown in Figure 4-19, this will open a large list of portal actions present by default. Some of these actions will seem familiar in that they represent parts of the Plone site.

Scroll through the actions until you find the Home item, and change the Name field to **welcome**. Then scroll down to the bottom of the page, and click Save. Returning to the Plone interface, you'll now notice that it says *welcome* on the tab.

The order of the tabs from left to right on the page is set by the order from top to bottom in the list of actions. So, to move the tabs, it's a matter of checking the tab and then scrolling to the bottom of the page to the Move Up and Move Down buttons. It's a little tedious, but by repeatedly checking the actions and then using the up and down buttons, you can alter the order. Do this, and you'll note that the tabs now appear in a different order on your Plone site.

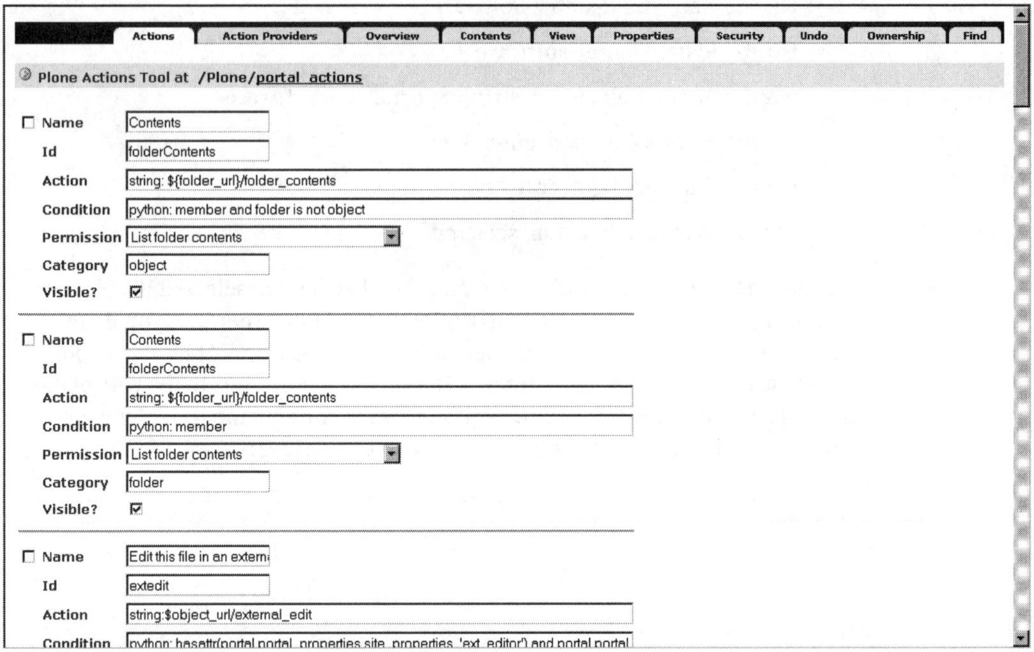

Figure 4-19. The portal actions for your Plone site

Why Is the Text in Lowercase?

Plone changes the case for many features, such as tabs, to lowercase in the style sheet. To turn off this option, you can alter the style sheet, which is discussed later in this chapter in the "Changing Images and CSS" section.

Book Web Site: Adding a New Tab

A nice navigation helper is to add a tab or remove one in the portal tabs. So, in this sidebar, you'll add a tab that points to the Software folder, and you'll remove the news and members tabs (which in my site is pointless). Return to the ZMI, and click *portal_actions*. Scroll to the bottom of the form to the add form. I filled out the form with the following values:

- For the Name field, enter **Software**.
- For the Id field, enter **software_tab**.
- For the Action field, enter **string:$portal_url/Software**.
- For the Permission field, enter **View**.
- For the Category field, enter **portal_tabs**.
- For the Visible field, enter **selected**.

Further, I found the actions for news and members and deselected Visible (not forgetting to hit Save, of course). Returning to the Plone interface, you'll now see those new tabs. The key value here is Action, which is a TALES expression. These are discussed fully in Chapter 5. The Action value points to the URL of the folder you're pointing to; in my case, it's Software and is in the root of my Plone site. Hence, the expression is string:$portal_url/Software.

Altering the Icons for a Document

If you're looking at a list of links or options in a Plone site, then chances are that a series of actions are producing that list. If it's not actions, then it's code, but many of the key features of the Plone interface are generated dynamically from settings in the ZMI. Two other examples of actions are the document actions and site actions.

The site actions appear in the top-right corner and are links to change the size of the text. These links could be anything but just happen to reference some client-side script functions. These links are again configured in portal_actions and are just actions that have a different category. If you look through the actions in portal_actions, you'll see these three actions at the bottom of the page. They have the category site_actions. If you want to remove them, just uncheck the Visible option. The icons come from the portal_actionicons tool, which is another simple tool that maps the icon to the action. Looking in portal_actionicons, you'll see a match for normal_text of site_actions that matches up an icon (see Figure 4-20).

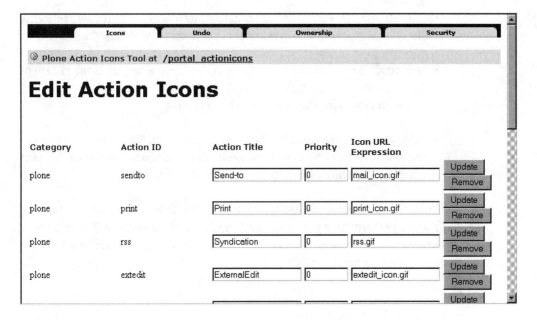

Figure 4-20. Site actions

Similarly, document actions are in portal_actions and have the category document_actions. You can again edit the order, icons, and text and add or remove icons from the interface all through editing those actions.

Changing Images and CSS

The look and feel of a Plone site is a big subject that takes three chapters of its own, Chapters 5–7. The following sections cover the basics and, rather than trying to explain everything, just show how to quickly make a few changes.

A *skin* is a series of CSS, images, templates, and scripts that come together to form a look and feel for the user. The idea of a skin is that you can change the skin and hence change the look and feel of a site without having to change the content.

Changing the Skin

You can change the default skin for a site using the portal skin form, which is accessible from the control panel. You can represent a Plone site in a few different ways by applying different colors, style sheets, and templates to a site.

The portal skin form provides the following three choices:

- **Default skin:** This is the default skin to show to a user when they access the site. There is only one skin that's given by default, which is Plone Default.

- **Skin flexibility:** This sets whether you're going to allow users the choice of choosing their skin. If this is enabled, a user can go to their preferences and choose a new skin. This is enabled by default.

- **Skin cookie persistence:** If a user can select a skin, then select this to have the cookie last indefinitely. This means that a user will always see this skin when logging into a site. This is disabled by default.

Select the changes you'd like to make, and click Save to commit the changes. To improve performance sites, use image and style sheet caching. To ensure that you're seeing the new skin as it should be, clear your browser's cache (on Internet Explorer, pressing Ctrl+F5 will do this).

Setting a Different Logo

Changing the logo of a Plone site from the Plone logo is a simple operation, but the steps can get a little confusing, so you should follow them carefully.

First, access the ZMI, click *portal_skins*, click *plone_images*, and then click *logo.jpg*. This will open the page for that object. It should look something like Figure 4-21.

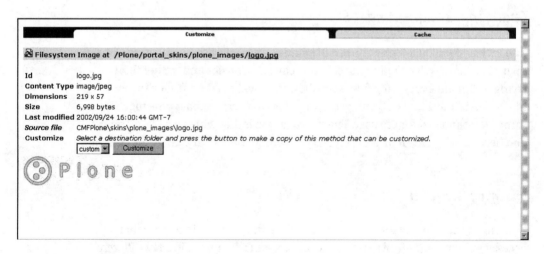

Figure 4-21. The default logo

This object represents the logo as it's used in Zope. In Figure 4-21 you can clearly see information about the image, its size, its type, and its location on the file system. In the middle of the page is the Customize button; click it. This will create a copy of the object called logo.jpg in the custom folder (see Figure 4-22).

NOTE   If at this point you get an error message about a bad request, return to portal_skins/custom, and you'll see an object called logo.jpg. Click that object. There can be only one object called logo.jpg in the custom folder, and the error is warning you that this procedure has been performed already. If you want to customize the original object (in other words, repeat these steps), you'll have to delete the object inside custom.

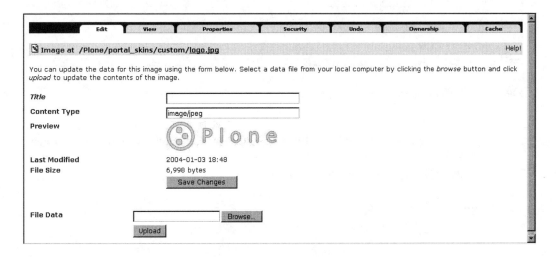

Figure 4-22. The customized image

This page may look similar to the previous page shown in Figure 4-21, but there are a couple of differences. First, if you look in the top-left corner of the page, you'll see that the meta_type and location of this object has changed. No longer are you in portal_skins/plone_images/logo.jpg; rather, you're in portal_skins/custom/logo.jpg. Second, you'll now see a Browse button that lets you select an image and upload it, meaning you can change this image. Click that button to find your new image, and click Save to commit the changes. In Figure 4-23, I'll add a Canadian Plone logo as an example.

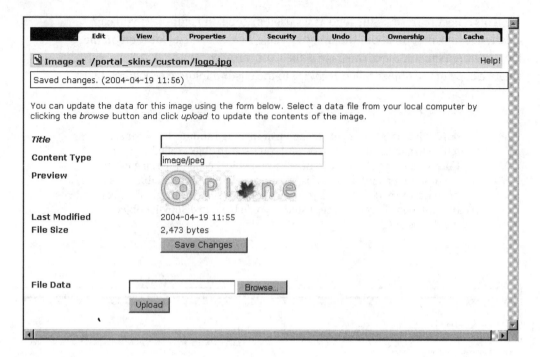

Figure 4-23. The Canadian Plone logo

Now return to the Plone interface, and you'll see that the image has changed. To ensure you're seeing the new image, clear your browser's cache (on Internet Explorer, pressing Ctrl+F5 will do this).

What If Your New Image Isn't in JPG Format?

Zope doesn't base the Multipurpose Internet Mail Extensions (MIME) type on the extension but rather on the content. So, you can upload a GIF image into logo.jpg, and it'll still work since the correct MIME type of image/gif is applied. However, you may want to rename the image to logo.gif or logo.png to be less confusing.

Changing the CSS Code

CSS determines the majority of the look and feel of your site, including the tabs, the images, the boxes, and the overall layout. The fact that Plone's CSS is totally customizable means that from a few style sheets users can completely customize many aspects of a site.

Again, Chapter 7 covers what all the elements do; in this section, I'll quickly show you how to change the CSS code for a Plone site. First, access the ZMI, click *portal_skins*, click *plone_styles*, and then click *ploneCustom.css*. This opens the page for that object. This style sheet is actually straightforward; in fact, it's empty. Plone is using the cascading property of CSS. Because the Hypertext Markup Language (HTML) for Plone first imports plone.css and then ploneCustom.css, any changes to the latter overrides the standard style sheet. Why is this a good thing? It means you can make small incremental changes to ploneCustom.css without breaking or altering the core style sheet.

So, to customize the ploneCustom.css object, click *portal_skins*, click *plone_styles*, and then click *ploneCustom.css*. Next, click the Customize button. Again, this object has been customized, and instead of being at portal_skins/plone_styles/ploneCustom.css, you'll notice you're now at portal_skins/custom/ploneCustom.css. Because file objects can now be edited through the Web, you can directly edit the style sheet through the Web.

As an example, make the background have an image in the middle of it (this isn't necessarily the best user interface, but it's a clear example of how to customize the CSS code). First, you need to upload an image to Plone. To do this, click *portal_skins*, click *custom*, click the Add button, and then select Image, as shown in Figure 4-24.

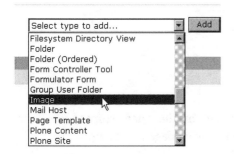

Figure 4-24. Adding the new image

For the file I chose an image I found on the Web (which is also available on the Plone book Web site), but you could choose any image you have. Make sure that the ID of the image is background.gif, as shown in Figure 4-25.

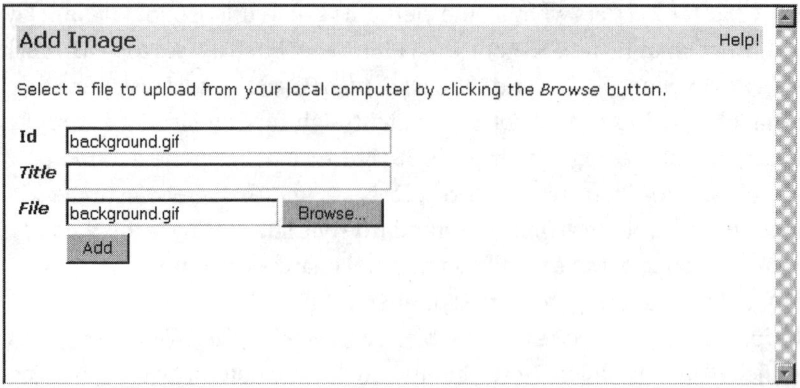

Figure 4-25. Checking the new image

Second, you need to change the CSS code to point to the new image. You've already customized the CSS code, so return to portal_skins/custom/ploneCustom.css and change the text from this:

```
/* DELETE THIS LINE AND PUT YOUR CUSTOM STUFF HERE */
```

to the following:

```
body {
    background-image: url(background.jpg);
    background-repeat: no-repeat;
    background-position: center;
}
```

Click Save Changes to commit changes to this file. Then return to the Plone interface. If all went well, you should see the new image (see Figure 4-26).

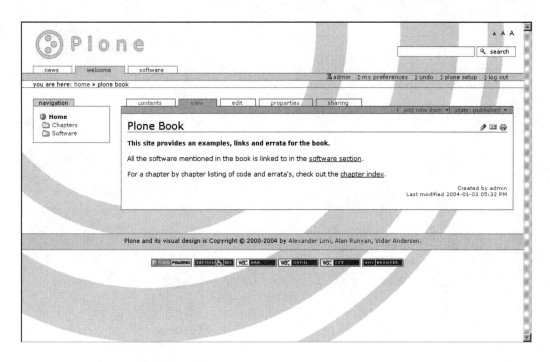

Figure 4-26. The new background image

Introducing Basic Plone Templating

PLONE PUTS TOGETHER three layers of technology to create a page. Python and page templates create some Hypertext Markup Language (HTML), which is sent to the browser. There, some Cascading Style Sheets (CSS) render the nice page with which you're now familiar. Those two first elements, the Python code and the page templates, are the main areas of discussion in this chapter and Chapter 6.

To understand how to generate and then edit a Plone template, you have to first learn about some key underlying concepts. Some of these concepts are particularly unique to Plone, and although they provide great advantages, it does take some time to get used to them.

In this chapter, I'll start by covering object publishing. I'll explain how to interact with objects inside Plone. Then I'll explain how to build expressions. Once you're familiar with those two concepts, I'll cover how Plone pages are actually put together. At the end of the chapter, you'll create a new page inside your Plone site that uses the techniques you've learned so far.

This chapter will make more sense if you're familiar with Python. However, at each stage I'll explain the concept behind the code, so even if you don't understand Python, you should be fine. The rest of the book references the Template Attribute Language Expression Syntax (TALES) and Script (Python) objects, so you should take the time to get familiar with them in this chapter. You should have a head start: I already introduced TALES in the previous chapter because it's used for generating portlets and actions.

Understanding the Underlying Templating Machinery

Diving straight into how Plone templating works would likely leave you confused, so I'll start by going through the underlying templating machinery. In an ideal world, this is something you shouldn't have to worry about, but in practice I've found that it's the first block people hit when trying to learn to use Plone.

Plone is rather unique in that everything in Plone is an object. If you're unfamiliar with the concept of an object, there isn't much to know; an *object* is just a "thing" that encapsulates some behavior. Each object has methods that you can call on the object. One example is a computer mouse. A computer mouse could have methods such as move, click, and right-click.

In Plone, a document is an object of a particular type. All this means is that the document isn't just a static bit of text; instead, it's something a little more complicated and far more useful. A document in Plone has a description method, for example, that will give you the description that the user added. When using the templating system, you'll see in more detail that everything is an object. You'll look first at some of the basic principles of object publishing.

Introducing Object Publishing

In Plone, you're actually publishing objects that are located in Zope; most of them are objects that are persisted in the object database. The concept is more complicated than standard Common Gateway Interface (CGI) environments, where a script is executed and passed a series of request variables. Everything in Plone is an object, everything in Zope is an object, and everything in Python is an object. Until now I've tried to avoid using the word *object*; instead I've used words such as *template*, *script*, and *item*, but all of these are really objects—just ones that behave differently.

When you request a Uniform Resource Locator (URL) from Plone, an object in the environment is called. Plone does this by translating the URL into a path. So, if the URL is /Plone/login_form, what Plone is going to do is break that URL down into a path and look up each of those objects in the database. It's going find the Plone object and then a login_form object inside the Plone object. Looking up this path is called *traversal*; essentially, Zope traverses across those objects and then calls the last one in the path.

When Zope calls the login_form object, the object is executed in its context. The term *context* is something you'll hear a lot of in Plone. It's merely the current context of the object being executed. In this case, it's /Plone. The context changes a lot as you move through a Plone site. If you called the URL /Plone/Members/login_form in a browser, then the context would be /Plone/Members.

As mentioned, *traversal* is how you can programmatically access objects in Plone in the same manner as you do in a URL. This is similar to accessing items in a file system—if you wanted to access a picture in My Documents on Windows, you'd enter a directory such as **c:\Documents and Settings\andym\My Documents\My Portrait.jpg**. You could access an object in Plone by entering **Members/andy/My Portrait.jpg**. This would work if you had a series of folders and objects that looked like the following:

```
Members
  |_ andy
     |_ My Portrait.jpg
```

In the file system version, you go through the computer's hard drive directory by directory. In Plone, the same thing happens; it's just that Members and andy are objects.

One catch is that Zope is case sensitive. In Windows, you can type **My Portrait.jpg** or **my portrait.jpg**. That won't work in Plone, however; you have to provide the same case as the object ID. For this reason, it's recommended that you try to keep all URLs lowercase so your users have less chance of making a mistake.

Plone and Zope have added a twist, called *acquisition*, to this whole publishing system. The concept behind acquisition is one of containment: Objects are situated inside other objects called *containers*. In the previous example, the andy object is a container inside the Members container inside the Plone site container (which in turn is inside the Zope application container).

In a standard object-oriented environment, an object inherits behavior from its parent. In Plone and Zope, an object also inherits behavior from its container. An object goes through a container hierarchy to figure out how to get these behaviors.

So, take the example of accessing Members/andy/My Portrait.jpg. What if the object Some Image.jpg didn't exist in the andy folder but instead exists higher up in the hierarchy? Well, acquisition would find it for you. Take the following hierarchy:

```
Members
  |_ andy
  |_ My Portrait.jpg
```

In this case, if you executed the URL, Plone would traverse to andy and then try to find My Portrait.jpg—but, sure enough, it doesn't exist in the container. So, it'd look in the containment hierarchy, which is the Members folder, and it finds and returns My Portrait.jpg. The result is that the user will see the image, just like usual.

However, if you compare this to the earlier example where the image was contained in the andy folder, you'd find that the following key differences exist:

- First, the context is the same, even thou gh the object is in a different place. Context is based on the location from where the object is called.

- Second, the container is diff erent, and the container of My Portrait.jpg is now different. It's Members, not andy.

So, what's the point of all this? Well, you can now put an object in the root of a Plone site, and any object can get to it because it's looked up through acquisition.

Although this probably makes sense, acquisition can be quite complicated, especially looking through the context hierarchy (which can occur). If you want to learn more about it, you can read Zope lead developer Jim Fulton's excellent discussion of acquisition at http://www.zope.org/Members/jim/Info/IPC8/ AcquisitionAlgebra/index.html.

Introducing Template Expressions

Before diving into the Zope Page Templates system, you must understand TALES. Often in an application you need to write expressions that can be evaluated dynamically. These aren't scripts; rather, they're *one liners*—simple expressions that can do something simple and easy in one line of code.

An expression is evaluated with a series of local variables passed into it. These variables are determined by what's calling the expression. Workflow passes one set of variables in, and the Zope Page Templates system passes another. For the moment, I'll use examples that have context. Remember, as discussed, the context is the context in which an object is requested.

So far you've seen some TALES expressions, such as string:${portal_url}/ Software. However, this is merely one example of a wide range of expressions. The main use of TALES is in Zope Page Templates, the HTML generation system for Plone. Although its name may suggest it's suitable only in templates, many tools in Plone use this syntax to provide simple expressions, such as actions, workflow, and security. Different kinds of expressions exist, and I'll run through them one by one.

Using Path Expressions

The path expression is the default and most commonly used expression. Unlike all the other expressions, it doesn't require a prefix to denote the expression type. The expression comprises one or more paths. Each path is separated by the pipe symbol (|). Each path is a series of variables separated by forward slashes (/). The following are some simple examples:

```
context/message
context/folderA/title
context/Members/andy/My Portrait.jpg
```

When the expression is evaluated, the path is split on the forward slashes. It then starts at the leftmost value and traverses to find that object, method, or value. It then places that object on the current stack and moves onto the next value; it repeats that process until it reaches the end of the expression or can't find a matching value. If the object it finds is a Python dictionary or mapping object, it'll call that value of the dictionary. One nice feature of a path expression is that the only restricted character is /, so names can contain spaces and periods and still be evaluated.

When the end is reached, it'll call that object (if it can be called). If it's a non-callable object, it'll get the object's string value, and this is what will be returned. If at any time there's an error in this lookup (the most common being that the requested attribute doesn't exist), then it'll move onto the alternate expression, if there is one. You can specify an alternate expression by separating it with a pipe symbol.

For example:

```
context/folderA/title|context/folderB/title
```

The previous example will render folderA's title if it exists or folderB's title if the first one doesn't exist. It'll repeat this process for each expression, until there are no more expressions or until one of them evaluates successfully.

Using Not Expressions

A not expression has the prefix not: at the beginning and simply inverses the evaluation of the TALES expression that follows the prefix. Because the Zope Page Templates system doesn't have an if statement, you can use this to test for the opposite of a previous condition.

For example:

```
not: context/message|nothing
```

Using Nocall Expression

By default, when a path expression reaches the last item in the path sequence, it calls the item, if possible. The nocall: prefix prevents this from happening. A nocall expression is rarely used in Plone, but it does have occasional uses. For example, you can use it to reference another object but not render it. Here's an example:

```
nocall: context/someImage
```

Using String Expressions

String expressions allow you to mix up text and variables into one expression. All string expressions start with the string: prefix. This is a useful function, and you'll see it used quite a bit. The text can contain anything that's legally allowed inside an attribute, which essentially includes alphanumeric characters plus spaces. Contained inside the text can be variables, prefixed with a dollar sign ($). Here are some examples:

```
string: This is some long string
string: This is the $title
```

In the latter example, the variable $title is evaluated. The variable can actually be any path expression. If the variable contains /, then the variable has to be wrapped with {} to signify the start and end of the expression.

For example:

```
string: This is the ${context/someImage/title}.
```

If a dollar sign in the text needs to be escaped, use another dollar sign immediately before the dollar sign you need to escape.

For example:

```
string: In $$US it costs ${context/myThing/cost}.
```

Using Python Expressions

Python expressions evaluate a line of Python code. All Python expressions start with a python: prefix and contain one line of Python.

For example:

```
python: 1 + 2
```

The Python code is evaluated using the same security model that a Script (Python) object uses, as discussed in Chapter 6. For these reasons, Python should be simple and limited to presentation functionality, such as formatting strings and numbers or performing simple conditions.

Further, almost all the other TALES expressions mentioned can be wrapped in Python and called. The following are the expressions:

- **path(string)**: Evaluates a path expression

- **string(string)**: Evaluates a string expression

- **exists(string)**: Evaluates a string expression

- **nocall(string)**: Evaluates a nocall expression

For example, the following code:

```
python: path('context/Members')
```

is equivalent to the following:

```
context/Members
```

A few convenience functions have also been added to assist developers. The test function takes three parameters: a statement to evaluate and the true and false conditions. The statement is evaluated, and the appropriate value is returned. For example:

```
python: test(1 - 1, 0, 1)
```

The same_type function takes two variables and compares if they're the same. For example:

```
python: same_type(something, '')
```

Some developers discourage using Python inside the Zope Page Templates system because it means adding logic in the presentation templates. Often, as a developer, for each piece of Python added, it can be useful to ask yourself if that piece of code would be better factored out and placed in a separate Script (Python) object. This doesn't mean you should move every piece of Python out—just think about it before adding anything.

Book Web Site: Revisiting Actions

In Chapter 4, you added an action for pointing to the software part of the site so it appeared as a portal tab. In that action, you added in the string expression `string: ${portal_url}/Software`. This may make a bit more sense now that I've explained the variable `portal_url`. This is the URL to your portal, which may vary depending upon if you're using virtual hosting. It does this by using acquisition to acquire the `portal_url` object and insert the resulting value into the string. The result is that you'll always get an absolute link to the `Software` folder.

Gotcha: Mixing Python and Strings

I've seen newcomers mixing up Python and strings a few times. All the expressions are different. In other words, you can't place path-like expressions inside a Python expression. For example, the expression `python: here/Members + "/danae"` doesn't make sense. The entire expression is interpreted as Python, so Plone will try to divide `Members` by `here`, and you'll get errors. This is an ideal situation to use a string expression (which lets you do variable substitution), so the variable can be a path expression. So, you could use `string: ${here/Members}/danae`.

Using the Zope Page Templates System

Now that you understand object publishing and expressions, you can get into the real meat of the system, Zope Page Templates. This is the templating system that Plone uses for generating HTML.

Many HTML generation systems are available, and some of the better known are JavaServer Pages, Active Server Pages, and PHP. To users of the other systems, the Zope Page Templates system at first looks rather odd, but quickly you'll see it's an extremely powerful system.

The simplest template looks something like the following:

```
<p tal:content="here/message">The title</p>
```

If the value of message resolved to *Hello, World!* then the following would be output when the template was rendered:

```
<p>Hello, World!</p>
```

For a moment I'll gloss over a few of the finer points and show what has happened here. A standard paragraph was written in HTML, yet the content of that paragraph isn't the text shown in the output. To the opening paragraph tag, a `tal:content` attribute was added, and the `here/message` expression was written for that attribute. The content of the paragraph was output, however, as the value of the message variable (in this case, *Hello, World!*).

At run time, the template is evaluated, and the `tal:content` attribute is called. The `tal` part stands for Template Attribute Language and has a range of commands, including `content`. You'll see all these commands later; with them, you can do almost anything you want to do the HTML tags. You can create loops, alter tags, alter attributes, remove tags, and so on. Before the template runs, this will show up as valid Extensible HTML (XHTML) and will show up in an editor as a paragraph with that text.

All these page templates are valid XHTML. This is a standard for HTML and is valid Extensible Markup Language (XML) code. This means you must follow these rules:

- All tags must be lowercase.

- Attributes must always be quoted (`<input type="checkbox" checked="1" />`, for example).

- Empty elements must be terminated (for example, `<br />`, not `<br>`).

To define a page as XHTML, you must give a DOCTYPE declaration and use the XML namespace set in the `html` tag. Plone uses the following declaration at the top of every page:

```
<!DOCTYPE html PUBLIC "-//W3C//DTD XHTML 1.0 Transitional//EN"
    "http://www.w3.org/TR/xhtml1/DTD/xhtml1-transitional.dtd">
<html xmlns="http://www.w3.org/1999/xhtml" xml:lang="en" lang="en">
```

For more information on the XHTML specification, go to `http://www.w3.org/TR/xhtml1/#xhtml`.

Another HTML Generation System?

In the first few years of the Web, programmers were the prime creators of HTML. Programmers rapidly threw together systems to generate HTML programmatically so they could get on with their real jobs. With tools such as Perl's CGI modules, programmers could write complicated server-side code for content.

However, soon everybody was generating content, and the process had to be made easier. This brought about the wave of escape coding languages. These languages used a special kind of HTML markup that was processed to produce output. As mentioned, some of the most popular are Active Server Pages, JavaServer Pages, and even whole languages based on the concept, such as PHP. Zope followed this trend with Document Template Markup Language (DTML).

These systems take HTML and intersperse it with custom tags such as `<% .. %>` or `<dtml-... />`. This system was popular because it was easy to understand, and users who already knew basic HTML could grasp the idea of a few more tags. Designers could ignore the content of these tags and let the programmers deal with them. Programmers could alter the relevant code parts without upsetting the content.

However, these systems have the following problems:

- The HTML templates can be hard to scale as more and more content gets added to the script. Pages quickly become huge and hard to manage.

- Logic and content aren't neatly separated. They can be separated with some of these systems; however, the ability to intersperse any HTML with a piece of programming code is too easy. Often, content, presentation, and logic become one large, entangled mess.

- Pages can't be easily edited. Often pa ges or templates come with the note "just leave these bits alone..." because editing them would break the code. What You See Is What You Get (WYSIWYG) editors can be set to not alter some tags, but they can easily break others. In large organizations, users with different roles all have to edit the same page.

- It can be hard to see a default resu lt. Take, for example, a database query that shows the result in a table. How can a designer see how that would look without actually running the code?

For these reasons, the Zope Page Templates system was created. Page templates present a novel approach; instead of providing another method of escape coding, code is added to existing tag attributes. Not only is the Zope Page Templates system free and open source, it doesn't require Zope. Currently, versions of the system exist in Python, Perl, and Java.

Introducing Page Templates and Content

As you're now aware, Plone is a content management system where users add content to a Plone site through the Web. Those content objects are stored inside Plone and then rendered back to the world using page templates.

Returning to the earlier example of accessing /Members/andy/My Portrait.jpg, I'll now discuss what actually happens to the content in Plone. First, Plone finds and calls the My Portrait.jpg object; it's called because there's no specific method being called on the object. When a content type is called, a certain template is located and rendered. The context for that template will be the image you want to access, and the template will be the one for that image.

If a different action was being called on the image, such as /Members/andy/ My Portrait/image_edit, then the action image_edit would be looked up for that object, and the corresponding template would be returned. Chapter 11 discusses how this works in more detail.

So, in all the templates in Plone, you'll see a referral to here or context. This is the context of the content being accessed. In a template, you can now say context/something or other, and this will be the something or other looked up relative to the piece of content, not the template. You'll now create your first template in Plone.

Creating Your First Page Template

The standard way to create a page template is through the Zope Management Interface (ZMI). Unfortunately, because it means editing the template through a text area in a Web browser, the ZMI is also the most painful to use as a developer. The text area provides limited functionality compared with most editors; it's lacking features such as line numbers, syntax highlighting, and so on. In Chapter 9, I show you how to use External Editor to edit content; this allows you to edit Web site content in local editors such as Macromedia Dreamweaver or Emacs. In Chapter 6, I show you how to make Plone read page templates off a hard drive as files, and then you can use any tool you'd like.

To create a template, go to the ZMI, click *portal_skins*, click *custom*, and then select Page Template from the drop-down box (see Figure 5-1). Click Add, and you'll see the page shown in Figure 5-2.

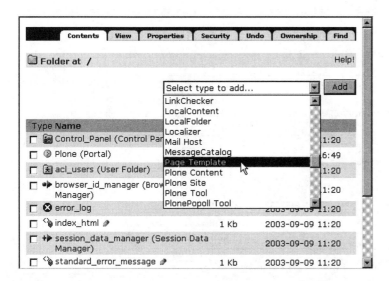

Figure 5-1. Selecting the Page Template option

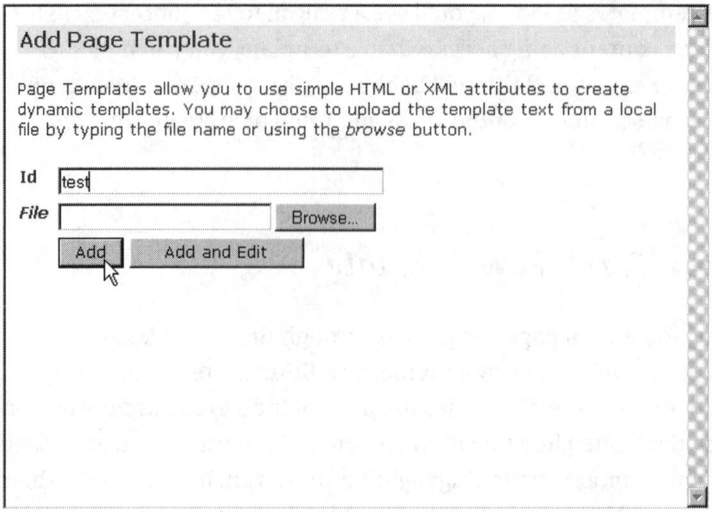

Add Page Template

Page Templates allow you to use simple HTML or XML attributes to create
dynamic templates. You may choose to upload the template text from a local
file by typing the file name or using the *browse* button.

Id `test`

File [   ] [Browse...]

[Add]   [Add and Edit]

Figure 5-2. Adding a page template

Enter **test** for the page template's ID. Then click the Add and Edit button,
which takes you to management screen (see Figure 5-3). You can then edit this
template through the Web by using the text area and clicking Save Changes to
commit your changes.

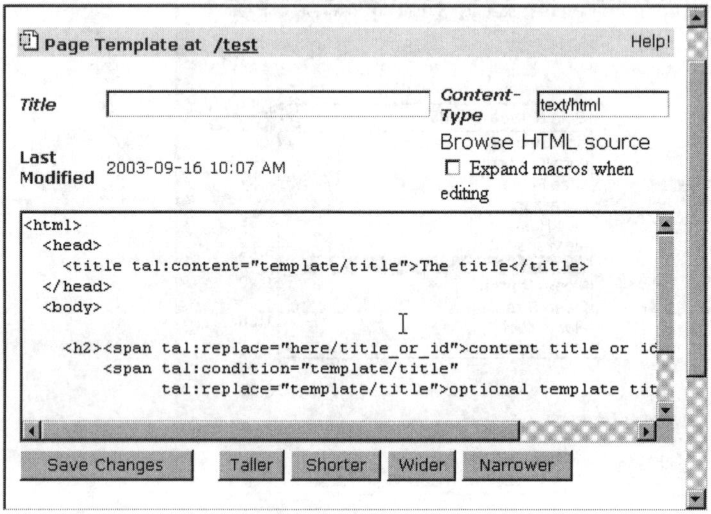

Page Template at /test   Help!

Title [   ]   **Content-Type** text/html

Last Modified 2003-09-16 10:07 AM

Browse HTML source
☐ Expand macros when editing

```
<html>
  <head>
    <title tal:content="template/title">The title</title>
  </head>
  <body>

    <h2><span tal:replace="here/title_or_id">content title or id
      <span tal:condition="template/title"
            tal:replace="template/title">optional template tit
```

[Save Changes]   [Taller] [Shorter] [Wider] [Narrower]

Figure 5-3. Editing a page template

NOTE   Before Zope 2.7, all the page templates passed through the variable here, which is equivalent to context. If you see here in any code in a page template, it means context. The new context variable was added to be clearer and bring the page templates in line with Script (Python) objects.

After clicking Save Changes, the page template will be compiled. If you've made any errors in the template, you'll see them highlighted at the top of the page. Figure 5-4 shows an error with an h1 tag that isn't closed. (As previously mentioned, page templates must be valid XHTML.)

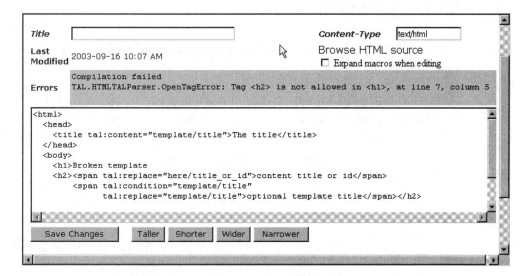

Figure 5-4. Page template error

Once you've saved the page template successfully, you can click the Test tab to see the rendered value of the template. In Figure 5-5, you'll see that the heading has been replaced with the ID of the template, and the main paragraph now includes the ID of the template.

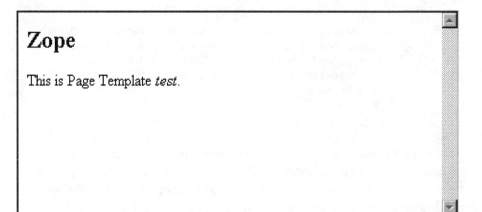

Zope

This is Page Template *test*.

Figure 5-5. Generating the page

The management screen for a page template also has the following important features:

Title: This is the title for this template, and it's optional. If you change this in the previous example, for instance, after clicking Test, you'll note that the resulting HTML has changed.

Content-Type: This is the content type for this template; it's usually text/html.

Browse HTML source: This will render the template unprocessed as HTML. This is how the template would appear if it were loaded into an HTML editor.

Test: This will process and render the template.

Expand macros when editing: This checkbox will try to expand macros. I recommend leaving this unchecked most of the time. Macros are an advanced feature and are discussed in Chapter 6.

Now that you've created a page template, you'll make a few modifications to it. This will demonstrate the topics covered so far in this chapter. For example, if you want your page template to demonstrate 1+2, you could add the following line to your page template:

```
<p>1+2 = <em tal:content="python: 1+2" /></p>
```

Then click the Test tab to see if it works. You should see the following:

```
1+2 = 3
```

To see an example of a path traversal, print the logo of your Plone site. You can include an expression in the logo of your Plone site by adding the following to your page template:

```
<p tal:replace="structure context/logo.jpg" />
```

This will create the appropriate HTML for the image and show it on the page.

Understanding the Page Template Basic Syntax

Now that you've seen how to make a page template, I'll explain the basic syntax of it. You can break the syntax of page templates into a few different components, which I'll cover in the following sections.

Introducing Built-In Variables

You've seen the expression syntax, so now you'll learn about the variables that are passed to it when you render a page template. All of the following happen in the context of accessing the image Some Image.jpg in the Members/andy folder, called with the URL /Members/andy/Some Image.jpg:

container: This is the container in which the template is located. With Plone this is usually the portal_skins folder. You should avoid using a container because portal_skins can do unexpected things to the meaning of container (for example, a reference to the andy folder).

context: This is the context in which the template is being executed. In Plone this is the object being viewed if you're viewing a portal object (for example, a reference to the Some Image.jpg object).

default: Some statements have particular default behavior. This is noted in each of the statements, and this variable is a pointer to that behavior.

here: This is equivalent to context.

loop: This is equivalent to repeat.

modules: This is a container for imported modules. For example, modules/string/atoi is the atoi function of the Python string module. This includes all the modules that are safe to import into the Zope Page Templates system. For more information, see "Scripting Plone with Python" in Chapter 6.

nothing: This is the equivalent of Python's None.

options: These are the options passed to a template, which occurs when the template is called from a script or other method, not through the Web.

repeat: This is the repeated element; see the tal:repeat element in the "Introducing TAL Statement Syntax" section of this chapter.

request: This is the incoming request from the client (all the values from the incoming request are visible using the following test context script). All the GET and POST parameters are marshaled into a dictionary for easy access. Here are some examples:

```
request/HTTP_USER_AGENT # the users browser
request/REMOTE_ADDRR # the users browser
request/someMessage    # the value of some message, in the query string
```

root: This is the root Zope object. For example, root/Control_Panel gives you the control panel for Zope.

template: This is this template being called. For example, template/id is the ID of the template being rendered.

traverse_subpath: This contains a list of the elements still to be traversed. This is an advanced variable, and it's recommend you understand traversal and acquisition before using this.

user: This is the current user object. For example, user/getUserName is the username of the current user.

CONTEXTS: This is a list of most of these values.

 NOTE   With the exception of CONTEXTS, any of these variables can be redefined in a tal:define statement if the user wants. However, this can be confusing for anyone using the code and isn't recommended.

The test_context page template shows all the values of these variables, plus the locations of some of the objects (see Listing 5-1). It can be useful for debugging and explaining the variables. Add it as a page template called test_context, and then click Test to see the results.

Listing 5-1. test_context

```
<html>
  <head />
  <body>
    <h1>Debug information</h1>
  <h2>CONTEXTS</h2>
  <ul>
```

```
    <tal:block
        tal:repeat="item CONTEXTS">
    <li
        tal:condition="python: item != 'request'"
        tal:define="context CONTEXTS;">
            <b tal:content="item" />
            <span tal:replace="python: context[item]" />
    </li>
    </tal:block>
  </ul>
  <h2>REQUEST</h2>
  <p tal:replace="structure request" />
  </body>
</html>
```

The test_context page template will produce the output shown in Figure 5-6.

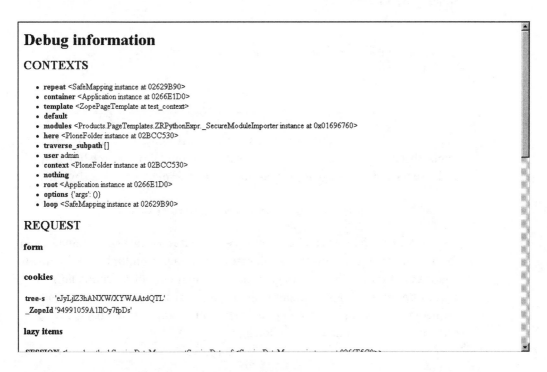

Figure 5-6. An example of all the default variables in a script

Introducing TAL Statement Syntax

The Template Attribute Language (TAL) provides all the basic building blocks for dynamic presentation. TAL defines eight statements: `attributes`, `condition`, `content`, `define`, `omit-tag`, `on-error`, `repeat`, and `replace`.

Since page templates are valid XML, all TAL attributes must be lowercase. Further, each element can have each statement only once. In the following examples, I've inserted new lines in the elements to increase legibility; this is perfectly valid code and quite common in the Plone source. However, this is optional and isn't required.

tal:attributes: Changing an Element's Attributes

The `tal:attributes` allows you to replace one or more attribute of an element. A statement contains the attribute to be changed, separated by a space from the statement. For example:

```
<a href="#"
   tal:attributes="href context/absolute_url">
   Link to here
</a>
```

This will change the `href` attribute of the link to the result of `here/absolute_url`. The `href` attribute has already been defined on this element, so if a designer opens this page, the designer will see a valid element (although the link may not make sense until the page is processed). Some example output is as follows:

```
<a href="http://plone.org/Members/andy/book">Link to here</a>
```

Since each element can have multiple attributes, `tal:attributes` allows you to alter one or more attributes simultaneously by having multiple statements. To change multiple attributes at once, separate statements with a semicolon (;). If the attribute or statement contains a semicolon, you can escape this with another semicolon immediately after it appears (;;). For example, to change both the `href` and `title` element, do the following:

```
<a href="#"
   tal:attributes="href context/absolute_url;
      title context/title_or_id">Link</a>
```

The example output is as follows:

```
<a href="http://plone.org/Members/andy/book">Plone Book</a>
```

The tal:attributes and tal:replace tag are mutually exclusive since replace eliminates the element. If the Zope Page Templates system detects this, it'll raise a warning, and it'll ignore the tal:attributes tag. If the expression evaluates to default, then no change will be made. For example:

```
<a href="#"
    tal:attributes="href
        python:request.get('message', 'change', default)">
    Link</a>
```

In this example, I'm using the get function on the request object. If the incoming request to the page has the message variable, then the first value will be used, which is of course change. If the message variable isn't present, then the second value, default, will be used. Hence, only by passing the message parameter will a change take place.

tal:condition: Evaluating Conditions

The tal:condition statement allows a condition to be tested before rendering the element. For example:

```
<p tal:condition="request/message">
    There's a message
</p>
<p tal:condition="not: request/message">
    No message
</p>
```

Here, the paragraph with the text for a message will be rendered only if the request variable has an attribute and it resolves to true. Being able to test for a condition is pointless if the opposite condition can't be tested for; this is what the not expression allows. The not: prefix inverts the statement, so not: request/message resolves to true if the request variable message resolves to false.

In TAL, the following evaluates to `false`:

- The number zero

- Any float or complex that evaluates to zero (for example, `0.0`)

- Strings of zero characters (for example, `""`)

- An empty list or tuple

- An empty dictionary

- Python's `None` value

- TALES's `nothing` value

The following evaluates to `true`:

- The default value

- Any number other than zero

- Strings that aren't empty

- Strings that are just spaces (for example, `"    "`)

- Anything else

tal:content: Adding Text

The `tal:content` statement is probably the most commonly used statement in a page template. This statement is also one of the simplest, replacing the content of an element with the value specified. For example:

```
<i tal:content="context/title_or_id">Some title</i>
```

The example output is as follows:

```
<i>The title</i>
```

This will replace the text *Some title* with the value of the expression `context/title_or_id`. If the text to be placed contains HTML elements, those elements will be escaped. By default, the text to be replaced is HTML escaped;

the structure prefix will allow the HTML to be entered without the elements being escaped. For example:

```
<i tal:content="structure here/title_or_id">Do not escape HTML</i>
```

If the element with the tal:content attributes contains other elements, then all those elements will be replaced. The tal:content and tal:replace tags are mutually exclusive; they can't both be placed on the same element, and an error will be raised if this is attempted. If the value is default, the content is unchanged.

tal:define: Defining Variables

The tal:define statement allows variables to be created and reused within the template. For example:

```
<p tal:define="title here/title_or_id">
    ... <i tal:content="title">The title</i> ...
</p>
```

In this example, the variable title is created and assigned the result of here/title_or_id; later the variable title is used in a tal:content statement. By default the variable is created only locally within the scope of the current element. So, in the previous example, only elements within the paragraph tag can use the title variable. You can redefine the variable anywhere within the statement or reuse it in other elements as many times as needed.

To create a variable to be used globally, you can use the prefix global. This will allow access to the variable anywhere within the template, not just within the defining element. For example:

```
<p tal:define="global title string:Foo bar">
    ... <i tal:content="title">The title</i> ...
</p>
<i tal:content="title">We still have a title</i>
```

Furthermore, Plone defines a large number of global definitions so that users can easily use them in their scripts. As with any such definitions, they're subject to change, so you should use them carefully. These *defines* mean a large number of global variables are available. For example, to get the title of your Plone site, you can just call the following:

```
<p tal:content="portal_title" />
```

You can find these defines in the ZMI by clicking *portal_skins*, clicking *plone_templates*, and then clicking *global_defines*. You can find a full list of all the defines, and an explanation of them, in Appendix A.

tal:omit-tag: Removing Elements

The tal:omit-tag is rather unusual. It allows the removal of a tag. Because the Zope Page Templates system requires the use of HTML tags, complicated pages can often need lots of elements and can result in extra tags being added. For this statement, the tag is removed, which just leaves the content of the tags. For example:

```
<p tal:omit-tag="">This is some text</p>
```

The output is as follows:

```
This is some text
```

In this example, the text *This is some text* will be rendered; however, the tag won't be rendered. Optionally, the tal:omit-tag statement can take an expression as an argument. If that expression evaluates to false, then the tal:omit-tag doesn't happen. For example, this does nothing:

```
<p tal:omit-tag="nothing">This is some text</p>
```

One alternative to using tal:omit-tag is using the tal namespace, as discussed in the "Useful Tips" section of Chapter 6.

tal:on-error: Performing Error Handling

The tal:on-error statement provides a method to handle errors. It acts rather like tal:content because it causes the content of the tag to replaced, but it's triggered only when an error occurs.

The following is an example:

```
<p  tal:content="request/message"
    tal:on-error="string: No message">Message</p>
```

If there's an error evaluating the request/message expression here, then the on-error attribute will be activated. This causes the contents of the tag to be replaced with the text *No message*.

Unfortunately, the on-error statement is rather limited. The tag can't distinguish between different errors and allows only one expression to be evaluated and used. This limitation is by design so that the tag won't be overused. Error handling should really be handled in the logic of your application.

Fortunately, for all expressions, you can supply alternatives in the statement if the first part of the statement evaluates to something other than true or false (in other words, if an error is raised). Each alternative is separated by the pipe character (|), and multiple alternatives can appear in a statement. If you're relying on variables from the incoming request, then always add a |nothing to the end to ensure that an attribute error isn't raised.

For example:

```
<p
  tal:content="request/message"
  tal:condition="request/message|nothing">
    There's a message
</p>
<p tal:condition="not: request/message|nothing">
    No message
</p>
```

This second example is more verbose but desirable for a couple of reasons:

- The designer is able to see the positive *and* negative condition.

- You can handle a more complicated error condition than just printing a string.

tal:repeat: Performing Looping

The tal:repeat allows looping through objects and is one of the more complicated statements. A statement contains the value to be assigned for each iteration of the results, separated by a space from the results being iterated through.

Here's an example of looping:

```
<table>
  <tr tal:repeat="row context/portal_catalog">
    <td tal:content="row/Title">Title</td>
  </tr>
</table>
```

In this example, the expression here/portal_catalog returns a list of results. Because the repeat starts on the table's row tag, for each row in the list of results, a new row in the table will be created. Rather like tal:define, each iteration of the results is assigned to a local variable (in this case, row). This example will show one row for every item in the list of results.

You can access some useful variables from the repeat statement, such as the number of the current iteration. You can access these through the repeat variable, which gets added to the namespace. For example, to access the current number, you use the following:

```
<table>
  <tr tal:repeat="row context/portal_catalog">
    <td tal:content="repeat/row/number">1</td>
    <td tal:content="row/Title">Title</td>
  </tr>
</table>
```

The full list of variables available in repeat is as follows:

- **index**: This is the iteration number, starting from zero.

- **number**: This is the iteration number, starting from one.

- **even**: This is true for an even-indexed iteration (for example, 0, 2, 4, ...).

- **odd**: This is true for an odd-indexed iteration (for example, 1, 3, 5, ...).

- **start**: This is true for the first iteration.

- **end**: This is true for the last iteration.

- **length**: This is the total number of iterations.

- **letter**: This is the iteration number as a lowercase letter (for example, a–z, aa–az, ba–bz, ..., za–zz, aaa–aaz, and so on), starting from one.

- **Letter**: This is the uppercase version of letter.

- **roman**: This is the number as a lowercase Roman numeral (i, ii, iii, iv, v, and so on), starting from one.

Two other values are available in the repeat namespace that are rather unusual and rarely used, first and last. These two variables allow you to store information about data in the iteration. By using the value you want to store in an expression, a Boolean value will be returned. For the variable first, true indicates that this is the first time the value has occurred in the iteration. Likewise, for the variable last, true indicates that this is the last time the value has occurred in the iteration.

Here's an example of this:

```
<ul>
  <li tal:repeat="val context/objectValues">
    First: <i tal:content="repeat/val/first/meta_type" />,
    Last: <i tal:content="repeat/val/last/meta_type" />:
    <b tal:content="val/meta_type" />,
    <b tal:content="val/title_or_id" />
  </li>
</ul>
```

tal:replace: Adding Text

The tal:replace statement is similar to tal:content with one difference—it removes the entire tag.

For example:

```
<p tal:replace="context/title_or_id">Some title</p>
```

This will render the result of the expression context/title_or_id but will remove the paragraph tags from the result. This is equivalent to the following:

```
<p
  tal:content="here/title_or_id"
  tal:omit-tag="">Some title</p>
```

If the element with the tal:replace statement contains other elements, then all those elements will be replaced. You can't use the tal:replace statement with tal:attributes or tal:content; they're mutually exclusive, and an error will be raised if you place both on the same element.

Introducing Execution Order

The order that TAL attributes are written isn't the order in which they're executed because they're really XML elements (and XML doesn't care about attribute order). The order in which they're executed is as follows:

1. `define`

2. `condition`

3. `repeat`

4. `content` or `replace`

5. `attributes`

6. `omit-tag`

You can't use the `content` and `replace` statements on the same element because they're mutually exclusive. Using the `attributes` statement on the same element as a `replace` or an `omit-tag` is meaningless since the attributes are removed. The `on-error` tag isn't mentioned because it'll be used when the first error occurs in any of the previous elements.

Example: Displaying User Information

To illustrate the points you've learned so far, you'll now create a page template that performs a simple task: displaying information about a user in the system.

In this example, a company is using Plone internally as an intranet. Each employee is registered in Plone and given a login; however, there's no simple page that shows employees or how to contact them. You'll create a simple user information page that shows a user's e-mail address, home page, picture, and when they last logged in.

The first prototype of this page is easily accomplished with TAL, TALES, and a bit of knowledge of the basic Content Management Framework (CMF) tools. Unfortunately, because the Application Programming Interfaces (APIs) are rather convoluted for those tools, some of this code is a little longer than it should be. At this stage, don't worry too much about the API of those tools; these will be covered in Chapter 9. If you just take the API for granted for the moment, you can concentrate on the TAL.

First, you need to create a page template; click *portal_skins*, click *custom*, add a page template, and give it the ID **user_info**. Second, you'll edit it as follows. For a full listing of this page template, please see Appendix A. Examining the full listing, you'll see that it starts with HTML and body tags.

For convenience, you'll put the main definitions in a `div` tag:

```
<div
  tal:omit-tag=""
  tal:define="
    userName request/userName|nothing;
    userObj python: here.portal_membership.getMemberById(userName);
    getPortrait nocall: here/portal_membership/getPersonalPortrait;
    getFolder nocall: here/portal_membership/getHomeFolder
  ">
```

In this div tag there are four defines: one to get the username passed in
through the request object and another to translate that username into a user
object. The last two defines ensure that you have a valid reference to the methods
that give you user pictures and folders; these again are convenient because they
make later code simpler. Making a div tag or other tag such as this that contains
a series of defines is quite a common pattern in the Zope Page Templates system.
It simply makes the code cleaner.

Next, you do two simple conditions to check that you have a user:

```
<p tal:condition="not: userName">
    No username selected.
</p>
<p tal:condition="not: userObj">
    That username does not exist.
</p>
```

If no username is given in the request, then the expression
request/username|nothing will result in a userName that's nothing and hence fail
the simple test. Further, if the username isn't valid, the userObj will result in None,
and error messages will be printed for both these conditions.

Now you're ready to actually process the user:

```
<table tal:condition="userObj">
  <tr>
    <td>
      <img src=""
      tal:replace="structure python: getPortrait(userName)" />
    </td>
```

Since you can only show the user if one is found, you'll ensure that there's a
simple condition on this table, tal:condition="userObj". To show a user's picture,
you'll use the getPortrait method defined early. This function returns the entire
tag, so the structure tag ensures the whole image is rendered correctly. Next, you
want to show a few properties such as name and email. The following shows one of
these options, getting the home folder:

```
<li
    tal:define="home python: getFolder(userName)"
    tal:condition="home">
    <a href=""
        tal:attributes="href home/absolute_url"
        >Home folder</a>
</li>
```

First, you use a define to get the folder and assign this the variable home. In a Plone site, creating a home folder for a user is optional, so you have to be sure that if you're linking to a folder, it exists. Fortunately, because of the TAL execution order, the define comes before the condition. Following this, you show a link to the folder using the absolute_url attribute of a folder.

The page template goes through a few more lines of finding other useful and exciting properties to show the user. As with most things in Plone, the key is finding the correct API calls and then processing the output accordingly.

Finally, the page ends by closing all the relevant tags. If all goes well, you should able to call the page by accessing the URL http://yoursite/user_info?userName=[someuser] where someuser is a username that exists in your Plone site.

At the moment, this page template is pretty limited. Only a user with the manager role can view this page, it can show only one member at a time, and the information for the user is rather thin. In Chapter 6, I'll show how to expand this example and add some component reusability, as well as the ability to translate the text into other languages.

CHAPTER 6

Introducing Advanced Plone Templating and Scripting

THE PREVIOUS CHAPTER covered how the Zope Page Templates system works. To understand page templates, Chapter 5 also covered the object hierarchy, acquisition, and Template Attribute Language Expression Syntax (TALES). Using the code from the previous chapter, you were able to generate dynamic Web pages. The chapter also showed an example page template that plugged the code together, covered the building blocks of the templating system in Plone, and provided the key information you'll need in order to use Plone.

It's now time to move onto some of the more advanced features of page templates and templating in Plone in general. First, I'll introduce the Macro Expansion Template Attribute Language (METAL) and Internationalization (I18N) namespaces. Like the TAL namespace, these provide functionality to the site developer. For those itching to know exactly how a Plone page is plugged together, the "Hooking Into Plone Using METAL" section provides many of the answers.

Up until now I've shown how you can use simple Python expressions in page templates. Of course, sometimes a one-line Python expression isn't enough. So in the "Scripting Plone with Python" section, I'll show you can take Python to the next level and increase the power of your scripting.

Finally, I'll cover a common example, showing how to put together a form in Plone. This example demonstrates concepts learned in the previous chapters and ties it all together while showing you exactly how Plone handles forms.

Understanding Advanced Plone Templating

One of the nice elements of page templates is that different functions are clearly separated into different namespaces. In the previous chapter, you looked at the TAL namespace. That's not the only namespace that page templates provide; two other namespaces are key to Plone.

The first is METAL. As the rather long name suggests, it's similar to TAL in that it's an attribute language and inserts itself into element attributes. However, its primary aim is to ensure that you can reuse chunks of other page template code. It does this using the slot and macro functions.

The second is I18N, which allows you to translate the content of page templates. This is used in Plone to localize the interface of Plone into more than 30 languages and for many users is one of the key features of Plone. As you'll see, the ability to localize text is of interest to all users, even those building a monolingual site. You'll start with METAL.

Hooking Into Plone Using METAL

So far you've seen how to use TAL to dynamically create parts of pages. However, this really doesn't let you do a great deal of complex templating. There really isn't a mechanism to put a standard header on top of every page, other than using a TAL statement. METAL is a method of allowing preprocessing of the templates and provides some more powerful functions than TAL. All METAL functions start with the `metal:` prefix.

metal:define-macro

The `metal:define-macro` command allows you to define an element to reference from another template. The name of the referenced chunk is the name of the macro. The following is an example that defines boxA as a piece you want to use elsewhere:

```
<div metal:define-macro="boxA">
   ...
</div>
```

That div element is now a macro that can be referenced from other templates. The macro refers only to the part of the page referenced by the element, which, in this case, is the div tag. So, it's common to use multiple `macro:defines` in one page and for the page to be a valid Hypertext Markup Language (HTML) page, like so:

```
<html xmlns:tal="http://xml.zope.org/namespaces/tal"
    xmlns:metal="http://xml.zope.org/namespaces/metal"
    i18n:domain="plone">
    <body>
        <div metal:define-macro="boxA">
            ...
        </div>
        <div metal:define-macro="boxB">
            ...
        </div>
    </body>
</html>
```

Corresponding with the earlier goals of page templates, this page is a valid HTML page that can be edited by a designer. When the macro is called, the HTML outside the div tags will be discarded.

metal:use-macro

The metal:use-macro command uses a macro that has been defined using the define-macro. When a template defines a macro using the define-macro command, it's accessible to other templates through a macros property. For example, if you want to pull the portlet macro out of the portlet_login template, you can do the following:

```
<div metal:use-macro="context/portlet_login/macros/portlet">
    The login slot will go here
</div>
```

This will fetch the macro and insert the result in its place. As shown, the use-macro command takes a path expression that points to the template and then to the specific macro in the template.

Example: Using the use-macro and define-macro Macros

As an example of this, the following is a template called time_template. This template shows the date and time on the current Plone server. This is quite a useful function to have, so you can wrap this in a macro to be reused. This is the example page template containing the define-macro:

```
<html>
    <body>
        <div metal:define-macro="time">
            <div tal:content="context/ZopeTime">
                The time
            </div>
        </div>
    </body>
</html>
```

If your template is called time_template, then you can reference this macro in another template. You can now reference this macro in multiple templates. This is an example template:

```
<html>
    <body>
    <div metal:use-macro="context/time_template/macros/time">
       If there is a message then the macro will display it here.
    </div>
    </body>
</html>
```

When this template is rendered, the HTML produced by Plone looks like this:

```
<html>
    <body>
    <div>
        <div>2004/04/15 17:18:18.312 GMT-7</div>
    </div>
    </body>
</html>
```

metal:define-slot

A *slot* is a section of a macro that the template author expects to be overridden by another template. You could think of it as a hole in your page template that you're expecting something else to fill in. All define-slot commands must be contained within a define-macro. For example:

```
<div metal:define-macro="master">
  <div metal:define-slot="main">
  ...
  </div>
</div>
```

metal:fill-slot

This completes a slot that has been defined with the use-slot command. A fill-slot must be defined with a use-macro command. When the define-macro part is called, the macro will attempt fill in all the define slots with the appropriate fill-slots. Here's an example fill-slot:

```
<div metal:use-macro="master">
<div metal:fill-slot="main">
The main slot will go here
</div>
</div>
```

Example: Using Macros and Slots

Returning to the previous example, you'll now enhance it a little. If you wanted to put a custom message at the beginning of the time, then you'd add a slot at the beginning of the time_template, inside the define-macro. The slot is called time and is as follows:

```
<html>
    <body>
        <div metal:define-macro="time">
            <div metal:define-slot="msg">Time slot</div>
            <div tal:content="context/ZopeTime">
                The time
            </div>
        </div>
    </body>
</html>
```

Now, in the calling page template, you can call the fill-slot:

```
<html>
    <body>
    <div metal:use-macro="context/time_template/macros/time">
      <div metal:fill-slot="msg">The time is:</div>
      If there is a message then the macro will display it here.
    </div>
    </body>
</html>
```

The end result is that you'll see the time-slot filled in as follows:

```
<html>
    <body>
    <div>
    <div>The time is: </div>
        <div>2004/04/15 17:18:18.312 GMT-7</div>
    </div>
    </body>
</html>
```

How Plone Uses Macros and Slots

Both macros and slots are similar inasmuch as they both extract content from another template and insert content, but they do this differently. The difference comes in how they're used: Macros are elements of a template that are explicitly called, but slots are like holes in a template that you expect other templates to fill in for you. For example, in Plone's case, the portlets such as the calendar, navigation, and so on are macros that are explicitly called.

In fact, if in the Zope Management Interface (ZMI) you look at the file by clicking *portal_skins*, clicking *plone_templates*, and then clicking *main_template*, you'll see that the entire page consists of macros and slots. At this stage, it's probably a little confusing, but when called, it runs through a series of macros and pulls everything together. This allows a user to easily change any part of a Plone site by overriding that macro, as you'll see in the next chapter. For example:

```
...
<div metal:use-macro="here/global_siteactions/macros/site_actions">
    Site-wide actions (Contact, Sitemap, Help, Style Switcher etc)
</div>

<div metal:use-macro="here/global_searchbox/macros/quick_search">
    The quicksearch box, normally placed at the top right
</div>
...
```

Continuing to scroll down through main_template, you'll encounter some define slots. Briefly I'll recap how a page in Plone is rendered. When an object is shown, a template for that view of that content is shown. When you view an image, the template image_view is shown, and that template controls how the image is shown. To do this task, the image template fills the main slot. If you look in the image_view template, you'll see the following code defined in that template:

```
<div metal:fill-slot="main">
...
</div>
```

If you jump back to the main_template, you'll see that it contains a define-slot definition for the slot main:

```
<metal:bodytext metal:define-slot="main" tal:content="nothing">
    Page body text
</metal:bodytext>
```

Each type of content has a different template, and each template defines how they'll use the main slot differently. So, then each content type has its own particular look and feel from the templates. Just one element is missing in the equation. Somehow when you called image_view, the template knew it should use main_template. In the image_view template, you use the macro from the main_template. This is defined in the following HTML:

```
<html xmlns="http://www.w3.org/1999/xhtml" xml:lang="en-US"
    lang="en-US"
    metal:use-macro="here/main_template/macros/master"
    i18n:domain="plone">
```

In this case, the main_template has the main slot filled in by the slot defined as main in the template being rendered. The following is a timeline of how the page is built for viewing an image:

1. The user requests the image_view template of an image.

2. The main_template macro at the top of the image_view template is encountered and called.

3. The main_template is processed.

4. The define-slot="main" is encountered, and the fill-slot is found in image_view.

5. The `fill-slot` is called, and the results are inserted into `main_template`.

6. The `main_template` continues processing.

7. The result is sent back to the browser.

This allows Plone to be flexible in terms of how each page is defined. For example, `main_template` defines just more than that one slot; there's also a slot for inserting Cascading Style Sheets (CSS) code:

```
<metal:cssslot fill-slot="css_slot">
    <metal:cssslot define-slot="css_slot" />
</metal:cssslot>
```

If a view needed a custom set of CSS, you could define this slot in the view, and it'd be filled in when rendering. Some of the macros in `main_template` define slots in them as well and then fill them back in the `main_template` so that if you really wanted, you could also fill in those slots. That's an advanced technique, however, so you'll want to ensure you have the basics down before going down that road.

Introducing Internationalization

Plone is always striving to maintain a large number of high-quality translations. The fact that Plone provides an accessible user interface in more than 30 languages is a key selling point for Plone. This also means that I18N is a key feature of the templates. To facilitate this, the I18N namespace is an extra namespace such as TAL or METAL that has specific statements.

This section details what users need to know in regard to the templates. In a template you can add an `i18n` tag to an element that will allow the translation of an attribute or its contents. Six statements exist: `attributes`, `data`, `domain`, `source`, `target`, and `translate`. The basic pattern is to wrap the piece of text you want to translate and add the appropriate `i18n` attributes. For example, if you want to translate the following:

```
<i>Some text</i>
```

it would become like so:

```
<i i18n:translate="some_text_label">Some text</i>
```

Each localization provides a translation of *Some text*, and the translation tool looks up a translation for a user. When performing the translation, each string to be translated must have a unique message ID that identifies the item to be translated. For example, a string such as *Search* may have a message ID of search_widget_label. The message ID allows the string to be identified uniquely and the translation to be repeated.

i18n:translate

This translates the contents of an element, with an optional message ID passed as a statement. For example, the following will create a message ID of title_string:

```
<h1 i18n:translate="title_string">This is a title</h1>
```

This example is for a piece of text that's static and doesn't change. However, in some situations, the piece of text could be taken from a database or an object and is dynamic. By leaving the translate statement blank, the message ID is composed of the value in the field. In the following example, if the title returned by the path expression here/title was *Alice in Wonderland*, then that title would be passed to the translation tool. If no translation exists, the original value will be inserted:

```
<h1
    tal:content="here/title"
    i18n:translate="">
    This is a title.
</h1>
```

The translation command is probably one of most common i18n tags you'll use, and you'll see it throughout the Plone templates. It not only enables you to translate static parts of your site, such as form labels, help messages, and descriptions, but also the more dynamic parts of your site that could change more often, such as page titles.

i18n:domain

This sets the domain for the translation. To prevent conflict, each site can have multiple domains or groups for translations; for example, there may be one domain for Plone and one for your custom application. Plone uses the domain plone, which is usually the default domain in Plone:

```
<body i18n:domain="plone">
```

You shouldn't have to use this tag much; however, if you're writing a custom application, you may find it useful to have a domain that doesn't conflict with other domains.

I18n:source

This sets the source language for the text about to be translated. It isn't used in Plone:

```
<p i18n:source="en" i18n:translate="">Some text</p>
```

i18n:name

This provides a way of preserving elements in a larger block of text so that the block of text can be reordered. In many languages, not only are the words changed but also the order. If you have to translate a whole paragraph or sentence that contains smaller chunks that shouldn't be translated, then they can be passed through:

```
<p i18n:translate="book_message">
    The
    <span
       tal:omit-tag=""
       tal:content="book/color"
       i18n:name="age">Blue</span>
    Book
</p>
```

This will produce the following message string:

```
The {color} Book
```

If the target language required these to be in a different order, these could then be moved around and still have the dynamic content inserted into the correct place. In French, this would need to be translated as so:

```
Le Livre {color}
```

i18n:target

This sets the target language for the text about to be translated. It isn't used in Plone.

i18n:attributes

This allows the translation of attributes within an element, rather than the content. For example, an image tag has the alt attribute, which shows an alternate representation of the image:

```
<img
    href="/someimage.jpg"
    alt="Some text"
    i18n:attributes="alt alternate_image_label" />
```

Multiple attributes should be separated with a semicolon, just like tal:attributes work.

i18n:data

This provides a way of translating something other than strings. An example is a DateTime object. An i18n:data statement requires a matching i18n:translate statement so that a valid message ID is available. For example:

```
<span i18n:data="here/currentTime"
    i18n:translate="timefmt"
    i18n:name="time">2:32 pm</span>... beep!
```

Translation Service

Now that I've covered the tags, I'll cover the mechanism for performing the translation. By default Plone comes with an I18N mechanism. This allows you to internationalize the user interface so that messages, tabs, and forms can all be translated. At this stage, this doesn't cover the actual content that users add. If you add a document in English and view the page asking for it in French, you'll get the English document with French text around the outside (see Figure 6-1).

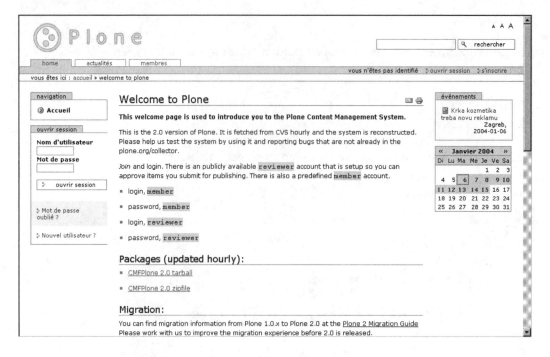

Figure 6-1. Plone.org in French

Plone reads the HTTP headers that a browser sends to the client requesting a language. If your browser is in English, then you won't see much.

To change the language settings in Internet Explorer, do the following:

1. Go to Tools ➤ Internet Options.

2. Click the Languages button at the bottom of the dialog box.

3. Click Add to add a new language, and select a language that Plone has a translation for—for example, French (France) [fr], and click OK.

4. Then make sure this language is at the top by using the Move up button.

5. Click OK and then OK again.

Once you've done this, pick your favorite Plone site and visit it in your browser. The translations for Plone are handled through a tool called Placeless Translation Service (PTS). You can locate the PTS tool in the Zope control panel; at the bottom of the page you'll see an option for Placeless Translation Service. Click this, and it'll open all the translations that exist. These translations are read in from the file system; click a translation to see the information about the language, such as the translator, the encoding, and the path to the file. All the files are actually stored in the i18n directory of the CMFPlone directory.

Translations are handled using two files for a translation, a .po and a .mo file. For example, plone-de.po contains the translations for German (de is the code for German). The .mo file is the "compiled" version of the .po file and is used by Plone for performance. You never need to look at the .mo file, so you can just ignore it. The .po is the file you can edit to change a translation. If you open that file in a text editor, you'll see a series of lines starting with the text msgid or msgstr. Above the msgid is actually the code where the i18n command occurs, so you can see which bit of a page you're translating. For example:

```
#: from plone_forms/content_status_history.pt
#.    <input attributes="tabindex tabindex/next;" value="Apply"
class="context" name="workflow_action_submit" type="submit" />
#.
#: from plone_forms/personalize_form.pt
#.    <input attributes="tabindex tabindex/next;" tabindex=""
value="Apply" class="context" type="submit" />
#.
msgid "Apply"
msgstr "Anwenden"
```

In the two parts of the previous page templates, the word *Apply* will be translated into *Anwenden* for German users. What gets translated is determined by the i18n tags that have been inserted into the page templates, as you saw earlier. If you want to change that translation or add your own variation, then merely change the .po file. If no msgstr is found, then the default English translation is found. Once you've made that change, restart Plone. When this happens, Plone will recompile that file into the .mo version, and your translation will be updated.

For Plone, the default translation is always to use the English translation file if no language is given or no translation is available. In fact, the plone-en.po file is blank, so no translation will be available. Therefore, Plone does the final fallback, does no translation, and shows the text in the page template. The text in all page templates is in English since most developers speak English. The long and short of this is that there's no English translation.

Therefore, you can make a new translation by copying the plone.pot file into a new file of the name plone-xx.po. The value of xx should match the country code of your translation. You can find a list of language codes at http://www.unicode.org/onlinedat/languages.html. Once you've started the translation, set the values at the top, including the language code, and start translating away. If you've done a new language file, then the Plone I18N team will happily accept it and help you complete it. The Plone team mailing list is at http://sourceforge.net/mailarchive/forum.php?forum_id=11647.

Translating the content that people add is actually quite a tricky task and something that Plone is working toward, but currently it hasn't completely ironed out. The favorite approach at the moment is to use two products, `PloneLanguageTool` and `i18nLayer`, both of which can be found on SourceForge (`http://sf.net/projects/collective`). However, both of these are for more experienced developers to fully understand and integrate; I hope something like this will be in the next release of the book.

Example: Displaying Multiple User Information

In Chapter 5 you used simple TAL commands to show a user's information in more detail. That template has a few drawbacks; one of them is that it shows only one user at a time. You've seen that a simple `tal:repeat` can enable you to repeat content, but you'll now use a macro to make this page more modular.

You'll change the `user_info` page template so that it lists every page member in the site. Instead of looking for a username being passed in the request, you'll use the function `listMembers`, which returns a list of every member on the site:

```
<div metal:fill-slot="main">
  <tal:block
   tal:define="
   getPortrait nocall: here/portal_membership/getPersonalPortrait;
   getFolder nocall: here/portal_membership/getHomeFolder
   ">
   <table>
     <tr tal:repeat="userObj here/portal_membership/listMembers">
        <metal:block
          metal:use-macro="here/user_section/macros/userSection" />
     </tr>
   </table>
  </tal:block>
</div>
```

You'll note that the code for `user_info` is now a great deal shorter. The member returned by `listMembers` is passed in to `tal:repeat`. For each member, there will be a table row and then a macro to show information to the user. In that table row, the locally defined variable `userObj` now contains the user information. Of course, you now need to make a macro called `userSection` in a page template, so you'll create a page template called `user_section` as referenced in the macro. This template contains all the code that was between the table's row tags. Again, you can find a full listing for this page template in Appendix B:

```
<div metal:define-macro="userSection"
    tal:define="userName userObj/getUserName">
    ...
```

The only real change is that the use-macro in the main template has to be removed and a new macro defined so that this macro can be defined. Because the username is no longer explicitly passed, you need to get the username from the user object by using the getUserName method. To test the resulting page, go to http://yoursite/user_info, and you should see a list of users.

The page now is user-friendly, showing multiple users on one page. The code is more modular, rendering the user's information in a separate macro that can be altered independently. This page is still not perfect but will be improved in later chapters.

Example: Creating a New Portlet with Google Ads

In Chapter 4 you saw how to easily edit portlets in a Plone site; adding your own portlet isn't much harder. To write your own slot, you need to make a new page template with a macro inside it. Then a TALES expression that points to macro will be added to the list of portlet, rendering the portlet to the page.

The basic template for a portlet is as follows:

```
<div metal:define-macro="portlet">
    <div class="portlet">
      <!-- Enter code here -->
    </div>
</div>
```

All you need to do is insert some suitable code into the portlet. Google set up a text-based advertising system in 2003 that places text on your site. The ads are based upon what Google thinks your site is about, based on the search results for your site. The Google system is available at http://www.google.com/adsense. To display ads (and get paid for them), you'll have to register with Google. On the Google Web site, it'll ask you to pick some colors and style. Since you'll put this in a slot, I recommend the "skyscraper" size—tall and thin. Make a copy of the JavaScript that the site produces.

Next, you have to create a portlet:

1. In the portal_skins/custom folder, make a page template called googleAds.

2. Take the previous base code template, and change the portlet name to googleBox.

3. Paste the code from Google, replacing the <!-- Enter code here --> section.

The end result should be something like Listing 6-1; however, your version will have a valid value for google_ad_client, rather than yourUniqueValue. That value tells Google which site ordered this ad and who to pay. Curiously enough, if you don't have a valid value there, Google will still happily show the ads but not pay you!

Listing 6-1. Displaying Ads from Google

```
<div metal:define-macro="portlet">
    <div class="portlet">
<script type="text/javascript"><!--
google_ad_client = "yourUniqueValue";
google_ad_width = 120;
google_ad_height = 600;
google_ad_format = "120x600_as";
//--></script>
<script type="text/javascript"
  src="http://pagead2.googlesyndication.com/pagead/show_ads.js">
</script>

    </div>
</div>
```

To then include this on your site, as detailed in Chapter 4, add the following portlet to your list of portlets:

```
here/googleAds/macros/portlet
```

Scripting Plone with Python

At least four different levels in Plone exist for creating logic. The simplest level for using Python in Plone is the Python TALES expression I discussed in the previous chapter. However, a Python expression allows you to do only one line of code; often you'll want to do something more complicated.

Even more common is the problem that you really don't want to cram all the logic into the template. Placing logic in your template is a bad idea in general; any time you can move anything that isn't explicitly presentation logic out of the template, you've saved yourself a headache. Separating logic and presentation allows you to easily allow different people to work on different parts of the project, and it improves code reuse. The other layers of adding scripting Plone happen roughly in the following order:

- **Template attribute expressions**: These provide expressions and a way of inserting little snippets of logic or simple paths in many places.

- **Script (Python) objects**: These are simple scripts that execute in Plone in a restricted environment.

- **External method objects**: These are more complicated modules that don't execute in restricted environments.

- **Python products**: This is the key source that the CMF and Plone is written in; this offers access to everything in Plone. Python products are an advanced subject and are covered in Chapter 14.

After an expression, the next level of complexity is Script (Python) object. This object allows for multiple lines of Python code, and you can call it from an expression. When you call a Script (Python) object, you're incurring a small amount of extra overhead as Plone makes a switch into that object. However, that overhead is minimal because there's a trade-off between clarity, separation, and performance. My advice is to put as much logic into Python as possible and keep page templates as simple and as clean as possible. It's easy to move it back later if there's a performance hit, but at least you'll understand what's happening later.

Using Script (Python) Objects

A Script (Python) object is may you might traditionally think of in Plone as a script. It's a snippet of Python that you can write and then call from other templates or through the Web directly. Plone actually has a large number of these scripts for performing various key functions. A Script (Python) is halfway between an expression and an external method in terms of power.

To add a Script (Python) object, go to the ZMI, select Script (Python) from the drop-down menu, and click Add, as shown in Figure 6-2.

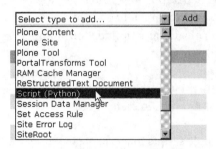

Figure 6-2. Adding in a Script (Python) object

Give the script an ID such as **test_py** and then click Add and Edit. This will open the edit page for the Script (Python) object, which looks like Figure 6-3.

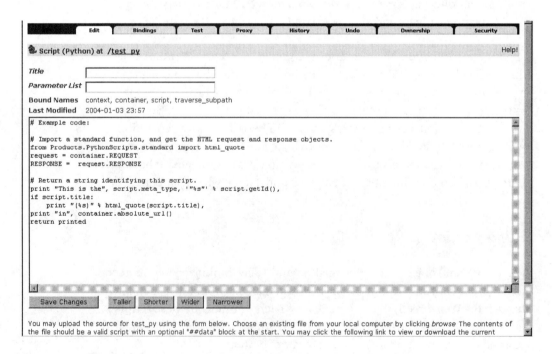

Figure 6-3. Editing a Script (Python) object

You can edit the script directly through the Web. If you make a syntax error, you'll be told about it after you've clicked Save Changes, as shown in Figure 6-4.

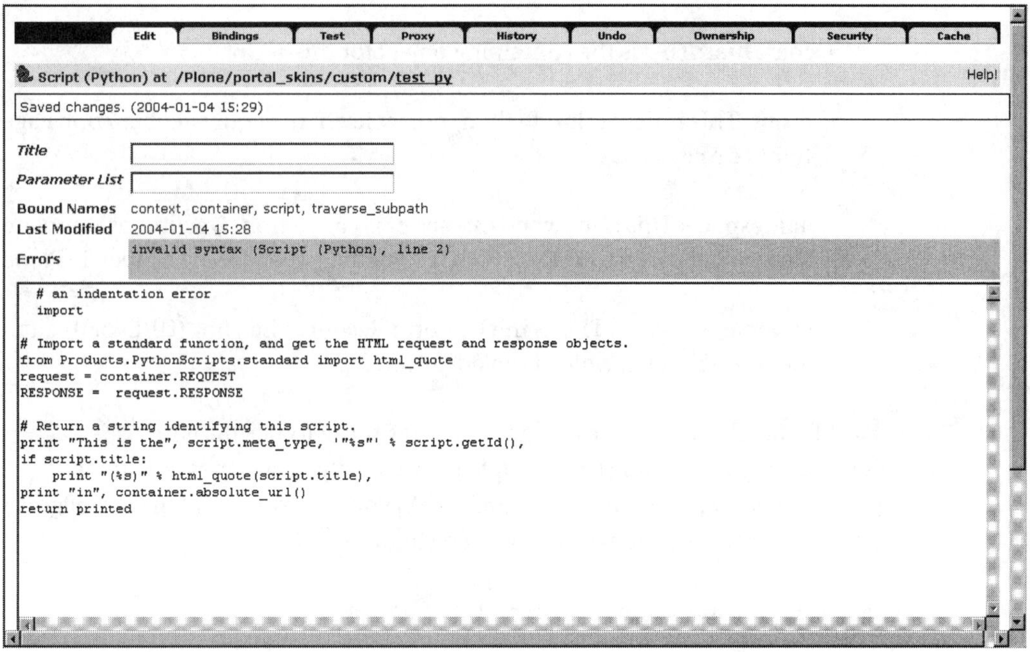

Figure 6-4. A deliberate indentation error in the Script (Python) object

If your Script (Python) has no errors, you can click the Test tab to see what the output is. In this case, the sample is rather boring; it prints the following text:

```
This is the Script (Python) "test_py" in
http://gloin:8080/Plone/portal_skins/custom
```

A script also has the following options:

Title: The edit form has a Title option, which is for you to give the script a title. This will show up in the ZMI, so it'll be easier to remember what it does.

Parameter List: This is a list of parameters that the script takes, such as variableA or variableB=None. In fact, this is a standard list of parameters you'd expect in a standard Python function. Some parameters are already defined for you in this object, however; you can see them by clicking the Bindings tab. In that tab, you'll see a list of the variables already bound into the object, which should have familiar names by now.

The following are the variables bound to the script that are accessible from a Script (Python) object:

- **context**: This is the object on which the script is being called.

- **container**: This is the containing object for this script.

- **script**: This is the Script (Python) object itself; the equivalent in Zope Page Templates is `template`.

- **namespace**: This is for when this script is called from Document Template Markup Language (DTML), which is something that doesn't happen in Plone.

- **traverse_subpath**: This is the Uniform Resource Locator (URL) path after the script's name, which is an advanced feature.

I'll now show a simple example that ties these topics into the Zope Page Templates system, using the example I gave of a Python expression in the previous chapter that adds two numbers. As you saw, you could make a page template for this that looks like the following:

```
<p>1 + 2 = <em tal:content="python: 1 + 2" /></p>
```

The equivalent using a Script (Python) object looks like the following. Change the `test_py` script to the following line:

```
return 1+2
```

As you saw at the beginning of the previous chapter, you call an object by giving its path as an expression. So, in a page template, you can now do the following:

```
<p>1 + 2 = <em tal:content="here/test_py" /></p>
```

The object `test_py` is acquired in the path expression and called, and it then returns the Python back to the template and prints. You've now called a script from your template! This is obviously a rather simple example, but my point is that there's a great deal you can do in a Script (Python) object that you just can't do in a page template.

In a Script (Python) object, you can specify the title, parameters, and bindings setting by using the ## notation at the top of a script. When you save a script with that bit of text at the top, Plone will remove that line and instead change the appropriate value on the object. This syntax is used a lot in the Script (Python) object in this book to ensure that you have the right title and parameters. So, you could rewrite the previous script as follows:

```
##title=Returns 1+2
##parameters=
return 1+2
```

Scripting Plone

Scripting Plone is a rather complicated subject because as soon as you're able to script Plone, you have to take into account the Application Programming Interface (API) of all the objects and tools you may want to use. Explaining APIs is beyond the scope of this book; instead, I'll demonstrate how to do some simple tasks using Script (Python) objects. Once you're comfortable with them, I'll describe more API-specific functions.

Page templates can loop through Python dictionaries and lists quite nicely. But often you don't have data in one of these convenient formats, so you need to jump into a Script (Python) object, format the data nicely, and then pass it back to the page template.

The most convenient data format is a list of dictionaries, which lets you combine the power of a tal:repeat and a path expression in one function. As an example, you'll see a function that takes a list of objects. Each of these objects is actually an object in a folder. For each of those objects, you'll see the object if it has been updated in the last five days. Listing 6-2 shows a useful little portlet I put together for a site that wanted to locate this type of information and then highlight exactly those items.

Listing 6-2. Returning Objects Up to Five Days Old

```
##title=recentlyChanged
##parameters=objects
from DateTime import DateTime

now = DateTime()
difference = 5 # as in 5 days
result = []

for object in objects:
  diff = now - object.bobobase_modification_time()
  if diff < difference:
    dct = {"object":object,"diff":int(diff)}
    result.append(dct)

return result
```

In this Script (Python) object I've introduced a couple of new concepts. First, you import Zope's DateTime module using the import function. The DateTime module, covered in Appendix C, is a module to provide access to dates. It's pretty simple, but if you make a new DateTime object with no parameters, then you'll get the current date and time; this is the now variable. When you subtract two DateTime objects, you'll get the number of days. You can compare that to the difference a user wants to monitor and, if it's longer, add it to the result list. The result of this is a list of dictionary objects, which looks like Listing 6-3.

Listing 6-3. The Result of Listing 6-2

```
[
  {
      'diff': 1,
      'object': <PloneFolder instance at 02COC110>
  },
  {
l       'diff': 4,
      'object': <PloneFolder instance at 02FE3321>
  },
  ...
```

So now that you have the results in the right order, you need a page template that will pass in the list of objects and process the results. An example of this is as follows:

```
<ul>
  <li tal:repeat="updated python: context.updateScript(context.contentValues())">
```

This template has a tal:repeat call at the top that calls the script (in this case, called updateScript). Into that function it passes one value, a list of contentValues from the current context. Previously you called the Script (Python) object using a path expression; you could do that here as context/updateScript. However, you can't pass parameters through to the script being called in that syntax, so you make a Python expression instead, which is python: context.updateScript(). The contentValues function returns a list of all content objects in a folder. Next, look at the code for each iteration:

```
  <a href="#"
     tal:attributes="href updated/object/absolute_url"
     tal:content="updated/object/title_or_id">
     The title of the item</a>
  <em tal:content="updated/diff" /> days ago
  </li>
</ul>
```

As shown, you can loop through this list of values, and you can then use path expressions to access first the repeated value (updated), then the object (object), and then a method of that object (title_or_id). This is an example of taking complicated logic processing and passing it off to a Script (Python) object.

Restricted Python

I've mentioned several times that Script (Python) objects and Python TAL expressions all run in *restricted Python* mode. Restricted Python is an environment that has some functions removed. These functions may potentially be dangerous in a Web environment such as Plone. The original reasoning is that you may have untrusted (but authenticated) users writing Python on your site. If you open an account at one of the many free Web hosts for Zope, you'll find you can do this. However, if you have given people the right to do that, you don't want them to get access to certain things such as the file system.

In restricted Python, some common Python functions have been removed for security reasons—most notably, dir and open aren't available. This means that, as with Script (Python) objects, they can't be introspected, and access is limited to the file system. A few Python modules are available to the user. Most of these are for experienced developers; for more information, see the relevant documentation or module code:

- **string**: This is the Python string module (http://python.org/doc/current/lib/module-string.html).

- **random**: This is the Python random module (http://python.org/doc/current/lib/module-random.html).

- **whrandom**: This is the Python whrandom module. You should mostly use random now (http://python.org/doc/current/lib/module-whrandom.html).

- **math**: This is the Python math module (http://python.org/doc/current/lib/module-math.html).

- **DateTime**: This is Zope's own DateTime module.

- **sequence**: This is a Zope module for easily sorting sequences.

- **ZTUtils**: This is a Zope module that provides various utilities.

- **AccessControl**: This gives access to Zope's Access module.

- **Products.PythonScripts.standard**: This gives access to the standard string-processing functions of DTML such as html_quote, thousands_commas, and so on.

If you want to import a module that isn't in the previous list, then you can find excellent instructions in the PythonScript module. You'll find them at Zope/lib/python/Products/PythonScripts/module_access_examples.py. However, a more simple method is available to you—using an external method.

Using External Method Objects

An *external method* is a Python module written on the file system and then accessed in Plone. Because it's written on the file system, it doesn't run in restricted Python mode, and therefore it conforms to the standard Plone security settings.

This means you can write a script that does anything you want and then call it from a page template. Common tasks include opening and closing files, accessing other processes or executables, and performing tasks in Plone or Zope that you simply can't perform in any other way. For obvious reasons, when you're writing a script that can do this, you need to be sure you aren't doing anything dangerous, such as reading the password file to your server or deleting a file you don't want to delete.

To add an external method, you go to the file system of your instance home and find the Extensions directory. In that directory, add a new Python script file; for example, Figure 6-5 shows that I added test.py to a directory on my Windows computer.

You can now open test.py and edit it to your heart's content, writing any Python code you want. The only catch is that you must have an entry function that takes at least one argument, self. This argument is the external method object in Plone that you'll be adding shortly. The following is an example entry function that reads the README.txt file out of the same Extensions directory and spits it back to the user (you'll have to change the path to point to your file):

```
def readFile(self):
    fh = open(r'c:\Program Files\Plone\Data\Extensions\README.txt', 'rb')
    data = fh.read()
    return data
```

Now that you've done that, you need to map an external method to this script. This is a Zope object, so return to the ZMI, click *portal_skins*, and then click *custom*. Finally, select External Method from the Add New Items drop-down list. When you add an external method, you need to give the name of the module (without the .py) and the entry function, so in this case the add form looks like Figure 6-6.

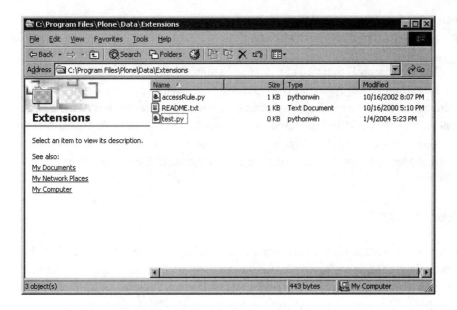

Figure 6-5. A new external method, `test.py`

Add External Method   Help!

External Methods allow you to add functionality to Zope by writing Python functions which
are exposed as callable Zope objects. The *module name* should give the name of the
Python module without the ".py" file extension. The *function name* should name a callable
object found in the module.

Id	test_external
Title	
Module Name	test
Function Name	readFile

       [Add]

Figure 6-6. The newly added external method

After clicking Save Changes, you can hit the Test tab to see what happens
when it runs. In this case, you should get a line or two of text. Since you have the
External Method module in Plone, you can access it from a page template in the
same way as any other object. A path expression to `here/test_external` would do
the trick in this case. For example:

```
<h1>README.txt</h1>
<p tal:content="here/test_external" />
```

The real power is that you can pass code off to the unrestricted Python mode and from there to any function you want, without having to worry about security. Although this may seem like a cool function, external methods aren't used a great deal in Plone because complicated logic is usually moved into a Product object, and simple logic is kept in a Script (Python) object. If you find yourself using External Method objects a lot, consider one of the tools discussed in Chapter 12.

Useful Tips

Because page templates are valid Extensible Markup Language (XML) and can be used independently of Zope or Plone, you have several useful scripts for cleaning up page template code and performing syntax checks. These are additional tools and checks; Zope actually performs all the necessary checks when you upload a page template. For a project such as Plone, it can be useful to run automatic checks on your code or verify it locally before committing changes.

To run these checks, you'll need to be able to edit these tools locally and have Python installed on your computer. For more information on External Editor, a method for editing remote code locally, see Chapter 10.

Introducing XML Namespaces

Page templates use XML namespaces to generate code. Programmers can use the rules of XML namespaces to make life easier. At the top of a page template, you'll see a declaration of the namespace in the starting tag:

```
<html xmlns="http://www.w3.org/1999/xhtml"...
```

This sets the default namespace to Extensible HTML (XHTML). For any containing element, if no namespace is defined, it uses that default namespace. For example, you know the next element is XHTML because it has no prefix:

```
<body>
```

Normally for TAL and METAL elements and attributes, you have been adding the prefix `tal:` and `metal:` to define the namespace. The following code is something that should be familiar by now:

```
<span tal:omit-tag="" tal:content="python: 1+2" />
```

This will render 3. However, the following is an alternative:

```
<tal:number content="python: 1+2" />
```

By using the tal: prefix on the element, you've defined the default namespace for this whole element as tal. If no other prefix is given, the tal namespace is used. In the example, using span tags, the default namespace is XHTML, so you have to specifically define the tal: prefix when using the Content tab.

Note that the element name is descriptive and can be anything not already defined the tal namespace (for example, content or replace). Because tal:number isn't a valid XHTML element, the actual tag won't display, but the content will—making the omit-tag unnecessary. This technique is used a lot in Plone to make code that's smaller, simpler to debug, and more semantic.

Introducing Tidying Code

HTML Tidy is an excellent tool for testing and cleaning up HTML code that can perform a few useful tasks. Versions of HTML Tidy exist for all operating systems; you can download it from http://tidy.sourceforge.net. For Windows users, find the appropriate download for your version of Windows, unzip the tidy.zip file, and place the tidy.exe in your PATH (usually your Windows directory, such as C:\up WINNT).

HTML Tidy can tell you if there are any XHTML errors in your page template. For these purposes, one flag can make a difference: -xml. This tells HTML Tidy to process the file as XML and report any XML errors. Given the example "bad" template shown in Listing 6-4, you can see a few errors. Not only is the code not indented, but it's missing closing elements and has invalid nesting.

Listing 6-4. An Example Broken Page Template: bad_template.pt

```
<!DOCTYPE html PUBLIC "-//W3C//DTD XHTML 1.0 Transitional//EN"
    "http://www.w3.org/TR/xhtml1/DTD/xhtml1-transitional.dtd">
<html xmlns="http://www.w3.org/1999/xhtml">
<head>
<title></title>
</head>
<body>
<p>
<div>
This is bad HTML,
XHTML or XML...<a tal:contents="string: someUrl"></a>
</p>
```

```
<img>
Further it isnt indented!
</body>
</html>
```

If you run Listing 6-4 through HTML Tidy, you'll see the errors in the template and get nicely indented code, as shown in Listing 6-5.

Listing 6-5. The Output from HTML Tidy

```
$ tidy -q -i bad_template.pt
line 11 column 1 - Warning: <img> element not empty or not closed
line 10 column 1 - Warning: missing </div>
line 10 column 39 - Warning: <a> proprietary attribute "tal:contents"
line 11 column 1 - Warning: <img> lacks "alt" attribute
line 11 column 1 - Warning: <img> lacks "src" attribute
line 9 column 1 - Warning: trimming empty <p>
<!DOCTYPE html PUBLIC "-//W3C//DTD XHTML 1.0 Strict//EN"
    "http://www.w3.org/TR/xhtml1/DTD/xhtml1-strict.dtd">

<html xmlns="http://www.w3.org/1999/xhtml">
<head>
  <meta name="generator" content=
  "HTML Tidy for Linux/x86 (vers 1st August 2003), see www.w3.org" />

  <title></title>
</head>

<body>
  <div>
    This is bad HTML, XHTML or XML...<a tal:contents=
    "string: someUrl"></a> <img />Further it isnt indented!
  </div>
</body>
</html>
```

The complaints about proprietary attributes can be a little annoying. To check that your page template is valid XML, pass the -xml flag. The output is less verbose and just points out the missing tags:

```
$ tidy -q -xml bad_template.pt
line 15 column 1 - Error: unexpected </body> in <img>
line 16 column 1 - Error: unexpected </html> in <img>
```

Conducting Syntax Checks

When you edit a page template in the ZMI, Zope performs a syntax check on the document for things such as invalid tags. If a tag is invalid, an error will be shown on the template while you're editing it through the Web. If, like me (and as I demonstrate in Chapter 7), you write most of your page templates on the file system, then a simple syntax check for a page template is really useful. Listing 6-6 is a Python script that resides on your file system and runs independently from Zope.

To run this, you must have a Python interpreter, and the Python module PageTemplate must be importable. To make PageTemplate importable to your Python interpreter, you must add the Products directory of your Zope installation to your Python path. You have several ways to do this (covered in Appendix B).

Listing 6-6. Error Checking Page Templates

```python
#!/usr/bin/python
from Products.PageTemplates.PageTemplate import PageTemplate
import sys

def test(file):
    raw_data = open(file, 'r').read()
    pt = PageTemplate()
    pt.write(raw_data)
    if pt._v_errors:
        print "*** Error in:", file
        for error in pt._v_errors[1:]:
            print error

if __name__=='__main__':
    if len(sys.argv) < 2:
        print "python check.py file [files...]"
        sys.exit(1)
    else:
        for arg in sys.argv[1:]:
            test(arg)
```

For every file passed through to the script, the ZMI will compile the page template and see if there are any TAL errors. Taking the bad_template.pt file from Listing 6-4, you'll get an error:

```
$ python zpt.py /tmp/bad_template.pt
*** Error in: /tmp/bad_template.pt
TAL.TALDefs.TALError: bad TAL attribute: 'contents', at line 10, column 39
```

In this case, it has picked up on the incorrect spelling of tal:content as tal:contents. This error is something HTML Tidy doesn't catch. Unfortunately, the processing stops at the first syntax error. If there are multiple errors, only the first is picked up, meaning sometimes you have to check the syntax several times.

Using Forms

Forms are an integral part of any site, and almost everyone needs to create a method for creating and altering forms in your Plone site. With the form framework in Plone, you can change the validation that process forms have, where they take the user to, and so on. This framework isn't just specifically designed for stand-alone forms that perform a simple task, such as request a password, login, and so on. The framework also works for all content types for tasks such as editing a content type, which I'll cover later in this book in Chapters 11–13.

All basic forms have at least two components that you've already seen so far: a Page Template object to show the form to the user, and a Script (Python) object to parse the results and perform some action on the results.

The form controller framework in Plone introduces a few new object types that are equivalent to the types you've seen in this chapter. These are the Controller Page Template object, the Controller Script (Python) object, and the Controller Validator object. These new objects have their equivalent objects, as shown in Table 6-1. These new objects have more properties and act in slightly different ways than the equivalent objects.

Table 6-1. New Object Types That the Controller Provides

Object Type	Equivalent Zope Object
Controller Filesystem Page Template	Page Template
Controller Python Script	Python Script
Controller Validator	Python Script

To add one of these objects using the ZMI, go to the drop-down box, and select the name.

The form controller framework creates a sequence of events for a form that a user can then define. The following is the sequence of events when executing a form:

1. A Controller Page Template object is shown to the user.

2. The user completes the form and submits it.

3. Any validations for the content submitted are executed.

4. The appropriate action for the data (often success or failure) is executed.

When this sequence of events occurs, a state object is passed around, which contains information about the status of the object, the success of any validations, and any messages that are to be passed.

The following sections run through these steps to show how a form can be validated, and then I'll show a full example in the "E-Mail Example: Sending E-Mail to the Webmaster" section.

Creating a Sample Form and Associated Scripts

The beginning of this process is a form. Although this is actually a Controller Page Template object, it's written using standard TAL code. To add one, select Controller Page Template from the now-familiar drop-down box and give it an ID of **test_cpt**.

A form in Plone is actually a rather lengthy piece of code if you want to utilize all the options available to you. This piece of code is reproduced in full in Appendix B and is the code used in the later example:

```
<form method="post"
      tal:define="errors options/state/getErrors"
      tal:attributes="action template/id;">

    ...
    <input type="hidden" name="form.submitted" value="1" />
</form>
```

Looking at this code, you should note that to work in the framework, a few minor differences exist between this and what you may consider a standard form. First, the form is set up to submit to itself; this *isn't* optional. Second, a special hidden variable exists called form.submitted.

The Controller Page Template object checks the request variable for the value form.submitted to see if the form has been submitted. If, instead, it has just been accessed—for example, via a link—this *isn't* optional. At the beginning of the form, you set the variable errors. The errors dictionary comes from the state object that's passed into the templates. The state object is a common object to all the templates and scripts in this system.

Creating Validators

Once the user clicks the Submit button on your form, the data will be run through the validators and be validated. Validators are optional. Data doesn't need to be validated, but of course any application should do that as appropriate. The Validator tab for a Controller Page Template object gives you a link to the possible validators.

A validation script is the same as a normal Script (Python) object that has one extra variable, state. The state variable is how you can pass results of the validation. Listing 6-7 shows a simple validation script for checking to see if you've been given a number.

Listing 6-7. Validating That a Number Has Been Provided

```
##title=A validation script to check we have a number
##parameters=
num = context.REQUEST.get('num', None)
try:
    int(num)
except ValueError:
    state.setError("num", "Not a number", new_status="failure")
except TypeError:
    state.setError("num", "No number given.", new_status="failure")
if state.getErrors():
    state.set(portal_status_message="Please correct the errors.")
return state
```

This state object contains basic information about what has happened during the validation chain. The state object stores the errors for each field, the status, and any other values. For example, if the number given can't be turned into an integer, you set the status to failure and give an error message for the field using the setError method. Later this error message will be shown for the field. At the end of the script, any errors returned so far are retrieved via the getErrors method.

To add the previous script, click *portal_skins*, click *custom*, and select Controller Validator from the drop-down box. Give it an ID of **test_validator**. You can now return to the Validation tab of your Controller Page Template object and add a pointer to this validation script, as shown in Figure 6-7.

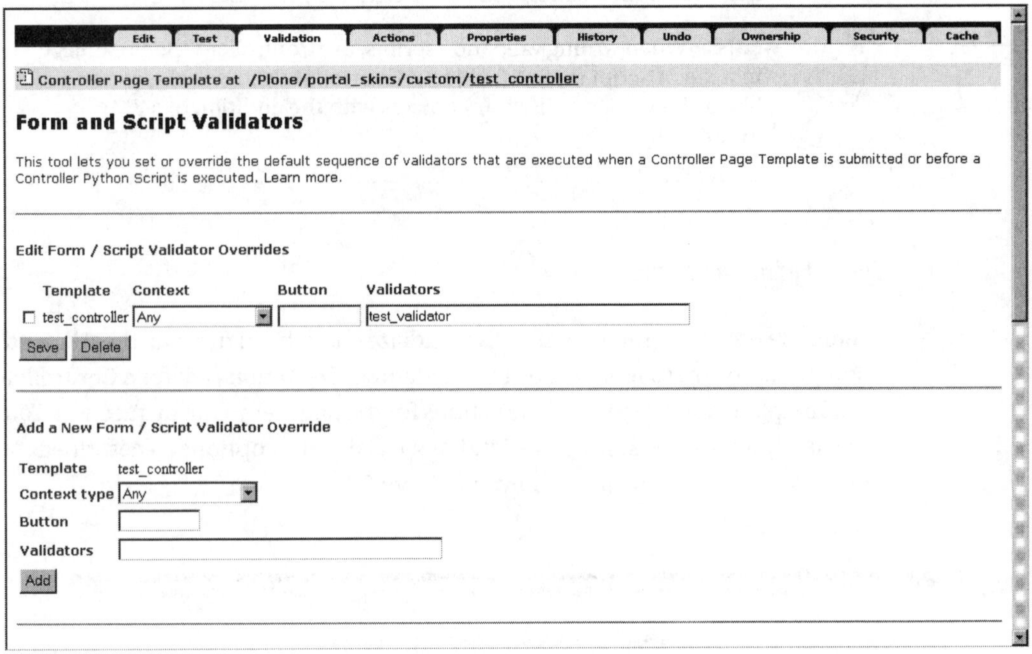

Figure 6-7. Adding the test_validator *to the Controller Page Template object*

You have a couple of choices for a validation. In the example I've ignored them since they aren't relevant, but the following is a list of the options:

contextType: This is the type of the context object, if any, that template is executed in. This is a shortcut to the content type of the context object. If you wanted only this validation to occur on a link, then you could set this value to Link.

button: This is the button, if any, that's clicked to submit the form. You could have different buttons on a form (for example, a Submit and a Cancel button). Each of these buttons could then map to a different action; clicking Cancel would take you to one place, and clicking Submit would take you to another.

validators: This is a comma-separated list of validators, which are Controller Validator objects that the template will acquire. In the previous example, you used the validator ID of test_validator.

NOTE   When writing validation scripts, use Controller Validator objects instead of Script (Python) objects. Controller Validator objects are just like ordinary Script (Python) objects with the addition of a ZMI Actions tab.

Specifying Actions

Actions are the ending actions after the validators have been run, and they depend upon the status that's returned by the validators. The Actions tab for a Controller Page Template object shows all the actions for the page template in question. You can specify actions with the same kind of specialization options as described previously via a Web form, as shown in Figure 6-8.

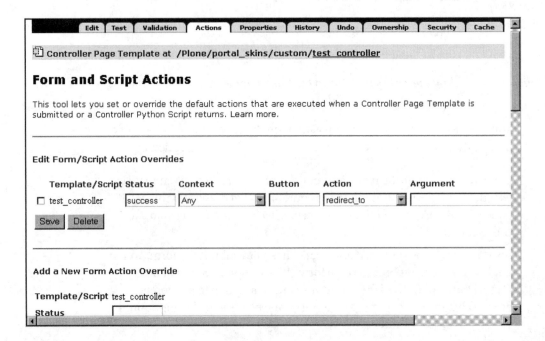

Figure 6-8. Adding an action

You have the following four choices for the actual resulting action:

redirect_to: This redirects to the URL specified in the argument (a TALES expression). The URL can be either absolute or relative.

redirect_to_action: This redirect to the action specified in the argument (a TALES expression) for the current content object (for example, string:view). At this stage I haven't covered actions yet, but each content object has actions such as view and edit. Chapter 11 covers actions for an object.

traverse_to: This traverses to the URL specified in the argument (a TALES expression). The URL can be either absolute or be relative.

traverse_to_action: This traverses to the action specified in the argument (a TALES expression) for the current content object (for example, string:view).

One example of this is if the completion of the form is a success, you traverse to a Controller Python Script object that you've written that processes the result of the form. If the page is a failure, you traverse back to the template and show them the error.

The difference between a redirect and a traversal is that the redirect is an HTTP redirect sent to the user's browser. The browser processes it and then sends the user off to the next page. Thus, the redirect actions lose all the values passed in the original request. If you need to examine the contents of the original form, then this isn't the best approach. Instead, I recommend the traversal to options. The result is the same; it's just that the traverse option does this all on the server. Doing this preserves the request variables and allows you to examine this in scripts.

E-Mail Example: Sending E-Mail to the Webmaster

You'll now see a real example and spend the rest of this chapter building it. A common requirement is a custom form that sends e-mail to the Webmaster. You'll build this type of form in the following sections. The complete scripts, page template, and assorted code are available in Appendix B. If you really don't want to type all this in, you can see this example online at the book's Web site; it's also downloadable as a compressed file from the Plone book Web site (http://plone-book.agmweb.ca) and the Apress Web site (http://www.apress.com), so you can just install it and try it. This example has just two fields in the form: the e-mail of the person submitting the form and some comments from that person. For this form, the e-mail of the person will be required so you can respond to their comments.

Building the Form

The form is the largest and most complicated part of this procedure, mostly because there's so much work that has to be done to support error handling. This form is a Controller Page Template object called feedbackForm. To ensure that it's wrapped in the main template, I'll start the form in the standard method:

```
<html
    xmlns="http://www.w3.org/1999/xhtml"
    xml:lang="en-US"
    lang="en-US"
    i18n:domain="plone"
    metal:use-macro="here/main_template/macros/master">
  <body>
    <div metal:fill-slot="main"
        tal:define="errors options/state/getErrors;">
```

One addition here is errors options/state/getErrors, which will place any and all errors into the errors local variable for later use.

Because of the requirement for the form to post back to itself, you set this action in TAL, with the expression template/id. This path will pull out the ID of the template and insert it into the action, so this path will always work, even if you rename the template. Note that you're also adding the i18n tags you saw earlier to ensure that this form can be localized:

```
<form method="post"
      tal:attributes="action template/id;">

<legend i18n:translate="legend_feedback_form">
    Website Feedback
</legend>
```

The following is the start of the row for the e-mail address. You'll define a variable here called error_email_address that's set to an error string if there's a suitable string in the errors dictionaries. That error value will be generated by the validator should there be an error:

```
<div class="field"
    tal:attributes="class python:test(error_email_address,
                                    'field error', 'field')">
    tal:define="error_email_address errors/email_address|nothing;">
```

The following is the label for the e-mail address field. In this label you'll include a div for the help text. The span element will become the now-familiar red dot next to the label so that the user knows it's required:

```
<label i18n:translate="label_email_address">Your email address</label>
<span class="fieldRequired" title="Required">(Required)</span>
<div class="formHelp"
     i18n:translate="label_email_address_help">
     Enter your email address.
</div>
```

Next you'll add the actual element:

```
<div tal:condition="error_email_address">
    <tal:block i18n:translate=""
                content="error_email_address">Error
    </tal:block>
</div>
<input type="text" name="email_address"
       tal:attributes="tabindex tabindex/next;
                       value request/email_address|nothing" />
</div>
```

At the top of this block, you test to see if there's an error. If there is, the class for the element changed to be the field error class; this class will show a nice orange box around the field. Next, if an error has occurred for this field (as you've already tested for), the corresponding message will be displayed. Finally, you'll show the form element, and if there's a value for email_address already in the request, you'll populate the form element with that value.

The tabindex is a useful tool in Plone. It contains a sequential number that's incremented for each element, and each time it sets a new HTML tabindex value for each element in a form. This is a nice user interface feature; it means each form element can be safely moved around without having to worry about remembering the tabindex numbers because that'll happen automatically.

That's a lot of work for one element, but it's mostly boilerplate code; you can easily copy or change it. You can find the remainder of the form in Appendix B.

Creating a Validator

In the example you have only one required element (the e-mail), so it's a simple piece of Python called validEmail.vpy that does the work. The contents of this script are as follows:

```
email = context.REQUEST.get('email_address', None)
if not email:
    state.setError('email_address', 'Email is required',
                   new_status='failure')
if state.getErrors():
    state.set(portal_status_message='Please correct the errors.')
return state
```

If no e-mail address can be found, this script adds an error to the dictionary of errors with the key of email_address and a message. This key is used in the page template to see if an error occurred on that particular field.

Processing the Script

This example has a simple e-mail script that gets the values (which are already validated) and forms an e-mail out of them. This is a Controller Python Script object; it's just like a standard Script (Python) object except that it has a state variable, and, like the Controller Page Template, you can give it actions for when it succeeds:

```
mhost = context.MailHost
emailAddress = context.REQUEST.get('email_address')
administratorEmailAddress = context.email_from_address
comments = context.REQUEST.get('comments')

# the message format, %s will be filled in from data
message = """
From: %s
To: %s
Subject: Website Feedback

%s
URL: %s """

# format the message
message = message % (
    emailAddress,
    administratorEmailAddress,
    comments,
    context.absolute_url())

mhost.send(message)
```

You've now seen a simple script for sending e-mail. This is a common script that you'll see again and again. Basically, the MailHost object in Plone will take an e-mail as a string, as long as it conforms to the Request for Comment (RFC) specification for e-mail that has From and To addresses.

In this e-mail, you take the administrator address you specified in the portal setup and send the e-mail to that person. The only extra part in this script is the addition of setting the state. This will set a message that provides some feedback to the user:

```
screenMsg = "Comments sent, thank you."
state.setKwargs( {'portal_status_message':screenMsg} )
return state
```

Binding the Three Parts Together

At the moment, however, three separate entities exist: a form, a validator, and an action script. These need to be tied together to form the chain, so you'll return to the Controller Template object. Click the Validator tab, and enter a new validator that points to the validEmail script. You'll also add a success action if the processing is correct to traverse to the sendEmail script. On the sendEmail script, you can now add another traversal back to feedbackForm so that after sendEmail happens correctly, the user will be sent back to the original page.

NOTE   A much more complete e-mail validation script appears in Plone called validate_emailaddr, which checks that the e-mail is in the right format. If you want to use this script instead, you can point the validator to this script.

That's it—you're done! You should now be able to test the form on the book's Web site. To make it even easier, I made a Feedback tab, which points to the feedbackForm template, and from there you can now give feedback to me about this book!

Customizing the Look and Feel of Plone

OVER THE PREVIOUS two chapters I've covered some of the core components of Plone's user interface, including Script (Python) objects and page templates. It's now time to cover exactly how you construct the look and feel of a Plone site. This chapter includes the objects from previous chapters and introduces some new ones.

To start, I'll cover all the key definitions and Plone elements that comprise a site. I'll define terms you may have already heard of, such as *skins* and *layers*. Then I'll cover customizing the Plone user interface, concentrating on the power that Cascading Style Sheets (CSS) bring to the site developer. I'll run through the key variables and show how you can change them. I'll then revisit the customization of logos and skin elements, pulling together all the topics I've briefly covered over the past three chapters.

Then, I'll show how to make a new skin and explain the techniques for developing all this on the file system.

Finally, I'll finish this chapter with an example site. Specifically, I'll show the Maestro site, which was used by NASA to distribute data about the Mars rovers. This is a high-traffic Web site built in Plone, and the skin provides an excellent case study for customizing a site. This real-life example of how you can customize and modify a Plone site will enable you to do the same on your own.

Introducing Plone Skins

When a document displays in Plone, the content of that document displays in the now-familiar Plone green and blue interface. A *skin* determines exactly how that document displays to the user, including the images and styles surrounding the content. A skin groups elements, wrapping that piece of content, and presents them in a certain manner.

To generate the representation that a user sees, a skin has many elements, including the static items, such as images, and the dynamic pieces, such as scripts. In the previous chapter, the feedback form was an example of adding a few elements to a skin to create new elements of a skin. That example contained logic in the format of a Python (Script) object and new pages in the format of page templates. You added those elements to the skin so that a user could interact with the form.

You can use as much or as little of an existing skin as you want to assemble a new skin with Plone. You can make the skin from minor tweaks or major changes, as you can see on community sites such as http://www.zopezen.org and http://www.zopera.org. Each Plone site must have at least one skin, which will be used as the default, but it can have as many skins as the site developer wants. A user may optionally flip between skins, should the site developer want to allow the user to do so, although I've found this is rarely the case.

The default Plone skin is the one you see on a Plone site such as http://www.plone.org, with the familiar blue and green interface. But Plone doesn't have to look at all like, or be even vaguely recognizable as, a Plone site; its look is entirely up to you. Take, for example, the list of sites available at http://www.plone.org/about/sites; these sites each provide a different and custom experience for the user. In most cases, these sites can easily flip between skins and provide different looks for users. Other sites use the power and flexibility of the Plone interface internally for creating and editing content while providing a totally different look to external users.

I've seen many questions on mailing lists such as, does Plone have to look like a Plone site? Can it look one way to one user and another way to another user? Can it look like my corporate site? The answer to all of these questions is "yes": The only limit is your imagination (and the amount of time you can spend on customizing your site).

Using Layers Within a Skin

A skin is divided into logical collections of templates and scripts called *layers*. Altering these individual collections allows a user to easily add components to a skin or remove them. The layers are represented in a skin by a hierarchical list of folders. Each layer matches a name of a folder, and each folder contains the skin elements.

For example, a skin can have the following layers:

```
custom, gruf, plone_ecmascript, plone_wysiwyg ...
```

The order of the layers in that list is the key factor to how Plone finds the elements. When an element, such as logo.jpg, is requested from the skin, the skin looks through the layers to find the element. The skin starts by looking at the first layer assigned to that skin (in this example, custom). If the skin can't find the element in the first layer, it moves to the second layer (in this example, gruf). It continues looking through the list of layers until it finds the element for which it's looking. If it can't find the element, then a 404 error is raised and returned to the browser.

A similar concept is the use of the PATH environment variable in most systems. When entering a command or looking for a program, the operating system looks through the directories on the file system as specified in the PATH environment variable. A similar approach happens for layers, where the layers are looked through in order to find that element.

By allowing higher layers to take precedence over lower layers, developers and administrators now have the ability to customize and manipulate their site through the layers. If you don't like a particular element of a Plone skin, then by moving that element up a layer, you can custom the result. You can sort your skins and layers in Plone with the portal_skins tool, which I'll cover next.

Managing Skins with the portal_skins Tool

You use the portal_skins tool in Plone to define the skin and layers behavior. The portal_skins tool also provides a service and application programming interface (API) for creating and using skins.

To access the portal_skins tool, go to the Zope Management Interface (ZMI) and click *portal_skins*. You'll see two key screens in the ZMI; the first, the Contents tab, shows all the folders and file system directory views (FSDVs) located within this tool (see Figure 7-1).

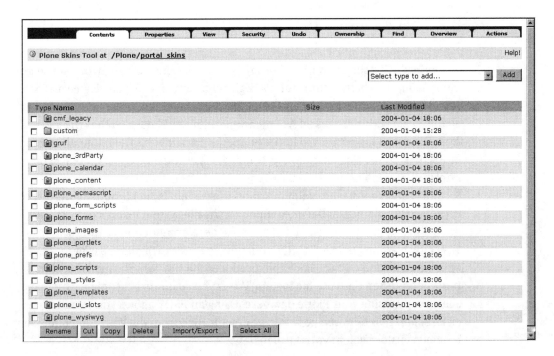

Figure 7-1. The contents of the portal_skins *tool in a standard Plone installation*

All of the folders and file system directory views on the Contents tab aren't layers by default, but now you can turn them into layers. Further, the second important screen, the Properties tab, shows all the skins and layers you've defined in your Plone site (see Figure 7-2).

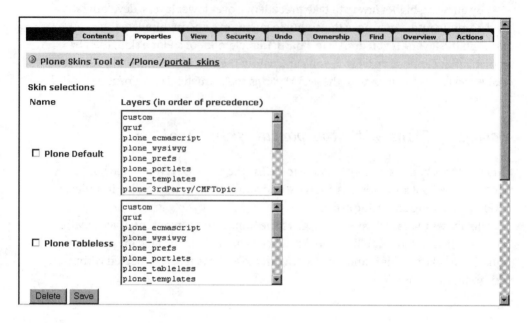

Figure 7-2. The skins and layers in a standard Plone installation

As Figure 7-2 shows, the list of these layers is quite long. Although this may seem intimidating, this hefty number of layers gives the developer a large degree of flexibility and reuse. Each skin displays on the left, with a text area to the right displaying all the layers within that skin. As I mentioned earlier, Plone searches the layers from the top to the bottom to locate elements. Each layer is the name of a folder or FSDV from the Contents tab. In Figure 7-2, you can see a plone_ecmascript directory, and in Figure 7-1 you can see the matching FSDV object.

An FSDV is a new object that provides a useful ability in Plone; it allows direct access to skin elements that are defined on the file system instead of from the Zope object database as usual. FSDVs make development and customization easier. By reading objects directly from the file system, it's much easier for developers to write and edit the code that produces the site. When you install Plone, the skin is written onto the file system. When you customize an object, you make a local copy inside your Plone database. Using an FSDV allows you to maintain clean separation between code you've downloaded from the Web and code that has been customized in your local instance.

Plone 2 ships with two skins, Plone Default and Plone Tableless. Plone Default uses tables to render the main body flanked by two table cells on either side, containing the left and right slots. For browser compatibility, this is the default setup. However, if you switch to Plone Tableless, then you'll get a skin that looks the same, except there are no tables used to produce the page, which gives you, as the site developer, more flexibility. At the time of writing, the Plone Tableless skin can be a little problematic on some browsers, such as Internet Explorer. I hope in the future that the Plone Tableless skin will become the default.

To change the skin, scroll to the bottom of the form where you see the Default Skin value and select the default skin from the list of choices. If you select the Skin Flexibility option, then users will be able to choose their own skin from the *my preferences* section.

Returning to the Contents tab of the `portal_skins` tool, you can see that some of the folders—for example, `custom`—are standard folders that exist in Zope. These have the normal folder icon. Others—for example, `plone_images`—are FSDVs that point to areas of the file system. These have the folder icon with a green lock inside it. This lock indicates that you can't add or edit elements in an FSDV through the Web; you can do it only through the file system.

To see where the files for an FSDV reside on your hard drive, click the Properties tab of the FSDV. For example, from the Contents tab of the `portal_skins` tool, click Properties, and it will list the file system path of `CMFPlone/skins/plone_images`. This path is the location of this directory on the file system relative to the instance home you specified in the installation process. Because you can see files through the Web in the FSDV or on the file system, you can access them for reading either way. Because viewing files through a file system is generally more friendly and easy to do, I'll refer to a file as a path in the file system, which can be accessed using familiar tools.

Customizing Skins

You've seen how skins and layers interact. Now you'll see how you can customize a Plone site. I'll start by returning to the example in Chapter 4, where you learned how to customize the logo. Using your new knowledge of how skins work, you'll be able to follow along and customize the skin. Then I'll move onto showing the power of the Plone CSS and how you can customize it. Finally, I'll cover the main template you saw in earlier chapters and go through all the elements of it.

Customizing the Logo, Revisited

In Chapter 4 you learned how to customize the logo in the top-left corner of a Plone site, but I skipped over what was actually happening. The section revisits that example.

The logo.jpg image is the image that appears in the top-left corner of every page. You'll now look at what happens when a browser tries to render this page. Once Plone receives the request for that image, it looks through the layers to find logo.jpg. In a default site, this is the item in plone_images, called logo.jpg. Because this is an FSDV, as I mentioned earlier, you're unable to alter the image through the Web. To guard your site against future changes, you don't want to be able to change it on the file system either. Instead, take a closer look at what the Customize button does. If you look at that button again, you can see that there is, to the left of that button, a drop-down list of folders in the contents of the portal_skins tool.

 NOTE The folders listed are ones that exist inside the Zope database. FSDVs aren't included in the drop-down list; by default, it shows only folders.

Clicking the Customize button makes a local copy of the item in the folder selected in the drop-down box. By default that folder is the custom folder, so now you have a copy in the custom folder. When Plone looks up the item, logo.jpg, it will access the version in the custom folder. Looking again at the layers for the Plone Default skin, the custom folder is the topmost layer of the skin. Hence, when logo.jpg is called, it will find the image in the custom layer. This is why the new logo.jpg is rendered.

Placing customized items into the custom folder is the quickest way to start tweaking your Plone site. The custom folder is a standard Plone folder, so you can put as many items in there as you want in order to override earlier elements.

Introducing Plone's Cascading Style Sheets

The visual representation of a Plone site in a browser is put together almost entirely using CSS. Perhaps the easiest way to see exactly what the CSS does for a Plone site is to compare Figures 7-3 and 7-4. The first shows Plone with style sheets, and the second shows Plone without any style sheets.

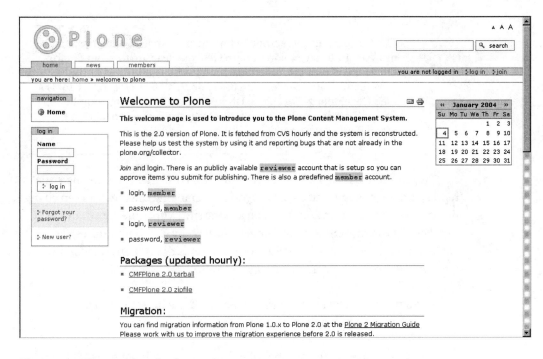

Figure 7-3. Plone with style sheets

Figure 7-4. Plone without style sheets

TIP   If you want to reproduce this, turn off style sheets in your browser. Internet Explorer doesn't let you easily do this, but Firefox (http://www.mozilla.org/products/firefox/), the Mozilla-based open-source browser, lets you easily do this. In Firefox, select Tools ➤ Web Developer ➤ Disable ➤ Disable Styles. With a large number of CSS and other developer tools, Firefox is the browser of choice for many Plone developers.

The difference is striking to say the least. CSS provides not only the visual representation of pages but also the layout. By changing the CSS, you can change this visual representation and layout on a Plone site (within the constraints of CSS).

Having the presentation of Plone produced by CSS is an impressive achievement used by many talented user interface developers. The following are some of the benefits of having a CSS layout:

- CSS provides a layer of separation between the presentation and the templates that generate the presentation.

- You can make a large number of ch anges without having to touch the underlying templates. All that's needed is an experienced CSS developer.

- CSS makes the site faster by sending smaller files. Each Hypertext Markup Language (HTML) file is smaller since the layout for the site isn't contained in HTML markup but in the CSS, which can then be cached.

- CSS allows you to customize the look and feel without breaking underlying accessibility work.

Code Layers

When a Plone page is rendered, at least three layers of code create a page. For the example of the tabs that appear across the top of a Plone site, this is how they're assembled:

1. First, the action providers (which I discussed in Chapter 4) create a list of the tabs to display. Security and other checks happen here.

2. Second, the Zope Page Templates system assembles the tabs and loops through the values returned by the action provider, creating HTML that's sent to the browser.

3. Finally, CSS creates the visual representation of the HTML in the browser on the user's client.

So rather than asking yourself, how can I customize the tabs? you need to consider exactly what customization you want to perform. This could mean changing the CSS, the HTML, the data, or the underlying tabs. The general rules are as follows:

- Plone presents data in some manner, either from a data set or content.

- CSS produces the visual representation.

- The HTML and templates provide the glue between the two.

In fact, Plone is so customizable, on so many levels, that it's easy to worry about which bit to customize. To make sure that future Plone template changes don't compromise your application's design, try not to customize the templates. Instead, I recommend you try the CSS or the actions first. This way, when the templates change in future versions of Plone, there will be less chance of a problem.

Customizing the Font, Colors, and Spacing

The actual style sheet that does most of the work, `plone.css`, has a number of variables in it populated using Dynamic HTML (DTML). I do not cover DTML in this book; this is probably the only use of it in Plone, so if you don't already know DTML, I recommend you avoid learning it, if possible! The Zope Page Templates system will give you everything you need. Excellent online references do exist for DTML for Zope, however; refer to `http://zope.org/Documentation/Books/ZopeBook/2_6Edition/DTML.stx`.

The DTML syntax for this style sheet is actually pretty simple; each variable relates to a corresponding attribute in a property sheet. To access this property sheet, click *portal_skins, plone_styles*, and then *base_properties*. In Figure 7-5, you can see how this file looks in the ZMI.

For example, `&dtml-fontColor;` locates the variable `fontColor` and places it in the style sheet, so the `fontColor` here will be black. Now you can see where that variable is referenced in the `plone.css` file. To access the CSS file, click *portal_skins, portal_skins*, and then *plone.css*. In this file you can see that `mainFontColor` is referenced in quite a few places; for example, it's referenced in the main body of a page, like so:

```
body {
    font: &dtml-fontBaseSize; <dtml-var fontFamily>;
    background-color: &dtml-backgroundColor;;
    color: &dtml-fontColor;;
    margin: 0;
    padding: 0;
}
```

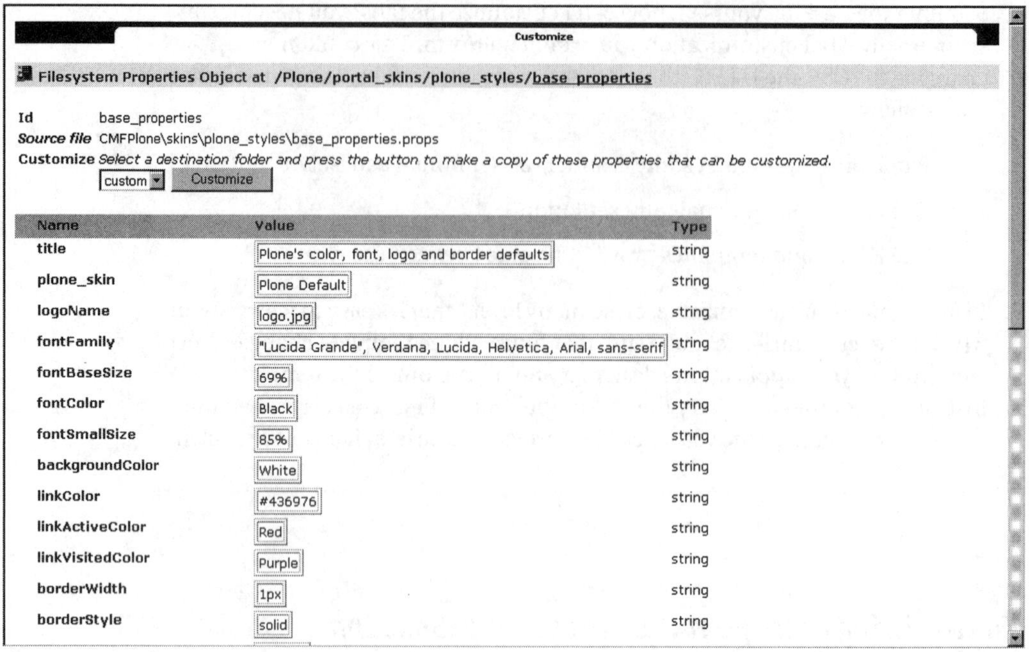

Figure 7-5. The base properties for the style sheet

You could keep reading through the style sheet, if you really wanted, but changing the variable is always a quick way to see exactly what it affects.

Returning to the ZMI, click *portal_skins*, click *plone_styles*, click *base_properties*, and then click the Customize button. As you've seen, this will create an object in the ZMI that you can customize. This time the customized object is actually a folder that has the properties contained in the folder. To access the properties you've just customized, click *portal_skins*, click *custom*, and then click *base_properties*. Next, select the Properties tab (see Figure 7-6).

This property list allows you to change the properties of mainColor to something different, for example, red or #cc9900. Change the value of that property, and click Save Changes. Returning to the Plone site, you should now see the nice, new color.

In Chapter 4 you saw an example where, to change a tab on the top of a page, users could change the actions. Although you may type an action with an uppercase first character (such as *Members*), it then displays in lowercase letters on the Web page. This because CSS transforms the text to lowercase because of the textTransform property in the property sheet. To stop this transformation, change the property for textTransform to none.

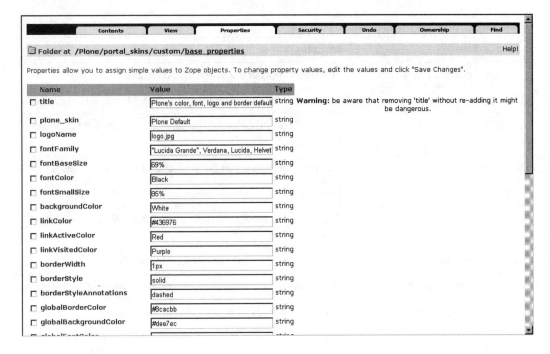

Figure 7-6. The properties of the folder

In the style sheet, properties are defined for all the colors, spacing, and fonts that are used in a Plone site. Table 7-1 describes all the parameters.

Table 7-1. CSS Properties

Variable Name	Description
logoName	The filename of the portal logo
fontFamily	The font family used for all text that isn't a header
fontBaseSize	The base font size from which everything is calculated
fontColor	The main font color
backgroundColor	The background color
linkColor	The color used on normal links
linkActiveColor	The color used on active links
linkVisitedColor	The color used on visited links
borderWidth	The width of most borders in Plone
borderStyle	The style of the border lines (usually solid)

Table 7-1. CSS Properties (Continued)

Variable Name	Description
borderStyleAnnotations	The style of border lines on comments, and so on
globalBorderColor	The border color used on the main tabs, the portlets, and so on
globalBackgroundColor	The background color for the selected tabs, portlet headings, and so on
globalFontColor	The color of the font in the tabs and in portlet headings
headingFontFamily	The font family for h1, h2, h3, h4, h5, and h6 headlines
headingFontBaseSize	The base size used when calculating the different headline sizes
contentViewBorderColor	The tabs' border color on the Contents tab
contentViewBackgroundColor	The content view tabs' background color on the Contents tab
contentViewFontColor	The font color used in the tabs on the Contents tab
textTransform	Whether to lowercase text in portlets, tabs, and so on
evenRowBackgroundColor	The background color of even rows in listings
oddRowBackgroundColor	The background color of odd rows in listings
notifyBorderColor	The border color of notification elements such as the status message and the calendar focus
notifyBackgroundColor	The background color of notification elements such as the status message and the calendar focus
helpBackgroundColor	The background color of the calendar pop-up widget
discreetColor	The color of the credits, document byline, form help, and other elements that are extra information and not meant to be shown at "full strength"
portalMinWidth	The minimum width of the portal
columnOneWidth	The width of the left column
columnTwoWidth	The width of the right column

Customizing the CSS

If you have small customizations, place them in ploneCustom.css. This is a second style sheet that's loaded after plone.css. By using the cascading functionality of style sheets, you can apply any changes to ploneCustom.css to the overall style sheet.

For example, to change the byline that appears on the bottom of every page, simply change `ploneCustom.css`. Again, access that file through the ZMI, and then click Customize. This will create a copy of that style sheet in the `custom` folder. To alter the byline, move it to the left side of the page and make it bold, as shown in Figure 7-7.

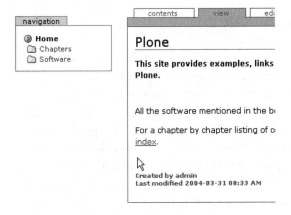

Figure 7-7. The new bold byline on the left

You do this by adding the following:

```
div.documentByLine {
    text-align: left;
    font-weight: bold;
}
```

Here you've set two attributes for the `byline` element: `text-align` and `font-weight`. Note that you haven't changed any other attributes of the `byline` element; the remaining attributes are inherited from the original style sheet. With a few simple lines of CSS, you've changed the site and made sure that other changes to Plone won't affect your site. Changing `ploneCustom.css` is the best bet for small changes.

By using different style sheets, you can use Plone to provide a different look to different clients. Often Web sites have a Click for Printable Page button that shows a simpler page, without much formatting. Plone alleviates this problem by providing a separate style sheet; when a browser prints the page, that style sheet formats the page. All the alternate style sheets are included at the top of a page; you can find them by clicking *portal_skins*, clicking *plone_templates*, and then clicking *header.pt*.

NOTE One style sheet that's a little unusual is the projection style sheet. It's supported only by Opera, and when the browser is used in full-screen mode, headings turn into separate pages and a presentation-like interface displays.

Customizing the Main Template

As you saw in the previous chapter, to get the Plone look and feel on a page, you need to use the master macro from the main_template. Every Plone page uses this macro and then fills in the appropriate slots. By taking a look at the main template in detail, you can see how a Plone page is constructed in a page template and then see exactly how you can customize those individual page elements.

If you look at the main Plone page, you'll see a number of elements in that page. Figure 7-8 shows a Plone page with all the key user interface elements marked. Table 7-2 describes each of the elements and their purpose. For each element in Figure 7-8, you'll find a corresponding number in the table.

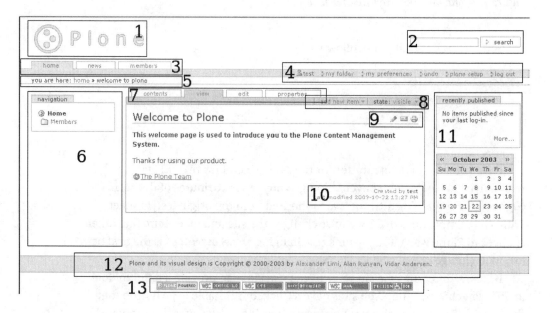

Figure 7-8. All the main elements in the Plone user interface

Table 7-2. User Interface Elements

Number	Name	Description
1	Site logo	Shows the top logo.
2	Search form	Shows the search form.
3	Portal tabs	Shows the tabs across the top of the site.
4	Personal bar	Shows the personal information for that user such as *login* and *my folder*.
5	Breadcrumbs	Shows the location of the current content.
6	Left slot	Determines where portlets added to the left_slot property display.
7	Content tabs	Shows the actions with the category content_tabs for that piece of content.
8	Content drop-down lists	Shows some drop-down menus for this content, workflow for the content, and new content types.
9	Document actions	Shows the actions for this particular piece of content, such as a printing or e-mail. These are the document_actions actions.
10	Byline	Shows a description of the content and its author.
11	Right slot	This is where portlets added to the right_slot property display.
12	Footer	Shows information at the bottom of the page.
13	Colophon	Shows more information below the footer.

I haven't covered one section of this template: the content. All the text from *Welcome to Plone* down to *The Plone Team* is content added and edited by the users. This is the main slot in the page template, which is filled in by a the particular content type or page template, as you've seen. Chapter 6 covered using slots; in that chapter, I showed how, by using the main slot, you can ensure content appears inside a Plone page.

So, given these components of your Plone page, how do you customize a particular part? The answer is to find the matching part of the main_template, see which part it calls, and then customize that. For this reason, I'll cover the main template in detail.

At first glance, the main template looks quite long and complicated, but it's mostly all macros, and its main purpose is simply to pull content from other areas. You can find the main template by clicking *portal_skins*, clicking *plone_templates*, and then clicking *main_template*.

The philosophy behind the main template is that a user shouldn't have to alter the actual configuration of the template, unless there are major changes planned. Because the main template pulls all the content from other places inside Plone, you can alter the assembled page by customizing those individual elements. This means you can alter just the sections you'd like to change rather than altering the whole template.

The main template uses Extensible Markup Language (XML) namespaces heavily to present the simplest possible `metal` code. For example:

```
<metal:headslot define-slot="head_slot" />
    <!-- A slot where you can insert elements in the header from a template -->
```

Here, the name of the tag isn't a standard Extensible HTML (XHTML) element; instead, it uses the `metal:` prefix to define a namespace as `metal:headslot`. This has the following advantages:

- The element `headslot` is semantic, in that it describes the element. It's easy to spot that this is the slot for adding anything you may want to add to the head of your page.

- Attributes in that element use the namespace in the element if not otherwise declared; so, instead of `metal:fill-slot`, you can just use `fill-slot`.

- The actual tag isn't a valid XHTML tag, so it won't display. However, if the rendering of the tag generates any valid XHTML, that XHTML will display.

When a macro is used, the content in the calling template is removed, so it's possible to place comments in the calling template as text inside the macro. For example:

```
<div metal:use-macro="here/global_searchbox/macros/quick_search">
    The quicksearch box, normally placed at the top right
</div>
```

Because of the comment, it's easy to determine that this macro refers to the search box in the top-right corner of a site (element 2 in Figure 7-8). To see the macro, find the script named `global_searchbox` and the `quick_search` macro contained within it. The main template continues through `main` macros, pulling information from different templates and scripts, and builds the page as it goes.

After this section, the main template reaches the main content of the page, which is the object being rendered. In Chapter 6 I explained the difference between a slot and a macro; recall that a template defines slots that are then filled by the content. Really there's only one slot of any importance for content, and I've mentioned it many times: the main slot.

One common pattern in Plone that may be confusing is how to define a slot inside a fill slot. For example, the following is the definition for the css_slot:

```
<metal:cssslot fill-slot="css_slot">
    <!-- A slot where you can insert CSS from a template -->
    <metal:cssslot define-slot="css_slot" />
</metal:cssslot>
```

This design pattern looks a little odd, but it defines the slot and then re-creates the fill slot. If you look at the main template carefully, those slots are actually inside the header use-macro, so the header macro may fill this slot. But you also want the end template to fill the slot, so for this reason the slot is redefined. This means one slot can now be filled in two places, which is a useful technique for changing the templates.

Scanning down through the rest of main template, you'll reach the left and right columns, the footers, and the colophon. Note that the left column may appear before the main content of a page (if your language reads from left to right anyway), but the style sheet moves it there. This ensures that if you visit the site in a text-only browser, the main content appears first, not after all the navigation options.

Table 7-3 describes the macros and slots in the main template.

Table 7-3. Main Template Macros and Slots

Name	Description	Slot or Macro?
Cache headers	Sets the Hypertext Transfer Protocol (HTTP) cache headers for the content.	Macro: cacheheaders in global_cache_settings
Head slot	Allows content to add to the head element of a page.	Slot: head_slot
CSS slot	Allows content to add custom CSS for the page.	Slot: css_slot
JavaScript head slot	Allows content to add custom JavaScript to the page.	Slot: javascript_head_slot

Table 7-3. Main Template Macros and Slots (Continued)

Name	Description	Slot or Macro?
Site actions	The site actions allow you to have a series of actions above the search. By default these allow you to change the font size.	Macro: `site_actions` in `global_siteactions`
Quick search	The quick search box show in the top-right corner.	Macro: `quick_search` in `global_searchbox`
Portal tabs	The (normally blue) portal tabs that are normally at the top left. The actual tabs shown are determined by actions. This determines how the tabs are rendered in HTML.	Macro: `portal_tabs` in `global_sections`
Personal bar	The personal bar in the top right: login, logout, and so on.	Macro: `personal_bar` in `global_personalbar`
Path bar	The path breadcrumbs that start with "You are here."	Macro: `path_bar` in `global_pathbar`
Content views	The (normally green) tabs across the top of content. This will show only if the content is editable by the current user. The actual tabs shown are determined by actions. This determines how the tabs are rendered in HTML.	Macro: `content_views` in `global_contentviews`
Content actions	The little drop-down actions in the top-right corner of the context bar.	Macro: `content_actions` in `global_contentviews`
Portal status message	A message shown whenever something changes.	Macro: `portal_message` in `global_statusmessage`
Header	The header on a piece of content.	Slot: `header`
Main	The main part of a piece of content.	Slot: `main`

Table 7-3. Main Template Macros and Slots (Continued)

Name	Description	Slot or Macro?
Sub	The bottom part of a piece of content where the comments on an object will appear.	Slot: `sub`
Left portlets	The slots or portlets shown on the left of a page. There are a few definitions here: `column-one-slot` is the whole left column, and `portlets-one-slot` is then the slot. If neither of these slots is defined, it calls the macro.	Macro: `left_column` in `portlets_fetcher`
Right portlets	The slots or portlets shown on the right of a page. See the left portlets.	Macro: `right_column` in `portlets_fetcher`
Footer	Copyright and other message.	Macro: `portal_footer` in `footer`
Colophon	Miscellaneous messages for the bottom.	Macro: `colophon` in `colophon`

Armed with this information, it's now a matter of customizing the macro or the slot to change the look and feel of the page. Again, it's recommended not to actually customize the main template itself but to instead customize the parts that the main template calls. The next section shows a few example customizations you can make to Plone.

Examining Example Customization Snippets

The following sections show some examples that demonstrate simple customizations you can do to your Plone site. Some solutions provide one or two different ways of performing the same task.

Removing a Block

One rather neat trick is to be able to easily remove a block from the user interface such as the path bar or the search box. You have two ways to do this; the most obvious is to customize the macro that displays the element. For example, to remove the breadcrumbs, you could click *portal_skins*, click *plone_templates*, click *global_pathbar*, and then turn off the element in the page template level; for example, you can change the following:

```
<div metal:define-macro="path_bar"
    id="pathBar"
    tal:define="breadcrumbs python:here.breadcrumbs(here);
        portal_url portal_url|here/portal_url">
```

To this, add the following bold line of code:

```
<div metal:define-macro="path_bar"
    id="portal-breadcrumbs"
    tal:condition="nothing"
    tal:define="breadcrumbs python:here.breadcrumbs(here);
        portal_url portal_url|here/portal_url">
```

This means customizing a page template, which isn't a problem at all and is by now something with which you should be familiar. The slightly different approach is that you can hide elements at the CSS level. This still means the item is rendered and HTML is generated, but it's then turned off for the client—they can't see it. Because the generation of the HTML still occurs, this is a suboptimal solution, but it's a neat trick.

Most elements in Plone have a unique Document Object Model (DOM) element ID; for example, in the case of the breadcrumbs, it's `portal-breadcrumbs`, as you can see in the previous code. To stop showing the `portal-breadcrumbs`, simply add the following to `ploneCustom.css`:

```
#portal-breadcrumbs {
    display: none;
}
```

Changing Portal Tabs

I've already shown you how you can change the text of the portal tabs if you change the actions. They're displayed using the style sheet, not using tables (although users may initially think so). Looking at Table 7-3, you can see that the code for the portal tabs is `portalTabs`. To make the border of the nonselected tabs dotted, you can simply change the `ploneCustom` style sheet to the following:

```
#portal-globalnav li a {
    border: 1px dotted;
}
```

The tabs are a series of HTML list (li) and anchor (a) elements, so by changing the CSS for these elements, you can change the tabs' appearance. Later in the "Case Study: Examining the NASA Skin" section I'll show how to change these tabs into images.

By using CSS you can also move any element's location with the position attribute. Next, move your tabs to the top of the screen, above the logo and search box. To do this, you use the absolute value of the position, which lets you define the position by using the left, right, top, and bottom attributes. Add the following to your ploneCustom style sheet to place the portal tabs at the top of your Plone site:

```
#portal-globalnav {
  position: absolute;
  top: 0em;
}
```

This is a powerful technique for moving elements. You have multiple options for positioning the elements, including relative positioning, but that takes a little work with CSS to get the positioning just right.

Moving the Left and Right Slots

I discussed the left and right slots in Chapter 4, and I've shown you how to add a new slot to the list of slots. You may have noticed that the terms *left* and *right* slots can be a little misleading. The default is to show the slots in those positions, but it's easy to move them.

 NOTE   This works only when you're using the Plone Tableless skin. This isn't the default setting, so you'll have to change the skin in the portal_skins tool, as discussed earlier in the "Managing Skins with the portal_skins Tool" section.

For example, if you wanted to move the left portlets to the right side of the page, then you could do this by changing ploneCustom.css to the following:

```
#portal-column-one · {
    float: right;
}
#portal-column-content {
    float: left;
}
```

This moves the leftmost column to the right and pushes the main section to the left.

Hiding Help in Forms

If you wanted to hide the help in all the forms, you couldn't realistically change all the templates. But you could employ a similar tactic to hiding the path bar—and just set display: none for the form elements. The following has the desired effect of not placing the input element on a new line:

```
div.formHelp {
    display: none;
}
```

Figure 7-9 shows the feedback page without breadcrumbs, with the help hidden, with dotted tabs, and with the left slot moved to the right of the page, all changed with only a few lines of CSS.

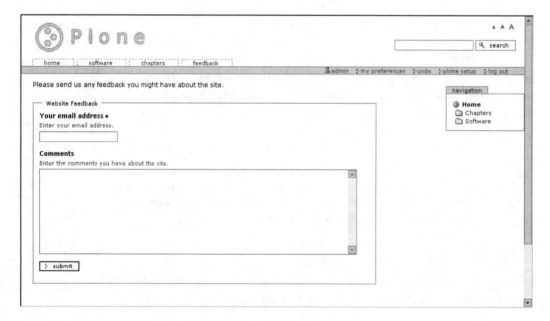

Figure 7-9. The combined effect of some of the examples

How Do You Find Element X?

As I've shown, the templates, scripts, and images contained in the skins directory of a Plone installation create a Plone skin. Many files live in that directory, so going through every file would be long and counterproductive when those files change. Instead, it's useful to understand some basic techniques for finding the elements you want to alter.

Bear in mind at which level you want to customize the element. As noted earlier, you have three levels for rendering an object. If you want to change the visual representation, or its placement, then chances are that you can change the CSS and do no further work.

If CSS isn't sufficient, then your next best bet is to search through the templates. For example, suppose you want to change the text that appears on the page when a user logs in, or you want to change the entire page. In this example, you'll alter the page shown in Figure 7-10 to make it a script that does something unusual.

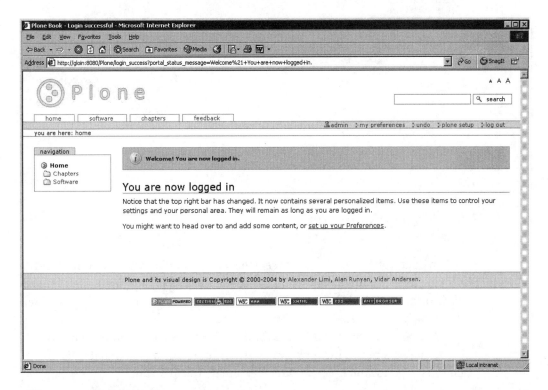

Figure 7-10. The "You are now logged in" page

Some clues exist to find this template so you can alter it; I'll run through each of them in turn now.

Searching by Using the URL

The Uniform Resource Locator (URL) to a page translates to a series of objects in Plone that are traversed. In Figure 7-11, I've traversed to the login_success page. In this case, the final part of the URL is login_success, as you can see in the address bar in Figure 7-11. When an object is loaded into an FSDV, the extension is stripped off, so you're looking for a template or script that starts with login_success.

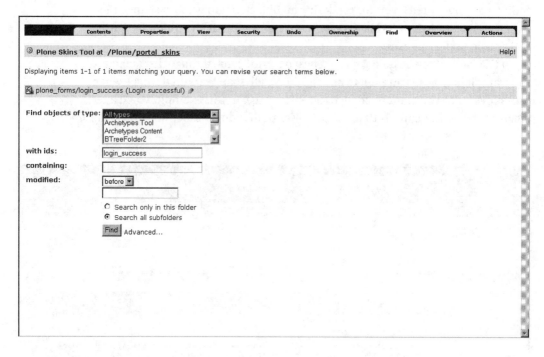

Figure 7-11. Searching for an ID

In Zope you can perform this search by going to the portal_skins tool and clicking the Find tab. Once there, enter **login_success** in the *with ids* field. Leave all the other settings the same, and click the Find button. Sure enough, you'll find the login_success template.

You can also conduct this search on the file system, depending upon your operating system and the tools available. The quickest way to find this file in Linux is to go to your CMFPlone directory and do the following:

```
$ cd skins
$ find -name 'login_success*' -print
./plone_forms/login_success.pt
```

On Windows, open the CMFPlone folder in Windows Explorer and click the Search tab. Then enter the name of the file as **login_success**, and click Search. This should give you a list of likely files.

This search should provide the result, CMFPlone/plone_forms/login_success.pt. If you perform the same search in the ZMI, you click *portal_skins*, click *plone_forms*, and then click *login_success*.

Searching for a Piece of Text

A rather crude approach that's somewhat successful is to do a full-text search on the code to find the element that renders the page. For example, looking at the page in Figure 7-12, you can see that it contains the text *Notice that the top*. The simplest way to find the bit that renders that text is to search for it.

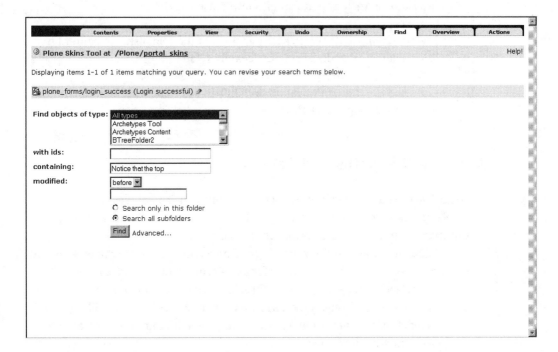

Figure 7-12. Searching for text

In Zope you can also perform this search by going to the portal_skins tool and clicking the Find tab. Once there, enter **Notice that the top** in the *containing* field. Leave all the other settings the same, and click the Find button. Sure enough, you'll find the login_success template.

You can also conduct this search on the file system, depending upon your operating system and the tools available. The quickest way to find this file in Linux is to go to your CMFPlone directory and do the following:

```
$ grep -ri "Notice that the top" *
plone_forms/login_success.pt: Notice that the top
```

On Windows, open the CMFPlone folder in Windows Explorer and click the Search tab. Then enter the contents of the file as **Notice that the top**, and click Search. This should give you a list of likely files. Using this rather crude technique, you've been given a template, login_success, that renders the message back to the user.

This technique has the following issues:

- Beware of lowercasing the content in CS S; always make your searches case insensitive (the default in Windows). It's annoying to search for *home* when it's *Home* in the template and it's lowercased in CSS.

- If you're trying to do this in a language other than English, the content may have been localized, causing the search to fail.

- Occasionally there may not be searchab le text that will match up; in this case, looking up via a URL is the recommended approach.

Making New Skins and Layers

So far I've talked about customizing the existing skin. The process for making a whole new skin or a new layer isn't actually that different. I'll cover one key point, putting your templates and scripts on the file system.

Making templates and scripts on the file system and creating new skins and layers are definitely the best way to go for long-term maintainability and flexibility. Not only is creating skin elements much easier in familiar tools on the file system, but it also allows you to easily redistribute your code. Writing on the file system is the style of choice for almost all Plone developers, with minor modifications in the custom directory if needed.

Making a New Skin

As you've seen, a skin is actually nothing more than a collection of layers. For my new skin, I wanted to place all my custom code in one place, so I went to the portal_skins tool, added a new folder, and gave it the ID of custom_chrome.

Then, to add a new skin, you have to click *portal_skins*, select the Properties tab, and add a new skin under the text *Add a new skin*. You'll need to enter a series of layers that you want to set up for this skin. In this example, I added a new skin called *Custom Chrome* and a series of layers, as shown in Figure 7-13.

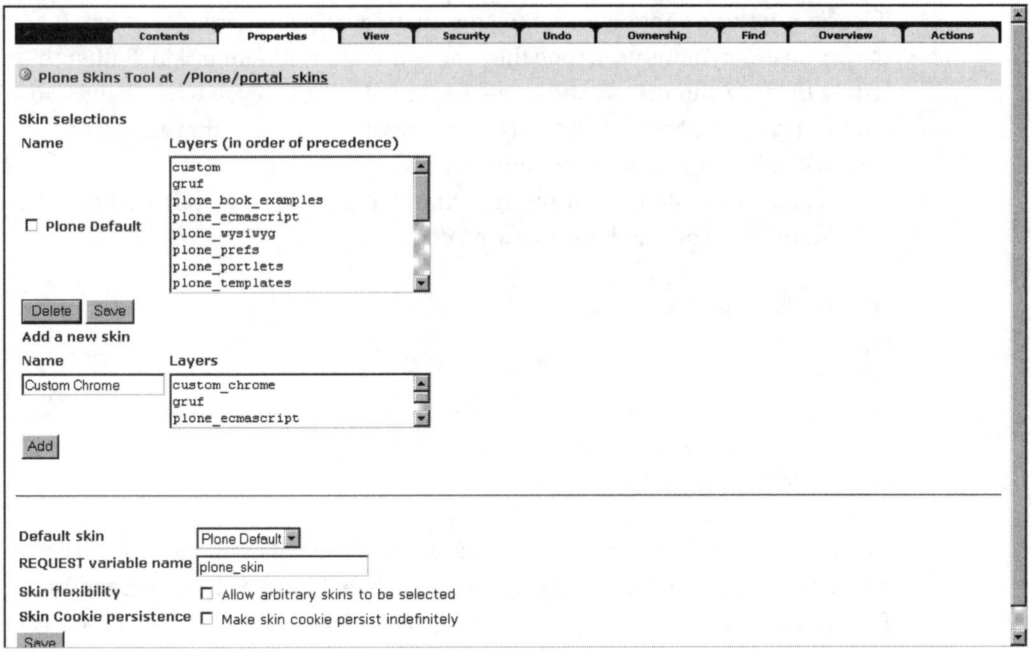

Figure 7-13. Adding the Custom Chrome skin

Then I added the layers for the skin. In this case, the skin didn't have a layer called custom in it; instead it had a folder called custom_chrome. You now have two skins that use two layers and two folders. Any objects added to the custom_chrome folder will affect that skin, not the Plone Default skin.

Using Multiple Skins

As mentioned, a standard Plone site has two skins, Plone Default and Plone Tableless. In the previous section, I added a new skin, Custom Chrome. As I discussed in Chapter 4, you can set the default skin using the Plone interface. Click *plone setup*, and then click the Portal Skin button. This mirrors the choices available in the ZMI after clicking *portal_skins*, selecting the Properties tab, and scrolling to the bottom of the page.

You have one more option, though: REQUEST *variable name*. This is the request variable that will contain the user's skin information. This is plone_skin by default, which is the cookie name. But it can also be passed through other request variables such as the query string. It's available only through the ZMI.

You can also set skins programatically. This allows developers to show different skins to different users depending upon certain business or site logic. For example, if a user is writing content for a site, they may see the standard Plone skin. If they're an anonymous user, then they can see a totally different skin. Rather than letting the user choose, the site is making that decision. If you really want, you could base the skin on the folder they're accessing; however, that approach can lead to confusion, so I don't recommend it.

To change the skin, add a Script (Python) object called setSkin in the root of your Plone site. Then add the following code:

```
##title=Skin changing script
##parameters=
req = context.REQUEST
if req['SERVER_URL'].find('internal.somesite.org') > -1:
    context.changeSkin("Plone Default")
context.changeSkin("Custom Chrome")
```

The actual logic for determining the skin will depend upon the site's business rules. In this case anyone accessing http://internal.somesite.org will get the Plone Default skin, and anyone accessing http://external.somesite.org will get the Custom Chrome skin. Unfortunately, one catch is that you can't determine the skin on the security level of the user (for example, authenticated users see one skin, and managers see another). This rather obvious need isn't possible at the time of writing without severely hacking a Plone site.

NOTE   Basing the skin on untrusted client information is common practice but not completely secure because you're trusting the information from the client. Making sure this is secure depends on your particular network settings. In most cases, you can handle this easily at the firewall or using a proxy server such as Apache, which could be configured to block all external requests to http://internal.somesite.org. I discuss integration with Apache in Chapter 10.

To activate this code, assign an access rule to this object. This means that each time this Plone site is accessed, this Script (Python) object will be executed. Each time the script is run, the skin will be set according to the script. To assign a rule to this script, select Set Access Rule from the drop-down menu and then enter the name of your Python (Script) object. Now test by visiting your site, and see what skin you get.

You do have to be careful with access rules because they occur on every invocation of that folder (or Plone site); you have to ensure that they're correct and that nothing bad can happen in them. If you've accidentally written a bad or incorrect Script (Python) object and can't even get access back into the ZMI to fix it, then you can turn off access rules by restarting Plone with the following environment variable:

```
SUPPRESS_ACCESSRULE = 1
```

Appendix B explains how to set environment variables if you're unfamiliar with this process.

Making a New Skin on the File System

Throughout these chapters I've been using the ZMI. But what most Plone developers use for any serious work is the file system. Making a skin on the file system is actually easy.

Go to the instance home directory of your Plone installation. Inside the Products directory, make a new directory; the name of this directory is the name of the product, so the convention is something short, with no spaces or underscores and mixed case. PloneBookExample, CMFPlone, and PloneSilverCity are all examples. Inside that folder, make a new file called __init__.py and a directory called skins. In the __init__.py file, you need to add the following two lines:

```
from Products.CMFCore import DirectoryView
DirectoryView.registerDirectory('skins', globals())
```

Next, restart Plone, and then click *portal_skins* to add an FSDV. This will open a list of the registered directories. Scroll down until you find the one that matches the directory you registered; this will be the name of the directory with /skins on the end. Enter an ID that makes sense, and click Add. You now have an empty directory where you can go to add layers of your skin.

Debugging Skins

Another reason I've repeatedly been using the ZMI with you, rather than the file system, is that it gives feedback about errors and gets you comfortable with placing objects inside others. A further positive feature about using the ZMI is that changes are instantaneous. If you change an object and then refresh, you see the change immediately (assuming you have no cache).

This isn't the case with the file system. If you change something in the file system, it isn't updated in Plone. This is for performance reasons. Plone has no way of knowing you made that change, so it must update the Zope cached copy of that object. Without getting into file system notification trickery, a Plone site has two states: production and debug mode. When Plone is in debug mode, it checks all the directories, finds files that have changed, and then updates Plone. This means you can make a change, and it will appear immediately. When run in production mode, however, your changes will not happen until you refresh the skin (see Chapter 11) or you restart Zope.

For obvious reasons, if you're developing skins in Plone, then running in debug mode is the way to go. Chapter 2 showed you how to change the configuration for Plone so that it runs in debug mode. As a quick recap, open the zope.conf file inside the etc directory of your installation and ensure the debug-mode directive is set to on.

Using File System Objects

The FSDVs allow the mapping of only those Zope objects that have been specifically configured to be used in this manner. It determines the Zope object based on the extension of the filename. The contents of that file are the contents of one attribute of the object—usually the main content, such as the binary contents of an image, or the text contents of the template.

To create an object in your empty FSDV, just go to the skins directory and start adding files that match the objects you want to make. Once the file is loaded into Zope as a Zope object, that extension is stripped off. For example, some_template.pt becomes a file system page template with the ID some_template. Table 7-4 describes the extensions.

So, to get an image in your directory view, dump in a .gif or .jpeg file. If you want a Script (Python) object, then add a file ending in .py.

Table 7-4. Extensions

Extensions	Object Type	Equivalent Zope Object
`.pt, .zpt, .html, .htm`	Filesystem Page Template	Page Template
`.cpt`	Controller Filesystem Page Template	Controller Page Template
`.py`	Filesystem Script (Python)	Script (Python)
`.cpy`	Controller Python Script	Controller Python Script
`.vpy`	Controller Validator	Controller Validator
`.doc, .pdf, .swf, .jar, .cab, .ico, .js, .css`	Filesystem File	File
`.gif, .jpg, .jpeg, .png`	Filesystem Image	Image
`.props`	Filesystem Properties Object	Folder with Properties
`.zsql`	Filesystem Z SQL Method	ZSQL Method
`.dtml`	Filesystem DTML Method	DTML Method

Setting File System Object Metadata

Extra content for an object such as title, security, or cache is stored in a separate file. That file is given the same filename as the original file, with `.metadata` added to the end. If the original file is `logo.jpg`, for example, then the metadata will be contained in `logo.jpg.metadata`.

The metadata file is in the Windows `.ini` format of `key` = `value` pairs. This format has been extended to contain information about forms for the Form Controller object, which you'll see in the next section. All the choices, even the presence of this file, are optional. The following is a sample file:

```
[default]
title = Test object
cache = RAMCache
proxy = Manager

[security]
Access contents information = 1:Manager,Anonymous
```

The following are the values you can set in that file:

title: This is the title that's applied to the object in the ZMI and in Plone; this will show up in the Plone templates.

cache: This is the ID of the cache object in which you'd like the object to be cached. By default Plone comes with two cache objects: a RAM Cache Manager and a HTTP Cache Manager. Chapter 14 discusses the function of these two objects.

proxy: This is the proxy role you'd like to apply to this object. See Chapter 9 for more information.

security: This is the security area, which allows multiple lines of security settings. The key contains the name of the permission. The right side contains the acquisition setting, followed by the roles delimited by commas. For example, View = 0:Manager means only users with the member and manager role can see an object, and security settings aren't acquired for that permission.

Using Validators in the File System

To specify validators on the file system, add the validator to the .metadata file. The validator section of the .metadata file would look like this:

```
[validators]
validators = validate_script1, validate_script2
```

This will run the two validation scripts: validate_script1 and validate_script2, in that order. A validation script will examine the data and add errors to the form controller state if there's a problem.

The contextType and button options need a slightly different syntax. Validations are run on the context being executed—for example, a document or image. You could have a different validator execute for the document and for the image. For example, to have a different validator script run when this is invoked as a document, add the following line:

```
validators.Document = validate_script2
```

You can vary the validator depending on the button clicked on the form by appending the name of the button in the form to the left side of the validator. The name of the button must begin with form.button. For example:

```
<input type="submit" name="form.button.button1" value="First" />
```

The metadata file would then look like the following:

```
validators..button1 = validate_script1
```

The `..` is a space for the context type, so if, as previously, you wanted this to occur for `button1` on a document, then the metadata file would look like the following:

```
validators.Document.button1 = validate_script5
```

Using Actions in the File System

Like validators, you can specify actions in the `.metadata` file. The syntax for the `actions` section of your file would look like this:

```
[actions]
action.success = traverse_to:string:script1
```

In the previous example, when the form is submitted and the validation scripts return a status of success, the traverse to action is called with the argument `string:script1`. That argument is actually an expression. The default action for the failure status is to reload the current form. The form will have access to all the error messages via the `state` object in its options.

Again, you can specify a particular action on a particular context; for example, to specify an action for success when on a document, you can do the following:

```
action.success.Documnent = traverse_to:string:document_script
```

Again, you can specify the action for the following button:

```
<input type="submit" name="form.button.button1" value="Button" />
```

by adding the following to the `.metadata` file:

```
action.success..button1 = traverse_to:string:script1
```

This example has no explicit context given, so it's valid for any type of context.

Finding Example File System Skins and the Book Examples

All the examples in this book have been collected in a skin for you to install. You can find this on the Plone book Web site at http://plone-book.agmweb.ca/Software/ PloneBookExamples and on the Apress book Web site at http://www.apress.com. It's available as a .zip file of the skin; after you've downloaded and unzipped it, you'll find there's a file structure similar to the one mentioned earlier.

You have an __init__.py file and skins directory. In the skins directory you'll find a series of page templates, Controller Validator objects, and all the matching metadata files. If you want to install this, then copy the PloneBookExamples folder into the Products directory of your instance home. Restart Plone, and then click *plone setup*. Select Add/Remove Products, and you'll see an entry for PloneBookExamples; check it, and then click install. You've now installed the templates and can go to feedbackForm and get the page template you saw in the previous chapter.

What the install procedure did was automate the process of adding an FSDV and then added a layer to each skin. If you click *portal_skins* and then select the Properties tab, you'll see that the new layer plone_book_examples has been added.

Case Study: Examining the NASA Skin

In January 2004 two NASA probes landed on Mars: Spirit and Opportunity. These remote-controlled robots scoured the surface of Mars, returning pictures and analysis of the surface. The probes were a great success, and sent back stunning pictures of the surface of Mars that thrilled the world.

One small part of this cog was a Web site at http://mars.telascience.org. This site published a program called *Maestro*. To quote the Web site, its purpose was the following:

> *You can download a scaled-down version of the program that NASA scientists use to operate Spirit and Opportunity. Updates are also available for Maestro that contain real data from Mars that you can add to your copy of Maestro.*

Turning to Plone, the group responsible for this site developed a site that looks great quickly and easily. In this case, a large number of community members and volunteers helped the members of the Maestro team develop the site. Figure 7-14 shows the working Plone site.

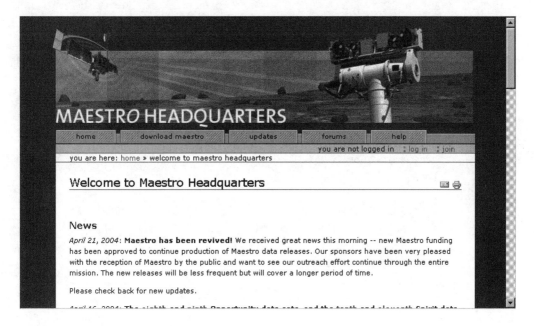

Figure 7-14. The Maestro site

You'll probably recognize some similar signs of a Plone site: the tabs across the top, the personal bar in the top-right corner, and the usual breadcrumbs. Other than that, the site looks quite different from the standard Plone site. In the following sections, I'll step through exactly how this was done. Well, actually, it's quite simple because most of the look and feel was put together using CSS. There were little to no changes other than changes to the custom style sheet and some new images.

You'll first look at the non-CSS changes to the site, which are changes to some of the templates and properties.

Removing the Portlets and Some of the Main Elements

The site has no portlets. These have been removed because in this site there aren't any that are relevant. Instead, news appears on the home page. To remove these portlets from your site, go to the root of the Plone site and click Properties. In the form fields next to left_slots and right_slots, delete all the values.

In the Maestro site, a few elements have been removed. Sometimes I've found that this the best thing to do for features that just aren't needed in a site. It can be a little hard to squeeze every user interface element into a Plone site, but really you don't always have to do that; instead, just remove the elements you don't need. A few elements here have been removed: the site actions, the search box, the footer, and the colophon.

To accomplish this, those templates that produced the code were customized and then altered so they rendered nothing. For example, to remove the search box, in the ZMI click *portal_skins*, click *plone_templates*, and then click *global_searchbox*. Next, click the Customize button. Then change the template to the following:

```
<html
    xmlns="http://www.w3.org/1999/xhtml"
    xml:lang="en" lang="en"
    i18n:domain="plone">
    <body>

        <div id="portal-searchbox"
                metal:define-macro="quick_search"
                tal:condition="nothing">
            Nothing to see here.
        </div>
    </body>
</html>
```

This is the technique I showed earlier for removing elements; just set tal:condition on the macro element to ensure that the condition is false.

Customizing the Colors

You set the base colors for the site in the base_properties object. This object has been customized, and the colors changed to the following colors (unless mentioned, all the other items are the same):

```
linkColor: #776a44
globalBorderColor: #776a44
globalBackgroundColor: #e0d3ad
globalFontColor: #776a44
```

The color change I most noticed is globalBackgroundColor, which affects the colors of the personal bar and has changed from blue to brownish. These minor colors changes will alter the base style sheet so that it matches the images and overall look and feel nicely.

Creating the Style Sheet

The big part of this site is the style sheet, which is reproduced in full in Appendix B. Here I'll highlight some of the main parts of the style sheet. This style sheet is based on ploneCustom.css, which was customized in the custom folder. Then, some of the elements of the Web page were overridden in the new ploneCustom.css file.

First, the entire background for the body is set to the color #343434.

```
body {
    background: #343434;
}
```

Second, the actual content of a Plone page, the part that you can edit, is contained in one class called documentContent. Because the background color of the documentContent element is set to white in the main plone.css file, the background of the text is white and produces the white area in the middle of the screen.

Next, the image of the satellite and robot at the top of the Web site is one large image. You place it at the top using CSS. The code for this is as follows:

```
#portal-top {
    background: url("http://mars.telascience.org/header.jpg") transparent no-repeat;
    padding: 162px 0 0 0;
    position: relative;
}
```

This CSS code sets the parameters for the element that has the ID of portal-top. If you look at the HTML code for a Plone site, you'll see the portal-top element at the top of the page, just below the body element. By setting the background for that image to the URL of the image in question, you can have the image appear. The image is 162 pixels high, which is why the padding for the top of the #portal-top element is set to 162px. If you don't do this, then all the items below will be pushed up, overriding the image.

The header image is 677 pixels wide, and you'll note that the text in the page fits cleanly underneath the image, rather than spilling out to the left or right. You can do this by setting the value for the element to 680px. The visual-portal-wrapper HTML element is actually just below the body, and it sets the width for the entire page body. The code for this is as follows:

```
#visual-portal-wrapper {
    width: 680px;
    margin: 1em auto 0 auto;
}
```

This sets the width for all the pages to be a fixed width, which is fine as long as you make sure the width is smaller than the industry-standard 800-pixel width. No matter how big the user makes the browser window, the main part of the page will never grow beyond those 680 pixels, ensuring it matches nicely with the image.

Probably the other obvious changes are the tabs at the top of the page, which are now images instead of just the standard Plone boxes. Three images make up the tabs at the top of the page: a spacer between tab, the left part of the tab, and the right part of the tab. By putting these three images together, you get the effect of the tab. Figure 7-15 shows these three images.

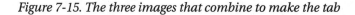

Figure 7-15. The three images that combine to make the tab

For editing the CSS, remember that each of the tabs is really a list item containing a link inside an element with the ID `portal-globalnav`. To set up the background spacer between each tab, the skin first sets the background for the entire element. Again, note that by setting the height of the image to 21 pixels, the same size as the image, you've ensured that there's the appropriate space for the image. The code is as follows:

```
#portal-globalnav {
    background: url("http://mars.telascience.org/listspacer.gif") transparent;
    padding: 0;
    height: 21px;
    border: 0;
    margin: 0 0 1px 6px;
    clear: both;
}
```

To set the image at the left end of the tab, you use the start image. You set the start image by setting the value on the li element, rather than the anchor element, like so:

```
#portal-globalnav li {
    display: block;
    float: left;
    height: 21px;
    background: url("/liststart.gif") transparent no-repeat;
    padding: 0 0 0 33px;
    margin: 0 0.5em 0 0;
}
```

Finally, you set the right part of the tab by adding an image to the anchor element. You do this by altering the anchor element inside the tab. The following code shows where you set the background image to be the right part:

```
#portal-globalnav li a {
    display: block;
    float: left;
    height: 21px;
    background: url("/listitem.gif") transparent right top;
    padding: 0 33px 0 0;
    border: 0;
    line-height: 2em;
    color: black;
    font-size: 90%;
    margin: 0;
}
```

Now, you've replaced the rather standard-looking Plone tabs with great-looking buttons.

Creating the Splash Page

This page has one other key element. The front page of the site is a *splash page*, which shows a nice graphic and invites the user to enter. You can add this by going into the ZMI and removing the index_html object that's normally there. Once removed, create a new file called index_html. In that file, create custom code to make the home page, including a custom CSS. The main element of that is one image, placed there by the following CSS:

```
div {
    background: url(/splash.jpg) transparent no-repeat;
    width: 260px;
    height: 335px;
    position: absolute;
    ...
}
```

The remaining CSS handles the placing of the text and links within that image. This page has no Plone elements at all; it's static HTML.

Conclusion

This looks like a reasonably complex site, with relatively simple CSS that does most of the hard work. By using CSS you've changed Plone's look and feel without having to know a great deal about Plone beyond the HTML. Also, by ensuring that the images are placed using CSS, you maintained key accessibility functions.

Thank you to NASA and all the people involved from the Plone community for helping with this site and case study. These include but are not limited to John Graham, Alma Ong, Joe Geldart, Michael Zeltner, and Tom Croucher.

CHAPTER 8

Managing Workflow

ONE OF PLONE'S many strengths is the workflow component. Workflow fits into one of the core themes of *content management*, which is the separation of logic, content, and presentation. This chapter therefore covers Plone's workflow in detail.

The chapter starts by covering some key definitions related to workflow, as well as the key tools involved, so that you can begin to conceptualize workflows. Once these concepts are clear, I then discuss how to add and edit your own workflows.

Throughout this chapter, I reference simple changes you can make to the workflow that comes straight out of the box with Plone. I also provide a series of examples to help you perform tasks such as creating notifications, moving content, and so on. Finally, I show some of the more advanced features of workflow development and some of the useful tools that are available.

What Is Workflow?

Workflow is a chain of actions or events that occurs on something to achieve an objective. Workflow often expresses business rules that may exist. Every business has different rules and policies about tasks that must happen within that company. Examples of this include the following:

- Before an employee's time sheet is approved, it must be viewed and acknowledged by a supervisor.

- In a widget factory, for each widget assembled, users must be notified of the order and any change in the state of the widget as it passes through the factory.

- Before a Web page is published on a Web site, it must be approved by marketing, approved by the Webmaster, and translated by a linguist.

Workflow separates the logic of these business rules and standardizes the concept of thinking about these changes. By having separate logic, it's now easy for businesses to change the application to fit their business and their business rules. Often applications try to enforce a workflow on a business because the workflow is hard-coded into the application.

Understanding Workflow in Plone

Plone's workflow tool provides certain features and limitations that are key to understanding workflow in Plone. The workflow product used in Plone is DCWorkflow, which is an open-source product released by Zope Corporation. Other workflow systems are available, and some of them are being incorporated into Plone, such as OpenFlow (http://www.openflow.it). However, for the moment, DCWorkflow is powerful and simple enough to provide all the functionality most users will need.

DCWorkflow assumes there's one object in the system that's the target of the workflow—for example, one piece of content or one widget. It further assumes that all objects of the same type go through the same workflow. By repurposing content (see Chapter 11 for more on this), you can have similar content use different workflows.

Since the DCWorkflow system is included in Plone, there's nothing extra to install. It's represented in the Zope Management Interface (ZMI) by the portal_workflow object.

Conceptualizing a Workflow

Before explaining a workflow, I'll explain a few simple pieces of terminology: states and transitions.

A *state* is information about an item of content at a particular moment in time. Examples of states are private, public, pending, and draft. All workflows have at least one starting state in which all the content starts. The workflow will then move the content through a series of states, either by user interaction or by some automation process. When the content reaches an end state, it'll remain in that state for a long time (usually forever). Content may reach one or more different end states in the process of a workflow.

For that piece of content to move from one state to another, a *transition* is needed. A transition connects a starting state and an ending state. A transition can have lots of different features associated with it, as you'll see later, but for the moment, you just need to know that a transition moves content between two states. Usually a transition is triggered by some external force, such as a user clicking a button on a Web page or a script interacting with a page.

Visualizing a workflow, especially when talking about something as nebulous as content, can be a little confusing. Thinking about an everyday occurrence will help. In this case, the following example shows the workflow of my credit card bill, which I have the joy of getting every month:

1. The credit card company prepares a bill and mails it to me.

2. I get the bill and put it on my desk. Sometimes the bill sits on my desk for quite a while as I wait for the end of month. Occasionally I have to query people about certain expenditures, such as "What were those clothes you bought?"

3. Any serious queries or questions then go back to the credit card company, perhaps causing a new bill to be created (although this happens quite rarely).

4. Usually at the end of the month, when I do all the accounting, I then pay the bill.

From this, then, you can come up with some states. Looking at the previous steps, you'll see you really have no need to create different states for receiving the bill, which includes opening it and putting it on my desk. Similarly, you don't need to bother with every review that happens. Although these are all valid steps that take place, trying to make a workflow for every state would be too cumbersome. Instead, you can summarize the workflow with the following states:

- **Draft**: The credit card bill has been prepared and sent to me.

- **Review**: The credit card bill has been received and is on my desk, being reviewed.

- **Paid**: The credit card bill has been paid, put in my filing cabinet, and forgotten about forever.

Now that you've come up with the states, you can think of the changes that need to occur. For each of these states, you'll have at least one transition that occurs to move the bill from one state to another:

- **Post**: The bank sends the credit card bill.

- **Pay**: I pay the credit card bill.

- **Reject**: Something is wrong on the bill, and it isn't approved.

Figure 8-1 shows this set of transitions and states. In the figure, boxes represent states, with the state written in them. Arrows represent the transitions from one state to the next, with the name of the transition in italics.

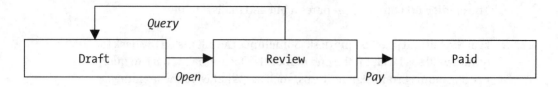

Figure 8-1. A simple state machine for paying credit card bills

You've now extracted this business process of paying a credit card bill into a workflow. The next step is to think about roles and security for this credit card bill. This workflow now contains the business logic for an application for processing credit cards.

Understanding Roles and Security in Workflow

In any complicated system, you'll have users of all roles and groups. These roles give Plone a large amount of flexibility with security, but they also can make it more complicated. Chapter 9 covers security, local roles, and groups, but this section covers some key points about how these topics relate to workflow.

When a piece of content moves from one workflow state to another, the workflow process can change the security settings on that content. The security settings determine what user can perform what action on what piece of content. By manipulating the security settings through workflow, you can cause the security to change on a piece of content through its life cycle. Users from static systems or Zope often get confused because in Zope, all pieces of content have the same security settings throughout their life cycle.

Returning to the credit card example, you can infer the security settings for the credit card bill. One way to represent this is to produce a table that expands the security in general terms for the transitions that can occur at each of the various states, as shown in Table 8-1.

Table 8-1. The Transitions and Entities That Can Make Them

State	Me	Bank
Draft		Post
Review	Pay, Reject	
Paid		

At this stage in Table 8-1, you've seen the transitions and who can make them. You haven't thought about the access that each user has to perform an action on an object at each point. For example, at which point can someone edit the bill, and when can it be viewed? These are called *actions* in Plone terminology, as shown in Table 8-2. I hope that only I have access to my own credit card statements! Likewise, at any stage, the bank is able to view the credit card bill and answer queries on it.

Table 8-2. The Actions and Entities That Can Make Them

State	Me	Bank
Draft		View, Edit
Review	View	View
Paid	View	View

Actually, as it turns out, I can't edit my credit card bill; only the bank can. I can send back my credit bill by rejecting it, but the bank is unlikely to want my edits. In this situation, assume the bank is the owner of the credit card bill. This demonstrates a concept called *ownership*. I may have several credit card bills from several banks, and in each case you can think of the bank as the owner. Each bank owns its own credit card bills, but Bank A isn't the owner of Bank B's bill. Table 8-3 combines the transitions and actions, changing the terms *Me* and *Bank* to *Payee* and *Owner*, respectively.

Table 8-3. The Transitions and Actions Combined, Plus the Roles of People

State	Payee	Owner
Draft		Post, View, Edit
Review	Pay, Reject, View	View
Paid	View	View

Of course, this is a rather contrived example, but it illustrates how you can apply workflow to basic states. More transitions can occur here—for instance, I'd be more than happy for someone else to pay my credit card bill for me—but that's so unlikely that you shouldn't add it to the workflow or security.

Before showing how to create and edit workflows, I'll now show you the default workflows that ship with Plone.

Introducing Plone Workflows

Plone ships with a set of default workflows for your Plone site. These workflows provide a logical way of moving content through a Plone site. A standard Plone site ships with two workflows: the default workflow and the folder workflow. The following sections present each of these in turn.

Default Workflow

Chapter 3 covered the default workflow and the default settings when publishing content. I discussed the security and settings for each state in the workflow. However, a picture is worth a thousand words, so Figure 8-2 shows the workflow state.

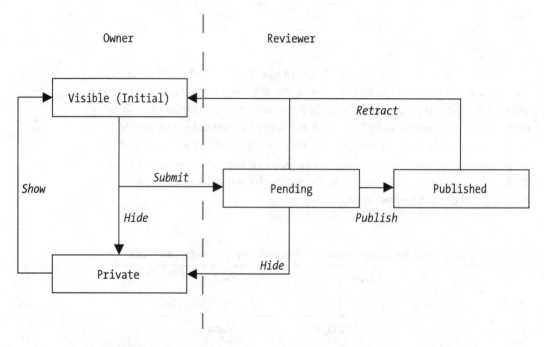

Figure 8-2. The default workflow for content that comes with Plone

Figure 8-2 shows the main states and the transitions. This figure has a gray dotted line that represents a sort of security divider. To the left of the line is where owners of the content usually interact with the content. To the right of the line is where reviewers usually interact with the content.

NOTE   The owner of the content is the person who created the content originally. An owner is one particular member of a Plone site. Although many members exist in a Plone site, only one person can be the owner of a piece of content in a Plone site. Because the owner role is calculated when an object is created, the owner role is special.

Just like with the credit card example, an associated set of permissions exists for the default workflow. Table 8-4 outlines all the permissions and the states.

Table 8-4. The Default Workflow Permissions

State	Anonymous	Authenticated	Owner	Manager	Reviewer
Pending	View	View	View	Edit	Edit
Private			Edit	Edit	View
Published	View	View	View	Edit	View
Visible	View	View	Edit	Edit	View

* View refers to the following permissions: Access Contents Information and View
* Edit refers to the following permission: Modify Portal Content

As you can see from Table 8-4, by default only when content is in the private state is it truly hidden from everyone else. When content is in the published state, only the manager can edit it. Later in the "Editing Permissions" section, I'll show you how to change these permissions easily through the Web.

Folder Workflow

I also discussed the folder workflow in Chapter 3, when I covered publishing content with you. However, as I noted in that chapter, no pending state exists for folders. Instead, you have a slightly simpler workflow, as shown in Figure 8-3.

Owner and Reviewer

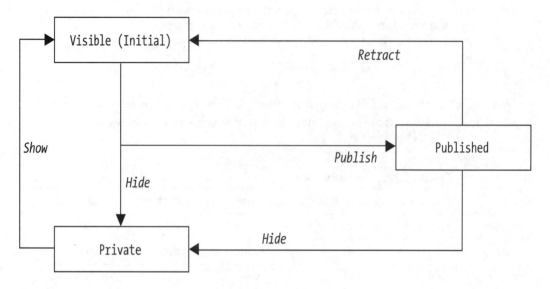

Figure 8-3. The folder workflow for content that comes with Plone

Other Workflows

Numerous workflows are available to a Plone site, including private workflow, community workflow, one-step publication workflow, and so on. ZopeZen comes with a workflow, and PloneCollectorNG also comes with a workflow. DCWorkflow comes with four workflows.

Currently, two workflows come in the PloneWorkflows product in the collective project on SourceForge (http://sf.net/projects/collective): the community workflow and one-step publication workflow. The community workflow is similar to the Plone workflow, with a few changes. The one-step publication workflow has two states: private and published.

At the moment, you have no easy way to install and uninstall workflows, and you have no real easy way to transition content between one state and another. For example, if you install the one-step publication workflow into an existing state, you also need to fix the states for all objects and move them into one of the new states. In this case, it's probably simple—everything in a published state should stay as it is, and everything else should move into the private state.

Adding and Editing Workflow

Now that I've discussed the default workflow, I come to the key point that's probably most on your mind: How can you change the defaults? Well, as with most of Plone, you can add, edit, and delete all workflow through the ZMI. The tool that controls workflow is portal_workflow. In the following sections, I cover how workflows are assigned and then go through all the settings for a workflow in detail.

Setting Workflows to a Content Type

After clicking *portal_workflow*, you'll see a list of workflow assignments. A feature of DCWorkflow is that each content type has one and only one workflow assigned to it; Figure 8-4 shows these assignments.

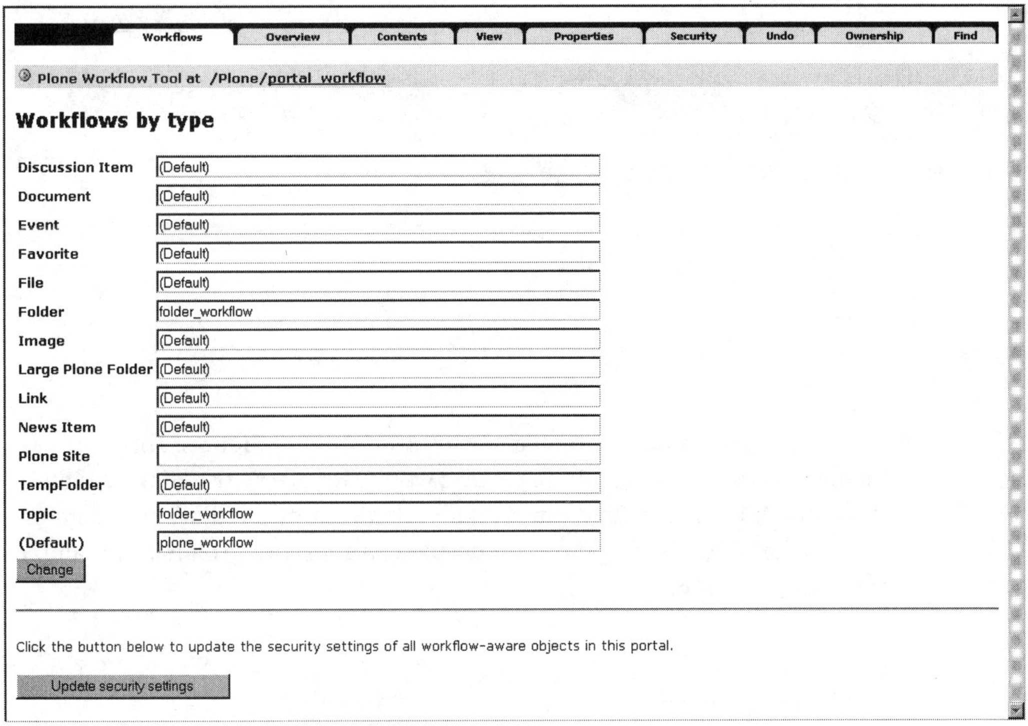

	Workflows	Overview	Contents	View	Properties	Security	Undo	Ownership	Find

Plone Workflow Tool at /Plone/portal_workflow

Workflows by type

Discussion Item	(Default)
Document	(Default)
Event	(Default)
Favorite	(Default)
File	(Default)
Folder	folder_workflow
Image	(Default)
Large Plone Folder	(Default)
Link	(Default)
News Item	(Default)
Plone Site	
TempFolder	(Default)
Topic	folder_workflow
(Default)	plone_workflow

Change

Click the button below to update the security settings of all workflow-aware objects in this portal.

Update security settings

Figure 8-4. The list of workflow by type

On this page you'll see a list of each content type and the workflow that has been applied to it. If a workflow isn't specified (in other words, the value is blank), then no workflow is applied. As an example, the default for the Portal Site type is blank. You really don't want to try transitioning the Plone site itself, just the objects in it. If the value is (Default), the default workflow at the bottom of the page is applied to that content type. In Figure 8-4, for topic and folders, the folder_workflow workflow is used, and for all other content types, plone_workflow is applied. The names of the workflow refer to the name of workflow objects imported or created inside the workflow tool. For more information on the workflows available, select the Contents tab. This opens a list of workflows that have been loaded into the system, as shown in Figure 8-5.

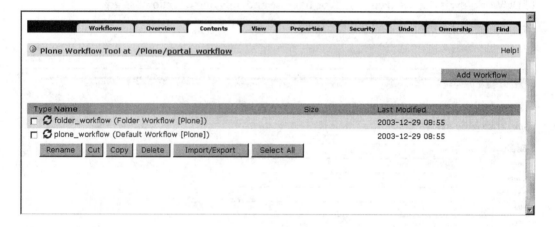

Figure 8-5. Workflows available

You can add workflows by clicking the Add Workflow button. This opens a list of the workflows available; to create a workflow, select a workflow type and enter a workflow name. To create workflow that's empty but that's configurable through the Web, select dc_workflow and enter an appropriate name; for example, enter **my_workflow**.

Editing a Workflow

From the Contents tab, you can click a workflow to access the management screens for that workflow: all the states, transitions, and associated features. The series of tabs across the top of the page outlines the functionality of a workflow quite well: States, Transitions, Variables, Worklists, Scripts, and Permissions. I'll run through each of these tabs and some of the other options available. Unless otherwise mentioned, all the following tabs are accessible from this main workflow page.

Creating or editing workflow can require lots of clicking and can be a little confusing. If you're a developer keen on using the file system, then you can do all this from Python if you want—I cover this for you later in this chapter in the "Writing a Workflow in Python" section.

Setting the Initial State

To set the initial state, go to the States tab and check out the states available; next to one of the states you'll see an asterisk, as shown in Figure 8-6.

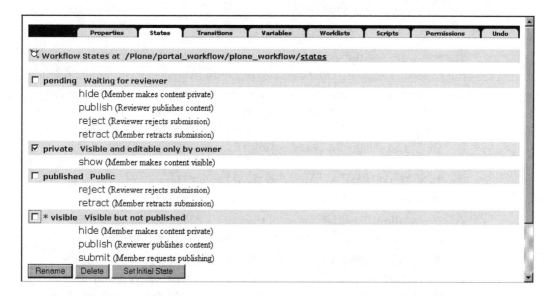

Figure 8-6. Setting the initial state for this workflow

You set the initial state for your workflow on this page by checking the box next to the state and then clicking Set Initial State. All content that uses this workflow will be created with an initial state. Any content that has already been created will remain in its initial state; changing the state afterward won't change that state. You can set only one initial state for each workflow.

How Can You Set the Initial State As Private?

On some sites it may make sense for content to not show up at all or be accessible to users other than administrators and owners only after it has been completed. The best way to do this is to set the default state for the object to something that provides this security—for example, private. In the private state, only reviewers, managers, and owners can actually see the item.

To set the default state to private in the ZMI, click *portal_workflow*, and select the Contents tab. Next, click *plone_workflow*, select the States tab, and then select the default state by checking the box next to *visible*. Finally, click the Save Changes button. New content will now be in the private state and not accessible to the general public.

Editing States

The States tab lists the states that are present in this workflow. At the beginning of this chapter, I explained that a state represents an object at a particular point in time. Each state has an ID that's unique; this is usually a simple verb such as *pending* or *published*. To add a state, enter an ID and click Add at the bottom of the page.

You'll also see the following options:

Title: The title of the state is displayed in your Plone site and is a user-friendly version of the state.

Description: The description of the state is a long description of the state. This isn't currently shown to users but may be in the future.

Possible transitions: This lists all the possible transitions that can occur from the state. This list will show only if you actually have a transition in the system. Simply select the transitions that need to occur on this state. By selecting a transition for this state, you're selecting the start point for this transition to be this state.

To alter a state, enter the changes and then click Save to commit the changes. The Permissions tab will open with the permissions that will be applied to an object while it's in this state. This may mean changing the permissions on an object when it transitions into that state. The form is rather self-explanatory; to enable an anonymous user to view the object, check the boxes that correspond to View and Anonymous and click Save Changes, as shown in Figure 8-7.

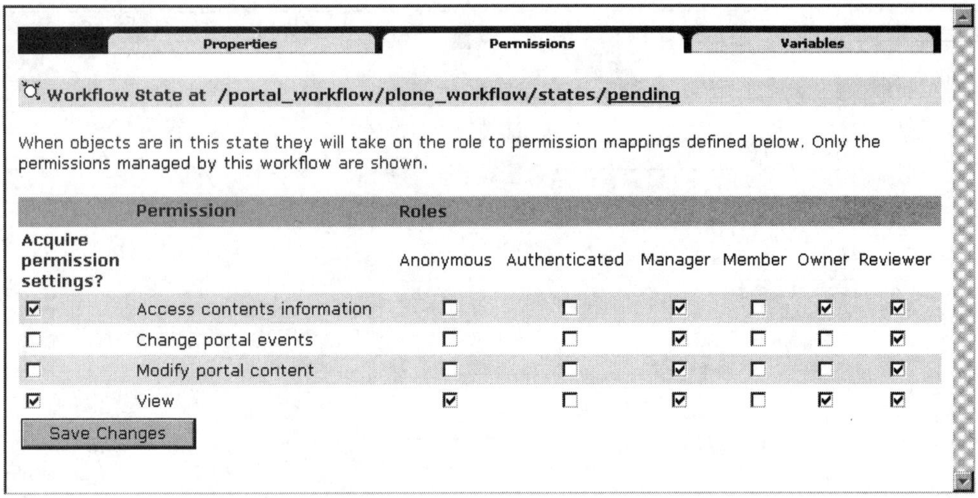

Figure 8-7. State permissions page

If you change the permissions for a particular workflow state, you've created an issue that needs resolving. Any existing content in that state won't have the new workflow permissions set on it. The content will have the old workflow permissions, and you'll need to update them. When you've finished making all your changes, go to the root workflow page and click Update Security Settings, as shown in Figure 8-4. Performing that update may take a while depending upon the number of objects to be altered.

The Variables tab allows you to assign a value to a variable when the object is in this state. The workflow determines the list of variables available to each state. For more information on these, see the "Editing Variables" section.

Editing Transitions

The Transitions tab lists the transitions that will occur in this workflow. In the beginning of this chapter, I showed you how a transition represents the changes that will occur to the object. Each transition has a few variables that are shown on the summary page. To add a transition, enter an ID and click Add at the bottom of the page, as shown in Figure 8-8.

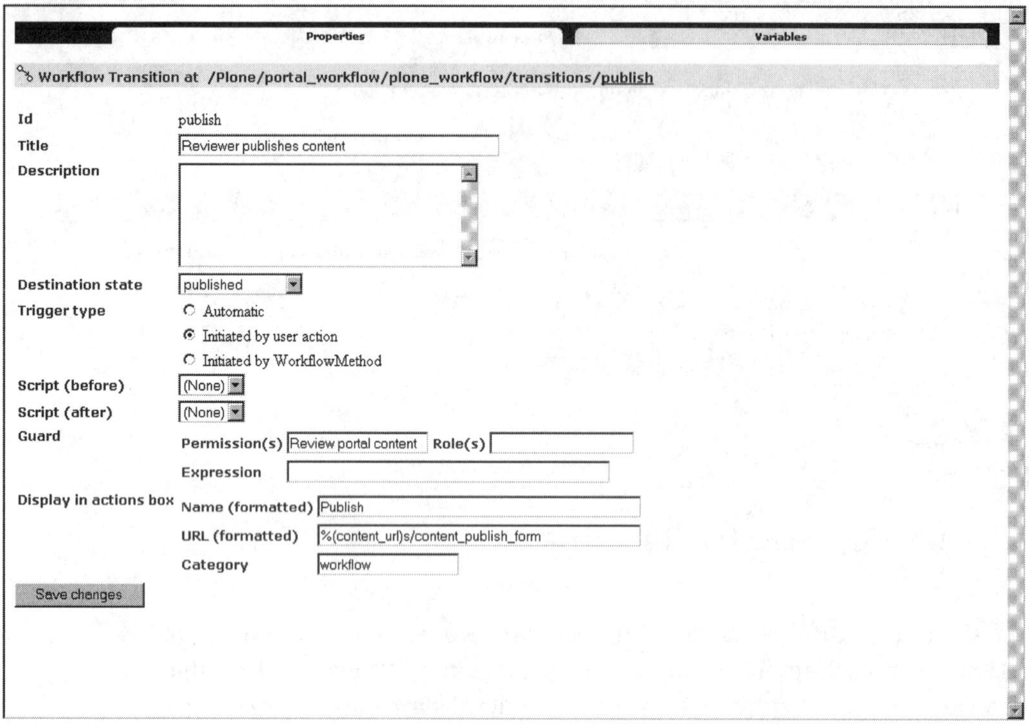

Figure 8-8. Transition details page

If you now click a transition, you'll open the following details for that transition:

Title: This is the title for this transition.

Description: This is the detailed description for this transition.

Destination state: This is the state that will be the target for this transition. The initial source state is defined by assigning the transition to the state.

Trigger type: This indicates how the transition will be triggered. *Automatic* means that this will happen as soon as it moves into this state. *Initiated by user action* is the most common choice and means a user has enacted the transition by clicking a link.

Script (before): This runs this script before this transition occurs.

Script (after): This runs this script after this transition occurs.

Guard: This is the security for this state (explained shortly).

Display in actions box: This is how this transition will be displayed in Plone. Entering a value here also ensures that the transition will be entered as an action. You can then get this transition as an action by querying for actions.

Of these values, the destination state is quite interesting. Although I've already mentioned that transitions normally change state, this isn't required. Because each transition can run scripts and write something into the history, it can be useful sometimes *not* to change state. For an example of this, see the "Using Workflow to Track Changes" section later in this chapter. If your transition does change the state, then select the new state as the destination state.

A transition can have multiple starting points but only one destination; if you need multiple destinations, you'll have to make multiple transitions. You can specify scripts to run before or after this transition. Two common examples are moving an object in workflow and sending an e-mail notification. The "Common Tasks and Examples" section covers both of these examples.

Before any transition can be executed, a security guard checks the entire transition to ensure that the user running the transition has the right to do so. The guard has the following three components:

Permission(s): These are the required permissions. Multiple permissions should have a semicolon (;) to separate them.

Role(s): These are the required roles. Multiple roles should have a semi-colon (;) to separate them.

Expression: This is a workflow expression. For more information on this, see the "Editing Workflow Expressions" section later in this chapter. For each value specified, the guard must evaluate as true before continuing. If a test of any of the values fail, then the transition won't execute. Usually you'll find most guards have only one or two values specified.

Editing Variables

The Variables tab lists the variables that will be created and changed in the workflow. I haven't discussed variables much with you up to this point; instead, I've focused on states and transitions. This section covers variables.

It isn't always possible, and I don't recommend that you try, to encapsulate all the information you'll need in a workflow within just states and transitions. Instead, you can use variables to store some workflow-related information. For example, in the credit card bill example, the bill could be paid by several methods (Internet banking, check, and so on). You could store the amount method ($100, for example) in a variable. Should the bill be rejected or altered, that amount would be updated. The point of a variable is to have something that changes between each state and transition.

So, returning to the main workflow page, click the Variables tab to get a list of all the variables. To add a variable, enter a variable ID and click Add at the bottom of the page. To determine what state an object is in at any time, DCWorkflow stores the current state in a variable on the object. The default name of that variable is review_state.

 NOTE If you need to change this because it conflicts with another name, you can do so at the bottom of that page. However, doing this will cause all your current objects to lose their state, so be careful about changing that value.

Each workflow variable has the following properties:

- **Description**: This is the variable description.

- **Make available to catalog**: These variables will be placed in a list exposable to the catalog. This doesn't add indexes or metadata to the catalog; you still have to do that manually.

- **Store in workflow**: This determines if the information is to be stored in the workflow or on the object.

- **Variable update mode**: This determines when to update the variable.

- **Default value**: This determines a default value as a string.

- **Default expression**: This is the default value as an expression. If this is present, it'll be used instead of default value (for more information, see the "Editing Workflow Expressions" section later in this chapter).

- **Info. guard**: These are security settings for accessing this variable. These guard settings are similar to the guard settings for a transition; however, the guard occurs when accessing the variable here.

Editing Worklists

The Worklists tab provides access to all the worklists that are assigned in this workflow. A *worklist* is a method of querying the workflow for information about the numbers of objects in that workflow. For example, I'd like to be able to easily ask the workflow for all the outstanding credit card bills I have.

To add a worklist, enter an ID and click Add. Each worklist has the following properties:

- **Description**: This is a description of the worklist.

- **Cataloged variable matches**: This is the value that the worklist must match to be added in this worklist. The variable matched is the workflow state variable given in the variables list (the default variable name for this variable is review_state).

- **Display in actions box**: This is information to display on the user interface. Entering a value here also ensures that the transition will be entered as an action. You can then get this transition as an action by querying for actions.

- **Guard**: This is a guard for accessing this worklist.

Returning to the credit card example, if I wanted to know all the credit card bills that need reviewing by me, then I could place this information in a worklist. First, the variable review_state would contain the current state for each item. All the credit card bills that need reviewing would be in the review state. Second, I'd add a worklist called review_queue, and the value for variable would be pending. I could now ask the worklist for all the items in the review_queue.

Although a worklist is a convenient way of storing this information, Plone doesn't use them. Instead, Plone uses ZCatalog directly to query objects that are workflowed. Since the DCWorkflow worklist uses the catalog tool, the end result is the same.

Editing Scripts

The Scripts tab lists the scripts that are available to this workflow. This list is actually a standard folder in the ZMI, and you can add almost anything there. Since the main reason you'd want to do this would be to add a script to perform advanced handling of transitions, you should add only Script (Python) objects here.

To add a script from the Scripts tab, select Script (Python) from the Add drop-down menu, and give the script an ID. The script is passed to one and only one object, which is the base workflow expression object; for more information on this object, see the "Editing Workflow Scripts" section later in this chapter. For example, if you need to access the actual object in the workflow, you can use a Python script such as the following:

```
##parameters=state_change
obj = state_change.object
```

What happens in this script is up to the developer—you can run almost anything here. You can trigger events, and you can access other workflows and transitions. For some example scripts, see the "Sending E-Mail Notifications" and "Moving Objects" sections later in this chapter. When the script executes, it will execute as the user who initiated the transition. You could assign proxy roles on the script if it needs to happen as someone else. Returning to the transitions, you can assign this script to any number of transitions in the *script (after)* and *script (before)* settings. You can run the script either before or after a transition.

Editing Permissions

The Permissions tab lists the permissions that are managed by this workflow. You've seen these permissions already when examining the states. You set the list of permissions manageable in those states in this tab. To add a new permission, select the permission from the drop-down box and select Add.

How Can You Edit a Published Document?

Well, you can't edit a published document in the default workflow unless you have the manager role. If you allow the owner of the document to edit it, then you really should review it again. However, this seems to be a common request and is a trivial thing to change. In the ZMI, click *portal_workflow*, and select the Contents tab. Then click *plone_workflow*, and select the States tab. Finally, click *published* and then select the Permissions tab. Check the box that corresponds to allowing the owner to modify portal content.

| | Properties | | | Permissions | | | Variables | |

🔍 Workflow State at /Plone/portal_workflow/plone_workflow/states/published

When objects are in this state they will take on the role to permission mappings defined below. Only the permissions managed by this workflow are shown.

	Permission	Roles					
Acquire permission settings?		Anonymous	Authenticated	Manager	Member	Owner	Reviewer
☑	Access contents information	☑	☐	☑	☐	☐	☐
☐	Change portal events	☐	☐	☑	☐	☐	☐
☐	Modify portal content	☐	☐	☑	☐	☑	☐
☑	View	☑	☐	☑	☐	☐	☐

Save Changes

Click Save Changes to save your permissions. Because you've updated the security settings, you'll have to click *portal_workflow*, select the Contents tab, and click *Update security settings*. This will update all the objects in your site and ensure that your permissions have been applied to existing objects. Now owners can edit their documents while they're in the published state.

Editing Workflow Scripts

Scripts are an opportunity for the developer to perform some logic upon a transition. That logic can be almost anything you want. You could be checking that some conditions have been performed (for example, is the document spell checked?) or that some special actions have been performed. When the object is transitioned, the script will be called.

When a script is called, one extra parameter is passed to that script. That extra parameter provides access to all sorts of transition-related elements and attributes. That parameter is called the state_change parameter, and it has the following attributes:

status: This is the workflow status.

object: This is the object being transitioned in the workflow.

workflow: This is the current workflow object for the object being transitioned.

transition: This is the current transition object being executed.

old_state: This is original state of the object.

new_state: This is destination state of the object.

kwargs: These are keyword arguments passed to the doActionFor method.

getHistory: This is a method that takes no parameters and returns a copy of the object's workflow history.

getPortal: This is a method that takes no parameters and returns the root Plone object.

ObjectDeleted(folder): This tells workflow that the object being transitioned has been deleted; it takes the object to which you'd like to return the user. Pass to the exception the folder you'd like the user to be redirected to (see the "Moving Objects" section later in this chapter).

ObjectMoved(newObject, newObject): This tells workflow that the object being transitioned has moved. Pass to the exception the folder you'd like the user to be redirected to (see the "Moving Objects" section later in this chapter).

WorkflowException: This raises an expectation back to workflow and aborts the transaction (and hence the transition).

getDateTime: This is a method that takes no parameters and returns the DateTime object that relates to the transition.

For example, to find out what state is being transitioned to and when, the following is a Script (Python) object that will tell you just that information. This script logs the information about the transition into the log file:

```
##parameters=state_change
st = 'From %s to %s on %s' % (
    state_change.old_state,
    state_change.new_state,
    state_change.getDateTime())
context.plone_log(st)
```

 TIP When you're writing a Script (Python) object, you may need to print to the log file to help with debugging. A script called plone_log does this, which takes a string and passes it to Plone's logging functions. Hence, calling context.plone_log is a useful tool for debugging.

When assigning a script to a transition, you have two choices: before and after. As the names suggest, a script that's set assigned to before runs prior to the transition running. This is suitable for scripts that may check if something should happen prior to the transition running, such as testing that another dependent object or page has been uploaded or there are no spelling errors. The script assigned to after runs once the transition completes—although if at any time an uncaught exception is raised on a script, this will cause the transition to fail, the object to remain in its original state, and the exception to display to the user.

Editing Workflow Expressions

Throughout this chapter you've seen values that can be expressed as workflow expressions. For example, the value assigned to a variable is the result of a workflow expression. This expression is nothing special; it's merely a Template Attribute Language (TAL) expression with a few different variables available.

You already learned about TAL expressions in Chapter 5, so you should be familiar with these expression and all their options, such as Python, string, and path expressions.

Unlike the standard TAL expression, a few extra parameters are passed through to the namespace, relating to the particular workflow. The namespace for a workflow expression contains the following:

- **here**: This is the object being transitioned in the workflow.

- **container**: This is the container of the object being transitioned in the workflow.

- **state_change**: This is the state change object referenced in the "Editing Workflow Scripts" section.

- **transition**: This is the transition being executed, identical to `state_change.transition`.

- **status**: This is the original state, identical to `state_change.old_state`.

- **workflow**: This is the workflow for this object.

- **scripts**: These are the scripts available in this workflow.

- **user**: This is the user executing this transition.

Common Tasks and Examples

I'll now present some common tasks you can achieve easily using workflow. When a user causes a workflow transition, this transition runs using that specific user's account. In many of these examples, a normal user may not have the correct permissions to perform the task. For example, members don't normally have the right to access the list of members unless this permission has been explicitly given to them.

To solve this permission issue, where noted, some of the following Script (Python) objects have been given a slightly different role. To set a proxy role on a script, access the Proxy tab on an object and then select the user to run the script, as shown in Figure 8-9.

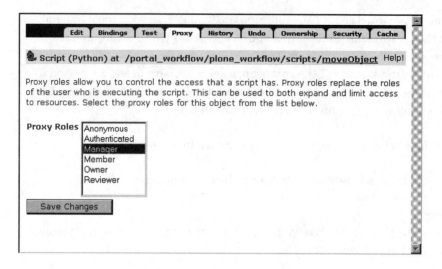

Figure 8-9. Setting proxy settings on a script

You would, of course, make sure your scripts executed with the minimum roles needed, depending exactly upon what your script does.

Example Workflow Expressions

The following are some useful examples of workflow expressions that can be used in various places.

To get the comments, or an empty string, with this transition, use the following:

```
python:state_change.kwargs.get('comment', '')
```

To obtain the title of the folder that the object is in, use this:

```
container/Title
```

To test if the old state is review state, use this:

```
python: state_change.old_state == 'review'
```

To get the user executing this transition, use this:

```
user/getId
```

So if you wanted to track who the last user to transition an object was, you could add a last user variable into the workflow. You do this by going to the workflow and clicking the Variables tab. Then add the variable last_user. If you set the Default expr variable to user/getId, each time the object changed, that value would be stored for you.

Using Workflow to Track Changes

For one particular application a client of mine wanted to keep track of every time an item was edited and any reasons for that edit so that when auditing the item later, there would be a comment for each change. Thanks to workflow, this was quite easy to achieve.

In this case, the workflow had only one state—but actually this will work for almost any workflow. To this one workflow, a transition was added called edit. That transition didn't actually change the object's state; the destination state for that transition was (Remain in state), meaning no change occurred.

When an object is edited, a method is called to perform the change. For example, when a document is edited, the method called is document_edit.cpy. You can find that script by clicking *portal_skins*, clicking *plone_form_scripts*, and clicking *document_edit*. All that's needed is to add one line to that script before the last line:

```
context.portal_workflow.doActionFor(new_context,
  'edit', comment='')
```

The doActionFor method of portal_workflow performs the transition given (in this case, edit) for the object passed in (in this case, context). Each time the object is edited, that edit transition will fire. That will cause a line to be added to the comments list showing who edited the object, when it was added, and any comments associated with it.

When an object is edited, there are actually no comments, so to be a little more advanced, you'd have to modify the document's edit template to include a comments field. You could then access this comments list by going to the State tab, where the list of changes displays at the bottom.

Moving Objects

One useful ability is moving an object during the workflow. For example, you could move all press releases into a folder called Press Release each time you publish one. Content could be created and edited anywhere and then on publishing moved into that folder. The example script in Listing 8-1 moves the object being workflowed into the Members folder. To add this script, go into the workflow tool in the ZMI, and select the Scripts tab. Then select Script (Python) from the drop-down box. Give the new object the name **moveObject**, and then enter Listing 8-1 into this script.

Listing 8-1. Moving an Object

```
##parameters=state_change
# get the object and its ID
obj = state_change.object
id = obj.getId()

# get the src folder and the destination folder
dstFldr = context.portal_url.Members
srcFldr = obj.aq_parent

# perform the move
objs = srcFldr.manage_cutObjects([id,])
dstFldr.manage_pasteObjects(objs)

# get the new object
new_obj = dstFldr[id]

# pass new_obj to the error, *twice*
raise state_change.ObjectMoved(new_obj, new_obj)
```

You need to do a few more things; first, assign this script to a transition. I'd normally use such a script in the publish transition. To do this, go to that transition and assign the value of script (after) to moveObject.

Second, one other small problem exists: This script moves objects into the Members folder. You'll probably have a better destination in mind, of course. To perform such a move, a user has to have the appropriate rights to move objects between these folders. Normally, only a manager can move objects into the Members folder. So you need to give the script the proxy role of manager. You can do this by clicking Scripts, clicking *moveObject*, and selecting the Proxy tab. Assign the role of manager to this script. You can find more information about security and local roles in Chapter 9.

Looking at the code, first the script gets the object and the object's ID from the transition namespace. Then it gets the source and destination folders. Then it utilizes Zope's ObjectManager Application Programming Interface (API) to perform the copy and paste. You could, of course, determine these folders programmatically—perhaps based on the user performing the transaction or on the type of content being moved. Finally, you get the object and pass it to an exception ObjectMoved.

The `ObjectMoved` exception is a special exception to DCWorkflow. By passing the new object twice as parameters into the exception, the new object will be passed up to the Plone front end. This is critical so that when the user is sent to the object in response to the change, it's to the new location of the object, not the old one. Of course, you may want to write a function that moves the function back after rejecting the object, perhaps to the member's home folder.

Another special case, and a more unusual one, is to delete an object in workflow. Usually deleting an object is an action from the containing object, so it's unusual to see in workflow. For this task, you can raise an `ObjectDeleted` exception. Listing 8-2 shows the script to perform a delete.

Listing 8-2. Deleting an Object

```
##parameters=state_change

# get the object
obj = state_change.object
id = obj.getId()

# get the parent folder, delete the object
srcFldr = obj.aq_parent
srcFldr.manage_delObjects([id,])

# raise the object deleted method and pass
# the folder you want to return to
raise state_change.ObjectDeleted(srcFldr)
```

You could call this script `deleteObject` and successfully delete objects in the workflow. Again, by ensuring the error is raised, Plone will know what to do; in this case, it takes the user to the folder containing that object.

Sending E-Mail Notifications

If you have a Web site that a user doesn't visit regularly, then putting information on the site about what has to be reviewed and when is rather pointless. You can turn workflow into a rudimentary notification system by using it to send e-mails to the users. The notification channel of e-mail is just one simple example; this could also be an instant message, a text message delivered to a phone, and so on. I'll leave other options to your imagination.

In this example, you'll send e-mail via the `MailHost` object on the server to every user who has the reviewer role in the system, telling them about a new item that has been submitted for review. This is actually a more complicated script than the ones I've shown you so far, since it runs through a few steps: defining the variables, finding the account name of every reviewer, finding an e-mail, and sending an e-mail. Listing 8-3 shows the script.

Listing 8-3. Sending an E-Mail Notification

```
##parameters=state_change
# the objects we need
object = state_change.object
mship = context.portal_membership
mhost = context.MailHost
administratorEmailAddress = context.email_from_address

# the message format, %s will be filled in from data
message = """
From: %s
To: %s
Subject: New item submitted for approval - %s

%s

URL: %s
"""
```

This sets up the message and objects you need. Apart from the object being transitioned, you'll also need a reference to the membership tool portal_membership and the Simple Mail Transfer Protocol (SMTP) server via MailHost. The message is easily configurable to send an e-mail in any format you like.

You then use the listMembers method of the portal_membership object to get a list of members. For each member, you can then see if the reviewer role is in the list of roles for that user by calling the getRoles method:

```
for user in mship.listMembers():
    if "Reviewer" in mship.getMemberById(user.id).getRoles():
```

The astute reader will note that looping through every member in a Plone site could be a little slow if you have thousands of users. In the next chapter, you'll modify this script to pull the list of users from a specific group.

There's no point in sending an e-mail if you don't have a user's e-mail address, so you should check here that there's a valid e-mail first. Now all that's left is to format the e-mail and send it. For this you can use Python's string replacement functionality and pass in four parameters that correspond to the %s in the `message` variable set at the beginning of the script. After this replacement, the `msg` variable will contain the e-mail you want to send. To send the e-mail, simply call the `send` method of the `MailHost` and pass through the e-mail string:

```
if user.email:
    msg = message % (
        administratorEmailAddress,
        user.email,
        object.TitleOrId(),
        object.Description(),
        object.absolute_url()
        )
    mhost.send(msg)
```

This will result in the following e-mail being sent:

```
From: administrator@agmweb.ca
To: andy@agmweb.ca
Subject: New item submitted for approval - Plone's great

We all know Plone is a great product, but with the newest release
it's gotten even better...

URL: http://agmweb.ca/Members/andym/News_Item_123
```

Appendix B shows the full listing for this script.

Using PloneCollectorNG

PloneCollectorNG is a bug tracker that's available for Plone. You'll find many other issue trackers out there, but this is the one I use and recommend for Plone. In fact, writing an issue tracker seems to be a common thing for developers to do. One of the really nice things about workflow is that it enables your users to significantly change the way an application works. As a developer, developing products hooking into DCWorkflow allows your application to remain flexible. You can find PloneCollectorNG at `http://www.zope.org/Members/ajung/PloneCollectorNG`.

The product adds a series of content types during installation; one of them is PloneIssueNG, which is an *issue* (or bug report). Rather than hard-coding exactly how the issue moves through the database, a separate workflow is assigned to the issue. That workflow contains appropriate states, transitions, variables, and worklists.

At any stage you can find out what state an object is in by calling the getInfoFor method of portal_workflow. This useful method accepts an object and the variable to be looked up. In PloneCollectorNG's workflow, that variable is called state, and in Plone workflow, it's called review_state. For example, to find the state for an object, you use this:

```
portal_workflow.getInfoFor(obj, "state")
```

You can find possible states for an object by examining the state's object directly from the workflow, like so:

```
portal_workflow['pcng_workflow'].states._mapping.keys()
```

The result of this is that if your user wants to have a simple issue-tracking system, then modifying this workflow through the Web is relatively trivial (if, when the application was developed, the workflow tools have been considered). Compare this to another popular bug-tracking system, Bugzilla, where changing a state or a transition requires hours and hours of a Perl programmer's time to find all the hard-coded references to a bug's state.

Distributing and Writing Workflow

If you've got a great workflow for your application, you have a couple of different ways to write and distribute workflow. The following sections close the discussion of workflow by presenting a couple of these options.

Writing Through the ZMI

Probably the simplest but most laborious way to write workflow is to use the ZMI. Although the ZMI drives many people crazy, it's a simple way to set up the options. Unfortunately, once you've started writing through the ZMI, you're stuck in that paradigm. In other words, there's no easy to edit or alter that workflow on the file system. I discussed editing a workflow through the Web with you earlier in this chapter, of course.

To export a workflow from the ZMI, click *portal_workflow* and select the Contents tab. Select the created workflows you'd like to export by checking the boxes on the left of the ZMI, and then click *import/export*. At the top part of the export page, select *Download to local machine*, and click *export*. A file with extension .zexp will be created that can be saved and redistributed. Selecting XML Format will provide a file in Extensible Markup Language (XML) format with an .xml extension.

If you're provided a workflow in a the .zexp or .xml format, then importing the workflow into your Plone is straightforward. Place that file in the import directory of Zope on the file system. This can be the instance home directory or the Zope directory.

Then click *portal_workflow*, select the Contents tab, and click *import/export*. At the bottom part of the page, you'll see a small form that takes an import filename. Enter the name of the filename there, and leave *Take ownership of imported objects* selected. Click the Import button to import the workflow. The workflow will now be imported and given the name specified in the export.

Writing a Workflow in Python

Using Python is probably the favorite way of programmers to write a workflow, since it can all be done in Python and easily distributed. First, make a Python module on the file system. At the top of the file, import the appropriate tools, as follows:

```
from Products.CMFCore.WorkflowTool import addWorkflowFactory
from Products.DCWorkflow.DCWorkflow import DCWorkflowDefinition
```

Second, make a function that creates the workflow. Appendix A lists the API for writing a workflow in a little more detail. But you could just cheat and look at all the great examples available in the PloneWorkflow's project in the collective (http://sf.net/projects/collective), or even the ones contained in Plone. For example:

```
def sample(id):
    """ Sample workflow """
    ob = DCWorkflowDefinition(id)
    ob.states.addState('private')
    ob.states.addState('public')
    # add transitions
    return ob
```

Finally, register the workflow in the system, like so:

```
addWorkflowFactory(sample,
                   id='sample_workflow',
                   title='Sample workflow')
```

This script will need to be as part of a product installation. Chapter 12 covers writing and installing products.

Now, of course, a shortcut is available, which is called DCWorkflowDump. This will take the code from the ZMI and dump it into a Python module for you. You can find the source code for DCWorkflowDump in the collective at http://sf.net/projects/collective, but you can also find a zip file of the code on the Plone book Web site at http://plone-book.agmweb.ca.

To install DCWorkflowDump, unzip the file and copy the directory called DCWorkflowDump into the Products directory of your Plone installation. To check that you're in the right directory, your Products directory should also contain a directory for DCWorkflow, among other things. Then restart your Plone instance.

Once you've restarted Plone, go to the particular workflow in the ZMI, and you'll notice a new tab called *dump*. Click that page to get the dump screen, and then click *Dump it!* to dump the workflow to the screen. This will take your workflow and format it in Python for you. Save that file to your product, and you now have a Python file you can manipulate. This product is a great tool because it allows you to create the workflow in the ZMI and then distribute and alter it through Python.

CHAPTER 9

Setting Up Security and Users

PLONE HAS A POWERFUL and fine-grained security model. It provides myriad options for security at all levels so each object can have custom security for a user, a role, a group, and so on.

To put this chapter in context, I'd like to share this interesting quote with you:

Security is hard.

—Jim Fulton, chief Zope architect

The security for Plone is so powerful and multifaceted that it can be quite hard to debug and manage. But perhaps no other part of a Plone site is as important as getting security right. A security breach in your site is probably the most serious blunder you can make, and for this reason, I cover Plone security quite comprehensively.

In this chapter I first cover all the user terminology and key interfaces with which your users will interact. Then I show how to add and edit users and groups through the Plone interface. I then step through the key tools and Application Programming Interfaces (APIs) that manage users and their security. Then I cover using Python tools to script changes to users and their properties. Finally, I cover server security and expand user authentication, providing a detailed example on how to incorporate users from a Lightweight Directory Access Protocol (LDAP) server.

Administering Users

One of the most common tasks you'll need to do as an administrator of a Plone site is to deal with the members of your site. Administration usually involves recovering passwords and changing member settings. You can perform quite a few simple tasks through the Web, but of course the best friend to any administrator is a scripting language such as Python to make changes en masse. If you have a large number of users, the "Scripting Users" section later in this chapter will be of particular interest to you.

Users, Roles, and Groups

Some of the key concepts in Plone are users, roles, and groups. Before I show you how to edit these, I'll cover in more detail exactly what these are.

Users

Each person visiting a Plone site is referred to as a *user*. The user may or may not be authenticated by Plone, and users who are not authenticated are called *anonymous users*. Users who are authenticated are logged into an existing user account. If they don't have an account, then usually they can create their own account.

Anonymous users are the *lowest* level of users in that they usually have the most restrictions. Once users log in, they gain the roles their accounts give them. A user is identified by a short identifier, for example, andym. By default, no users are created for you in Plone, except for the one added to Zope by the installer to give you administrator access. The name of that user is whatever you set up in the installer, usually admin.

Roles

A Plone site has a series of roles; a *role* is a logical categorization of users. Instead of setting every user's permissions individually, each role is assigned permissions individually. Every user can be assigned zero to many roles; for example, a user can be a member and a manager. Each role is identified by a simple name, for example: Member.

A Plone site has five predefined roles, split into two groups: assignable roles and not-assignable roles. Assignable roles are roles you can give to users so that when they log in, they have this role. Not-assignable roles are roles you don't grant specifically to a user but that occur within a Plone site. For example, you don't assign the anonymous role to a user.

The following are the not-assignable roles:

Anonymous: This is a user who hasn't logged into the site. This could be a user who has no account or one who has merely not logged in yet.

Authenticated: This role refers to any user who is logged into the site, whatever their role. By definition a user is either anonymous or authenticated; the two are mutually exclusive. Because the authenticated user doesn't provide much in the way of granularity, it isn't recommended for most applications.

The following are the assignable roles:

Owner: This is a special role given to users when they create an object. It applies to a user for that object only; the information is stored on the object. You don't normally explicitly assign someone as an owner. Plone does that for you.

Members: This the default role for a user who has joined your site. Anyone who joins using the *join* button in the Plone interface has this role.

Reviewer: This is a user with more permissions than a member but less than a manager. Reviewers are users who can edit or review content entered by a member; they can't change the site's configuration or alter a user account.

Manager: Managers can do almost anything to a Plone site, so you should give this role only to trusted developers and administrators. A manager can delete or edit content, remove users, alter a site's configuration, and even delete your Plone site.

Groups

Groups are a different concept from roles. Roles imply that a user has different permissions from someone with a different role, but a *group* is a logical categorization of users. For example, the marketing department may be one group, and the engineering department may be another group. Each user can belong to zero to many groups. Groups are optional; you don't need to use them, but the Plone team found them useful enough to integrate them.

Site developers can use the groups in anyway they choose, such as to group a department or a certain class of users. For most users using Plone for the first time, I recommend leaving groups unchanged; by default no groups are created for you.

NOTE You implement groups using Group User Folder (GRUF). The groups aren't part of Zope but are an extra tool for Plone. GRUF was developed and contributed by Ingeniweb.

Sharing Tab

When I discussed publishing documents in Chapter 3, I skipped past the Sharing tab because it's a more advanced feature you may not always want to use. The Sharing tab is an action in portal_actions, so if you don't want it to appear, go to that tool in the Zope Management Interface (ZMI) and uncheck the *visible* option. However, the Sharing tab is quite useful because it lets you give different local roles on an object in Plone to users or groups.

If you've got a piece of content you've added to a Plone site and you want another person to be able to edit it, then you need to give them more permissions for that one object. This is called a *local role*, and it allows you to give a user expanded rights on an item. If I write a document in Plone, I become the owner of that document and gain certain rights. If I wanted to collaborate on this document with my colleague Ralph, prior to publishing, then I need to give Ralph more permissions so he can edit that document. To do this, I go to the Sharing tab and give Ralph more permissions.

 NOTE　You can assign local roles on a folder or document basis. If you give users a local role on a folder, then they get that local role for every object in that folder.

The Sharing tab appears only in places where you have the rights to alter sharing—your folder being one such place. Click *my folder*, and then click *sharing*. Figure 9-1 shows the form for the Sharing tab. It has three main components; you can assign a user to have a local role on this object, you can assign a group to have a local role on this object, and you can see who has certain roles already.

To find a user to assign a role to, enter a search term (such as *Gavin*), which opens a list of users that match your search criteria; you can then click the user and select the role from the drop-down list. For example, in Figure 9-2, I'm giving Gavin the owner role on this folder.

contents | view | sharing | properties
add new item ▼ | state: visible ▼

Assign local roles to folder Chapters

A local role is a way of allowing other users into some or all of your folders. These users can edit items, publish them - et cetera, depending on what permissions you give them.

Local roles are ideal in cooperation projects, and as every item has a history and an undo option, it's easy to keep track of the changes.

To give a person a local role in this folder, just search for the person's name or email address in the form below, and you will be presented with a page that will show you the options available.

Search Terms
Search by

| User Name ▾ |

Search Term

| |

| ⋗   perform search |

View groups

Groups are a convenient way to assign roles to a common set of users.

| ⋗   view groups |

Currently assigned local roles in folder Chapters

These users currently have local roles assigned in this folder:

Assigned Roles Chapters

| ⋗   delete selected role(s) |

Figure 9-1. Accessing the Sharing tab

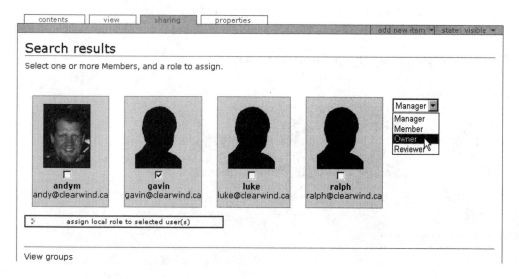

contents | view | sharing | properties
add new item ▼ | state: visible ▼

Search results

Select one or more Members, and a role to assign.

Manager ▾

Manager
Member
Owner
Reviewer

☐   ☑   ☐   ☐
andym   **gavin**   **luke**   **ralph**
andy@clearwind.ca gavin@clearwind.ca luke@clearwind.ca ralph@clearwind.ca

| ⋗   assign local role to selected user(s) |

View groups

Figure 9-2. Assigning a role to a user

In my earlier example, I wanted to assign rights to an individual user, but that can be annoying with large numbers of users...unless you've assigned them to groups. If I wanted to allow the whole marketing team to edit my document, I could do so. To get the groups available, just click *View groups*, which opens a list of groups for this site, and you can assign a local role to a group. In Figure 9-3 I'm giving Development the owner role on this folder.

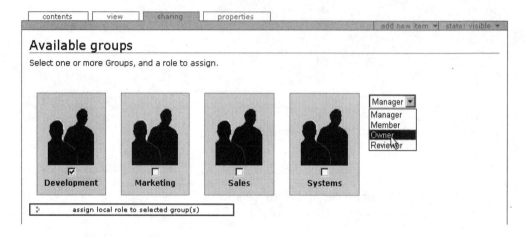

Figure 9-3. Assigning a role to a group

Finally, in Figure 9-4, you can see which users and groups have the roles for this page and then remove them if you want. Once you've given someone else local roles on an object, you allow them to access the Sharing tab. Then nothing is stopping them from removing roles for you from the content.

Figure 9-4. Viewing and removing roles

Administering Through the Web

Using the Plone interface you can easily modify the user who is assigned to certain groups, alter user information, add groups, and so on. You can do most of this through the Plone control panel; just click *plone setup* and then select Users and Groups Administration. You'll see two tabs: Users and Groups.

Click the Users tab to access the list of users in the system. The form is rather self-explanatory: You can remove a user, reset a password (resetting the password sends the user an e-mail anyway), or change an e-mail all from this form, as shown in Figure 9-5.

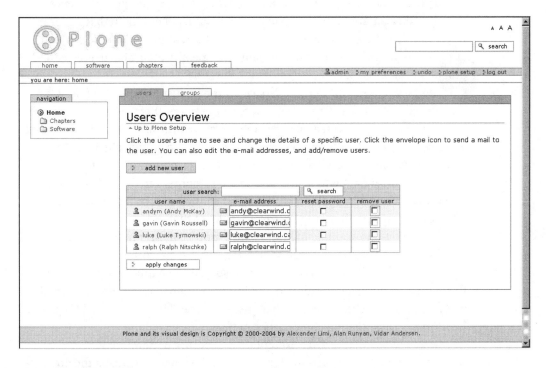

Figure 9-5. Editing users

By clicking a user, you can access the preferences form for that user, make any changes, and then click Save. To add a new user, click *add new user*. This opens the form to register the user and allows you to edit the data for that user. Because the number of users in a site can become quite large, the data will be batched in the familiar Plone manner. You can enter a search string, which will search through all the users to find matching names and e-mail addresses.

You can add, edit, and remove groups by clicking the Groups tab. To add a group, click the Add New Group button. This opens a form for a group; the only required field is Title, which should be a short, descriptive name for the group; usually a group is directly related to a business or site activity.

Now that you've added a group and have some users, you can match users and groups. Again, you can do this using the Plone control panel. You can either click a user and give that user some groups or click a group and put users into that group.

When to Use Groups?

Using groups is optional, and you may not ever choose to use them. One strong use of groups, however, is to make a *workspace*. In a basic Plone site, users can add and edit content in their own folder; each item of content in that folder is thus owned by the person who created it. But this really doesn't scale too well; after all, the whole point is that you want a few people to be able to edit a document and share it, of course!

This is where groups and workspaces come in. Just like there's a folder for members that contains all the user folders for members, there's also a folder called GroupWorkspaces. This is created by default whenever a group is added, and in that folder is another folder for each group. So, if you add a group called *Marketing*, you'll be able to find a folder at GroupWorkspaces/Marketing. Any user in the Marketing group will have the right to add, edit, and delete content in the Marketing workspace; in other words, you now have a folder for that group. This is the same as adding a group and then assigning a local role for that group to that folder.

This is just one example of how useful a group can be; another is using groups in workflow. In the previous chapter I discussed workflow and how you can send an e-mail to certain people when something happens. If a member of the Marketing group added an item, for instance, then you can send an e-mail to all the users of that group, rather than just everyone. The "Calculating the Other Users in a Group" section shows how you to do this.

On the Plone Web site, for example, the users are in development groups that are responsible for parts of Plone, such as the release team and the documentation team.

Administering Groups

You can administer groups in two ways from the Plone control panel. You can either go to a user and click the groups for that user or go to a group and click the users for that group. Either way you can easily add and remove the groups for a user. To add a user to a group, however, go to the user search page and click a user; then click the Groups tab, which will show the groups for that user. For example, Figure 9-6 shows the groups for the user andym.

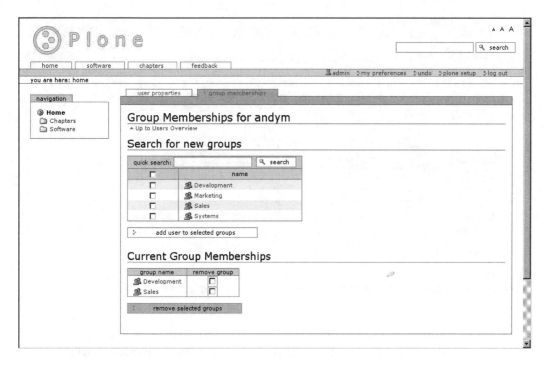

Figure 9-6. Groups for this user

To add the user to a new group, select the checkbox for the group and then click *add user to selected groups.*

Likewise, you can remove a user from a group by checking the box next to the group and then clicking *remove selected groups.* You'll see a similar interface for group management if you click *plone setup,* select User and Groups Administration, and click *groups.* Click a group, and then click *group members;* you'll get a list of the members in that group, and you can add and remove members from there.

Giving Groups Roles

So you've seen that users can have roles but also that groups can have roles. This may seem a little odd to you, but think, for example, of a group of supervisors that needs to be able to do anything to the content added by one of their staff members. To do this in a site, they'll need to have the reviewer role. To set up a group of supervisors, click *plone setup,* select User and Groups Administration, click *groups,* and then click *add new group.* Give that group the name **Supervisor** and complete the form. On the next form, you get a list of the groups and the roles assigned to them. To assign the reviewer role to this group, select the checkboxes that correspond to the reviewer role for that group, as shown in Figure 9-7.

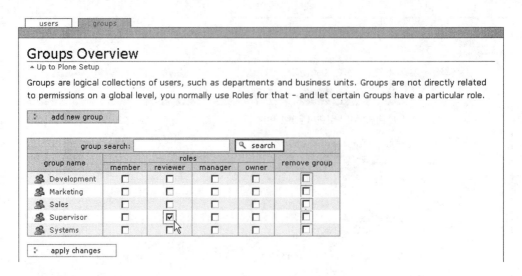

Figure 9-7. Setting up reviewer role for the Supervisor group

You've made it easy to give out the reviewer role to users, and you can now manage and administer the reviewers through the Plone interface. Furthermore, it's easy to programmatically calculate the reviewers because you can examine the group and get a list of its members.

The idea of groups having roles is actually a minor paradigm shift from standard Zope development, since in that scenario you're used to individual users being assigned roles. You can still do that in Plone, of course, but assigning roles to a group is easy in Plone.

NOTE By definition, when the permission for a user on an object is calculated, a few factors are taken into account. First, the roles assigned to a user are calculated. Second, the roles a user gets from its groups are calculated. This gives a total set of roles that a user may have.

User Registration Tools

Before users are members of your site, they must register with your site. Users can register themselves quite easily by clicking the *join* link in the top-right corner of a Plone site. I covered this in detail at the beginning of Chapter 3, where I showed you how users can join and register for a site. The registration process for users is actually pretty straightforward, but quite a few options are available. This process is controlled by three key tools: `portal_registration`, `portal_memberdata`, and `portal_membership`. The following sections present these three tools now.

Portal Registration

The portal_registration tool is an action provider and provides one key action in Plone: joining. Clicking this link will open the join form. By default, any user (anonymous included) that hasn't already logged in can click this link to join.

When users register using the join form, they'll get two simple options for a Plone site: to either validate e-mail or not validate it. The only true way to validate an e-mail address is to send an e-mail to the address and see if an appropriate response is returned. By default, e-mail validation is turned off; that is, when a user registers, by default they provide their name, e-mail, and password in Plone. They can then log in and use the site as usual. This is the form you've seen in Chapter 3. If e-mail validation is turned on, however, then users can give only a name, username, and e-mail, as shown in Figure 9-8.

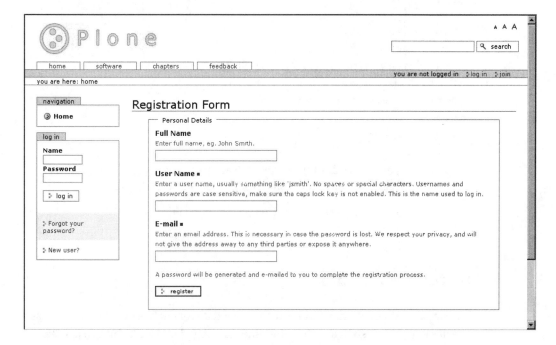

Figure 9-8. Registering a user with e-mail validation turned on

After clicking the link in the e-mail, they'll then be taken to a login screen, and the registration process can continue as normal.

To enable validation in the Plone interface, click *plone setup* and select Portal Settings. Under Password Policy, select *Generate and e-mail members' initial password*, and click Save to commit the changes.

If you'd like to view or edit the e-mail users get, then you can edit the page template that generates it. You can find the template by clicking *plone_skins*, clicking *plone_templates*, and then clicking *registered_notify_template*.

Adding an Action for Users

If you want to add any other actions for users, before they join, this is the best place to add them. For example, if you wanted to add a page that outlined a privacy policy, this could be a good place. To do this, first add the page and all the information you want to contain in that policy. It would make sense to make the ID of the page something useful, such as privacy.html, and put it in the root of your Plone site.

In the ZMI, go to portal_registration and add a new action with the following information:

```
Name: Privacy
Id: privacy
Action: string: ${portal_url}/privacy.html
Condition: not: member
Permission: Add portal member
Category: user
Visible: selected
```

You'll now get the privacy link to your privacy page if you aren't logged in. By making the category user, you'll ensure it appears in the personal bar.

Portal Member Data

The portal_memberdata tool holds the member data for each user. A Plone user has a series of options, such as skins, the time last logged in, What You See Is What You Get (WYSIWYG) editor, and so on. When a user joins a site, a default record in portal_memberdata is created. You set the actual properties created in that record in this tool; click *portal_memberdata*, and select Properties to see the default set of properties. In Plone these are the following:

- **e-mail**: This is the user's e-mail address.

- **portal_skin**: This is deprecated; ignore this property.

- **listed**: Show this user in the Members directory (Boolean). By default this is enabled.

- **login_time**: This is the date the user logged in for this session.

- **last_login_time**: This is the date of the last time the user logged in.

- **fullname**: This is a user's full name.

- **error_log_update**: This is used by the error log form; ignore this property.

- **formtooltips**: In old versions of Plone, there were options for displaying form help. This is now no longer relevant, so ignore it.

- **visible_ids**: This shows the IDs (or names) for objects. By enabling this, the first field on the edit form for each content type is Name, and by changing this users can rename objects. By default this is enabled.

- **wysiwyg_editor**: This is the editor to use in forms.

You can add or remove items from this list using the Zope interface. However, adding or removing elements from here doesn't automatically make the user interface form that users actually edit. In Chapter 3 you saw that by clicking *my preferences*, users can access and alter most of these properties. If you want to alter these preferences, then you'll have to customize that form. The values given for these fields are the default values for a newly registered user; for example, by default all members are listed in the Members tab, unless users explicitly decide otherwise.

So, for example, if you wanted all members not to be listed on the search by default, then you need to change the setting in this form. In the portal_memberdata form, find the *listed* property and uncheck the value in the form. Then click Save Changes, and all new users will no longer be selected.

The portal_groupdata tool contains the corresponding data for groups. The default properties for a group are as follows:

- **title**: A title for the group

- **description**: A description for the group

- **email**: An e-mail address

- **listed**: Whether to list the group to users

These tools store the user and group data on these tools and not in the main acl_users folder. If you want to move user information between Plone servers, then you'll need to move these tools as well; just moving the acl_users folder isn't enough. You can do this by importing and exporting these tools; however, before you import into the new Plone site, you must delete the existing tool, or an error will be raised.

Portal Membership

The portal_membership tool handles a few more properties; specifically, it matches the member data with the members. Accessing portal_membership from the ZMI gives a large number of options; the following are the most important:

- **Set members folder**: This is the folder to put member folders into. This folder must exist. By default this is Member.

- **Control creation of member areas**: By default, a member area for each user is created when joining. That creation is optional, however. Uncheck *Turn folder creation off* to disable this. The default is that it's on.

Under the Actions tab you'll find a whole series of actions that relate to users when they're logged in, such *my favorites*, *my preferences*, and so on. These all have the category user so that the actions will appear in the top-right corner.

The portal_groups tool provides similar tools to portal_membership, but for groups. Likewise, when a group is created, a group workspace is created where all members of that group can add and edit content.

Useful APIs

The portal_membership tool has one of most commonly used set of API functions. Often you'll want to find out key information such as the currently logged in user, whether the user is anonymous, and so on. The portal_membership tool provides you with these methods; the following are some of the most important:

- **isAnonymousUser()**: This returns true if the user is anonymous.

- **getAuthenticatedMember()**: This returns the currently logged-in user wrapped with portal_metadata properties. If no user is logged in, it returns a special nobody user with null mappings for portal_metadata properties.

- **listMemberIds()**: This returns the IDs for all the users.

- **listMembers()**: This returns all the user objects.

- **getMemberById(id)**: This returns the user object for a given ID.

- **getHomeFolder(id=None)**: This returns the home folder for a given ID. The ID is optional and if not provided gives the current member's home folder.

- **getHomeUrl(id=None)**: This returns a URL to the member's home folder. The ID is optional and if not provided gives the current members home folder's URL.

The user returned by these functions is "wrapped" in the data from the portal_memberdata tool so that the properties are attributes of the user object. So, for example, the following is a little Script (Python) object to get the e-mail address for the user Bob:

```
##parameters=
u = context.portal_membership.getMemberById("Bob")
return u.email
```

Cookie Authentication

By default Plone uses cookie authentication for its users, meaning that users must have cookies turned on in their browser to log in. This authentication is provided in a Plone site by the cookie_authentication object, which contains the necessary functionality for users to log in. If you really want to use Hypertext Transfer Protocol (HTTP) authentication, then you can simply remove this object; however, I really don't recommend it, because HTTP authentication isn't good for most sites.

This object provides the following items that you can edit from the ZMI:

- **Authentication cookie name**: This is the name of the cookie that will be used to persist user authentication. It does this by persisting a token for the user, which preserves a user's login. The default is __ac.

- **User name form variable**: This is the name of the variable in the login form that will contain the username. The default is __ac_name.

- **User password form variable**: This is the name of the variable in the login form that will contain the password. The default is __ac_password.

- **User name persistence form variable**: This is the name of the variable in the login form that will contain the persistence token. The default is `__ac_persistent`.

- **Login page ID**: If a user needs to log in, this is the page that they will be sent to in order to complete the login. The default is `require_login`.

- **Logout page ID**: If a user is to be logged out, then they will be sent to a nice page with a message. The page is this ID. The default is `logged_out`.

- **Failed authorization page ID**: When the authorization fails, this is the page that will show. By default, this is blank, as Plone does something different.

- **Use cookie paths to limit scope**: This sets the cookie to be local to the current folder and all folders below this. Leave this at the default of blank so that you'll authenticate for the entire site, regardless of where you actually click *login*.

To change the cookie that's being used, rather than the default, just change the value in this form and click Save. However, let me warn you that if you change the name of the cookie, all the existing cookies on your users' computers will be ignored, and they'll all have to log in again. If you wanted a different login page, then you could either customize the `require_login` page template or change the value of that variable.

The Actual User Folder

You can get access to the actual user folder for a Plone site by clicking the `acl_users` folder in the ZMI. This opens the Group User Folder (GRUF) interface, which gives you a variety of options.

The GRUF interface is actually quite similar to the user options you have through the Plone control panel. You can add and edit users and groups through a pretty straightforward interface. Clicking Users and Groups will allow you to edit these items. If you click the Contents tab, you'll get a choice of users or groups; click Users and then click *acl_users*. Finally you'll get to the actual user folder for a user. This looks like the standard user folder. You'll see a list of users, and to edit a user, you just click the username, as shown in Figure 9-9.

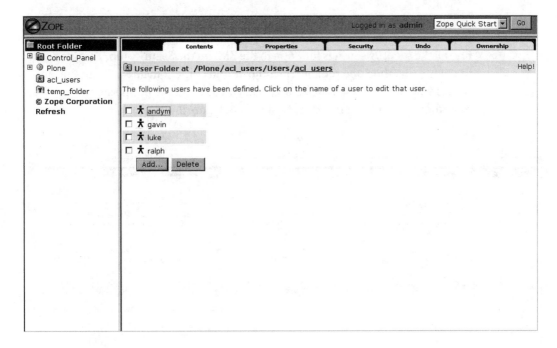

Figure 9-9. Editing the user record

From here you can alter a user's password or the roles. You'll note that at this point the group Management is actually represented as a role to ensure that no name collisions occur. The name is mangled to be group_Management. If you wanted to make this user a member of this group, then you could do so here. There isn't much you can do here, though, that you can't do at the highest level, so I wouldn't go down to this level unless you have to do something such as change the password or set a domain.

Setting Permissions

I've now covered users, roles, and groups with you, but there's more; the lowest level of settings for security is a permission. As the name suggests, giving a user a *permission* means giving them the ability to do something, such as view an object, add a document, get a listing of the contents of a folder, and so on. Each permission is identified uniquely by a meaningful name such as *View*, *Add portal content*, or *List folder contents*.

Permissions aren't applied to an individual user, but to a role. Each role gains particular permissions, and then the user gains those particular roles. You can find all the security settings for Zope in the ZMI on the Security tab. This includes the Plone site, the Zope root, all the objects and content inside a Plone site, and the skins. When clicking the Security tab, you'll see all the permissions and the roles that map to them in a grid, as shown in Figure 9-10.

| Contents | View | Properties | Security | Undo | Ownership | Find | Workflows |

Plone Site at /Plone   Help!

The listing below shows the current security settings for this item. Permissions are rows and roles are columns. Checkboxes are used to indicate where roles are assigned permissions. You can also assign **local roles** to users, which give users extra roles in the context of this object and its subobjects.

When a role is assigned to a permission, users with the given role will be able to perform tasks associated with the permission on this item. When the *Acquire permission settings* checkbox is selected then the containing objects's permission settings are used. Note: the acquired permission settings may be augmented by selecting Roles for a permission in addition to selecting to acquire permissions.

Acquire permission settings?	Permission	Roles					
		Anonymous	Authenticated	Manager	Member	Owner	Reviewer
☑	Access Transient Objects	☐	☐	☐	☐	☐	☐
☑	Access arbitrary user session data	☐	☐	☐	☐	☐	☐
☑	Access contents information	☐	☐	☐	☐	☐	☐
☑	Access future portal content	☐	☐	☑	☐	☐	☑
☑	Access inactive portal content	☐	☐	☐	☐	☐	☐
☑	Access session data	☐	☐	☐	☐	☐	☐
☑	Add Accelerated HTTP Cache Managers	☐	☐	☐	☐	☐	☐
☑	Add Archetypes Tools	☐	☐	☐	☐	☐	☐
☑	Add BTreeFolder2s	☐	☐	☐	☐	☐	☐
☑	Add Browser Id Manager	☐	☐	☐	☐	☐	☐
Acquire?		Anonymous	Authenticated	Manager	Member	Owner	Reviewer
☑	Add CMF Action Icons Tools	☐	☐	☐	☐	☐	☐
☑	Add CMF Caching Policy Managers	☐	☐	☐	☐	☐	☐

Figure 9-10. Security settings

In Figure 9-10 you can see that this object has a series of security settings. This is displayed as a grid of checkboxes; on the left are the permissions in alphabetical order, and across the top are the roles again in alphabetical order. This page is rather large and cumbersome, so there are two useful shortcuts. Click the permission to get all the roles for that permission; for example, Figure 9-11 shows the settings for the *Access future portal content* permission.

And you can click a role to get all the settings for that role, which is much easier than a long list, as shown in Figure 9-12.

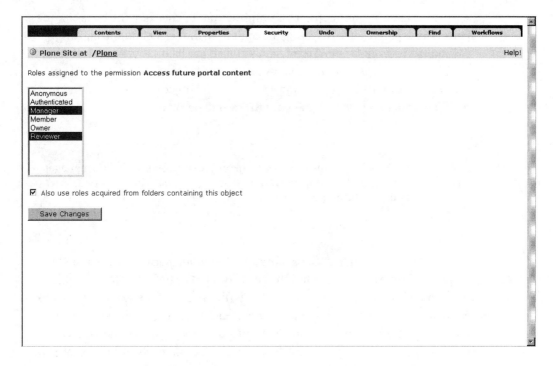

Figure 9-11. Settings for a permission

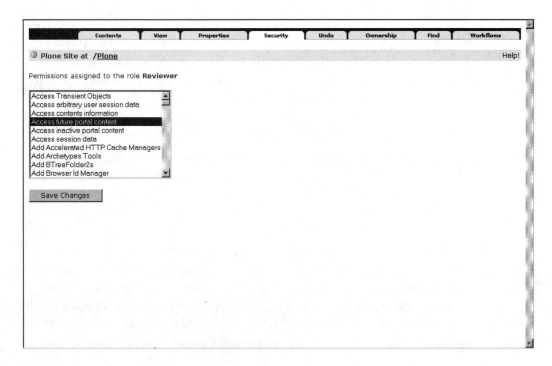

Figure 9-12. Settings for the reviewer role

For all these permissions, it's a simple matter of checking the boxes for the permissions you want or selecting the options in the select box and clicking Save Changes. When the Acquire Permission setting is checked, security settings for this permission will be acquired; when it's unchecked, permissions will not acquired. *Acquisition* is the ability of an object to search the object hierarchy to find permissions and then combine them for the overall permission.

NOTE The permissions page will turn on the security for the manager user for you; locking out your manager user would be really bad, so it's good for this to be on by default.

Now take a look at the *Access contents information* permission. In the ZMI, go to the root Plone object and click the Security tab. The default setting for this permission is that no roles are enabled; that is, the settings for each user are blank. However, the Acquire Settings option is checked, meaning you have to look in the parent objects in the hierarchy to determine this object's permissions. Go now to the root Zope folder, and click the *Security* tab. This opens the list of permissions for the root folder, and sure enough there are some settings for the *Access contents information* permission in this folder; namely, the anonymous and manager roles have this permission.

Since permissions are acquired, all subfolders will also acquire these permission settings. This means the Plone site and every object in the Plone site will have these permissions. Therefore, if you want to set a security permission for the whole site, all you have to do is configure the permission in the root Plone, and most of objects will acquire those permissions.

NOTE The exception is workflowed objects, which specifically turn off acquisition. This is covered in the "Security and Workflow" section later in this chapter.

You can set permissions on any object in Zope through the ZMI. This may be the Zope root, a Plone site, a folder such as the Members folder, or even a piece of content. Each object has it own set of permissions, but not all objects have the same choice of permissions. For example, the Add... permission is provided on all folders. But since these permissions don't make sense to a nonfolderish object (by definition, an object must be a folder to have items added to it), they aren't present.

Any product or piece of Python code in your Zope site can define its own security permission, so it can be a little difficult to define exactly what a permission lets you do. Table 9-1 describes some of the key permissions and what they do.

Table 9-1. Common Plone Permissions

Permission	Description
Access contents information	This permission allows access to an object, without necessarily viewing the object. For example, a user may want to see the object's title in a list of results, even though the user can't view the contents of that file.
Add...	There are numerous add permissions, each relating to the type of object a user may like to add. For a normal Plone site, all the permissions are grouped together as *Add portal content*.
Add portal member	This gives the ability to join a Plone site and get a user account.
Copy or Move	This gives the right to copy or move an object. Although users may have this right, they still need to have the permission to paste the object into a destination.
Delete objects	This gives the right to delete an object. In standard Zope, this permission is checked on the folder; in Plone this check is made on each object.
List folder contents	This gets a list of the contents of a folder; this doesn't check if you have right to view the actual object listed.
List portal members	This gives the right to see a list of members in the site and search through the members.
Modify portal content	This is a catch-all permission for any changes to an object, such as changing the content, its keywords, or other properties. This permission applies to nearly all objects.
Set own password	This gives the right to change your password in a Plone site.
Set own properties	This gives the right to change your properties in a Plone site.
View	This allows a user to view the object in question. *View* doesn't just mean only HTML views but also File Transfer Protocol (FTP), WebDAV, and other forms of access.

Adding a Role

Placing users in roles means you have to find a compatible set of permissions for each role so that grouping the permissions makes sense. This isn't always possible. Sometimes a certain user may need something different from similar users.

However, from a development point of view, the fewer and simpler you can keep the roles, the easier it will be. It's not too complicated, but an initial urge to create a role for every conceivable security option is a really bad idea. You'll get yourself into a total mess quickly. Instead I urge you to leave the number of roles sparse and keep them generic to the entire site.

To add a role, go to the root Plone folder, click the Security tab, and scroll down to the bottom (it's a long way). At the bottom is a simple form to add more roles or remove a role. Add the name of the new role, and click Add Role.

Performing Common Tasks

You can set some security options quickly and easily to perform regular tasks. Before you make a lot of security settings changes, however, I urge you to back up your Plone site. I show you how to do this in Chapter 14.

Stopping Users from Joining Your Site

To stop users from joining your site, you set the Add portal member permission in the root of your Zope for anonymous users. You can either deselect this for anonymous users there or go to your Plone site and turn off the Acquire Permission setting.

Stopping Users from Searching Your Site

To stop users from searching your site, you set the *Search ZCatalog* permission to anonymous users in the root of a Plone site. So, change the permission there by deselecting Anonymous or any other user.

Stopping Anonymous Users from Accessing Your Site Altogether

Ah, well, stopping anonymous users from accessing your site is a little tricky because it's quite complicated to remove anonymous access to your site completely; users still need to be able to access your site to be able to log in! What you really want, in this situation, is to be able to restrict access to your content. You can do this by restricting the permissions on your workflow.

Security and Workflow

As I pointed out in Chapter 7, workflow manages the security of each object in the workflow. It does this by changing the actual permissions on an object. I've just shown you how to view the security settings for each object, so you can now see how the security settings for objects in one state can be different from the security settings of an object in another state. If you click *portal_workflow*, select the Contents tab, click *plone_workflow*, and then select the States tab, you'll see all the states available. Click a state, and then select Permissions, and you'll see the permissions for that state, as shown in Figure 9-13.

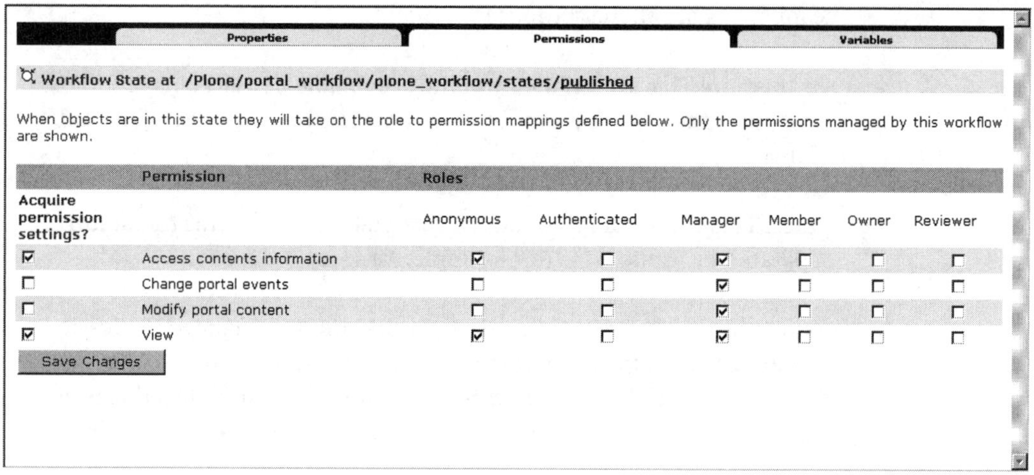

Properties	Permissions	Variables

Workflow State at /Plone/portal_workflow/plone_workflow/states/**published**

When objects are in this state they will take on the role to permission mappings defined below. Only the permissions managed by this workflow are shown.

Acquire permission settings?	Permission	Roles					
		Anonymous	Authenticated	Manager	Member	Owner	Reviewer
☑	Access contents information	☑	☐	☑	☐	☐	☐
☐	Change portal events	☐	☐	☑	☐	☐	☐
☐	Modify portal content	☐	☐	☑	☐	☐	☐
☑	View	☑	☐	☑	☐	☐	☐

Save Changes

Figure 9-13. The permissions for the published state

As you can see, when an object is moved into the published state, anonymous users will be allowed the *Access contents information* and *View* permissions. This means people can view the content. You'll note that members or owners can't edit their own content because they don't have that permission. The permissions applied by workflow are set on the Permissions tab, where you can set all the permissions that will be managed by the workflow.

After you've changed the security settings, you need to go to the plone_workflow tool and click *Update security settings*; otherwise, the object's security and the workflow will be different.

NOTE   Because the permissions change when the object is transitioned, any other permission changes to the object you may make through the ZMI are removed if (and only if) those permissions are managed by the workflow. For this reason, you should always resist the urge to make minor tweaks to the security of content types in the ZMI; stick to changing the Plone site object and the workflow.

Guards

All the transitions have a guard on them that lets the administrator select the permissions allowed before a user can perform the transition. When checking if a user can perform the transition, it will check in the following order: check the permissions, check the roles, and then check the expression. If any of these checks pass, then the transition will be run.

The following are all the settings for a guard:

- **Permission**: This is a list of any of the acceptable permissions separated by semicolons (;)—for example, `Review portal content; Modify portal content`.

- **Roles**: This is a list of roles that are acceptable roles for this transition separated by semicolons (for example, `Manager; Reviewer`).

- **Expression**: This is a workflow Template Attribute Language Expression Syntax (TALES) expression that will let you come up with a custom condition. For example, the following transition will occur only if this is in folder called `Members`; it's not really a permission, but it's a neat trick:

```
python: if 'Members' in state_object.getPhysicalPath()
```

NOTE   `getPhysicalPath` is a method of all objects in Zope that returns the location inside the Zope object hierarchy, ignoring any virtual hosting that may occur.

Proxy Roles

In the previous chapter I disscused some neat methods of notifying users and moving content around when content is workflowed. When this happens, the script is executed as the user performs the workflow transaction. In this case, your script may do something your user may or may not have the right to do. For example, you may not want to allow a user to add anything to a folder called public, except for workflow. This is a problem; you need to ensure the script can be executed with a higher role.

A *proxy role* is something your users won't interact with or know about, but it's a method for you to get around this problem. For example, say you want a user to be able to pick a user from all the other users in a site. You don't want to give the user the right to view all users, just list the users in this particular context. To execute the script, a user will need the *List portal members* permission to be able to get a list of members, but you don't want to give this to anonymous users.

The script that executes that command will need to be given a higher proxy role, probably Member. To do this, go to the script in the ZMI, click the Proxy tab, and click Member. If this script is based on the file system, then this information can be added in the metadata file. For example, the .metadata file would have the following line: proxy = Member. Now this script would be executed as a member, solving your security problem!

Scripting Users

So, you've got a whole bunch of users in your Plone site.now you'll need some scripts on that site to aid in the administration of the users. After a few hundred users, it can be really hard to make changes through the Web, so the following sections give a few example scripts that perform some important tasks.

Registering Users in Bulk

If you have a large number of users to register, then you need a script to import them. These users could be from any system you're upgrading to Plone. However, if you already have users in an external source such as LDAP, a relational database, or other source, you could integrate directly with that source.

For now, take a bunch of users in a comma-separated file, with the following content: username, full name, e-mail, and groups. In this example, you'll run through that list, add each user with those settings, and then change their properties so that they will have the correct settings. The .csv file will therefore look something like the following:

```
"User Name", "Full Name", "Email", "Groups"
"Andy", "Andy Mckay", "andy@enfoldsystems.com", "Systems,Sales,Development"
...
```

A `.csv` file is a file of comma-separated values, and it can be created and edited in most spreadsheet programs, such as Microsoft Excel or OpenOffice.org. You can then export the file as a comma-separated file and finally import it into Plone. Because this requires lots of methods that are restricted, you'll need to make this an external method:

```
# An external method to import user
import csv

# the full path to your csv file
fileName = "/var/zope.zeo/Extensions/test.csv"

def importUsers(self):
    reader = csv.reader(open(fileName, "r"))
    pr = self.portal_registration
    pg = self.portal_groups
    out = []

    # if your csv file contains a header line that
    # explains the contents of each column
    ignoreLine = 1
```

This is just the setup code; in other words, it sets up all the variables you'll use in this script. At the beginning, you import the `csv` module, which is a module that ships with Python 2.3 and provides fast parsing of `.csv` files. The `.csv` file is in the variable `fileName`, which is a full path to the file; if you make it a relative path, Plone may end up looking in the wrong place. As you saw earlier, `self` is passed to the method, and from that you can get to the two tools needed: `portal_registration` to provide access to the registration API and `portal_groups` to provide access to the groups API:

```
for row in reader:
    if ignoreLine:
        ignoreLine = 0
        continue

    # check we have exactly 4 items
    assert len(row) == 4
    id, name, email, groups = row
        groups = groups.split(',')

    # make a password
    password = pr.generatePassword()
```

Next you loop through each row and get the ID, name, e-mail, and groups. Then you make a random password by calling generatePassword. This generates a random six-character password composed of uppercase and lowercase characters and numbers. If you wanted to base the ID or password on provided information, such as the username or e-mail, then this is the opportunity to do that. In this case, I've entered each group in the same field, separated by a comma (for example, "Sales,Marketing"). Therefore, I need to split that into a list of individual names, like so:

```
try:
    # add in member
    pr.addMember(id = id,
        password = password,
        roles = ["Member",],
        properties = {
            'fullname': name,
            'username': id,
            'email': email,
            }
        )
    # groups are separated by commas
    for groupId in :
        group = pg.getGroupById(groupId)
        group.addMember(id)

    out.append("Added user %s" % id)

except ValueError, msg:
    # if we skipped this user for a reason, tell the person
    out.append("Skipped %s, reason: %s" % (id, msg))

# return something
return "\n".join(out)
```

Given that you now have all the user information you need to register the user, you can perform the actual registration. You do this by calling the addMember function, which is a function of portal_registration and which registers the user. A dictionary of key/value pairs, such as e-mail and name, is passed through to the function. Then, for each group you call getGroupById to get the group and call addMember on the group. As the name suggests, this will register the user with that group. When you're done, it's a matter of printing something out to the person running the import.

To run this on your site, you'll need to put this into the Extensions directory of your Plone server and call it import_users_with_groups.py. Then you'll need to manually add the groups that you'll have for your site; this script doesn't create the groups for you. Then prepare the .csv file; if you have your users stored in some other system, you'll need to find some way to get them into this format. Change the filename in the script to point to your filename. Next, add an external method to your Plone site, with the following values:

- **ID:** import_users_with_groups

- **Module name:** import_users_with_groups

- **Function name:** importUsers

Once you've added this external method, click Test to run the method, and you'll get the result!

Changing User Settings

If you install a new product or make a new setting, it can be necessary to change user metadata in bulk. For example, if you install a new WYSIWYG editor and want this to be default for every user, then two things need to occur:

- Change the default setting for every new user. To do this, click *portal_metadata* and select the Properties tab. Set the default there, and all new users will get this value.

- Alter the settings for every existing user, which can be done only with the following external method:

```
def fixUsers(self):
    pm = self.portal_membership
    members = pm.listMemberIds()

    out = []
    for member in members:
        # now get the actual member
        m = pm.getMemberById(member)
        # get the editor property for that member
        p = m.getProperty('wysiwyg_editor', None)
```

```
        out.append("%s %s" % (p, member))
        if p is not Noneand p != 'Epoz':
            m.setMemberProperties({'wysiwyg_editor', 'Epoz',})
            out.append("Changed property for %s" % member)
    return "\n".join(out)
```

Put this code in a Python module in the `Extensions` directory of your Plone instance. Call the module `fixUserScript.py`. Then in the ZMI, add an external method with the following parameters:

- **ID**: `fixUsers`

- **Module name**: `fixUserScript`

- **Function name**: `fixUsers`

Click the Test tab to run the code. It'll run through every member in your site and set the value for the WYSIWYG editor to `"Epoz"`. It does this by first getting a list of every member; there's a method on `portal_membership` called `listMemberIds` that does this for you. For each of the members, it examines the property used by Plone to determine the editor (in this case, the `wysiwyg_editor` property). If that property isn't `"Epoz"`, then it calls `setMemberProperties` to change it.

This is a useful way to loop through all your members. Then using the `setMemberProperties` and `getProperty` methods, you can examine or alter any of the member properties that a user may have.

Calculating the Other Users in a Group

I discussed earlier the possibility of sending an e-mail to all the people in a work-group for an object. You could add this to workflow, but first you need a script to do that. This example uses a couple of functions to get at the users. The following is the `getGroupUsers` script, which takes an object and returns a list of users:

```
##parameters=object=None
# object is the object to find all the members of the same group for
users = []
# get the creator
userName = object.Creator()
user = context.portal_membership.getMemberById(userName)
pg = context.portal_groups
```

```
# loop through the groups the user is in
for group in user.getGroups():
  group = getGroupById(group)

  # loop through the users in each of those groups
  for user in group.getGroupUsers():
    if user not in users and user != userName:
      users.append(user)
```

```
return users
```

In this script, you're given an object, so you need to find the creator of that object by calling the method Creator. Once you have that user, you can call getGroups, and a method of the user object lists all the names of all the groups a user is in. After that, you get each of those groups, and from that list you get the usernames for a group. So, finally, you have each username. Now for each of those users, you want only users who aren't duplicates or aren't the original person who made the change to the object. The user list will contain all the other users in the same groups as the person who owned the object.

You could plug this into your workflow e-mail notification script from Chapter 7 to enhance it. For example, for the workflow e-mail notification script, you may recall that you did the following:

```
for user in mship.listMembers():
    if "Reviewer" in mship.getMemberById(user.id).getRoles():
```

This loops through every user and checks if they have the membership role. The previous script was called getGroupUsers and placed in the portal_skins/custom folder. This means you can access it through the context namespace through acquisition; in short, context.getGroupUsers(object) will return you the users:

```
users = context.getGroupUsers(object)
for id in users:
    user = mship.getMemberById(id)
```

Now you're sending an e-mail to everyone in the group instead of all reviewers!

User Information in Page Templates

In Chapter 6, you made a page template that allowed a user to give feedback to the site administrator through a form. In that form, an input box allowed a user to type in an e-mail address, which you then validated. However, if a user is logged in and you know the e-mail address, then it'd be nice to fill it in automatically for the user.

The existing code for the input box is as follows:

```
<input type="text" name="email_address"
       tal:attributes="tabindex tabindex/next;
                       value request/email_address|nothing" />
```

Now, if a value for e-mail exists in the request from an earlier attempt at filling out the form, then you should show that. If not, then you can see if an e-mail address exists for the current user. The following changes to the form will ensure that the e-mail address is filled in:

```
<input type="text" name="email_address"
tal:define="user context/portal_membership/getAuthenticatedMember;
            email user/email|nothing"
       tal:attributes="tabindex tabindex/next;
                       value request/email_address|email|nothing" />
```

Debugging and Understanding Security

I've found that security is not only one of the hardest parts of Plone to understand, but it's one of the hardest to debug and test. Because the model is granular and complicated, it can be extremely difficult to find why and where an error occurs. Sometimes the error message or information given is hard to decipher or is hard to find any information about at all.

Testing security is also slightly harder because in sites with lots of roles, you should do a full regression test with each of those users in each of the situations. Because of the cost involved, though, people often don't do these full regression tests. Furthermore, having a bug in security is probably the worst thing that can occur on a site if it leaks confidential information. Plone will let you do whatever you want; it will happily let you shoot yourself in the foot, so be careful!

VerboseSecurity

VerboseSecurity is an add-on product included by default with the installers. You can also download VerboseSecurity from http://hathaway.freezope.org/Software/ VerboseSecurity. As the name suggests, it provides a detailed error message when you can't do something in Plone because you aren't authorized. If you have given too-lax security settings, this product won't help you, though.

VerboseSecurity can run on a Plone server without causing a performance hit, so you can happily run this on your production and development server. There might be a minor bit of extra overhead caused when someone isn't allowed to perform something and an error is raised and the new security modules kicks in.

However, since the error message is detailed, you won't want to expose this to users. It explains far more about your system than a user should ever know! It'll never reveal passwords—just information about the users, roles, and permissions. Of course, your production server will always be working perfectly, so there will be no need to install it on your production server.

The original implementation of the permission-checking routines were written in Python. As the API stabilized, and the developers realized the overhead that security caused, it was rewritten in C. By default, the faster C implementation is running, but this means that VerboseSecurity can't patch the permission module to be more verbose. I've rarely had to turn to this level of detail, though; usually I've found I can get enough information already. However, if you need more information, you'll need to run Plone with the following environment variable:

```
ZOPE_SECURITY_POLICY=PYTHON
```

To get VerboseSecurity to work, all you need to do is ensure that VerboseSecurity is in your Products directory (for more details on this, see Chapter 10) and then restart Plone. Go to the cookie_authentication object, which is the list of options for your site authentication, and in the form, change the option for login_page from require_login to empty, as shown in Figure 9-14.

Now you can go and re-create the circumstances for the error you'd like to debug. *Remember to log in as the user who got the error.* This is where it's handy to have two different browsers accessing your Plone site: one for administering, one for testing. When the error occurs, an HTTP authentication dialog will pop up on the screen. At that point, hit Cancel, and you should now get a detailed error message, such as that shown in Figure 9-15.

The message is rather long and self-explanatory. At this point I normally pop into the other browser and examine the permissions settings for the objects involved to see what the cause may be.

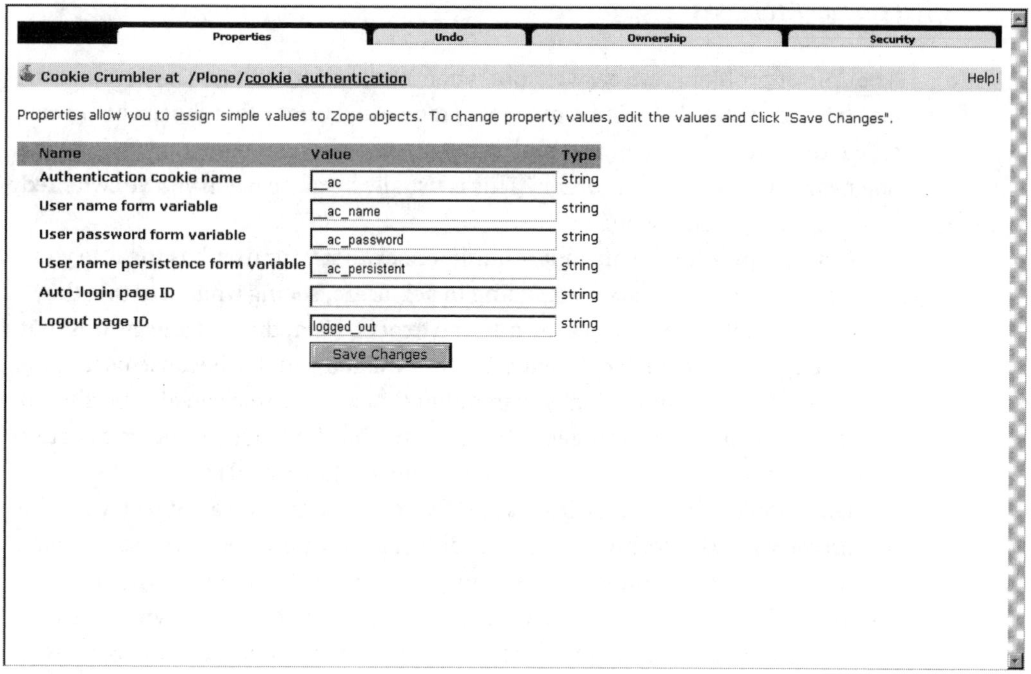

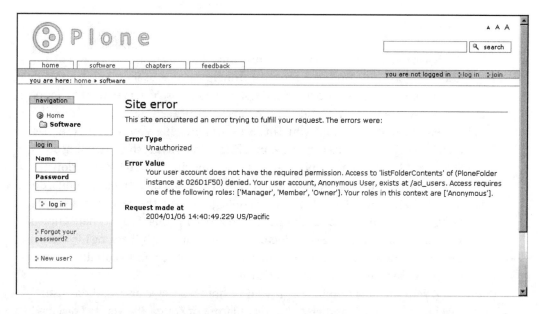

Figure 9-14. Changing the login settings for your site

Figure 9-15. A nice detailed error message

Common Problems

A couple of problems are easy to spot when dealing with Plone. The first one is unrelated specifically to Plone but worth repeating: Check that the user who can create the error is the one you think it is. Often I've heard people say, "Works in one browser and not in the other." This is usually because when you've switched browsers, you've also switched users.

Continuing with the obvious, double-check that your user has the role you expect it to have. This may mean going to acl_users, seeing what user role they have, and double-checking it's the one you expect. Next, think of any groups that a user may be in. Again, looking at acl_users will tell you this because users can get extra roles in a group. Finally, remember that a user's role can also be altered by local roles on folders or objects; this is a little harder to narrow down because there's no easy to way to tell what folder or objects have local roles.

Once you're sure who the user is and the role they have on an object, you'll be able to see what the permissions for an object actually are. As you've seen, two similar objects (for example, two documents) can have different permission and different roles. The user who creates the document will have the owner role for that document, and another user will just have the member role on it. Because workflow changes the permissions on a document as it moves through workflow states, this will also change the permissions.

Locking Down Plone

There isn't really an easy way to do this since there really is no concept of a "locked-down" site. However, the basic principle is that users should be able to do the minimum they need to do and nothing more—so you may want to double-check the default settings and remove those security settings they don't need.

For the really paranoid, you can also start removing features from the User Interface (UI) to stop users going wandering by modifying the Cascading Style Sheets (CSS). Of course, remember that just removing the tab for an action or denying access to a page template isn't enough if a user could still, say, edit a document. With knowledge of Plone, they could go and run the page from a script or other malicious mechanism. Often in Plone you'll find that if you try hard enough, you can get to the edit page of a document you're viewing by hacking the uniform resource locator (URL). However, you won't actually be able to edit the page; you'll just be able to call up the edit form.

If your server is running in the wild without restricted access, then ensure that you're running another Web server in front of Zope's ZServer. As I discuss in Chapter 10, the ZServer that comes in the package is a simple implementation without all the checks and security a real Web server needs. Consider proxies, if possible, for other Zope services such as FTP and WebDAV if you're going to let untrusted users at these services (this isn't normally the case).

Integrating Plone with Other Services

The following sections cover security outside of a Plone instance (for example, all the security settings you need to actually run Plone on a server). Then I cover using Plone with LDAP so that you can have users from an external server be used in Plone.

Security on Your Server

I've covered the security of users within the Plone system, but there's one other important issue: the security and setup of your Plone server within your operating system. As with any Web application, getting the security right for your server before exposing it to the world is critical. The install process for Zope 2.7 is pretty good and gets most of this right for you, but there are a few things to note, which I'll present to you now.

User Running Zope

You should ensure that the user running Zope has the minimum amount of security needed to complete the task. The user running Zope will need to read and write to all Zope directories on the file system. The user will need to write the directories that contain the logs and database of your Zope instance; those are the var and log directories of your Zope instance.

The best way to do this on Linux is to add a dedicated user account called, say, plone, that will handle this; you can then limit the access of that user in the unlikely event of Plone being hacked.

On Linux, if you want to have Plone bind to low-numbered ports (below 1024) such as 21 or 80, then you'll normally need to run Plone as root. It'll bind to these ports as root and then change to another effective user. To do this, you must specify a value for effective-user in the configuration file, zope.conf. It'll then do the bind and change to that user; an example of this is effective-user zope. The best alternative isn't to do this at all but instead to run Zope on a high port such as 8080; you can then protect that port at the firewall and use Apache or other Web server to run on port 80 and proxy through to port 8080. Chapter 10 covers more about this topic.

The equivalent on Windows is the user who runs the service; by default, this is the LocalSystem account. Again, you can change the user that Plone runs as.

If you're trying to run Plone on a Windows computer that doesn't have services (which I don't recommend or support), then Plone will be running locally as the user who started the server manually.

Some products may require the installation of extra software that provides features such as image manipulation, document conversion, and so on. If you've installed any of these tools, then bear in mind that they may require a bit of work so that they'll interact with your Plone site successfully. For example, I installed pdftohtml on Windows for Portable Document Format (PDF) conversion, but for the command to be read, I had to run the service as a user with more privileges so Zope could interact with this software. In this case, since the server was behind a firewall, this wasn't a problem.

Getting Emergency Access

If you've got a Plone site but can't access the ZMI because you don't know or have forgotten the password, then you can get an emergency access account. To do this, you need to have file system access to the instance of your Plone site. If you don't have this, you'll need to find some way to do this first.

To do this, go to the root of your instance and call the zpasswd.py script. You'll find this script in your Zope directory (in ZOPE_HOME). On my computer the script zpasswd.py is located in /opt/Zope-2.7/bin/zpasswd.py. So, to create a password, you'd do the following:

```
$ cd /var/zope
$ python /opt/Zope-2.7/bin/zpasswd.py access

Username: emergency
Password:
Verify password:

Please choose a format from:

SHA - SHA-1 hashed password
CRYPT - UNIX-style crypt password
CLEARTEXT - no protection.

Encoding: SHA
Domain restrictions:
```

This will create a file access in your Zope instance. Now restart Zope, and log into the ZMI using that username and password entered in that script. This user has a special meaning in Plone and is called the *emergency user*. Once you've logged in as an emergency user, you can't create objects, but you can now create a new user for yourself and log in as that user. For security reasons, you should then delete the access file.

Getting Emergency Access on Windows

The Windows installation of Plone features a Graphical User Interface (GUI) application for easily getting emergency access. Select Start ➤ Program Files ➤ Plone ➤ Plone, and click the Emergency User option. This allows you to create a new user, alter the current emergency user's password, or remove any emergency user, as shown in Figure 9-16.

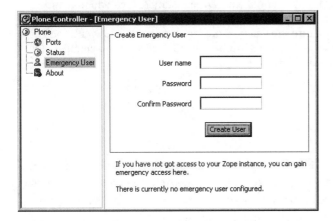

Figure 9-16. Creating a new emergency user

To create a new user, click Create User. In the pop-up dialog box, add a username and password. This will create a file that contains the username and password on the file system. Similarly, clicking Change Password will alter that user's password. After adding or altering a password, you'll need to restart Zope. To restart Plone, go to the Control tab, click Stop, and then click Start. Next, click Manage Root, and give the username and password you just entered. You'll be logged in as the emergency user, which means you can't create objects, but you can now create a new user for yourself and log in as that user.

Using External Authentication Systems

Plone stores all its users inside the Zope object database in a separate user list, as you saw in Chapter 8. As ever, this isn't perfect, and at some point you may want to use another service to authenticate your users. The most common alternative system is LDAP or Microsoft's Active Directory, which communicates using LDAP.

However, you may actually want to integrate with another application that stores its users in a relational database. At the time of writing, ActiveState's ASPN site uses Zope for all the content, but users can authenticate by using Microsoft's Passport system. Actually installing extra user authentication schemes is pretty straightforward thanks to excellent work by many developers. In the process of setting this up, I found that the hardest part was building the software and setting up the integration between systems.

 CAUTION   In the next section, you'll be playing around with the `acl_users` folders inside a Plone site. Never delete or alter the `acl_users` folder in the root of your Zope instance. If you do that and your user folder breaks for some reason (the server goes down, for example), your entire site will be blocked, and you'll no longer be able to get any access, even as an administrator. Make sure you change only the user folder in the Plone site!

Using LDAP

First, you need to set up an LDAP server, or something that communicates with LDAP, such as Active Directory (although apparently Active Directory has a few of quirks). In this example, I installed openLDAP on my Red Hat server and on my Windows server. For Windows, you'll find a precompiled version at `http://www.zope.org/Members/volkerw/LdapWin32`. I tested it for Python 2.3.

Download and unzip the file, and then place the contents inside `c:\Program Files\Plone\Python\lib\site-packages`. Then install `LDAPUserFolder`.

On Linux, you can find the openLDAP downloads at `http://www.openldap.org/`. The tested version includes the RPMs `2.0.27-2.8.0` and `2.0.27-2.8.0`. After building this by following the instructions, I went to `http://python-ldap.sourceforge.net/`, downloaded the appropriate Python LDAP libraries, and built those. In my case, the tested version was `2.0.0pre05-1.i386.rpm`. Make sure you use the same Python interpreter you're using to run Plone.

After you've gone through those particular hoops, you need to make sure the `_ldap.so` module is importable by Python. The easiest way to test this is to run the following:

```
$ python -c "import _ldap"
```

If you get no error messages, then it imported correctly. If you do get errors, then you'll have to retrace your steps. Then go and get LDAPUserFolder from http://www.dataflake.org/software/ldapuserfolder. The tested version was 2.1 beta 2. Download the file, untar it, and move it into the Products directory of your Zope installation. For example:

```
$ tar -zxf LDAPUserFolder-2_1beta2.tgz
$ mv LDAPUserFolder /var/zope/Products
```

Now restart Plone, go to the control panel, and ensure that it shows up correctly in the Products page of the control panel. I provide more details on this in Chapter 10.

Next, in Plone you should be able to click *acl_users*, click Sources, and then scroll down to the *Users source #1* option. Then select LDAPUserFolder, and check *I'm sure*, as shown in Figure 9-17. This will create a new user folder and replace the existing one, so make sure you aren't about to lose anything critical. In fact, now is a good time to do a backup. Then click OK.

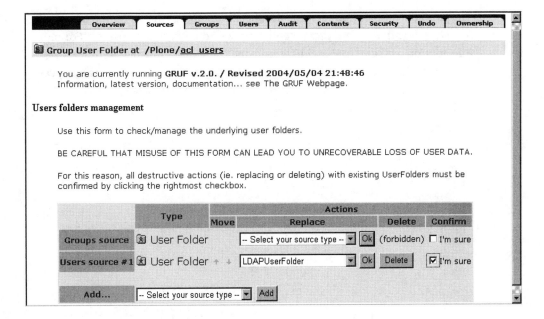

Figure 9-17. Adding an LDAPUserFolder

In the LDAPUserFolder settings, add the settings that match your existing LDAP settings. You should now be able to click the Users tab and search for users that already exist in your LDAP directory.

Relational Databases and Others

An excellent user folder replacement is called exUserFolder, which stands for *extensible user folder*. This one is easy to install; just download it from http://prdownloads.sourceforge.net/exuserfolder/exUserFolder-0_20_0.tgz, do the usual unzip dance, and copy it into your Products folder. Again, after restarting Plone, you should be able to click *acl_users*, select Sources, and then scroll down to the *Users source #1* option. Then select exUserFolder, and check *I'm sure*.

Actually, exUserFolder will authenticate against the following:

- Radius

- SMB

- LDAP

- Relational databases

To do this, you'll need to install the specific database adapter for the relational database; fortunately, adapters for all the major databases are covered. For more information, you can find excellent information in the exUserFolder directories with ReadMe files on almost every subject. The Zope book covers setting up access to a relational database at http://zope.org/Documentation/Books/ZopeBook/ 2_6Edition/RelationalDatabases.stx.

CHAPTER 10

Integrating with Other Systems

INTEGRATION IS A huge issue in any enterprise that has a large number of other systems already in place. Because Plone is an open-source project, it has a lot of products, add-ons, skins, and tools that provide extra functionality for free. That's right—often these extra products are given away to anyone who wants them. Additionally, as an open-source language, Python has a whole host of free, excellent products (often called *packages*). Most of these products don't directly affect Plone, though. In other words, they don't give functionality to Plone out of the box—that's what Plone products do. However, people often ask, "Can Plone do X?" The answer is often, "Yes, if Python can do it."

The following are some of the most popular Python products:

- **Python Imaging Library (PIL):** This allows you to manipulate, convert, and analyze images (http://www.pythonware.com/products/pil/).

- **ReportLab:** This allows you to create Portable Document Format (PDF) files dynamically with images, graphs, and other goodies (http://www.reportlab.org/).

- **Windows extensions:** This gives an interface to all the Windows Application Programming Interfaces (APIs); for example, it offers the ability to use Component Object Model (COM) objects (http://sourceforge.net/projects/pywin32/).

- **Pygame:** This is a framework that allows users to write games in Python. People have used it in Plone to get access to the media layer interfaces it provides for creating images or sounds (http://www.pygame.org/).

- **OpenOffice.org bindings:** This provides bindings so that you can do almost anything to OpenOffice.org documents, even parsing Microsoft Office documents, for example—as you'll see in Chapter 13 (http://udk.openoffice.org/python/python-bridge.html).

- **mxTidy**: This package locates and corrects problems in Hypertext Markup Language (HTML) files, including page templates (`http://www.egenix.com/files/python/mxTidy.html`).

These excellent add-ons usually have graphical installers for Windows that allow you to step through the installation. If you aren't using Windows, then the `distutils` module for Python offers a simple command-line interface for installing any of these products. As ever, the real key to installing anything is to read the instructions contained in the download. This chapter focuses on installing products that provide extra functionality to Plone. You'll find a directory of Python packages at `http://www.python.org/pypi`.

Open-Source Licensing

Most open-source packages are released with a particular license that describes how the package may be used. Before you use any third-party code, you should check the license to see if it's compatible with your needs.

Plone is licensed under the General Public License (GPL), which you can find at `http://www.gnu.org/copyleft/gpl.html` and inside the `LICENSE.txt` file of your Plone installation. If you're the developer of a Plone Web site, then you can happily create and develop Web sites without any issue. Users of your Web site will never have to worry about the license for the code; they just use the Web site normally. As with most licenses, the license limits the redistribution and sale of other people's code.

Usually licenses are easy to read and understand, but if you're unsure, you should probably have a qualified legal professional look at the license. I'll limit myself to describing the main licenses that exist in the Zope world and point you to where you can find more information:

- **Zope Public License**: This is the license for the Zope application server and the license of choice for many add-on products written for Zope. You can find a copy of the license at `http://zope.org/Resources/ZPL`.

- **Python License**: This is the license for Python; you can find a copy at `http://http://www.python.org/2.3/license.html`.

- **GPL**: This is the license for Plone; you can find a copy at `http://www.gnu.org/copyleft/gpl.html`.

- **Lesser GPL**: The is the Lesser GPL; you can find a copy at `http://www.gnu.org/copyleft/lesser.html`.

Installing Plone Products

A *product* is a module to install into Plone that provides more functionality to Plone. Although the name *product* implies a cost, that isn't the case—most products are free and open source. The term *product* actually describes something written on the file system and distributed for other Plone sites to use.

Installing a product generally involves the following two steps:

1. Installing it so that it's registered inside Zope

2. Installing it into each Plone instance that wants to use it

The large variety of add-ons available means that it's pretty hard to give any hard and fast rules about what exactly needs to be done to install them. As I'll repeatedly point out in this chapter, always read the product's installation files, which will usually explain how to install the product. If you do need further help, contact a mailing list or the product author for more information; however, ensure that you've read the instructions first.

When you're installing products, remember that you're installing code that could be incomplete and has no warranty on the quality. The nature of open source is that people tend to write products and then leave them as they move onto other projects. In an ideal world, before you install anything, you'd take the time to have someone you trust read through it line by line. In reality, you can't do this. Still, most products are pretty good. Just be careful to test products before you install them into your million-dollar site.

Finding Products

Finding the right products to meet your needs is probably the hardest part about integration. The Zope.org Web site contains many products created and uploaded by users. You can find these products primarily at http://www.zope.org/Products, but if you look at the home page of Zope.org, you'll see product announcements on the right side of the page. Some of these products are Plone related, and others are Zope, Content Management Framework (CMF), or Python related.

The other main area to find products is in the Collective project at SourceForge (http://sf.net/projects/collective). The products in the Collective project reside in SourceForge's Concurrent Versioning System (CVS). Although products often get released as tarballs, CVS access is the best way to see the products there.

At this time, no comprehensive product directory exists for Plone products or their state. (I hope one will be online at Plone.org by the time this book is published.) As products are released, people tend to put packages on the Files page, but the best bet is to look in the CVS. You can find a visual view of all the available files at `http://cvs.sourceforge.net/viewcvs.py/collective/`.

One final CVS repository that contains useful code is Zope Corporation's CVS repository. Almost all code that's made public is placed in this CVS repository. If you're looking for the source to Zope 2, then this is also the place to go. The `Products` directory contains all the products (`http://cvs.zope.org/Products/`). You can find more information on how to check out code at `http://dev.zope.org/CVS/ReadOnlyAccess`.

What Is CVS?

CVS is a system for maintaining control over source code. Most development happens in a source code control system, such as CVS or one of its many similar competing products, such as Subversion, Perforce, BitKeeper, and so on.

Checking files out of CVS is simple, and most Unix and Linux users will be familiar with using CVS from the command line. To check out all the products in the collective to your computer (this may take a while), do the following:

```
cvs -d:pserver:anonymous@cvs.sourceforge.net:/cvsroot/collective login
```

Supply a blank password and continue with the following command:

```
cvs -z3 -d:pserver:anonymous@cvs.sourceforge.net:/cvsroot/collective co .
```

Most of the Plone development team using Windows uses TortoiseCVS, which hooks directly into the Windows Explorer shell—from Explorer you can right-click to check in and check out code. For more information on TortoiseCVS, visit `http://www.tortoisecvs.org`.

Installing in Zope

Once you've found and downloaded a suitable product, you need to install it. You'll first need to install it into Zope so that Zope can recognize the new product. To do this, you need to find the area that contains all the existing products. To find the directories, go to the control panel in the Zope Management Interface (ZMI). There you'll see a list of the directories for your Plone instance. If you have a value for INSTANCE_HOME, then your Products directory will be located in that directory. If you don't have a value for INSTANCE_HOME, you'll find the Products directory inside SOFTWARE_HOME. It's worth noting that almost all methods of installing Plone create INSTANCE_HOME for you. As shown in Figure 10-1, my INSTANCE_HOME is /var/book, so my Products directory is /var/book/Products.

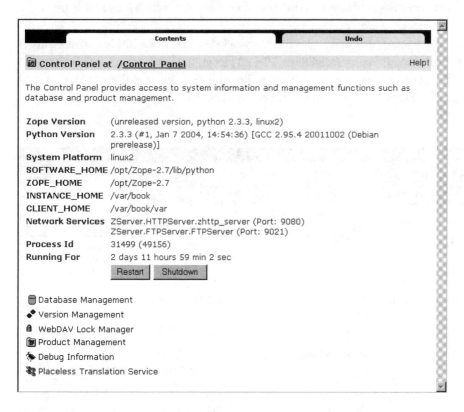

Figure 10-1. Locating your Products *directory*

To do the Zope part of the install, take the downloaded product, decompress it, and place it inside the Products directory for your server. Actually doing that is a little tricky and depends greatly upon how the product you're trying to install is packaged. To show this in more detail, the following section explains how to install an example product, CMFExternalFile, which itself is covered in the "Managing a File in Plone" section.

One of the nice things about CMFExternalFile is that it actually comes in two parts, with two downloads. First, you have the Zope-specific code called ExternalFile. If you ever wanted to use this product outside of Plone, in plain Zope, you could do so. Second, you have the Plone- and CMF-specific code called CMFExternalFile. Most products don't need two installs; they come self-contained as one product.

Performing an Example Installation on Windows

First, you'll need to download the product from Zope.org at `http://zope.org/Members/arielpartners/ExternalFile/1.2.0/ExternalFile-1-2-0.zip` and save it to your computer.

Second, unzip the file. For this you could use WinZip, which you can find on most Windows computers these days (I prefer 7-Zip, which is available from `http://www.7-zip.org/`).

After unzipping, you'll get a directory called `ExternalFile`. Inside that directory is the product directory (see Figure 10-2). You can tell this because inside that directory is a whole bunch of Python files and text files, including `INSTALL.txt` and `README.txt`, which contain information about how to do the install.

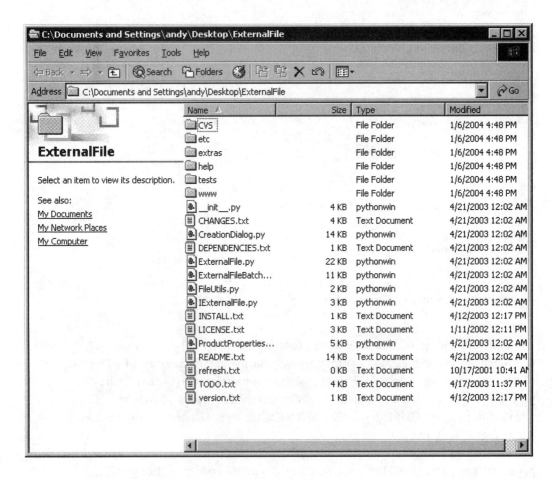

Figure 10-2. The `ExternalFile` *directory contents*

Next, move the ExternalFile folder (not its contents) into your Products directory. In Windows that directory is located at c:\Program Files\Plone 2\ Data\Products. In that directory you'll see a series of other directories including CMFPlone, CMFCore, and so on. The directory ExternalFile should now be one of those directories. You can now skip to testing the installation in the server.

Performing an Example Installation on Unix

First, you'll need to download the product from Zope.org at http://zope.org/ Members/arielpartners/ExternalFile/1.2.0/ExternalFile-1-2-0.zip and save it to your computer. Second, unzip the file; most Unix systems have an unzip program already installed. If so, execute the following commands:

```
$ unzip ExternalFile-1-2-0.zip
Archive:  ExternalFile-1-2-0.zip
   creating: ExternalFile/CVS/
...
```

After unzipping, you'll get the directory ExternalFile. You know that the ExternalFile directory is the product directory because inside that directory is a whole bunch of Python files and text files, including INSTALL.txt and README.txt, which contain information about how to install.

Now move the ExternalFile folder (not its contents) into the Products directory. This command will depend upon the configuration of your server, but in my case this is as follows:

```
$ mv ExternalFile /var/zope/Products
```

Testing the Installation in the Server

After installing a product, you'll need to restart Plone for the products to be registered in Plone. Once you've restarted your server, go to the ZMI and access the Product Management screen of the Zope control panel. This screen will list all the products installed on the server. If you installed the product successfully, you'll see that it's now listed, as shown in Figure 10-3.

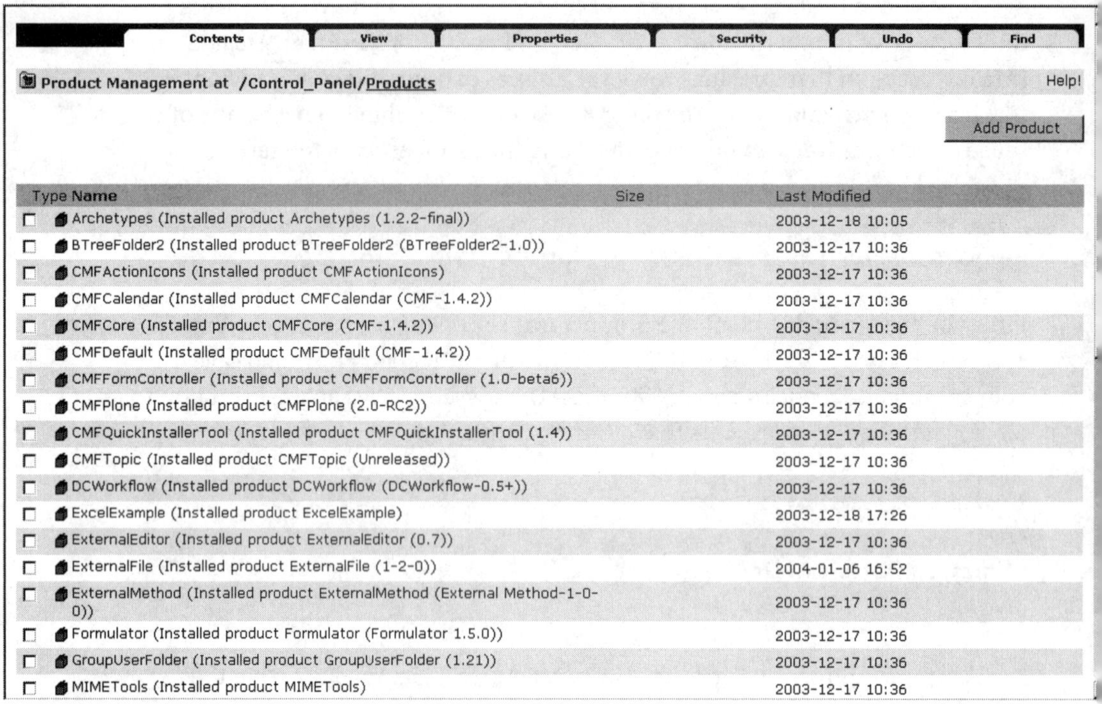

Figure 10-3. Correctly installed products

Incidentally, you have three things that could go wrong at this point. First, if nothing shows up in the management interface, then you've placed the directory in the wrong place. To correct this, double-check the installation instructions and the location of your Products directory, as explained earlier.

Second, you could get a "broken" icon appearing in the product list; this means the product was attempted to be registered in Zope, but an error occurred. Click the broken icon to get a traceback, which will tell you the error and should give you a chance to fix it.

Finally, if you've been unable to access the management interface after restarting, it could be that you have a more serious problem. Zope wasn't able to start because Plone found a serious error. To find out what the problem is, start Plone from the command line in debug mode, and a traceback will print to the screen.

Installing in Plone

Now that you've correctly installed into Zope, the next step is easy. To completely install CMFExternalFile, you'll now need to install the CMFExternalFile product

(http://prdownloads.sourceforge.net/collective/
CMFExternalFile.0.5.zip?download) the same way you installed ExternalFile.
You'll also have to restart Plone.

You have to install CMFExternalFile into *each* Plone instance. Not all Plone
products require this, but most do. The only real way to tell is to read the installation instructions. If you see anything about "install in the standard CMF way"
or "in your Plone instance make an external method," then you need to complete
this step.

Fortunately, you can actually disregard the instructions to make an external
method because Plone has a much simpler way to do this. In Plone, click *plone
setup* and then click Add/Remove Products. You'll see a list of products that are
installed on your server and that need configuring in Plone. Simply click the
check box next to the product (in this case, CMFExternalFile), and click *install*, as
shown in Figure 10-4.

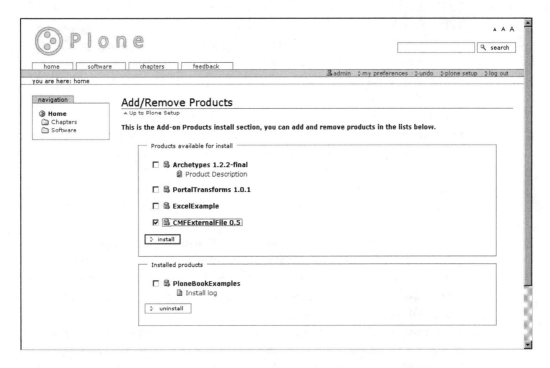

Figure 10-4. A list of products available to the user

Just like that, the product will be installed. Well, it may be—if there's an error,
then it won't show up in the installed products list. You may be able to solve the
problem by reading the log, so click the link next to the name of the product to
get a log. This installation is a service provided by the portal_quickinstaller tool

contained inside Zope. For a look at what this product actually does, skip to the "Integrating Plone with the File System" section.

Using a Different Web Server

If you're in an organization that already serves Web sites, then you'll likely have a Web server platform that you use. *Virtual hosting* is the ability to server multiple Web sites on one server, differentiating sites based upon their Internet Protocol (IP) address or name. It allows one initial server, such as Apache, to pass requests to one or more Plone instances.

Virtual hosting is usually achieved by *proxying*, although using a proxy server is a desirable approach with Plone no matter how many sites are hosted. A proxy server sits between a client and a server and forwards requests from the client and the server. A proxy server should be transparent to the user. In Chapter 14, I'll show you how you can use proxy servers to dramatically increase Plone's performance.

Although Plone uses Zope's underlying Web server, ZServer works just fine—it's not a complete, industry-strength Web server that should be exposed to the world. The server has several issues regarding possible Denial of Service (DOS) attacks; however, these are obscure and hard-to-find items within ZServer. No known attacks have been performed against ZServer that exploit these issues, but perhaps this is because of its relative obscurity in the real world. ZServer isn't specifically designed to be an industry-strength server, and since it's feature complete, it's no longer being developed. By keeping a server such as Apache up to date, you're ensuring that a robust secure server is facing the world. Of course, if you're developing an intranet or other application with trusted users, this may not be an issue.

Figure 10-5 shows how such a setup would exist; the figure doesn't show actual computers, just services. A request would normally come from the Internet to the firewall and then go to Apache and then to Plone. It could be that these are all different boxes. The essential point is that there should be no access to Plone from untrusted users except through a proxy.

Putting a Web server, such as Apache, in front of Plone provides a whole host of useful services that ZServer doesn't have. For example, Apache can provide the following: Uniform Resource Locator (URL) rewriting, Secure Sockets Layer (SSL) support, caching, content deflation, virtual hosting, proxying to other Web services, incoming request sanitation, and so on. The most commonly asked question is how to change a URL from `http://localhost:8080/Plone` into something more friendly such as `http://yoursite.com`. This is called *URL rewriting*. Whilst a proxying server isn't required for this, it's much easier with one.

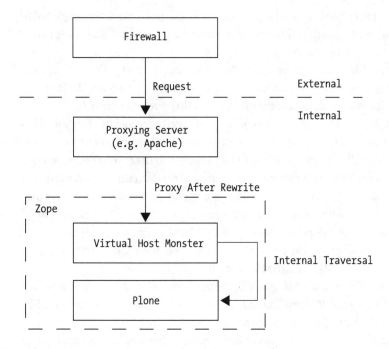

Figure 10-5. How virtual hosting works

A favorite method for proxying to Plone is to use an Hypertext Transfer Protocol (HTTP) proxy. Apache achieves this using the mod_proxy module. When a request for a page comes into the proxying server, it performs various functions. Then a new request is created and sent to the ZServer. That response is passed back to the server and then onto the client. Of course, this all transparent to the client, which just makes requests as normal to a server.

NOTE   The old way to connect Apache to Plone is via Fast CGI or Persistent CGI. These are harder to configure and actually slower when running. Although lots of old documentation exists on these subjects, more efficient solutions now exist, and I *don't* recommend these methods.

Configuring Plone

Before configuring your proxy Web server, you need to configure Plone. Since only one server can connect to a port at once, alter Plone so that it's listening to a high-numbered port. Usually this port would be something that's blocked at the firewall and isn't accessible from the outside. Example ports are 8080, 9090, 9673, and so on. Chapter 2 provides information about how to change the ports on which your Plone server runs.

Next, you probably want to perform URL rewriting to change the URL of your site. Because the Plone object lives inside the Zope Object Database (ZODB) and has an ID, it's accessed by putting that ID in the URL, such as `http://localhost:8080/Plone`. To make this friendlier, you need to translate the request to the Web server from `http://yoursite.com` into a request for a correct object inside Zope. You have two slightly different ways to do this, based upon your requirements. If you're using a proxy Web server or basing sites upon domain names, then you can use a Virtual Host Monster (VHM). This is a friendly and powerful object that will make your life so much easier, so I fully recommend using it. You need only one VHM in the root of a Zope instance. The VHM object sits at the root of a Zope site and intercepts all incoming requests; it then alters the request so that the request goes to the part of Zope that you want.

To create a VHM, in the ZMI, go to the root of your Zope and select *Virtual Host Monster* from the Add drop-down box; in the form that opens, enter an ID. For example, enter **vhm** (the actual ID doesn't matter).

At this point, if you're using a proxy Web server in front of Plone, continue to the configuration for that Web server in the "Configuring the Proxy Server" section.

This next step is necessary only if you *aren't* using a proxy Web server. Click the VHM object you added in the ZMI, and then select the Mappings tab, which will present a list of the available mappings for hosts on this object. The mapping takes an incoming request and maps it to Plone, with the following syntax:

```
host/path
```

where `host` is the hostname being mapped and `path` is the actual path to the object in Zope. For example:

```
www.somesite.com/Plone
```

To ensure that all variations on the name are mapped to the path, you can use wildcards in the mapping. For example, the following maps all subdomains of `somesite.com`:

```
*.somesite.com/Plone
```

To add this mapping, go to the Mapping tab, enter each mapping on a new line, and click Save. This means you'll no longer be able to access the root of your Zope site using the addresses you've mapped. Fortunately, you can still access the root of your Zope server using an IP address; this will still work because the mapping isn't applied to numeric addresses. Figure 10-6 shows how Figure 10-5 changes when you access the server through the IP directly and bypass the rewriting.

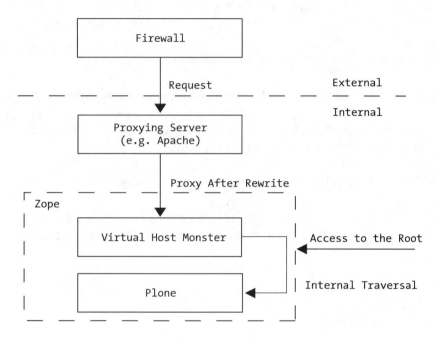

Figure 10-6. Virtual hosting with access to root

You've now mapped a named domain such as somesite.com to point to a particular Plone instance. If an incoming request is sent looking for that site name, it will be forwarded to the Plone instance.

Configuring the Proxy Server

Now that you've added your VHM into Plone, it's time to configure the proxy server. But proxy server configuration depends upon the actual server you're using. The following sections cover the specifics for each server. However, to get virtual hosting to work, you'll have to pass a URL to Plone that the VHM object understands.

It's worth noting that there's one other advantage of virtual hosting using a proxy server. You do all the configuration of the domains outside of Plone in the proxy server. This means your system administrator can now administer and use a familiar tool, without having to worry about Plone.

Proxying works by taking an incoming request and manipulating it so that a request with a special URL is sent to Plone. That request will be manipulated and contains all the information Plone needs to know to produce a response. When that response is produced and sent back to the requesting person, all the URLs have to point to your site correctly. This will ensure that links within your pages are all correct.

A URL has the following three main components:

- The IP or hostname and port for the server on which Plone resides

- The IP or hostname for where Plone is meant to be residing so that all links in resulting documents have the correct URL

- The actual object in Zope to access and the URL passed to it

This information is passed to Plone by transforming the URL into one big, complicated URL of the following format (line breaks have been added to make this clearer):

```
http://[URL to server]:[port]
/VirtualHostBase/[protocol]/[URL]:[port]
/[path to virtual host root]
/VirtualHostRoot/[actual URL]
```

Take the following example:

- Plone is on a box at the IP address 192.168.2.1 on port 8080. Note that the IP address is one that the proxy server can access; it's not the IP address to the outside world—the proxy server handles that.

- Plone should appear to be at www.mysite.com on port 80.

- The actual Plone object is at /Plone.

- The incoming request is for /Members/andym.

This translates into the following long URL:

```
http://192.168.2.1:8080 ➡
/VirtualHostBase/http/www.mysite.com:80/Plone ➡
/VirtualHostRoot/Members/andym
```

The point of doing this is that when the VHM object sees that URL, it knows exactly what to do with it. It munges it and sends the request to the Plone object. Obviously, the actual page fragment (`/Members/andym`) will be different for each request and needs to be calculated. But if you know what you're aiming for, you can now configure your server.

Configuring Apache

Apache is probably the most popular choice for placing in front of Plone, and it's available for all Linux, Unix, and Windows platforms (`http://httpd.apache.org/`). After installing Apache, you need to pass requests onto Plone by using HTTP proxies.

For configuring Apache, you'll need to access Apache's configuration files; where they are depend upon your installation of Apache, so consult the Apache documentation. In Windows, the configuration is accessible from the Start menu. In Linux, you can usually find the Apache configuration in the `/etc` directory at `/etc/apache/httpd.conf` or `/etc/apache2/httpd.conf`. To alter these files, you'll usually need you to gain root or privileged user access.

 NOTE This example uses Apache 2, but all these commands are backward compatible with earlier versions, such as Apache 1.3.2. However, some earlier versions of Apache (before 1.3.2) are known to have issues with cookies.

The easiest way to rewrite a URL in Apache is to use the built-in rewrite and proxy modules. This means enabling Apache's mod_rewrite and mod_proxy modules. In Apache, each site is usually contained within a virtual host directory that starts with the following:

```
<VirtualHost *:80>
    ServerName yoursite.com
    # other configuration options
```

All you need to do is enable rewrites and add the rewrite rule, like so:

```
    RewriteEngine On
    RewriteRule ^/(.*)  http://192.168.2.1:8080 ➠
/VirtualHostBase/http/www.mysite.com:80/Plone ➠
/VirtualHostRoot/$1 [L,P] ➠
</VirtualHost>
```

The key rewrite rule here takes any request string passed to it and appends it to the end of your hard-coded rewrite rule. The [L,P] tells Apache that this is the last rewrite rule, and it should proxy to the server given. After doing this, you'll need to restart Apache to update the configuration. You can find more information about rewriting in the mod_rewrite documentation at http://httpd.apache.org/docs-2.0/misc/rewriteguide.html. Note that in this case you've placed the rewrite rule information inside a virtual host directive. You could have multiple such virtual hosts in Apache so that PHP, Perl, and Java sites all sit side by side on one server.

Squid

For its powerful caching and configuration options, Squid is a popular choice for users. Squid is available for Unix, and there are Windows builds using cygwin available. Although I haven't tested the Windows version specifically, people who have report that it works well. You can find the downloads at http://www.squid-cache.org/. These notes cover the latest stable version at the time of writing, which is version 2.5.

Installing Squid from the source distribution is quite simple. After downloading, the following commands install Squid:

```
$ tar -xvf squid-2.5.STABLE3.tar.gz
$ cd  squid-2.5.STABLE3
$ ./configure --prefix=/usr/local/squid
...
$ make all
...
$ make install
...
```

Unfortunately, Squid doesn't have a rewrite rule that allows you to alter incoming requests before proxying. Squid Guard (http://www.squidguard.org) can do this job, though. I tested the 1.2.0 version. After downloading, the following commands perform the install:

```
$ tar -zxvf squidGuard-1.2.0.tar.gz
$ cd squidGuard-1.2.0
$ ./configure
...
$ make
...
$ make install
...
```

Now both Squid and SquidGuard are ready to go; however, both configuration files still need setting up. You can find the Squid configuration file at `/etc/squid.conf`. It's a long configuration file that fortunately explains in great detail all the options. The following are the essential options to set:

```
http_port 80
httpd_accel_host virtual
httpd_accel_port 0

http_access allow all
http_access allow localhost
```

These last two lines are security rules for allowing access from browsers. Because this was tested behind a firewall, these are lax rules. If you're running Squid externally, you should read up on access rules in detail. The easiest way to secure this is to change `http_access allow all` to `http_access deny all`. Finally, add the following line to the configuration file:

```
redirect_program /usr/bin/squidGuard -c /etc/squid/squidGuard.conf
```

This sets up the redirect through Squid Guard using the configuration file at `/etc/squid/squidGuard.conf`. SquidGuard doesn't come with a configuration file, but a standard one that uses the virtual host configuration looks like the following:

```
dbhome /var/lib/squidguard/db
logdir /var/log/squid
acl {
    default {
            redirect http://192.168.2.1:8080 ➥
/VirtualHostBase/http/www.agmweb.ca:80 ➥
/Plone/VirtualHostRoot/%p ➥
  }
}
```

Finally, Squid has the configuration you need to redirect traffic so that the host monster understands it. Incoming requests will be handled by Squid and then passed to Plone.

Microsoft Internet Information Services

Using Internet Information Services (IIS) isn't my preferred server of choice; however, many companies use IIS, so I've included this section. Unfortunately,

IIS can't perform proxying in the same way as Squid and Apache; you need a separate plug-in. Just before this book was published, a free proxy was written called IIS2Zope that provides this functionality. However, I haven't had chance to try it in a high-performance site. For more information, see http://zope.org/Members/freshlogic/index_html.

Instead, I'll cover a solution that's simple to set up and free. Earlier Zope users recommended PCGI, but over the years this has been slow and complicated to install. By using Microsoft's ASP language and some IIS properties, you have a quicker solution. It's called ASP 404 and does the redirect through Microsoft's ASP programming language.

From http://www.zope.org/Members/hiperlogica/ASP404, download the latest version. I tested ASP404_1-0-b2.zip. Unzip the downloaded file, and you'll find a file, default.asp, inside it. Take that file and put it in the root of the site you want to proxy; on my server, that's c:\inetpub\wwwroot.

Next, you need to configure that script with the appropriate information for the location of your Plone site. You have to open the script in a simple text editor and change two lines that contain the variables for the site configuration. Specifically, change line 18 from this:

```
zopeAddress = "http://127.0.0.1:8080"
```

to the address of the destination server. In this example, it's as follows:

```
zopeAddress = "http://192.168.2.1:8080"
```

Then change line 27 from this:

```
zopePath = "/"
```

to the ID of the Plone object, like so:

```
zopePath = "/Plone"
```

Save the file, and close the editor. Finally, you need to tell IIS to speak to Plone; this is where you have to use a bit of trickery. Open the Internet Services Manager, usually found somewhere in the Windows Control Panel. Find the site you want to proxy and access the sites properties, as shown in Figure 10-7.

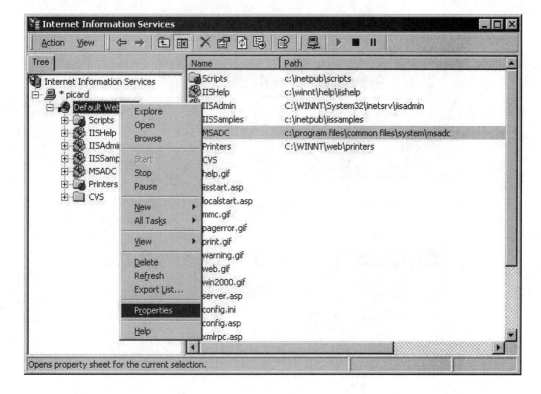

Figure 10-7. Accessing a site's properties

In the properties, select the Custom Errors tab, and scroll down until you find the error for 404. Double-click the 404 error and alter it as follows:

- **Message Type**: URL

- **URL**: /default.asp

Figure 10-8 shows the settings.

Save the changes by clicking OK. At this point, your list of errors should look like the list of errors in Figure 10-9. If this is the case, then you should be set up correctly. Access IIS through the browser and bingo—you'll see Plone.

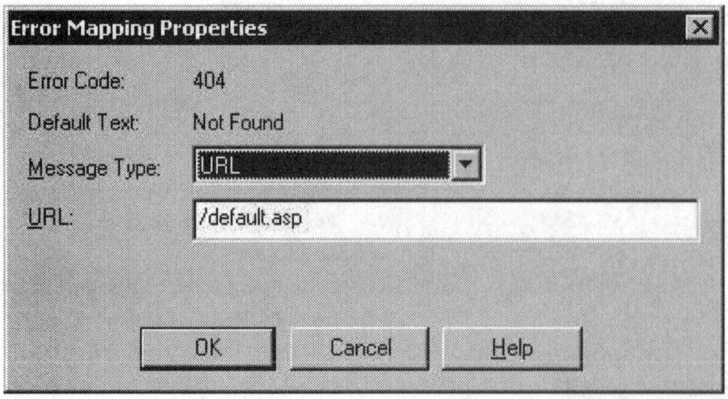

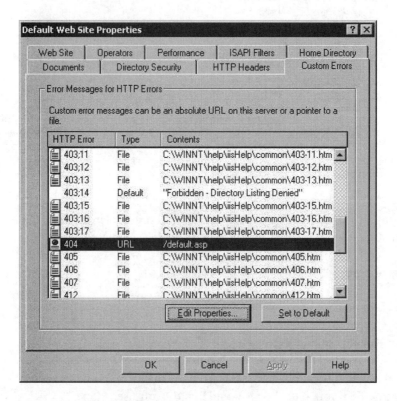

Figure 10-8. Setting up the redirect for 404

Figure 10-9. The error list

What's happened here is that you're capturing the error for when an item can't be found in IIS. The ASP script you installed then reads the request and forwards it to Plone. It takes the response and passes it back to IIS and down the line back to the browser. This means you've added a simple proxy program to IIS.

You have a few key concerns here, though. The first is that a page can't be found in order for the proxy to occur; otherwise the script will not be triggered. This is good and bad. You can add folders and images to IIS, and they will be served out instead of Plone if the names match the request from the browser. Second, the incoming request is parsed and sent on; this gets a little confusing in several situations with all the possible HTTP request configurations. You'll also find that all your Plone requests are actually logged as 404 errors, by IIS, which confuses log file analysis tools.

Overall, this setup has worked for most people who've used it, but whether it's an enterprise solution that could cope with every situation is unlikely. However, it provides a strong base for people to work with and develop.

Debugging Proxy Servers

Once you've set the server up and restarted everything, you'll want to test the server by using your browser to visit the site. After doing this a few times, you can use the following tips for when things don't seem to quite work as they should:

Testing the site: The golden rule of debugging proxy servers is to *always* test the site by logging in and bypassing your proxy server. You can do this by accessing the IP and port of your Plone server directly. In the case of the previous example, you can access the site by going to `http://192.168.2.1:8080/Plone`, and you've circumvented the proxy server completely. If you don't have any problems accessing and logging into Plone this way but do when you try through the proxy server, chances are any errors are occurring in the proxy's server side. Some older versions of Apache 1.3 do give problems with cookies when logging in, so you should upgrade to the latest 1.3 version.

Checking the URL: Double-check that your proxy server is sending the right URL, which can be quite long and complicated. Break it down by the forward slashes to examine each part. Remember that for Plone to return the correct URL, it must be passed the correct values. So you have to ensure that the `/[protocol]/[URL]:[port]` section is correct. If your site is using SSL, for example, ensure your protocol part is `https`, not `http`.

Integrating Plone with the File System

Integrating Plone with the file system may sound a little odd, but I'm talking about enabling the use of content on the file system with Plone. Of course, Plone already exists as a series of files that's installed and run on the file system.

However, all content in a Plone site is stored in the ZODB, but many people tell me they want to store and serve their content from the file system directly.

Actually, a lot of people look at Zope and Plone, see little folder icons, and assume they directly relate to the folders and items on the file system. However, this is really not the case. If you were using a relational database, as most Content Management Systems (CMSs) do, would you still want to do this? Many people jump into this thinking it's a problem, but the following are reasons why you'd want to do this:

You have lots of really large pieces of content: Plone can manage really large files without a lot of problems. Databases of more than 10 gigabytes aren't uncommon and work just fine. If you're getting really large pieces of content (for example, one client I work for uses Plone to manage its DVDs—the actual content of the DVDs, that is), then take a look at CMFExternalFile and Apache. For really large stuff, using Apache or another service to serve your content is a good way to go.

You want to manage content using programs that read from the file system, such as Microsoft Word: You can use External Editor to edit content stored in a Plone site using your local programs. If you have Microsoft Word installed, you can upload a Microsoft Word document and then edit it in Microsoft Word on your computer.

You're sick of editing code through the Web in little text areas: Again, look first at External Editor. Second, why are you doing work through the Web anyway? As I demonstrated in Chapter 7, you can write all skins and CSS templates on the file system.

You can use my file system tools on the content: Well, you can mount Plone via File Transfer Protocol (FTP) and WebDAV. Both of these provide file system–like interfaces that work with Plone.

You want to back up the content easily: In Chapter 14 I show how to back up and administer Plone and how to do simple incremental backups. An alternative storage called Directory Storage can handle this (http://dirstorage.sf.net).

You want to use CVS/Subversion/BitKeeper or some other source control system on the content: Ah, that makes sense but, unfortunately, isn't fully integrated yet. In future versions, one tentatively called Plone 3, this may be fully integrated.

With these points in mind, you'll now look at various ways you could serve content that exists on the file system through Plone.

Using the Proxying Web Server

So you've set up the Web server as described earlier in this chapter. At the risk of repeating myself, that Web server is better at serving plain content than Plone ever will be. If you have a large number of downloads, simply put them in a directory on your server that won't be proxying to Plone and then link to them from Plone. The users will just click the link and download as usual.

Doing this in IIS is easy because IIS first automatically checks to see if the file exists before raising the 404 error. Apache requires only two extra lines in the configuration, highlighted in the following code in bold:

```
<VirtualHost *:80>
    ServerName yoursite.com
    # other configuration options
    DocumentRoot /var/downloads
    RewriteEngine On
    RewriteRule ^/download(.*) - [L]
    RewriteRule ^/(.*)  http://192.168.2.1:8080 ➡
/VirtualHostBase/http/www.mysite.com:80 ➡
/Plone/VirtualHostRoot/$1 [L,P]
</VirtualHost>
```

In this example, you'll put the content in /var/downloads, and the URLs to the downloadable through Apache content will all start with /download.

The rewrite engine will see that the URL starts with /download and then not apply any change to it—that's what the dash (-) means. By specifying the [L] at the end of the line, no more rewrite rules will apply, so the proxy doesn't occur and Apache carries on like usual, serving the file.

This trick is useful if you want to host other services in the same virtual host. In one site I host—Mailman, a mailing list manager—all the Mailman URLs start with /mailman and /pipermail. After setting up Mailman correctly and doing all the configuration, I added the following two lines to the configuration so that it'd work nicely:

```
RewriteRule ^/mailman(.*) - [L]
RewriteRule ^/pipermail(.*) - [L]
```

Again, the only catch here is that you can't add objects to Plone where the names may conflict with your rules, such as adding folders with similar names. For example, mailman, pipermail, or download in this example would be forbidden because users could never view those objects. You could use this method to restrict access to certain parts of your site, but I recommend using security within Plone for this. At this point, Plone isn't actually managing content, so it has no security, workflow, or metadata. The content is entirely outside of Plone. This may be a good solution, though.

Managing a File in Plone

CMFExternalFile is a product that allows you to manage content from within Plone and still have the core content on the file system. If you installed ExternalFile and CMFExternal earlier in the chapter, then you're all set. If not, return to the earlier "Installing Plone Products" section.

After installing these, return to your Plone interface. You'll note that if you go to Plone, you can now add a new content type called *External File*. You add the External File type in the same way as a normal file, as I described in Chapter 3. In fact, if you dig into the program code, you'll note that it uses the same templates.

However, you'll notice one small difference here. The file has actually been added to the file system. It's placed in a new directory located in the var directory of your Plone installation. If you aren't sure where this is, go to the control panel and look for the directory listed by the instance home; my var directory is located in /var/zope/var. Inside that directory is a directory called externalfiles. In this directory, all the files you upload into Plone will be created. If you look in that directory, you should find the file you uploaded.

What you've got now is a hybrid storage solution that stores the file on the file system and the metadata about the object (description, keywords, and such) in Plone. This is better than the Web server-only solution because it allows the content to have security, metadata, and so on. If you really wanted, by configuring your Web server correctly, you could have the content served by Apache by reading the directory from the externalfiles directory.

FTP Access into Plone

Using FTP is one good way to put and get content so that you can edit it without having to use a browser. To enable FTP in Plone, ensure that it's enabled in the server. Returning to Chapter 2, you can see how to add and edit services like this. In short, make sure your Zope configuration file, zope.conf, has the following in it:

```
<ftp-server>
    address 21
</ftp-server>
```

NOTE If you're going to have your server use port 21, you must ensure that nothing else is listening to that port. Furthermore, for most Unix systems, you'll need to start your service as root so that it has permissions to connect to the low-numbered port. To do this, you'll need to set the effective user in your Zope configuration file. See the "Security on Your Server" section in Chapter 9.

Next, you'll need an FTP client to access the server. If you're on Windows, then you can just use Internet Explorer by entering the address of the server in the address bar. For example, set the address to the path of your Zope server (such as ftp://localhost:8021/), and you'll get access to the objects in your site, as shown in Figure 10-10.

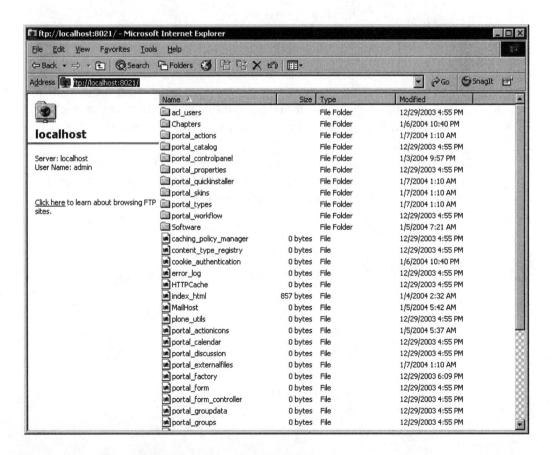

Figure 10-10. FTP access in Internet Explorer

If you need a username and password to access the server, you'll need to add them to the URL in the following format: ftp://user:password@localhost:8021/. Many other FTP clients are available that will allow you to have a more sophisticated interface if you'd like. Many FTP clients are available in Linux, for the command line, or with GUIs, such as gFTP and Konqueror.

WebDAV Access into Plone

WebDAV is a system for authoring content in systems such as Plone using HTTP. This allows you to map a Plone server as a file system. To enable this, you'll have to edit the Zope configuration file as I detailed in Chapter 2 so that the zope.conf file has the following in it:

```
<webdav-source-server>
    address 1980
</webdav-source-server>
```

In Windows, the WebDrive program is available at http://www.webdrive.com/. A free trial is available, so you can give it a try. After installing WebDrive, add a connection to the Plone server, and then all you need to do then is access your Plone directly from the file system by going to Windows Explorer, as shown in Figure 10-11.

For Unix, you can get Cadaver (http://www.webdav.org/cadaver), which is a full-featured command-line client. After installing Cadaver, you can connect to a Plone site from the command line. For example:

```
cadaver http://192.168.2.1:8080/Members/Plone
```

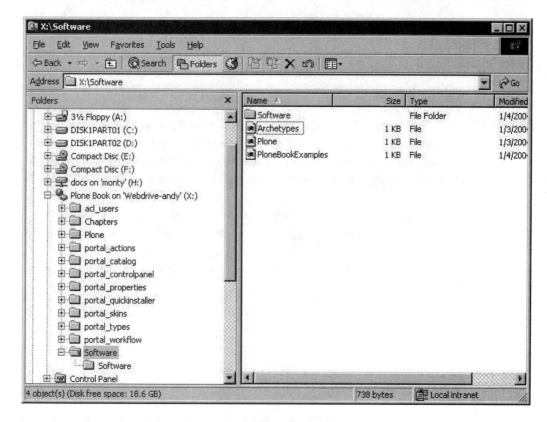

Figure 10-11. Accessing your Plone contents using WebDrive

Editing Content with Rich Editors

Editing content in a text area is a really bad way to force users to write and edit content—something I've commented on several times. Some editors provide a solution for this.

One is Epoz, which allows users to edit and alter documents directly in the browser without having to know HTML. If you have lots of users entering content, then installing Epoz allows your users to alter HTML content without having to actually understand HTML. For really advanced editing, you could use External Editor, which would allow you to edit content in a local program such as Microsoft Word.

Browser WYSIWYG Editor

You can find the tested version of Epoz 0.7.4 at http://zope.org/Members/mjablonski/Epoz/0.7.4. Epoz requires a modern browser, which most Plone users will need anyway. The required browsers are Internet Explorer 5.5+, Mozilla 1.3.1+, and Netscape 7.1+.

Download and install Epoz as usual; after installing, you'll need to change your personal Plone preferences so that you can use Epoz. Log into Plone, click *my preferences*, and select Personal Preferences. On the preferences page, open the Content Editor drop-down list, select the Epoz option, and then click Save to commit your changes.

Now you've chosen your editor, go to a document (any document will do) and click the Edit tab. You'll note that the *Body text* field has now changed significantly into a rich editor. The editor should be pretty self-explanatory to you, with familiar buttons such as B for bold, I for italics, and so on (see Figure 10-12).

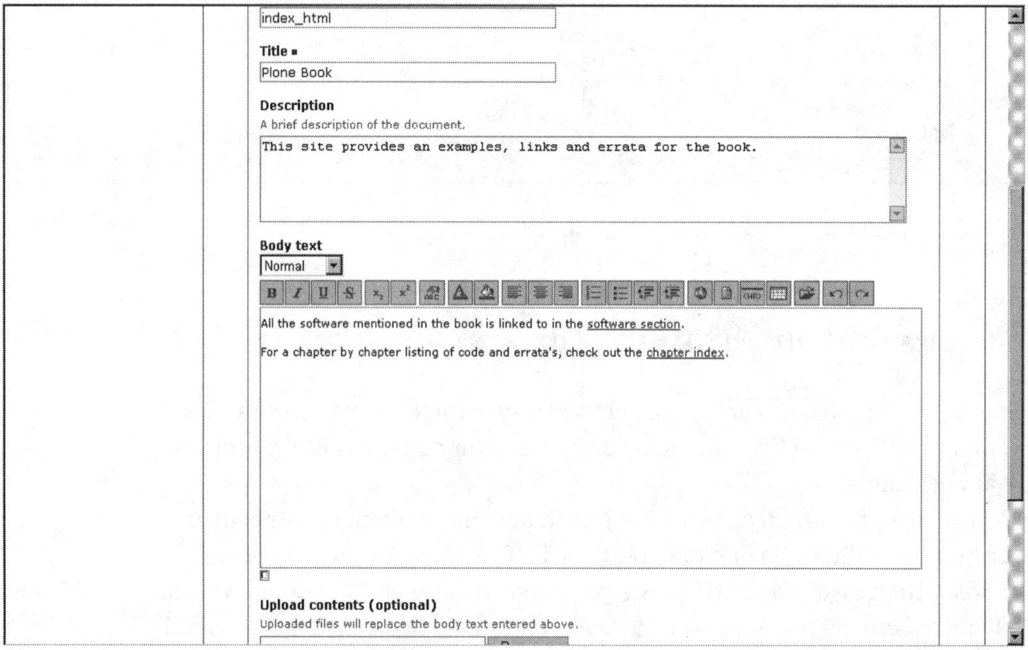

Figure 10-12. Editing a document in Epoz

External Editor

External Editor is a tool you can use on all sorts of Plone content, templates, and code. It allows you to edit Plone objects stored on a Plone site locally in programs of your choice. For example, you can edit a Microsoft Word document stored on your Plone site locally in Microsoft Word. When you save the document, it's automatically sent to Plone.

External Editor comes with the Plone installer packages and sets up automatically on the server. The application is unusual in that it has two components: one for the server and one for *each* client that wants to use the product.

Installing the Server Product

Installing the server product isn't necessary if you used an installer to install your Plone site. If this isn't the case, the server-side product is available at http://zope.org/Members/Caseman/ExternalEditor. Install the product in the standard way I discussed at the beginning of this chapter, and then restart your Zope.

Then, in Plone, log in as the administrator, click *plone setup*, and then select Portal Configuration. Select the Enable External Editor option to make sure you can edit objects with this tool.

Installing the Client Product

For every computer accessing the Plone site, you'll need to install this product on the client computer. Just like you'd install Flash or QuickTime in your browser, you install the client-side External Editor code. This is manageable in intranets or on your computer but can be a little harder for a public site.

For Windows 2000 and XP, download the executable Windows installer named zopeedit-win32-0.7.1.exe. Double-click the installer, and the graphical install will proceed. You just need to select all the defaults. This will set up the options for Internet Explorer. To verify that this has worked, do the following:

1. From the My Computer window, choose Tools ➤ Folder Options.

2. In the File Types window, scroll to the bottom, where you should see the extension Zope, as shown in Figure 10-13.

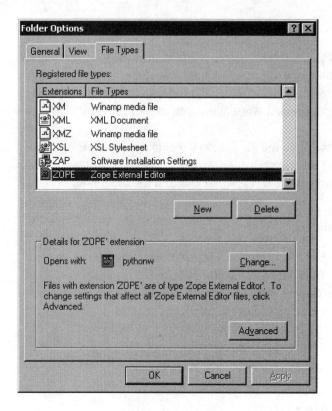

Figure 10-13. File type configuration on Windows

For Unix, download the tarball named `zopeedit-0.7-src.tar.gz`. You'll need to then unpack and run the setup as detailed in the Unix installation instructions at `http://zope.org/Members/Caseman/ExternalEditor/install-unix`. The following is an example with version 0.7:

```
$ tar -zxf zopeedit-0.7.1-src.tgz
$ cd zopeedit-0.7.1-src
$ python setup.py install
...
```

After you've installed the client, you'll need to configure each browser you want to use. Instructions for Konqueror, Galeon, and other browsers are available online at Zope.org. The following are the step-by-step configuration instructions for Mozilla:

1. Select Edit ➤ Preferences.

2. Under Navigator, choose Helper Applications.

3. Click the New Type button.

4. Enter a description, such as **Zope Editor**.

5. For MIME type, enter **application/x-zope-edit**.

6. For Application, select the helper application Python file.

7. Click OK, and then close Preferences.

External Editor opens an editor based on the contents of a configuration file. To have an editor of your choice invoked, alter that file. You can find it under different names in the following places, depending on your setup:

- On Windows, if you installed Plone using an installer, you can find this file at `c:\Program Files\Plone\Zope\pwi\zopeedit.ini`.

- On Windows, if you used the stand-alone External Editor installer, you can find this file in the directory you installed External Editor to; by default this is `c:\Program Files\ZopeExternalEditor\zopeedit.ini`.

- On Unix, this file will be called `.zope-external-edit` and located in the home directory of the user running the program, for example, `/home/andy/.zope-external-edit`. It's in the home directory of the user because each user may have different settings.

This file contains a mapping of extensions and the editor invoked; to change the editor for page templates, for example, find the following lines that have `meta-type:Page-Template`:

```
[meta-type:Page Template]
extension=.pt
```

For example, you can use Scite, a free text editor. To use this editor for page templates, you'd have to change the file to read as follows:

```
[meta-type:Page Template]
extension=.pt
editor=scite
```

For External Editor to work, each invocation of the editor must open a separate process. This means that the External Editor client program can monitor that process to see when it's finished. This causes problems for some editors that try to open multiple files in the same process. For example, to load VIM in KDE, you must run a separate shell as follows:

```
editor=konsole -e vim
```

Editing a Word Document

Editing a Microsoft Word document is actually really easy to set up; all you need is Microsoft Word installed on your local computer. Upload your Microsoft Word document to Plone as a standard file and then view the file in Plone. Click the little pencil icon in the top-right corner of your page. Microsoft Word will open on your computer, and the document from the server will display. You can now edit the content as much as you want, and clicking Save will automatically save the file into Plone.

Editing Page Templates Through External Editor

To create a page template, use the ZMI. Sure enough, when viewing the folder containing the page template, you'll see an extra pencil icon to the right of the object. Clicking the pencil will activate External Editor and open the page template in the editor you've selected. All you need to do is find a good editor for editing the page templates. Since page templates are just Extensible HTML (XHTML), I use a simple editor that supports Extensible Markup Language (XML). The following sections discuss two example editors: Dreamweaver and HTML-Kit.

Dreamweaver MX

Change the [meta-type:Page Template] part of the configuration file to point to Dreamweaver. For example, in my installation this is as follows:

```
[meta-type:Page Template]
extension=.pt
editor=C:\Program Files\Macromedia\Dreamweaver MX\Dreamweaver.exe
```

Clicking the pencil icon to edit in External Editor now opens it directly in Dreamweaver, as shown in Figure 10-14. Unfortunately, Dreamweaver will not open in each file in a separate instance, which means you can edit only one file at a time.

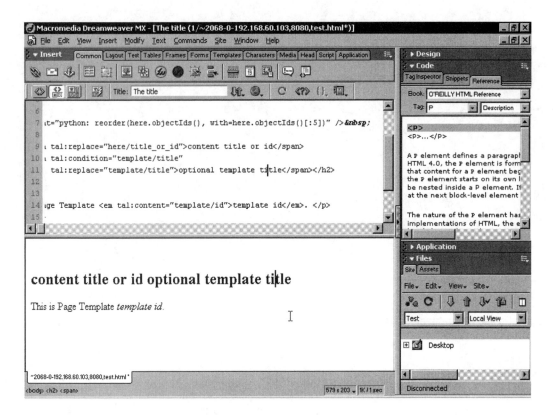

Figure 10-14. Editing page templates in Dreamweaver

HTML-Kit

HTML-Kit is a free and powerful HTML editor and is the favorite of many Plone developers. To use HTML-Kit with External Editor, alter your configuration file to point to HTML-Kit. For example, in my installation this is as follows:

```
[meta-type:Page Template]
extension=.pt
editor=C:\Program Files\Chami\HTML-Kit\Bin\HTMLKit.exe
```

Clicking the pencil icon to edit in External Editor now opens it directly in HTML-Kit. You can also edit a setting to open each file in a separate process; select Edit ➤ Preferences ➤ Startup, and check *Limit to a single HTML-Kit instance*. Each file will now open a new process.

CHAPTER 11

Manipulating and Categorizing Content Types

THROUGHOUT THE BOOK I've shown you how to add content to your site, and I've discussed the content types that come with Plone, such as documents, images, and so on. So far, however, you've been restricted to just these content types and the ones provided as products that you can find on the Internet. But the most powerful part of Plone is the core topic of this chapter: manipulating these content types.

In this chapter, I compare and contrast the different object types in Plone. This provides some insight into development tactics for your own projects. Then I cover the content types and how they're registered inside Plone. This registration provides the basis for customizing the types into the format you'd like. Then I move onto content categorization and searching—tasks you'll want to know how to perform. Armed with this knowledge, you'll be able to make key decisions about how to develop your site and create new content types.

So, I'll now whet your appetite about manipulating content types. Once you can customize an entirely new content type, you can have users adding and editing almost anything you want! Some of the examples include the following:

- Users can upload an image of a cell culture that's dissected and manipulated using imaging libraries and is then presented to the user in a certain format.

- Users can upload an MP3 audio file, extract the title and artist from the audio file, and place it inside Plone.

- You can build an entire e-commerce store, letting Plone users add items such as clothes for sale, including information such as shipping costs, dimensions, and warranty.

- Users can upload a Microsoft Word document and then manipulate it so that certain parts of it are blanked out. Users with a low security setting can see only those documents with blanked-out parts.

All these options and more are available to you in Plone! You really have few limits. This is why Plone is probably one of the most extensible and flexible frameworks available. The only real limit is your ability to program Python (or being able to afford someone to do it for you).

In this chapter, I thus cover content types in detail, including how to register and manipulate them through the Web. Although the following parts don't specifically require knowledge of Python, I recommend you at least become acquainted with it. I also include in this chapter information about the forms and how to validate them.

This chapter is required reading for anyone who wants to develop their own content types, no matter if they do it through the Web or in Python, because the chapter covers the areas needed to understand content type registration.

The next chapter will continue this journey—I'll take you into the really gory details of using Python to write content types. After that you'll use Archetypes to do the same thing with a tenth of the effort and then do some really cool and advanced stuff with Archetypes. But right now, you'll get straight into content types, from the top!

An Overview of Content Types

To begin with, I've been using certain terms throughout this book. The explanations I've given have been a little superficial, and it's time for me to expand on these to improve your understanding of them. The following are important concepts:

Content type: This is a type of content registered in a Plone site. Usually, but not always, a content type is something that can be added and edited through the Plone interface by users of the given security. In Plone it's recommended to separate content types such as documents, files, and images. This separation of content into different types is a basic Plone concept.

Item and object: These terms refer to the actual instance of something, and they're overloaded terms, so their definitions normally depend upon their context. So far in this book, I've used these terms to refer to a particular instance of a content type, such as one particular document or image. From now on, I'll use the specific term, *content type*, to refer to actual content types.

Tool: A tool is a service that sits inside a Plone site. There will be only one instance of each tool in a Plone site. In itself, the tool doesn't do anything, and external users of the application will never know how many tools exist or what they do. However, content types or requests that the users make will interact with the tools. You've already seen some key tools—`portal_workflow`, `portal_skins`, and `portal_actions`, for example.

Zope object: This is an object that lives inside Zope. It can be accessed through the Zope Management Interface (ZMI) and provides functionality for users. However, it isn't something that's accessed or controlled by Plone. If you go to a Plone site and access the ZMI, you'll see a large number of these objects in the ZMI. Tools are one such object, the Plone site is another, and the cache managers are another. A great deal of overlap exists between these objects; for example, Plone has an image content type, and Zope has an image object. The two do similar tasks and work in a similar way, but only one can be accessed through Plone.

NOTE Although everything inside a Plone site in the Zope Object Database (ZODB) is a *Zope object*, I use this term to describe objects that aren't tools or instances of a content type.

When to Make Content Types

So, you're building your killer application in Plone that's going to bring you fame and fortune. How do you structure it, and what do you build? Well, this depends upon what you're building, and you've factored out development so far. The following questions may help you decide:

Are you just changing skins and simple behaviors, such as portlets? You can do almost anything you want, except write a tool or a content type in a skin. You can change all the Cascading Style Sheets (CSS), templates, and scripts that come with a Plone site if you really wanted to do so.

Will members of your site add multiple copies of this item? If yes, then you probably want to write a content type.

Is this a service that other content types could use? If yes, then you probably want to write a tool.

Will you want multiple copies of something but don't want members of your site to be able to add and edit it? If yes, then you probably want a Zope object. However, you may want to rethink exactly what you're doing.

What usually happens is that an application is broken down into several bits: one or two tools and one or two content types. Chapter 12 covers writing a content type that takes source code, such as a snippet of Python, and then syntax highlights the code. If you needed that syntax highlighting in other places, then you could turn it into a tool that multiple content types could use. In short, tools are the best way to add functionality to a site rather than to any particular content type.

The definition for creating a content type is usually dictated by the requirement that users need to add, edit, and control these objects. It can be tempting to start creating a content type for every type of object, but as with all development, you need to be careful. Would it possible to use one content type instead of two, with only minor differences? Knowing how to configure this will come from experience, but the next few chapters will certainly help.

Content Type Configuration

So, your Plone site contains content types, but how does the Plone site know how they're configured? The answer is that for each content type, its attributes, methods, security, and skins are all defined on the file system in Python and associated code. This information is enough for Plone to understand how to use the product. The only exception to this, as you've seen, is workflow, which is normally defined externally from the content type. Some products have their own workflow that's added to the content type for its behavior.

Chapter 10 showed you how content types are installed in Plone through a two step-process: First, the product is installed in Zope. Second, the content type is installed in *each* Plone instance. The second step installs information about the content type, which is taken from the file system and then installed into your Plone site.

Why is this a two-stage process? In the second stage, a local copy of the product in your Plone site is made, and now you can change how the content behaves for you. Want a document object to have different tabs at the top? Want a document object to be manipulated differently, look differently, and even be called something completely different? No problem—you can now change your instance of Plone through the Web.

This approach is the same as it is for portal_skins, where you can customize a skin in your local instance. When changes occur in the product and you install a new version of Plone, those changes will affect the file system. But you can now download and install those changes; because you've customized it in your database, you'll keep the customized version.

Each content type in Plone will have a setting in the portal_types tool. Although each content type in the portal_types tool has only one setting, that type can have an unlimited number of actual objects in your database. The configuration is looked up when needed, so if you change the configuration, you'll update all the objects of that type in the database.

Content Type Registration in the portal_types Tool

To access the registration information, go to the portal_types tool in the ZMI. You'll be presented with a list of all the content types registered in this Plone site. Most of these content types are recognizable as something you'd add through the Plone interface with a few exceptions, such as Plone Site, TempFolder, and so on.

Each of these objects is an instance of factory type information, which is the name for a particular type of configuration. Click any of these objects to access the type's information; for example, when you click an event, you get the local copy of the information about the content type. You can alter this through the Web to change your configuration. The following are the values in that form:

- **Title**: This is a title for the content type. This isn't used in Plone.

- **Description**: This is the description that appears for this content type. This is used if you go to folder contents and click *add* without selecting a content type to add—a list of all the content types and their descriptions will appear.

- **Icon**: This is the ID of the icon that's used for this content type.

- **Product metatype**: This is the metatype for this content type. This matches up the Plone content type with a Zope metatype.

- **Product name**: This is the product name where this metatype is defined.

- **Product factory method**: This is the method that's called by the product factory to create this piece of content.

- **Initial view name**: This is the action that will be called when the item is clicked in the folder lists, folder contents, and so on. Usually this is the view, so enter the name of the view template.

- **Implicitly addable**: This indicates whether this content can be added to Plone. If this is selected, then it'll be addable, unless explicitly specified otherwise.

- **Filter content types**: If this content type is a folder, then enable this to filter the content types that can be added by users to this object.

- **Allowed content types:** If this content type can contain other items and *Filter content types* is enabled, only the types of content specified in this list will be allowed.

- **Allow discussion:** This sets the default status for discussions for all types of content. If this is enabled, then users will be able to discuss the content. Which users will be able to do this is based on the permission *Discuss content*.

You'll now look at some of the aspects of this registration information in a bit more detail, including some examples.

How Do You Change the Icon for a Content Type?

As an example, if you don't like the icon that appears for a content type, then it's a pretty simple matter of uploading a new image and then making sure that the value for the icon is set in the form described previously. Icons work best if they have a transparent background and are 16 pixels wide and 16 pixels high.

Click *portal_skins*, click *custom*, and add a new image. Then in the portal_types tool, set the value for the icon to be the same as the ID of the object uploaded. To test that the icon has changed, go to the Plone interface and look for where the object may appear; for example, do a search or look in the content add form.

Actions

When you're looking at the content type configuration in portal_types, you'll see an Actions tab. These are the actions that can be performed on the content type. You briefly looked at actions in Chapter 4, which contains a detailed list of what the Actions tab contains.

Recall that an *action* is a way of storing a list of information that can be easily edited and then accessed with multiple conditions. In the Plone portal, the actions display as blue tabs across the top of the site. For each content type, the actions appear as the green tabs that display in the middle of the page.

As you've seen, actions are stored on tool objects. Many of the tools contain actions, but you really don't have a great way to search for the location of an action. If you want to change a particular action on your Plone site, you have to find the tool that stores it.

Once you've found that action, you can then customize as much as you'd like. For instance, if you want to add a new action as a green tab for a document, you have to go and find the correct place. Luckily, the following tips help you find an action:

- If you're looking at an action on a pi ece of content such as view or edit, then it's on the particular content type in the portal_types tool.

- If you're looking at an action for the site, then it's in the portal_action tool.

- If you can't find it so far, look in a related tool; for example, joining and logging in are in portal_membership.

- If you can't find the action you're look ing for after trying the previous tips, go to portal_actions to see the list of tools and look through all the action providers.

Plone looks up the actions for content types in the following manner:

- For an object, all the actions are queried.

- For each action, the conditions, permissions, and visible properties are checked; if they pass, then the action will be returned.

- Each action will be shown in the user interface, usually in the form of tabs at the top of the content or the top of site.

- The URL for this action is the URL of the object with the actual Action appended to the end.

For example, on a document at http://localhost.com/Plone/Document123, the URL for an edit would be http://localhost.com/Plone/Document123/ document_edit_form. You should notice an important security issue here—the values for the conditions, permissions, and visible properties relate to showing the action in the list of actions. This means if users really wanted, they could alter the URL and go to http://localhost.com/Plone/Document123/document_edit_form even if the action permissions didn't allow this. For this reason, you should always have permissions on the actual actions that will be performed. If you were a user who could view an object but couldn't edit it, you could still alter the URL to get to the document edit form. No real harm has been done yet, because once you submitted it, the security would be rechecked and you'd be denied permission.

Normally actions are used as tabs in Plone, but since they can be called programmatically, they could be used in any way. To call an action programmatically, you call the listFilteredActionsFor method of the portal_actions tool. Given an object, this will return to you a Python dictionary keyed on category for all the actions for an object:

```
actions = context.portal_actions.listFilteredActionsFor(object)
```

This gives you the following:

```
{'site_actions': [
   {'category': 'site_actions', 'name': 'Small Text',
    'url': "javascript:setActiveStyleSheet('Small Text', 1);",
    'visible': 1, 'id': 'small_text',
    'permissions': ('View',)
    },
... and so on
```

The green tabs at the top are a combination of two categories: object and object_tabs. The actions returned from the method are a Python dictionary whose keys are the groupings of the category for that action. So, to get just the actions object for one category—for example, all actions in the object category— you could just access that key of the dictionary. For example, actions["object"] will give you a list of all these actions:

```
{'category': 'object',
 'name': 'Contents',
 'url': ' http://localhost:8080/Plone/folder_contents',
 'visible': 1,
 'id': 'folderContents',
 'permissions': ('List folder contents',)},
... and so on
```

You'll note that as long as you provide the object you're examining, it goes to the portal_types tool and finds all the actions for your particular portal_type, as well as any other actions that may be relevant.

If you wanted to add a new tab for a content type, all you need to do is go to portal_types, click the content type, and select the Actions tab. Then add your action. If the action were to appear as a green tab for the content type, then you'd have to ensure you made the category object_tabs.

Other Objects in the portal_types Tool

Looking at the portal_types tool, you'll probably notice you can add other object types to the folder such as DTML Method, External Method, Script (Python), and Scriptable Type Information. The first three of these options are present to provide support for the last option in the list, Scriptable Type Information.

Scriptable Type Information lets you define a type but create your own constructor permissions and construction script through the Web, instead of having them defined for you. If the default permission for a content type isn't sufficient, this may be an option. Although it's a useful-sounding option, I've never seen a good use for Scriptable Type Information over the standard factory-based type information, so don't worry about it.

Storing Content Type Information on the File System

You've now seen how this information is stored in Zope, but it does of course come from somewhere on the file system. This information is normally stored on the product in a dictionary, usually called *factory-based type information*. Listing 11-1 shows the factory information about Folder, which is a product that shows folders in Plone. This was taken from PloneFolder.py file located in the CMFPlone directory.

Listing 11-1. Factory-Based Type Information

```
factory_type_information = {
    'id':'Folder',     'meta_type':'Plone Folder',
    'description':"""\
Plone folders can define custom 'view' actions,\
 or will behave like directory listings without one defined.""",
    'icon':'folder_icon.gif',
    'product':'CMFPlone',     'factory':'addPloneFolder',
    'filter_content_types':0,
    'immediate_view':'folder_listing',     'actions':
      ( {
          'id':'view',              'name':'View',
          'action':'string:${folder_url}/',          'permissions':
(CMFCorePermissions.View,),           'category':'folder',        }
    ...
      )
    }
```

The Python dictionary closely maps the forms you saw in the Plone interface; for example, 'meta_type': 'Plone Folder' is the product's meta_type and will appear in that field. The actions appear as a list of dictionaries for each action, and it's again straightforward with key/value pairings for all the properties of an action. I just showed the first action here, View, but by now this information should be familiar to you.

Creating a New Content Type from an Existing Type

Repurposing is taking the information for an existing content type and creating multiple, slightly different copies of the same type. If you wanted to make a type that was almost the same as a news item, but not quite, then repurposing may be a quick and simple option.

The one big drawback of this approach is that you can't really change much beyond the actions, the skins, and some of content type settings. So before you proceed down this path, please be aware that you're limited to these points; you can't add new fields or attributes, for example. I've seen many e-mails on the mailing list saying, "I've done this much, but now I want to change the attributes of my press release." So consider this a warning: You can't! If you want to do more, check out writing content types in the next two chapters.

Say you wanted to make a press release type that's like a news item but it does the following:

- It has the name *Press Release* in the drop-down list.

- It has a different icon.

- It has a different workflow from a news item.

- It has a different view.

- It keeps the same data structure as a news item.

- It retains the news item type.

Well, in this case, repurposing a content type is ideal. For this example, take the factory-based type information for a news item, load it into the portal_types tool, and then call it a press release. This will allow you to reuse all the existing code and information while giving you new options. In the ZMI, access portal_types and complete the following steps:

1. Select *Factory-based Type Information*.

2. Enter an ID of **Press Release**, and in the *Use default type information* field, select CMF Default: News Item.

3. Click Add to complete this form.

This is now an instance of the configuration for a news item, but it's called *Press Release*. What advantage does this give you? Well, you now have another type of object that can be added through the Web by a user. This gives the users of your site a really easy way to distinguish between a news item and a press release, without mucking around with keywords or metadata. It will also show up in searches and all other places as a press release. You can now change the configuration for the press release, and this will leave the configuration for the news item intact.

Changing the icon was discussed earlier in this chapter—simply upload the image into your custom directory and then alter the Icon property in the portal_types page for a press release. If you go to portal_workflow, you can see that each content type has its own workflow. Because this is now a new content type, you can change the workflow for press releases only. Perhaps press releases require an extra stage of review or, when published, send e-mails to certain users. You can now make a new workflow, as I described in Chapter 8, and assign it to your press release.

Adding a new view means customizing the newsitem_view page template and renaming it to something meaningful such as pressrelease_view. You may want to alter that file to add some information about the company at the bottom of the page. For example:

```
<h2>About ACME Widget Company</h2>
<p>Our company is the prime maker of widgets in the world. Founded
in 1980 we've been providing excellent widgets to all parts of the
globe. For more marketing information, please contact: Joe Bloggs,
marketing director.</p>
```

After you've saved your changes to your new page template, return to the settings for the press release in portal_types and go to the Actions page. Change the action for viewing a press release from pointing to newsitem_view to pointing to pressrelease_view. Now whenever you view a press release, that view page will display, as shown in Figure 11-1.

In this case I've added a Press Release object, and the footer about ACME Company is in the template, so users don't need to remember to type this in every time.

Figure 11-1. An example Python script uploaded into Plone

Creating a Scripting Object

Once an object is registered in the portal_types tool, you can then create the object in your Plone site. You can also script the creation of the object programmatically. This is useful for making objects based on certain other factors or creating objects en masse. Plone has two useful Script (Python) objects for this:

generateUniqueId: This creates a new unique ID for the type of object, for example, Folder.2003-12-19.7359814582. It's unique only to the folder it's created in; if you create a lot of objects quickly, then it's possible that they couldn't be unique. For most normal usage, this is good enough.

invokeFactory: This takes an ID and a type name. This will create an object of the type given and give it the ID specified.

You'll make an example script that creates a folder and a default page in that folder, and into that default page you'll put some specific content. If this sounds familiar, this is what happens when you join a site and a home folder is created for you. The type names match the registration inside the portal_types tool, so if you wanted to create a folder and inside that create a document, you'd need to pass the parameters Folder and Document to the invokeFactory script.

Listing 11-2 shows a script that gets a unique ID and that creates a folder based on that ID. It will then step inside the folder and create a new document.

Listing 11-2. Getting an ID and Creating a Folder

```
##title=Create
##parameters=
# create with a random id
newId = context.generateUniqueId('Folder')

# create a object of type Folder
context.invokeFactory(id=newId, type_name='Folder')
newFolder = getattr(context, newId)

# create a new Document type
newFolder.invokeFactory(id='index.html', type_name='Document')

# get the new page
newPage = getattr(newFolder, 'index.html')
newPage.edit('html', '<p>This is the default page.</p>')

# return something back to the calling script
return "Done"
```

If you add this as a Script (Python) object and test it by using the Test tab, you'll get a folder made for you. One interesting thing to note is that this creates the folder and document in the current context, wherever the context object may be.

Content Type Registry

I've shown you a variety of ways to access Plone, including File Transfer Protocol (FTP) and WebDAV. When Plone receives a piece of content from one of these sources, it has to deal with the content in an appropriate manner. This negotiation is performed by the content type registry, which is visible in the ZMI as the content_type_registry tool. If you visit the content_type_registry tool in Zope, you'll probably be dazzled by yet another badly designed form in the ZMI.but don't let that put you off!

When a piece of content is added to Plone via FTP or WebDAV, the rules in the registry are executed from the top to the bottom, until a match is made. The match is based on the criteria in that rule, and when met, the appropriate content type for that rule is created. The following are the four different types of criteria:

major_minor: This takes the two parts (either side of the forward slash) of the Multipurpose Internet Mail Extensions (MIME) type of the incoming file and matches against them. If you leave either part blank, then it will match everything. For example, a major_minor of image (that's one empty space on the end) matches image/jpeg, image/gif, image/png, and so on.

extension: This matches the filename extension; each extension is separated by a space. So, for example, doc pdf matches invoices.doc and report.pdf.

mimetype_regex: This performs a regular expression match on the MIME type. For example, _,^j matches image/jpeg, image/jpg, application/java, and so on.

name_regex: This performs a regular expression match on the filename. For example, ^Invoice will match Invoice-123.pdf but not Not_an_Invoice-123.pdf.

To add a type, in the form at the bottom of the page, enter the name of the rule and the type from the drop-down and click Add. This will create a rule at the bottom of the page and allow you to enter a pattern that matches the type of rule you created and select the content type you want to create from the drop-down list. You can then click Up and Down to move your item up and down, respectively, to increase its importance.

As an example, I recently bought a digital camera. Because the Plone Windows installer has CMFPhoto and PIL all set up, it seemed a way to dump my pictures into an online photo album with minimum ease. First, I enabled the FTP server, and then I went to content type registry and made a new rule, based on extension that maps image/jpeg to the photo content type. I then moved the rule up above the existing rule for images. Then all I had to do was drag and drop the photographs into my FTP client, and they were automatically loaded into Plone, thumbnailed, and displayed.

Searching and Categorizing Content

You've seen how you can search for content in Plone, but I'll now go into detail and show how the underlying categorization and searching of content occurs. The main tool that stores all this information is a tool called the portal_catalog, which is a slightly different and extended version of the underlying ZCatalog tool. You'll find an excellent online reference to the ZCatalog at http://zope.org/ Documentation/Books/ZopeBook/2_6Edition/SearchingZCatalog.stx.

The catalog provides three key elements to a Plone site: It creates indexes of content, it holds metadata about the content in the index, and it provides a search interface to quickly examine the content of your Plone site. Of all the different objects present in your Zope site, only the actual instances of your content types are cataloged. Zope objects, tools, and other objects aren't placed in the catalog. For this reason, the catalog tool is closely tied to the content types and their usage. You can access the catalog by accessing the portal_catalog tool in the ZMI.

Indexing Content

The first part of the catalog's job is to build indexes of the content. An index primarily provides a method for quickly and efficiently searching the content. For this reason, the content of the index isn't designed to be clear or make sense; it's designed rather for fast and efficient searching. When you search in a Plone site, you search the indexes, and the catalog will return matching result sets for that query.

An index queries a Plone object for a particular value, a method, or an attribute, and then it indexes whatever that object returns for that query. How it actually indexes the content depends upon the type of the index. Table 11-1 lists all the indexes that come with Plone.

Table 11-1. Available Index Types

Name	Description
DateIndex	This is designed to index dates, and it lets you do searches based on dates and times.
DateIndexRange	This is a more efficient implementation of DateIndex for cases where you have two dates, such as start and end dates and doing lots of searches in those dates.
FieldIndex	This treats every result automatically and allows you to search on whatever the index may contain. It matches any search that matches the index.
KeywordIndex	This takes a sequence of keywords and splits them into separate words. This will return a result if any of the keywords in the index match the given query. This is ideal for searching subjects or keywords on objects.
PathIndex	This indexes the path of an object, such as /Members/ jane/myDocument, as a list of the objects. This allows you to query the catalog for all the contents of Members without having to ask the folder. A Path index will return everything below the Members folder.
TextIndex	This is an old text index that takes text, splits it up, and indexes that. See ZCTextIndex.
TopicIndex	This builds up predefined result sets at cataloging time. This is useful for often-repeated queries.
ZCTextIndex	This is a new index that provides full-text searching capabilities efficiently on pieces of text. It supports a large number of features, discussed in detail later.

You can see what indexes are defined in a catalog by clicking portal_catalog and selecting the Indexes tab. This will give you a list of all the indexes defined in your Plone site. The columns are the name of the index, the type, the number of hits, and when the index was last modified. The types of indexes were briefly covered previously, but Table 11-2 describes what all the default indexes are in a Plone site.

Table 11-2. Default Indexes That Are Set Up in Plone

Name	Type	Description
Creator	FieldIndex	This is the username of the person who created the object.
Date	FieldIndex	This is the effective date; if not present, it's the last modified date.
Description	TextIndex	The description field.
SearchableText	ZCTextIndex	The description, title, and body of the object as one searchable lump of text.
Subject	KeywordIndex	The keywords for an item.
Title	TextIndex	Item's title.
Type	FieldIndex	The portal type as defined in the portal_types tool.
allowedRolesAndUsers	KeywordIndex	Who can view this content; this is an efficient way to examine this so you can filter the search results.
created	FieldIndex	When the item was created.
effective	FieldIndex	When the item will become effective.
end	FieldIndex	For events only, when the event will end.
expires	FieldIndex	When the item will expire and no longer be viewable.
getId	FieldIndex	The ID for an item.
id	FieldIndex	Same as getId.
in_reply_to	FieldIndex	For discussions, gives the item to which this comment is responding.
meta_type	FieldIndex	The underlying metatype of the item.

Table 11-2. Default Indexes That Are Set Up in Plone (Continued)

Name	Type	Description
modified	FieldIndex	When the item was last modified.
path	PathIndex	The path to the item.
portal_type	FieldIndex	Same as Type.
review_state	FieldIndex	The state of the object in workflow.
start	FieldIndex	For events only, when the event will start.

If you're ever unsure of the contents of an index, then you can see the contents of the indexes in the ZMI. Click portal_catalog and select Catalog, and this will list every object cataloged at this time. Click an object, and a window will pop up with the contents of the index and the metadata. The metadata comes first so scroll down to see the indexes.

To add, remove, or alter the indexes, return to the Indexes tab. Use the usual Add drop-down box to add a new index or remove an index. If you want to run a reindex of a particular index, then select the indexes on the left and click the reindex button. If you add an index to the catalog, it isn't populated, meaning you then need to click the reindex button to ensure that there's some content in your index.

 NOTE If you have a large site, this indexing can be quite time and processor consuming, so you may want to avoid doing this during peak load times.

Metadata

When the catalog returns a result, it doesn't return to you the object; instead, it returns the metadata stored in the catalog. This metadata is a series of fields or columns for each value on the object. Likewise, a set list of columns for a Plone site are created, as described in Table 11-3.

Table 11-3. Default Metadata That's Set Up in Plone

Name	Description
CreationDate	The date when the object was created.
Creator	The username of the person creating the object.
Date	This is the effective date; if not present, it's the last modified date.
Description	The description field.
EffectiveDate	The effective date.
ExpiresDate	The expires date.
ModificationDate	The modification date.
Subject	The keywords on an object.
Title	The object's title.
Type	The object's portal_type.
created	Same as CreationDate.
effective	Same as EffectiveDate.
end	For events only, when the event will end.
expires	When the object will expire.
getIcon	The objects icon.
getId	The object's ID.
getRemoteUrl	Only used for links; this is the URL pointed to by the link.
id	Same as getId.
location	For events only, where the event will take place.
meta_type	The object's meta_type.
modified	When the object was modified.
portal_type	The object's portal_type.
review_state	The state of the object in workflow.
start	For events only, when the event will start.

How an Object Is Indexed

Content types are indexed automatically because they inherit from a class called PortalContent, which inherits from a class called CMFCatalogAware. The CMFCatalogAware class handles all the code to ensure that when you add, edit, cut, copy, delete, or rename an object, the catalog (and also workflow) are kept up to date. Essentially the object is passed to the catalog, and the appropriate instruction for the catalog is called (index, remove from index, and so on).

The catalog then runs through each index and for each index queries the object by looking for attributes or methods on the object. For most indexes, the attribute or method looked up is the same name as the index. For the index name Title, it would look for an attribute or method named Title and populate the index with the result. It then repeats the process with each of the metadata columns.

Two exceptions to this process are the FieldIndex and TopicIndex types. When you add a FieldIndex, you can specify that the index examines a different value than the name of the index. For example, you could make an index with the ID getVersion, which looks at the value of version. As you'll see later, some indexes have advantages over others, so it can be useful to have two different indexes pointing to the same value.

TopicIndex is a different type of index in that it builds up a series of sets at the time the content is indexed. If you wanted to do a lot of searches for all images, then you could add a search for o.portal_type == 'Image'. To do this, you need to create a TopicIndex and then click the index from the Indexes tab; you can even add multiple expressions to build up an index. At this time, TopicIndex indexes aren't used anywhere in Plone.

How Do You Reindex All the Content on Your Plone Site?

If you've made a large number of code-level changes, put in a new product, or renamed or moved your root Plone object, then you may need to reindex all the content on your site. In the ZMI, click portal_catalog, click Advanced, and click Update Catalog. This will run the process of updating your catalog.

 CAUTION   This is an even more intensive task than reindexing just one index, and it can take a long time and use a lot of memory and processing power if you have a large database.

Relational Databases vs. Plone

The development of content types in Plone is slightly different from developing using a relational database. A common development paradigm these days is LAMP—a combination of Linux, Apache, MySQL, and PHP or Perl. In this paradigm, data is stored in a table in the database, and a scripting language provides the application layer to pull the content out of the database and put it into templates. You search the content by sending queries to the database in SQL, using SELECT statements.

Plone does this differently with the use of an object database. Any content item can contain any attributes of any type, and the underlying object database takes care of persisting those attributes in the database. For searching, all the objects are then indexed in the portal_catalog tool. You have to specifically tell the catalog exactly what attributes you'd like to index. Instead of doing SQL calls, you'd instead use the catalog to examine the indexes.

This difference can be confusing in the development stage, especially since relationships between objects aren't created and maintained as they would be in a relational database application. Instead, there are two common ways to maintain a reference: using a catalog to maintain the relationship through keywords or other values or using a folder to group content. Archetypes, which I'll discuss in Chapter 14, allows you maintain relationships easily. It does so through the catalog.

Searching the Catalog

Of course, the biggest question is how to search the catalog and use the results. The first of these tasks depends upon the indexes, so I cover each of the indexes and show how to search them. The second of these tasks involves manipulating the results, so I then show you how to do this.

All of the following examples are in Python because this is the best way to search a catalog. I also show a quick example of how to hook this into a page template. I fully recommend using Python for manipulating the catalog because it really is the best place to do things, allowing you the best flexibility without having to worry about the syntax.

In general, you achieve searching by calling the method searchResults on the portal_catalog object and passing through a series of keyword parameters. A couple of reserved keywords exist, but the rest are mapped directly to the indexes of the same name. So if you wanted to search the SearchableText index, you'd pass through to the search method a keyword parameter for SearchableText. The reserved keywords are as follows:

- **sort_on**: This is the index to sort the results on, assuming that the index allows sorting (full-text indexes don't allow sorting).

- **sort_order**: This is reverse or descending; if not specified, the default is ascending.

- **sort_limit**: This is an optimization hint to make sorting a little quicker.

So, a general search for all items that mention Plone and are published in Date order looks something like this:

```
context.portal_catalog.searchResults(
    review_state = "published",
    SearchableText = "Plone",
    sort_order="Date"
)
```

The search will return the intersection of the index results, so this will find all items that mention Plone *and* are published. You can't do searches that are the union of results; however, you could do multiple results and then add the results together, but this is a rather unusual case, though.

TIP If you do a search with no values, then the entire contents of the catalog are returned. By default, all searches add values for effective and end dates, ensuring that you see content only between these times, unless the user calling the search has the *Access inactive portal content* permission.

Searching a Field or Date Index

To search a FieldIndex, pass through the value of the field. Any hits that match will be returned; for example, to search for all the image's in a site, use the following:

```
results = context.portal_catalog.searchResults(
    Type = "Image"
)
```

A field index can take a range of objects as well, and the index will attempt to find all the values in between by performing a comparison of the values. This range could be between two dates, two numbers, or two strings—it really depends upon the value of FieldIndex. You do this by passing a dictionary to the index, rather than just a string. The dictionary should contain two values: a list called *query*, which contains the values to be tested, and a range, which defines a range of the values. The range is a string of one of the following:

- **min**: Anything larger than the smallest item

- **max**: Anything smaller than the largest item

- **minmax**: Anything smaller than the largest and bigger than the smallest

For example, to find all events that have a start time bigger than now (in other words, anything in the future), use the following:

```
from DateTime import DateTime
now = DateTime()
results = context.portal_catalog.searchResults(
        Type = "Event"
        end = { "query": [now,],
                "range": "min" }
)
```

To search on a range, such as all news items in December, you'd need to calculate the start and end dates for the month. From those dates, you can then construct the following query:

```
from DateTime import DateTime
start = DateTime('2004/12/01')
end = DateTime('2004/12/31')
results = context.portal_catalog.searchResults(
        Type = "News Item",
        CreationDate = { "query": [start, end],
                         "range": "minmax" }
)
```

Date indexes work in the same manner as field indexes, and often you'll see dates placed inside field indexes, which works just fine.

Searching a KeywordIndex

By default, a `KeywordIndex` returns all the values that match in the keyword index. `Subject` is the only `KeywordIndex`; this is the keyword that a user has assigned to an object through the Properties tab of the Plone interface. To search for all items with the keyword *Africa*, use this:

```
results = context.portal_catalog.searchResults(
        Subject = "Africa"
)
```

Similar to a `FieldIndex`, a `KeywordIndex` can be passed a more complicated query, with several objects and an and/or operator (or is the default). This would allow you to find all objects that have almost any combination of keywords. To find all objects that have the subject *Africa* and *sun*, use the following:

```
results = context.portal_catalog.searchResults(
        Subject = { "query": ["Africa", "sun"],
                    "operator": "and" }
)
```

Searching a PathIndex

A path index allows you to search for all objects in a certain path. It will return every object below a current location, so if you ask for all objects in `Members`, it'll return everything in everybody's home directories. For example, for all objects that have `Members` in their path, use this:

```
results = context.portal_catalog.searchResults(
        path = "/Plone/Members"
)
```

If you want to further restrict this, you can do so by passing through a level parameter that sets where you expect the value to be. The level is a number representing its position in the path, from the left when splitting it up by forward slashes. For example, in the previous code, `Plone` is level 0, `Members` is level 1, and so on. Similarly to `KeywordIndex`, you can pass through an and/or operator. To get all objects in the /Plone/Members/danae folder and the /Plone/testing/danae folder, use the following:

```
results = context.portal_catalog.searchResults(
        path = { "query": ["danae"],
                "level" : 2 }
)
```

Searching a ZCText Index

ZCTextIndex is the most complicated of all indexes and takes a whole host of
options. Each ZCTextIndex requires a lexicon; fortunately, Plone creates and con-
figures all this out of the box. If you click *portal_catalog*, select the Contents tab,
and click *plone_lexicon*, you can see the default configuration of the lexicon.
Clicking the Query tab will show you all the words that are in the lexicon built out
of your Plone site content.

The ZCTextIndex is searched using the format I described in Chapter 3. It takes
similar terms to the searching that you can use on Google or other search engines.
At its most basic, you can search for any term (note that this is case insensitive),
like so:

```
results = context.portal_catalog.searchResults(
        SearchableText = "space"
)
```

But you can also search for all of the following:

- **Globbing**: Use an asterisk to signify any letters. For example, tues* matches
  tuesday and *tuesdays*. You can't use the asterisk at the beginning of a word,
  though.

- **Single wildcards**: Use a question mark to signify one letter. For example,
  ro?e matches *rope*, *rote*, *role*, and so on. You can't use the question mark at
  the beginning of a word.

- **And**: Using *and* signifies that both terms on other side of it must exist. For
  example, rome and tuesday will return only a result with both those words
  are in the content.

- **Or**: Using *or* signifies that either terms can exist. For example, rome or
  tuesday will return a result if either of those words are in the content.

- **Not**: Using *not* returns results where this isn't present (a prefix and is required). For example, welcome and not page would return matches for pages that contained *welcome*, but not *page*.

- **Phrases**: You can group phrases with double quotes (") and signify several words one after the other. For example: "welcome page" matches *This welcome page is used to introduce you to the Plone Content Management System*, but not *Welcome to the front page of….*

- **Not phrase**: You can specify a phrase with a minus (-) prefix. For example, welcome -"welcome page" matches all pages with *welcome* in them, but not ones that match the phrase *welcome page*.

 TIP   If you perform a search with no text, then no results are returned.

Using the Results

So you've got some results, now what do you do with them? The first thing a lot of people do is look at the results and assume that it's a list of the objects that were cataloged. Well, it isn't; rather, it's a series of "catalog brains." These brains are actually lazy objects that contain the metadata columns defined earlier. You can access any of these columns as if it were an attribute. For example, to print all the IDs of result objects, use the following:

```
results = context.portal_catalog.searchResults()
for result in results:
    print result.getId
return printed
```

In this example, getId is the name of a metadata column, so it'll display the value for getId that the catalog had for that object. If you try to just access a value that doesn't exist as a metadata column, then you'll get an AttributeError. The following are a few methods available from a brain that are useful:

- **getPath**: This returns the physical path for this object inside Zope.

- **getURL**: This returns the URL for this object with virtual hosting applied.

- **getObject**: This returns the actual object.

- **getRID**: This is a unique ID for the object in the catalog, and it changes each time the object is uncataloged. It's for internal purposes only.

So, if you wanted to get the object for each result, you can do so, as you'll see in the following example. However, there's a reason the catalog doesn't do this— it's expensive (in terms of computation) because it involves waking up an object from the database (and all the objects in between) and making lots of security checks. If you can try to make your metadata contain the right information, you'll have a much faster application. Obviously, sometimes metadata can't contain everything, but it's worth considering in the design. To get each object, use the following:

```
results = context.portal_catalog.searchResults()
for result in results:
    object = result.getObject()
    print object
return printed
```

Since you have a Python list of these brains, it's now straightforward to manipulate the results in a manner that you see fit. To find out how many results were returned, you can just call the len function on the list, like so:

```
results = context.portal_catalog.searchResults()
print "Number of results", len(results)
return printed
```

 NOTE len is a Python function that tells you the length of an item.

To get just the first ten items, use a Python slice, like so:

```
results = context.portal_catalog.searchResults()
return results[:10]
```

To do further filtering, you could manually filter the whole list, like so:

```
results = context.portal_catalog.searchResults()
for result in results[:10]:
    # Title returns a string so we can use the find method of
    # a string to look for occurence of a word
    if result.Title.find("Plone") > -1:
        print result.Title
return printed
```

To get a random object from the catalog, use the random module, like so:

```
import random
results = context.portal_catalog.searchResults()
r = random.choice(results)
object = r.getObject()
return object
```

Tying It All Together: Making a Search Form

In the previous discussion, I showed you how to get some results out of the catalog, and I used Script (Python) objects to demonstrate that. But you're probably asking yourself, how can I do this from a page template?

I'll start at the other end and first assume you have the results from a catalog query and loop through them in a page template using tal:repeat. This is how a lot of portlets are put together—the published and events portlets both just do queries and then show the results. Those portlets embed the query in a page template either by calling it directly:

```
<div tal:define="results python:
here.portal_catalog.searchResults(Type="Event")">
```

or by calling a separate Script (Python) object that returns the results. For example, in the following, the script is called getCatalogResults:

```
##parameters=
kw = {}
# enter your query into the kw dictionary
return context.portal_catalog(**kw)
```

In a page template, you'd get the results in the following manner:

```
<div tal:define="results here/getCatalogResults">
```

After doing this, you need to loop through the results using the standard tal:repeat syntax. You can access each metadata column directly in the Template

Attribute Language (TAL) by making a path expression to the column. So, given a brain, you could get the title from the metadata by calling `result/Title`. Listing 11-3 shows an example page that loops through the contents of `getCatalogResults` and displays each item in a simple unordered list.

Listing 11-3. Looping Through `getCatalogResults`

```
<html xmlns="http://www.w3.org/1999/xhtml" xml:lang="en-US"
      lang="en-US"
      metal:use-macro="here/main_template/macros/master"
      i18n:domain="plone">
<body>
<div metal:fill-slot="main">
<ul tal:define="results here/getCatalogResults">
    <li tal:repeat="result results">
        <a href=""
           tal:attributes="href result/getURL"
           tal:content="result/Title" />
        <span tal:replace="result/Description" />
    </li>
</ul>
</div>
</body>
</html>
```

One property of the `searchResults` method is that if you don't pass any parameters to the function, it'll look them up from the incoming request. So if you wanted to allow a form to post parameters to your results, then all you have to do is change the previous results line to the following:

```
<ul tal:define="

  results python: here.portal_catalog.searchResults(REQUEST=request)
  ">
```

Now you can redo your query and append any index to the URL. For example, if you called this page template `testResults` and appended `?Type=Document` to the end of the URL of your browser, only the documents in your site would appear. Since you can pass in almost any request values, you can set up a search form that would pass this information through to the search form. This is what the search and advanced search pages do; you'll note that if you go to a Plone site and search for *beer* in the search box, your URL will now have `?SearchableText=beer`.

So, Listing 11-4 shows a form to call your page template.

Listing 11-4. A Form to Call Your Template

```
<html xmlns="http://www.w3.org/1999/xhtml" xml:lang="en-US"
      lang="en-US"
      metal:use-macro="here/main_template/macros/master"
      i18n:domain="plone">
<body>
<div metal:fill-slot="main">
  <p>Select a content type to search for</p>
  <form method="post" action="testResults">
    <select name="Type">
      <option
        tal:repeat="value python:here.portal_catalog.uniqueValuesFor('Type')"
        tal:content="value" />
        </select>
        <br />
        <input type="submit" class="context">
    </form>
</div>
</body>
</html>
```

This script uses a method called uniqueValuesFor on the catalog, which will return all the unique values that exist for an index. This lets you perform a task such as populating a little drop-down box in a form, which is a pretty useful thing to have.

At this point, it becomes an exercise in HTML and page templates to make the pages as complicated as you'd like. Of course, the best place to look for all this is in the actual templates of Plone, which give lines upon lines of great examples. All the portlets you're familiar with in Plone (such as the calendar, events, related, and so on) are all built using catalog queries to determine what to show.

In this chapter, I've provided you with an overview of ways to develop a Plone site and how content types work in your site. I demonstrated how a content type is constructed and then referenced through the catalog. This is a key development methodology in Plone.

In the next chapter, I'll show how to develop a new content type pretty much from scratch. You'll see how you can integrate that new content type with the catalog register in the portal_types tool.

Writing a Product in Python

WRITING A PRODUCT for Plone allows you to do almost anything you'd like to do with Plone. Using Python to write content types or tools is the best way to provide ultimate flexibility. If you have a burning need for Plone to do something specific and it isn't covered elsewhere, then this is your opportunity to add this feature by writing a product. This could be storing some type of content specific to your company or some manipulation unique to you. In the previous chapter, I showed how you can customize a content type. This customization can take you only so far, though; you can't actually add new attributes to your content type, for example. Instead, you'll probably want to write your own content type.

In this chapter, I run through two examples: a content type and a tool. Both of these examples will be relatively straightforward but will get you ready for the next chapter, where I'll show you how to use Archetypes, a framework for Plone that allows you to generate content types quickly and simply with a minimal amount of code.

Specifically, I create a custom content type in Plone and step through all the code used to create this content type. It's a quite interesting content type—it uses several building blocks it pulls from a third-party C module and incorporates them into your Plone site. I show how to create the content type initially and then add permissions, search integration, new user interface elements, and installation scripts. Finally, I cover how to create a Plone tool, which is a way to add new tools to a site. Both of the examples in this chapter are available online for you to download, install, and study. Also, Appendix B lists all the code.

Writing a Custom Content Type

For the Plone book Web site (http://plone-book.agmweb.ca), I wanted to be able to show the code from this book online. I could've taken the code and simply placed it into documents, but that code would just show up without syntax highlighting. Also, all the whitespace in Python would have been removed. For a great product such as Plone, I needed something that looked good. So I needed a content type that would take code, syntax highlight it nicely, and allow users to easily view it online. Figure 12-1 shows the sample finished product.

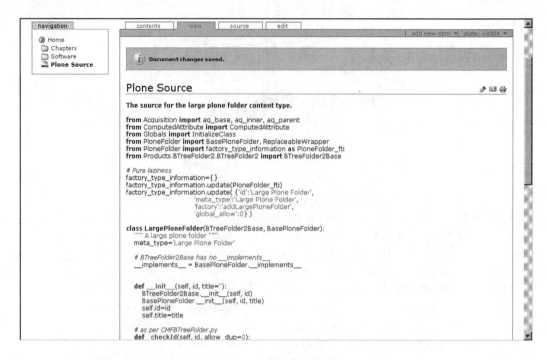

Figure 12-1. An example Python script uploaded into Plone

From this design, you can extrapolate a few requirements for this product. Specifically, this product will have the following attributes:

- **ID**: Each piece of code will have a unique ID. This attribute is required.

- **Title**: Each piece of code should have a title. This attribute is required.

- **Description**: Each piece of code should have a description describing what it should do. This attribute is optional.

- **Source code**: Each piece of code will have one source code attribute that contains the source for that content type. This will be optional, but making it required is reasonable.

- **Language**: This is the language for the source code—for example, Perl, Python, Hypertext Markup Language (HTML), and so on.

Of course, the content type should interact with Plone so that you can use the power of Plone. You'll need to ensure that the product can be searched, can interact with security, can interact with workflow, and is correctly persisted. Further, it'd be nice if users could upload scripts directly from their hard drives rather than trying to cut and paste into a text area.

When investigating this code, I needed to find a simple way to turn code into HTML. This is pretty easy to do for a language with simple syntax such as Python (in fact, Python can "lex" its own code), but really you want to be able to do this for multiple languages, such as HTML (page templates), JavaScript, Cascading Style Sheets (CSS), and so on. Fortunately, the SilverCity module does this already and is available from SourceForge (`http://silvercity.sf.net/`). It uses C libraries from the Scintilla text editor to lex the code. Without having to worry too much implementation, the upshot is that it'll happily spit out syntax-highlighted HTML for nearly a dozen programming languages.

Looking at the list of requirements, you'll see that they're pretty straight-forward. In fact, the ID, title, and description are all defined in the Dublin Core implementation in Plone. So you have to worry only about the source code and language. Plone requires an ID and a title, and it really helps to have a description.

Starting the Content Type

Now that you have an idea of the content type you'll create in this chapter, you can start building it by writing Python on the file system. This content type is also a product, so you create a new directory in your product directory. The name of the directory you'll create is the name of the product that Zope will import, so choose your name wisely. I toyed with the idea of calling the product *SourceCode* or *PloneSourceCode* but decided those would be too confusing (they could also mean that the product is the actual source code for Plone). Instead, *PloneSilverCity* seemed to be a nice name that gave credit to its origins and was sufficiently obscure that no one would confuse it with something else.

Developing with ZClasses

You're creating the content type using Python, but you've probably heard about ZClasses in other documentation or on the Internet. ZClasses are an existing framework in Zope 2 for developing classes through the Web. Many people have developed and distributed ZClasses successfully, and there can be a role for them for rapid development. However, I really don't recommend them. It's hard to develop them using existing tools, place them in source code, distribute them, and so on. Almost everyone I've talked to about ZClasses agrees that it's worth the effort to learn how to develop with Python, and I've seen more than one presentation that has ZClasses in the list of mistakes people have made.

If you do see documentation or other information relating to ZClasses, then I really recommend resisting the temptation to use it. For this reason, there's no mention of developing using ZClasses. If you're looking for a quick way to develop, then take a look at Archetypes, which is a slightly different approach.

After creating the directory, I usually add a few files and directories that I'll need. Every package needs an __init__.py file in it. The name of this file comes from Python and indicates that this directory is a Python package and hence importable. When the package is imported, Zope executes this file. Inside that file, you'll insert the product registration code so that the product will be registered with Zope.

Being user friendly, you can also add a few text files such as readme.txt, install.txt, and so on. One other text file that's also useful to add is refresh.txt. This file lets you hook into Zope's Refresh module and lets you dynamically reload the product as you write it. This is mind-bogglingly useful for your first few steps in writing a class, and I'll show how to configure this in Zope later.

At the moment, you have a directory called PloneSilverCity in the product directory that contains the following files, all empty: readme.txt, refresh.txt, install.txt, and __init__.py. This is now a valid Python package that does absolutely nothing (but not for long).

Integrating SilverCity

Before you get too far into the Zope code, it may be useful to figure out how to use SilverCity. In any software development, writing layers that allow testing at atomic layers is absolutely vital. For this reason, you should start by making sure that you can use SilverCity from a Python module. If that works, you then simply have to add the Zope layer.

So, look into SilverCity for a moment. First, you have to install SilverCity; fortunately, this module corresponds to the install instructions for Python modules as outlined in Chapter 10. To install on Windows, download the file SilverCity-0.9.5.win32-py2.3.exe from http://silvercity.sf.net and run the graphical installer. To install on Linux, download the file SilverCity-0.9.5.tar.gz from http://silvercity.sf.net and save it to disk. Then unpack it and run the setup.py program. For example:

```
$ tar -zxf SilverCity-0.9.2.tgz
$ cd SilverCity-0.9.2
$ python setup.py install
...
```

After doing this, you can quickly test that it works from the following Python prompt in Windows or Linux:

```
$ python
Python 2.3.2 (#1, Oct  6 2003, 10:07:16)
[GCC 3.2.2 20030222 (Red Hat Linux 3.2.2-5)] on linux2
Type "help", "copyright", "credits" or "license" for more information.
>>> import SilverCity
>>>
```

This means SilverCity has been successfully installed. If you don't get a similar result and can't import SilverCity, stop and solve this issue first; otherwise nothing else will run.

Now you need to figure out the Application Programming Interface (API) for this module; being lazy, I went and read an example script located in PySilverCity/Scripts called source2html.py. This script does exactly what you want: It spits out HTML for a given piece of code. A really cheeky way to see this in operation is to feed this script to itself, like so:

```
$python source2html.py source2html.py --generator=python

<?xml version="1.0" encoding="utf-8"?>
<!DOCTYPE html PUBLIC "-//W3C//DTD XHTML 1.0 Transitional//EN"
    "http://www.w3.org/TR/xhtml1/DTD/xhtml1-transitional.dtd">
<html xmlns="http://www.w3.org/1999/xhtml">
<head>
  <title>source2html.py</title>
  <meta http-equiv="Content-Type" content="text/html; charset=utf-8" />
  <link
    rel="stylesheet"
    href="default.css" />
</head>
...
```

This means you just need to look at this API and alter it slightly. Add a module called source.py in the PloneSilverCity directory. In this you'll write the code that will provide the interface to the library; this new module contains no Zope-specific or Plone-specific code at this point. This module has three main modules: it'll tell you all the possible languages you can use, it'll take some text and return the correct parser, and finally it'll actually perform the translation.

First, add the following create_generator function, which gives you the correct parser:

```
from SilverCity import LanguageInfo
from StringIO import StringIO

def create_generator(source_file_name=None, generator_name=None):
    """ Make a generator from the given information
    about the object, such as its source and type """
    if generator_name:
        return LanguageInfo.find_generator_by_name(generator_name)()
    else:
        if source_file_name:
            h = LanguageInfo.guess_language_for_file(source_file_name)
            return h.get_default_html_generator()()
        else:
            raise ValueError, "Unknown file type, cannot create lexer"
```

Second, when you're in Plone, you need to be able to figure out exactly what languages are available so you can show them to the users. Write the following function to return that list, and call it list_generators:

```
def list_generators():
    """ This returns a list of generators, a generator
    is a valid language, so these are things like perl,
    python, xml etc..."""
    lexers = LanguageInfo.get_generator_names()
    return lexers
```

Finally, the generate_html function takes a source file as a string, an optional generator, and an optional filename. SilverCity requires a file such as buffer to write the content out, so you can use Python's StringIO module to accomplish this. The following is the generate_html function:

```
def generate_html(source_file, generator=None, source_file_name=None):
    """ From the source make a generator
    and then make the html """

    # SilverCity requires a file like object
    target_file = StringIO()
    generator = create_generator(source_file_name, generator)
    generator.generate_html(target_file, source_file)

    # return the html back
    return target_file.getvalue(), generator.name
```

You'll note that this calls the create_generator function you wrote earlier to figure out the correct generator for this language. That's all the code you need to able to generate the HTML for a file. I haven't gotten into any of the specifics of actually lexing through the source or producing the HTML; the SilverCity library does this all for you. To reiterate the earlier point, in this module you have no reference to Zope or Plone; this module is completely independent. The actual details of this module aren't necessary to know, as long as you understand you're importing a third-party library.

It's traditional in Python scripts to put in at least one piece of test code. You could write a complete unit test suite, but that's outside of the current topic. Instead, you'll add a little bit of code to test two things: that this works and the languages that are available, like so:

```
if __name__ == "__main__":
    import sys
    myself = sys.argv[0]
    file = open(myself, 'r').read()
    print generate_html(file, generator="python")
    print list_generators()
```

If you run this script, it'll open itself and feed that into the HTML syntax highlighter. A bunch of HTML will be spit out. You could just place this in the Zope-specific module you're about to write; however, having it all in a separate script makes it easy to test and alter later.

Writing the Class

A content type in Plone is just an object that has some particular attributes and some particular base classes. You don't even need to worry about reading and writing from the database—that's all handled by the Persistencebase classes. For the moment, create a module called PloneSilverCity.py in the package.

First, import the source.py module you wrote a few moments ago. That's one simple line because the module is in the same package. The line to import the functions is as follows:

```
from source import generate_html, list_generators
```

Second, you'll need a PloneSilverCity class that allows you to encapsulate the functionality you need. You need to worry about the following four attributes on this class:

- **id**: This stores the unique ID of this instance of the PloneSilverCity class.

- **_raw**: This stores the raw source code in the class.

- **_raw_as_html**: This stores the source code after it has been lexed into HTML.

- **_raw_language**: This stores the language of this source code.

For each of these attributes, you'll write an *accessor*, which is a function that returns the value of that attribute so that rather than calling the attribute, you call the accessor function. An example accessor function is getLanguage, which returns the value of the language. Writing an accessor is usually a good idea, especially because you'll apply security to these accessor methods later. In Zope, any method or attribute that begins within an underscore isn't available to Web-based methods such as page templates or Script (Python) objects. A good practice is to start all your attributes with an underscore and then put security on the accessing method.

Listing 12-1 shows the basic class.

Listing 12-1. The Basic Python Class

```python
class PloneSilverCity:
    def __init__(self, id):
        self.id = id
        self._raw = ""
        self._raw_as_html = ""
        self._raw_language = None

    def getLanguage(self):
        """ Returns the language this code has been lexed with """
        return self._raw_language

    def getRawCode(self):
        """ Returns the raw code """
        return self._raw

    def getHTMLCode(self):
        """ Returns the html code """
        return self._raw_as_html

    def getLanguages(self):
        """ Returns the list of languages available """
        langs = []
        for name, description in list_generators():
            langs.append( {'name':lang, 'value':language} )
        langs.sort()
        return langs
```

You'll have to add one other method, which is an edit method that allows you to upload a file or a string. This one method will read the file and see if there's anything in the file; if there is, then it will be read and a filename determined. Then the code, language, and filename will be passed to the generate function. You'll store all this in the attributes mentioned earlier, as shown in Listing 12-2.

Listing 12-2. The Method for Handling Edits

```
def edit(self, language, raw_code, file=""):
    """ The edit function, that sets
    all our parameters, and turns the code
    into pretty HTML """
    filename = ""
    if file:
        file_code = file.read()

        # if there is a file and it's not blank...
        if file_code:
            raw_code = file_code
            if hasattr(file, "name"):
                filename = file.name
            else:
                filename = file.filename
            # set the language to None so set by SilverCity
            language = None

    self._raw = raw_code

    # our function, generate_html does the hard work here
    html, language = generate_html(raw_code, language, filename)
    self._raw_as_html = html
    self._raw_language = language
```

> **NOTE** Well-versed Python developers may raise an issue with using
> file.name and file.filename. Zope file objects have an attribute called
> filename, which represents the filename, while in Python the attribute
> is called name. This code will then work in straight Python or Zope.

So now you have a Python class that encapsulates the object. At this point, you should be able to run this from the Python prompt quite easily and test that it does what you want. For example:

```
$ python
Python 2.3.2 (#1, Oct  6 2003, 10:07:16)
[GCC 3.2.2 20030222 (Red Hat Linux 3.2.2-5)] on linux2
Type "help", "copyright", "credits" or "license" for more information.
>>> from PloneSilverCity import PloneSilverCity
>>> p = PloneSilverCity("test.py")
>>> p.edit("python", "print 'hello world'")
>>> p.getRawCode()
"print 'hello world'"
>>> p.getHTMLCode()
'<span class="p_word">print</span>
<span class="p_default"> </span>
<span class="p_character">>\'hello world\'</span>'
>>> p.getLanguage()
'python'
```

Turning the Package into a Product

Now you have a simple package, but this isn't yet a Plone product. You have to initialize it with Plone. This means adding extra information to the PloneSilverCity.py
module. Specifically, you need to add a factory function. Using a factory is a well-
known pattern in object-oriented design, and it defines how an object will be
created. So, to the PloneSilverCity.py module, add the following constructor to
the module:

```
def addPloneSilverCity(self, id, REQUEST=None):
    """ This is our factory function and creates
    an empty PloneSilverCity object """
    obj = PloneSilverCity(id)
    self._setObject(id, obj)
```

The addPloneSilverCity function isn't part of the PloneSilverCity class. As a
constructor for the class, it's placed in the module outside the class. This function
is the first Plone-specific function. Three parameters are passed to the method:
the self object, the ID string for the object, and REQUEST. The self object is
actually the context you've seen before, just by a different name. Since the objects
will always be created inside folder, self will refer to the folder in which this
object will be created. This function creates an instance of PloneSilverCity called
obj and passes it to the _setObject method of the folder. The _setObject method is
particular to Zope; it instantiates the object in the database and registers the
object in the containing folder.

Next, add the factory type information covered in Chapter 11 (this is your first chance to create it yourself). The factory type information contains all the information about the content type in a dictionary; this information is loaded into portal_types when the product is installed into your Plone instance. This information will mirror what you saw in earlier, where you altered factory type information through the Web.

Before building the factory information, I usually create a configuration file that contains all the repeated variables for the product. This file is called config.py, and in there you put the names of the product, the name of its layer in the skins, and the name as it will appear to the user, like so:

```
product_name = "PloneSilverCity"
plone_product_name = "Source Code"
layer_name = "silvercity"
layer_location = "PloneSilverCity/skins"
```

Then you can set up the factory type information and use these strings. For example, the ID will be Source Code since this is shown in Plone to the users. The actions section of the type information is a tuple of dictionaries of all the actions that can occur with this object. When this factory is loaded into Plone, the Actions tab inside the portal_types tool will be populated with this content. Each of those actions has a corresponding method, template, or script that will be called; most of these directly correspond to page templates, which I discuss later in this section.

As you know by now, an action is something that users can do to an item in the Plone database. Thinking of this example application, users can do two obvious things to the source code. They can view it and see the nicely highlighted code, and they can edit the item and upload some source code. Actually, Plone requires that there's one action called view and one called edit, so these two fit nicely. You also want a third action—it's nice to be able to download the source in its original form. With languages such as Python where the formatting is key, this is really useful. This action points directly to getRawCode, which is the method for getting the raw code back again.

Each action has a permission associated, as shown in Listing 12-3 (I show exactly where that comes from later in this section).

Listing 12-3. The Factory Type Information and Actions

```
factory_type_information = {
    'id': plone_product_name,
    'meta_type': product_name,
    'description': ('Provides syntax highlighted HTML of source code.'),
    'product': product_name,
    'factory': 'addPloneSilverCity',
```

```
'content_icon': 'silvercity.gif',
'immediate_view': 'view',
'actions': (
                {'id': 'view',
                 'name': 'View',
                 'action': 'silvercity_view_form',
                 'permissions': (view_permission,)},
                {'id': 'edit',
                 'name': 'Edit',
                 'action': 'silvercity_edit_form',
                 'permissions': (edit_permission,)},
                {'id': 'source',
                 'name': 'Source',
                 'action': 'getRawCode',
                 'permissions': (view_permission,)},
                ),
    }
```

 NOTE   At this point, the product can't be imported from the Python prompt because the code is incomplete.

Setting Up Permissions

A fundamental concept when dealing with Web sites is that everything and everybody is untrusted. Before any property is accessed or any method is called, you must first check if the party wanting to perform an action is allowed to do so. In most systems, three permissions exist: the permission to add an item, the permission to delete an item, and the permission to edit an item. One other permission applies to Plone: the right to view an item through the Web (or other protocol). The containing folder handles deleting, which is a permission handed out in Plone to the containing folder. If you can delete anything in the folder, you can then also delete the content type you're adding here.

This leaves you with three permissions to worry about. It's normal to use the ones that come with the CMFCore package: *Add portal content*, *Modify portal content*, and *View*. Returning to the config file, you can add the permissions you need, like so:

```
from Products.CMFCore import CMFCorePermissions
```

```
add_permission = CMFCorePermissions.AddPortalContent
edit_permission = CMFCorePermissions.ModifyPortalContent
view_permission = CMFCorePermissions.View
```

This means the `add_permission` variable references the permission imported from CMFCorePermissions. There's nothing magical about the permissions— each permission is just a string. Using the built-in permission is convenient and understandable for your users. Plone is already configured to allow the right person to add content using the *Add portal content* permission. Further, the default workflow is defined to use and alter these permissions. These permissions were the ones you added to the factory type information.

If you wanted to make your own permission, you could do so quite easily. Suppose you wanted the Add. permission to be Add Source Code and have its own permission. Then you'd change the file to read as follows:

```
add_permission = "Add Source Code"
```

After importing the product, you'd have a new permission in the Security tab matching that Add Source Code permission. Why would you want to do this? Well, using a permission that everyone else uses is convenient. However, it may be that you want more granularity or different security. For this reason, you can just create your own security settings.

Completing the Initialization

Now you need to set up the initialization of the product. You do this in the __init__.py module so that when Zope reads this file at startup, it'll complete the initialization of the product, as shown in Listing 12-4.

Listing 12-4. The __init__.py Module

```
import PloneSilverCity

from Products.CMFCore import utils
from Products.CMFCore.DirectoryView import registerDirectory

from config import product_name, add_permission
```

```
contentConstructors = (PloneSilverCity.addPloneSilverCity,)
contentClasses = (PloneSilverCity.PloneSilverCity,)
contentFTI = (PloneSilverCity.factory_type_information,)

registerDirectory('skins', globals())

def initialize(context):
    product = utils.ContentInit(product_name,
        content_types = contentClasses,
        permission = add_permission,
        extra_constructors = contentConstructors,
        fti = contentFTI)
    product.initialize(context)
```

What's happening in this code? Well, actually not that much—it's just a little verbose. First, you make references to the classes and constructors that are going to be used in `contentClasses` and `contentConstructors`. These map to the factory function for creating the objects and the actual class. These are then passed into the `ContentInit` function, inside `initialize`, which is a special function that's called during the product initialization. `ContentInit` does all the work to set up the product within Plone. The parameters to this function are as follows:

- **product_name**: This is the name of the product, as defined in the config file (in this case, `PloneSilverCity`).

- **content_types**: This is the tuple of classes that this product defines; usually this is just one class, but it may be more.

- **permission**: This is the permission that's needed to create an instance of this object; in this case, it's the `add_permission` variable I've defined in `config.py`.

- **fti**: This stands for factory type information and is the dictionary of factory type information you defined in the `PloneSilverCity.py` module for the content.

Altering the Product Modules

Now you can return to the `PloneSilverCity.py` module and complete the task of turning this into a Plone product. At the start of the module, you'll create the `import` statements. These `import` statements pull various Plone initialization requirements from various locations, as follows:

```
from Globals import InitializeClass
from AccessControl import ClassSecurityInfo
from Products.CMFDefault.DublinCore import DefaultDublinCoreImpl
from Products.CMFCore.PortalContent import PortalContent
```

These imports provide the base functionality for the product and are common across most content types. The definitions of imports are as follows:

InitializeClass: This function initializes the class and applies all the security declarations that it'll have. You specify those security declarations by using the ClassSecurityInfo class.

ClassSecurityInfo: This class provides a series of security methods that will allow you to restrict access to methods of the content type.

DefaultDublinCoreImpl: This class provides an implementation of Dublin Core metadata. Chapter 11 covered Dublin Core; this gives an object all the Dublin Core attributes and methods to access them such as Title, Description, Creator, and so on.

PortalContent: This provides the base class for all content in a Plone site and some of the key attributes it needs. Using this base class gives the object a whole host of functionality such as making the object persist inside the database, cataloging the object for searching inside the portal_catalog object, and making it registerable with the portal_types tool.

You'll also need to import the configuration variables and permissions as well. So that takes the following two lines:

```
from config import plone_product_name, product_name
from config import add_permission, edit_permission, view_permission
```

Returning to the class, you have to add two base classes to make it fully Plone compatible: PortalContent and DefaultDublinCoreImpl. You also need to give the class a meta_type. Each product in Zope has a unique meta_type:

```
class PloneSilverCity(PortalContent, DefaultDublinCoreImpl):
    meta_type = product_name
```

One requirement of Plone is that it knows what base classes the content type implements. Other parts of the application will need to know what classes are implemented. So, explicitly state what classes the content type implements, like so:

```
    __implements__ = (
        PortalContent.__implements__,
        DefaultDublinCoreImpl.__implements__
        )
```

Adding Security to the Class

If you've already decided to give the actions security, you also need to apply this security to the class. In an object-publishing environment such as Plone, anyone can call any method of the class through the Web, unless it begins with an underscore. This is obviously bad, and you need to protect all your methods.

To do this inside the class, make an instance of the ClassSecurityInfo class. You do this with the following line:

```
security = ClassSecurityInfo()
```

This security object provides an interface into Zope security machinery. You can then apply methods to the object. My favorite method for doing this is to add a line applying the security directly above the method. This way it's easy to remember where the security is applied, and you won't forget to update it later, if you need to do so. The declareProtected method takes the permission and the method name to protect the edit method. So that only people who actually have the edit permission can call it, you do the following:

```
security.declareProtected(edit_permission, "edit")
```

Repeat this for each method, giving the appropriate permission and method name. The only one that needs to be protected is __init__ because this begins with an underscore. To apply all this security, you must initialize the class. Without doing this one step, all the security further declared *won't* be applied, and your object will be public.

In other words, don't forget this line:

```
InitializeClass(PloneSilverCity)
```

The API for ClassSecurityInfo provides the following methods for the class:

- **declarePublic**: This takes a list of names. All the names are declared publicly accessible for all users through restricted code and through the Web.

- **declarePrivate**: This takes a list of names. All the names are private and can't be accessed through restricted code.

- **declareProtected**: This takes a permission and any number of names. All the names can be accessed only with the permission given.

- **declareObjectPublic**: This sets the entire object as publicly accessible.

- **declareObjectPrivate**: This sets the entire object to private and inaccessible to restricted code.

With these methods it's possible to set almost any security you'd like. However, I've almost always found that explicitly setting the protection of each method with a permission has been sufficient.

Integrating with Search

In the previous chapter I showed you how the search works and the indexes that exist. Since the indexes work against Dublin Core objects and you've used Dublin Core as a base class, your object's title, description, creator, modification date, and so on, will all be indexed for you—no extra work is needed. Further, by inheriting from the PortalContent class every time the object is altered, the catalog will be updated for you; again, you don't need to worry about anything.

However, one index does need a little help, and that's SearchableText. As I demonstrated previously, the SearchableText index provides the full-text index that Plone uses when a search is run. It'd be nice if the search would also index the source code, so if somebody uploaded a piece of code with import in it, the search would pick it up. Because the catalog looks at the object and tries to find an attribute or method matching the index name, all you need to do is provide a method with that name that returns the value you want.

The easiest way to do this is to make a string out of the fields you want—for example, the title, the description, and the raw code. This can be protected by the *View* permission, since anyone viewing the object can happily see the contents anyway. The following is a SearchableText method that performs this task:

```
security.declareProtected(view_permission, "SearchableText")
def SearchableText(self):
    """ Used by the catalog for basic full text indexing """
    return "%s %s %s" % ( self.Title()
                        , self.Description()
                        , self._raw
                        )
```

The Difference Between a Python Class and a Plone Class

As you can see, there's quite a difference between a normal Python product and one registered in Plone. However, most of those differences are about registering the product and asserting the security. The actual class remains similar. Listing 12-5 highlights all the differences between the pure Python implementation and the Plone implementation.

Listing 12-5. The Plone Version of the Class

```python
from Globals import InitializeClass
from AccessControl import ClassSecurityInfo
from Products.CMFDefault.DublinCore import DefaultDublinCoreImpl
from Products.CMFCore.PortalContent import PortalContent

from config import meta_type, product_name
from config import add_permission, edit_permission, view_permission
from source import generate_html, list_generators

factory_type_information = {
    'id': plone_product_name,
    'meta_type': product_name,
    'description': ('Provides syntax highlighted HTML of source code.'),
    'product': product_name,
    'factory': 'addPloneSilverCity',
    'content_icon': 'silvercity.gif',
    'immediate_view': 'view',
    'actions': (
                {'id': 'view',
                 'name': 'View',
                 'action': 'silvercity_view_form',
                 'permissions': (view_permission,)},
                {'id': 'source',
                 'name': 'View source',
                 'action': 'getRawCode',
                 'permissions': (view_permission,)},
                {'id': 'edit',
                 'name': 'Edit',
                 'action': 'silvercity_edit_form',
                 'permissions': (edit_permission,)},
                ),
    }
```

```python
def addPloneSilverCity(self, id, REQUEST=None):
    """ This is our factory function and creates
    an empty PloneSilverCity object inside our Plone
    site """
    obj = PloneSilverCity(id)
    self._setObject(id, obj)

class PloneSilverCity(PortalContent, DefaultDublinCoreImpl):
    meta_type = product_name

    __implements__ = (
        PortalContent.__implements__,
        DefaultDublinCoreImpl.__implements__
        )

    security = ClassSecurityInfo()

    def __init__(self, id):
        DefaultDublinCoreImpl.__init__(self)
        self.id = id
        self._raw = ""
        self._raw_as_html = ""
        self._raw_language = None

    security.declareProtected(edit_permission, "edit")
    def edit(self, language, raw_code, file=""):
        """ The edit function, that sets
        all our parameters, and turns the code
        into pretty HTML """
        filename = ""
        if file:
            file_code = file.read()

            # if there is a file and its not blank...
            if file_code:
                raw_code = file_code
                if hasattr(file, "name"):
                    filename = file.name
                else:
                    filename = file.filename
                # set the language to None so set by SilverCity
                language = None
```

```python
        self._raw = raw_code

        # our function, generate_html does the hard work here
        html, language = generate_html(raw_code, language, filename)
        self._raw_as_html = html
        self._raw_language = language

    security.declareProtected(view_permission, "getLanguage")
    def getLanguage(self):
        """ Returns the language that code has been lexed with """
        return self._raw_language

    security.declareProtected(view_permission, "getLanguages")
    def getLanguages(self):
        """ Returns the list of languages available """
        langs = []

        for name, description in list_generators():
            # these names are normally in uppercase
            langs.append( {'name':lang, 'value':language } )

        langs.sort()
        return langs

    security.declareProtected(view_permission, "getRawCode")
    def getRawCode(self):
        """ Returns the raw code """
        return self._raw

    security.declareProtected(view_permission, "getHTMLCode")
    def getHTMLCode(self):
        """ Returns the html code """
        return self._raw_as_html

    security.declareProtected(view_permission, "SearchableText")
    def SearchableText(self):
        """ Used by the catalog for basic full text indexing """
        return "%s %s %s" % ( self.Title()
                            , self.Description()
                            , self._raw
                            )


InitializeClass(PloneSilverCity)
```

Adding Skins

So now that you've got the main code, you have two things left to do: build the skins and create an installation method. The skins are actually one of the easier parts because so much of the work has been done already in the Plone framework. I covered skins in detail in earlier chapters, where I discussed how to make a skin for the Plone site on the file system. Each product that needs to provide custom User Interface (UI) does so by making its own File System Directory View (FSDV), so you'll do the same again here.

The skins are placed in the `skins` directory of the product. This directory name is defined in the `__init__.py` file where you register the directory using the `registerDirectory` function. If you wanted to change the name, make sure to register it—you can register as many directories as you like, but it's recursive and will register everything in and below that registered directory.

The easiest of all your jobs for this product is to add an icon for the object that will appear in Plone. The name of this icon is already defined in the factory type information with the line `'content_icon': 'silvercity.gif'`, so all you have to do is add an icon to the `skins` directory called `silvercity.gif`. This icon will display whenever you see the object in the Plone user interface. When SilverCity lexes a file, it outputs HTML using CSS tags, so you have ensure that the particular CSS file is available. For this product you simply copy the CSS out of the SilverCity product and place it in the `skins` directory with the name `silvercity.css`.

These two items are now done. Next, you actually have to write the view and edit pages. Previously I discussed how this is similar to a document, so when you're looking for view and edit pages, the best place to look is the pages for a document. Those pages are `document_view.pt` and `document_edit_form.cpt` and are located in the `CMFPlone/skins/plone_content` directory.

Making the View Page

To alter the view page, you take the view page for a document, copy it into your product's `skins` directory, and rename it to `silvercity_view.pt`. There's no point in re-creating the entire page when the view page is so similar; all you need to do is to make two minor changes.

As mentioned, SilverCity spits out HTML where all the code has been highlighted using CSS and you have a custom style sheet. You need to make sure that the view page inserts that CSS, and the main template has a slot for CSS called `css_slot`. To put the custom CSS file into that slot, you just have to provide a value for it. For example:

```
<metal:cssslot fill-slot="css_slot">

<link
    rel="stylesheet"
    href=""
    tal:attributes="href string:$portal_url/silvercity.css" />
</metal:cssslot>
```

Here you're referencing a CSS file called `silvercity.css`. That file is located in the `skins` directory, and you'll be accessing it from the skin when it's rendered. The original document shows a property called `cookedBody`, which is an attribute of a document. I removed that part of the code and instead inserted the code. As you've seen by now, the function `getHTMLCode` returns the HTML, so all you have to do is the following:

```
<div id="bodyContent">
    <div tal:replace="structure here/getHTMLCode" />
</div>
```

If you want to change anything else specific in this page template, now is your opportunity. It could be nice to show the language that it was written in, to show an icon, or to change history, for example.

Making the Edit Page

Like the view page, you can take the edit page, copy it into the skin, and rename it to `silvercity_edit_form.cpt`. The biggest problem is that the edit form is designed to be used with a What You See Is What You Get (WYSIWYG) editor such as Epoz. Until a good WYSIWYG editor for source code is available for Web browsers, you'll have to turn this off because you can't write SQL in an HTML editor.

This is quite a lengthy change of the page template—remember, you can get this off the Web site. In this template, remove all mentions of the editors and replace them with a simple text area. Keep the name of the HTML field the same because there's no real need to change it. Also, leaving it the same means it plays nicely with the script for handling the form later. A document has at the bottom a series of selections for the format, which are normally items such as Plain Text, HTML, and so on. You'll replace this with a drop-down box for all the languages that the main SilverCity library has available. The `getLanguages` method written earlier returns a list of all the languages. Each item is a dictionary that contains the value (for example, CPP) and a nice name (for example, C or C++).

Listing 12-6 loops through the getLanguages method written earlier. You can also define a variable for the current language so that as it loops through the languages, you can highlight the current language.

Listing 12-6. Adding a Drop-Down List for Selecting the Language

```
<div class="field">
  <label
   for="language"
   i18n:translate="label_silvercity_language">
Language</label>

    <div class="formHelp" i18n:translate="help_silvercity_language">
        Select the name of the language that you are adding
    </div>
    <select name="text_format"
            tal:define="l here/getLanguage">
        <option tal:repeat="item here/getLanguages"
            tal:content="item/name"
            tal:attributes="value item/value;
                            selected python:test(item['value'] == l, 1, 0)" />
    </select>
</div>
```

When the edit page gets submitted, you need to set up the validators and actions to do something with the form. The validation should check that a valid title and a valid ID have been given. To the silvercity_edit.cpt.metadata file, add the following:

```
[validators]
validators..Save = validate_id,validate_title
validators..Cancel =
```

Where did those validations come from? Well, I was cheeky and again looked at the validations for a document. That calls three validations, but you need only two of them. By checking what that validation evaluated to, you can see which ones are needed and which ones aren't. You'll find all the validations in plone_skins/plone_form_scripts, and the object name starts with validation.

So now you need the action, so take the edit script for a document (document_edit.cpy) and copy it into SilverCity. Mostly the script is just fine, so you can keep it with one modification. Change the messages to *Source code* instead of *Document*. Listing 12-7 shows the edit script.

Listing 12-7. The Edit Script

```
##parameters=text_format, text, file='', SafteyBelt='', ➡
title='', description='', id=''
##title=Edit a document

filename=getattr(file,'filename', '')
if file and filename:
    # if there is no id, use the filename as the id
    if not id:
        id = filename[max( filename.rfind('/')
                        , filename.rfind('\\')
                        , filename.rfind(':') )+1:]
    file.seek(0)

# if there is no id specified, keep the current one
if not id:
    id = context.getId()

new_context = context.portal_factory.doCreate(context, id)
new_context.edit( text_format
                , text
                , file
                , safety_belt=SafetyBelt )

from Products.CMFPlone import transaction_note
transaction_note('Edited source code %s at %s' % ➡
  (new_context.title_or_id(), new_context.absolute_url()) ➡
  )

new_context.plone_utils.contentEdit( new_context
                                   , id=id
                                   , title=title
                                   , description=description )

return state.set(context=new_context, ➡
 portal_status_message='Source code changes saved.')
```

The script does a few things. First, it gets the filename if one exists; if no ID is given, then the ID is set to that filename. This means if a user uploads library.c, the ID for that object will be library.c. Second, it tells portal_factory to create an object (see the "Portal Factory" sidebar for more information on what that means). Then it calls the edit method on the object (something you wrote earlier), and it calls contentEdit on the plone_utils tool. Without looking into the depths of the

plone_utils tool, contentEdit takes the keywords given, and if the class implements Dublin Core, then it will change those attributes. Since you set up the
__implements__ attribute earlier, the edit method in Listing 12-7 will do the work
for you. Any changes to title, ID, or description will be changed in the object.

Portal Factory

One problem exists with the way objects are created. Before you can even get to
the edit form, you have to create an object. Then the edit form for that object
will display. In practice, people accidentally create objects, get to the edit form,
and then realize it was the wrong type. This is annoying and leaves spare objects
lying around in your database. It's like creating a file on the file system, realizing
it's wrong, and then leaving it there.

To solve this, the portal_factory tool allows you to temporarily create objects.
It'll create a temporary object and then let you edit it. Only once you've clicked
the edit button will your object be created. To assign an object to portal_factory,
go to the portal_factory tool, and in the form select all the content types for
which you'd like to use this tool. The only catch is that you must ensure your
edit scripts correctly integrate with the tool, as shown in this example.

Installing the Product into Plone

You have a standard way for installing a product into Plone—you go to the
Plone control panel and click the product to install it. That script uses the
portal_quickinstaller tool to do the installation. For this product to work, you
need to expose functionality that the tool can read. After all, you want as many
people to use the product as possible. If you're writing something that's for
internal use only and you're never going to distribute to anyone else, you can skip
this stage. But you'll need to do these steps by hand anyway, and it's always better
to have a script for the installation.

NOTE   Quick Installer makes an external method of this install function and runs it for you behind the scenes. It performs a few other
tasks, as well. This means you could make an external method to do
this if you wanted. That's why the installation instructions for many
products tell you to create an external method.

To integrate with the Quick Installer, you need to make a specific module called `Install.py` in the `Extensions` directory. That module has to contain a function called `install`. The Quick Installer tool runs the `install` function, and the output is placed in a file on the server. The `install` method has to install the product into the portal types, so add an FSDV that points to the `skins` directory, and add this new directory to the skin layers.

Now import the functions and set up the variables as usual. You have to import the `factory_type_information` from the product so that you can use it in the script, as shown in Listing 12-8.

Listing 12-8. The Start of the Installation Function

```
from Products.CMFCore.TypesTool import ContentFactoryMetadata
from Products.CMFCore.DirectoryView import createDirectoryView
from Products.CMFCore.utils import getToolByName
from Products.PloneSilverCity.PloneSilverCity import factory_type_information

from Products.PloneSilverCity.config import plone_product_name, product_name
from Products.PloneSilverCity.config import layer_name, layer_location

def install(self):
    """ Install this product """
```

After this, everything is generic and could be run on any product—unless of course you want it to do something special on the installation. To add your product to the `portal_types` tool, you first check that your product isn't already registered. It could be that someone has registered another product of the same name. For this you'll call the `manage_addTypeInformation` method, as shown in Listing 12-9.

Listing 12-9. Remainder of the Installation Function

```
out = []
typesTool = getToolByName(self, 'portal_types')
skinsTool = getToolByName(self, 'portal_skins')

if id not in typesTool.objectIds():
    typesTool.manage_addTypeInformation(
        add_meta_type =  factory_type_information['meta_type']
        id = factory_type_information['id']
        )
    out.append('Registered with the types tool')
else:
    out.append('Object "%s" already existed in the types tool' % (id))
```

Next you need to add an FSDV to the `skins` directory. Again, the first thing you check is that you don't already have one; then you add the directory view with the following:

```
if skinname not in skinsTool.objectIds():
    createDirectoryView(skinsTool, skinlocation, skinname)
    out.append('Added "%s" directory view to portal_skins' % skinname)
```

Finally, you loop through all the skins and add your new FSDV to each of the skins. This is a generic function; each skin is listed as string with each layer separated by commas. All you have to do is split the string up and insert your new skin after the layer named `custom`, as shown in Listing 12-10.

Listing 12-10. Setting the Skin in the Installation Method

```
skins = skinsTool.getSkinSelections()
for skin in skins:
    path = skinsTool.getSkinPath(skin)
    path = [ p.strip() for p in p.split(',') ]
    if skinname not in path:
        path.insert(path.index('custom')+1, skinname)

        path = ", ".join(path)
        skinsTool.addSkinSelection(skin, path)
        out.append('Added "%s" to "%s" skins' % (skinname, skin))
    else:
        out.append('Skipping "%s" skin' % skin)
return "\n".join(out)
```

That's it. Your product is now ready to run.

Testing the Product

To test, restart your Plone instance so that it'll read the product directory in. If you haven't already developed your product in the appropriate products folder, then place it there now as part of your standard installation process. If there are any problems with your product, then Zope may start, but the product may show up as broken in the control panel.

Then install into Plone using the Add/Remove Products page in the Plone control panel. Now you should be able to go to a folder and add a source code object. The icon will be your icon in the skin, and the name is what you defined in the file system. After adding this, you'll get the edit page. Note that the URL now has `silvercity_edit_form` on the end and shows the nicely altered edit form.

You could add some code, select a language, and click Save, or you could upload a file from your computer. After clicking Save, you'll be taken back to the view function, and, sure enough, the code will be shown with the syntax highlighted.

This product is a little example of how simple writing a product in Plone is. Although it has been a lot of pages, most of it has been setting up the infrastructure and the skins. One of the first things people do is compare this to other Web scripting languages such as PHP. You have to remember that by having your code in Plone, you've achieved quite a few things without having to rewrite them. Specifically, you've achieved the following:

- Full-text searching of the content

- Integration with the workflow

- Integration with portal membership and authentication

- Persistence through the Plone database without having to write SQL or do other work

Further, it really does let your complete product scale later. For example, if you need a bug-tracking system, drop in the Collector product, and if you need a photo management product, drop in CMFPhoto. By utilizing the framework, you can give your overall site a great deal of flexibility and scalability.

Although this product is a little cheeky by using lots of existing code, it demonstrates quite a few key functions of writing a product in Plone.

Debugging Development

If you're developing your own product, then two things will happen to you at some point (unless you have so much Zen that you should be writing the Zope core code): your product will break, and you'll need to debug it.

During development, you may want to try importing the product into the Python prompt to see how it works. Unfortunately, you'll probably get an error. This is because when you do this import, you'll get a cascade of Zope-related imports. You can cope with some of this but not all of it. One of the common problems is that you'll get the following error:

```
Traceback (most recent call last):
  File "<stdin>", line 1, in ?
  File "PloneSilverCity/__init__.py", line 1, in ?
    import PloneSilverCity
```

```
File "PloneSilverCity/PloneSilverCity.py", line 4, in ?
  from Globals import InitializeClass
File "/opt/Zope-2.7/lib/python/Globals.py", line 23, in ?
  import Acquisition, ComputedAttribute, App.PersistentExtra, os
File "/opt/Zope-2.7/lib/python/App/PersistentExtra.py", line 15, in ?
  from Persistence import Persistent
ImportError: cannot import name Persistent
```

You can solve this by making sure that before you import PloneSilverCity you import Zope and run the startup method. To be able to import Zope, you must have the directory containing Zope in your path; on my computer, this is /opt/Zope-2.7/lib/python. However, you'll then run across errors trying to import CMFCore if you have an instance home configured, which you probably will.

The easiest way to import PloneSilverCity is to run Zope from the command line in debug mode using zopectl. This will open a Python prompt that will let you access the Zope database directly from Python. Chapter 14 covers this in more detail, but it can be done easily now (assuming your Zope isn't currently running). You can find the zopectl script in the bin directory of your Zope instance; for example, on my computer, this is /var/zope/bin. Listing 12-11 shows an example running zopectl with PloneSilverCity.

 NOTE At the time of writing, zopectl doesn't work on Windows. However, on Linux, it's a convenient way to test your code. Unfortunately, using zopectl requires locking the Zope Object Database (ZODB) and, unless you're running ZEO (something I'll discuss in Chapter 14), can't be done while Zope is running.

Listing 12-11. Debugging the Product Using Zope

```
$ cd /var/zope/bin
$ ./zopectl debug
Starting debugger (the name "app" is bound to the top-level Zope object)
>>> from PloneSilverCity.PloneSilverCity import PloneSilverCity
>>> p = PloneSilverCity("test")
>>> p.edit("python", "import test")
>>> p.getRawCode()
'import test'
>>> p
<PloneSilverCity at test>
```

When your product breaks, you'll get a traceback to one of two places, either the error log page or one of the event logs. If you've really broken it, then Plone won't start; this normally happens when an import fails. If that's the case, then Plone will just not start at all. I recommend starting Plone from the command line, be it Windows or Linux. Having the console output of that error will give you an immediate output of the error. For example, Listing 12-12 shows what happens when you try to run Plone SilverCity with a deliberate error in the import.

Listing 12-12. An Example Error on Startup

```
$ bin/runzope
------
2003-12-19T17:44:05 INFO(0) ZServer HTTP server started at Fri Dec 19 17:44:05
2003
        Hostname: laptop
        Port: 8080
------
2003-12-19T17:44:05 INFO(0) ZServer FTP server started at Fri Dec 19 17:44:05
2003
        Hostname: basil.agmweb.ca
        Port: 8021
------
2003-12-19T17:44:16 ERROR(200) Zope Could not import Products.PloneSilverCity
Traceback (most recent call last):
  File "/opt/Zope-2.7/lib/python/OFS/Application.py", line 533, in import_product
    product=__import__(pname, global_dict, global_dict, silly)
  File "/var/zope.zeo/Products/PloneSilverCity/__init__.py", line 1, in ?
    import PloneSilverCity
  File "/var/zope.zeo/Products/PloneSilverCity/PloneSilverCity.py", line 1
    import ThisModuleDoesNotExist
                      ^
ImportError: No module named ThismoduleDoesNotExist
```

At this point, Zope stops; you'll have to fix this import before starting again. This is probably the easiest error to fix but will likely occur only when you install that a whiz-bang new product off the Internet only to find it has a dozen dependencies.

The next kind of error that can occur is a programming or logic error, which occurs inside the code. Suppose your product adds two numbers together, but one of them is a string (this is an error in Python). An error will be raised, which Plone will report back to the user interface with an error value and error type. At this point, you should click *plone setup* and click Error Log to see the traceback, find the bug, and fix the issue.

If you change something in a product, the change doesn't get reflected in Python right away; you need to use a product called *Refresh* to force that change. This is an amazingly useful tool for new developers, and you enable it by having a file called refresh.txt in your Products directory. You'll note that PloneSilverCity has one. Next, in the ZMI, select Control Panel, select Products, select PloneSilverCity (or your product name), and click the Refresh tab. If your product has a refresh.txt file, you can click the Refresh button. Plone will then dynamically reload your product with all the new code. If you're running Zope in debug mode, then you can set the product to dynamically check every time it's run, rather than having to come back to this screen each time.

Unfortunately, everything with refresh isn't all rosy. It does do some rather "interesting" things behind the scenes to Python to enable this to happen. In fact, the Refresh product can produce unexpected results in your product—nothing that restarting Zope won't fix, though. Relatively simple products that just do data manipulation will be fine, but some products aren't. Chances are if you're just starting out, your products will be simple, and you'll be fine.

Finally, if it something goes wrong and you can't figure it out, you'll need to pull out a debugger. You have so many ways to debug Zope that I'll just discuss the one I use the most—the Python debugger. You can call the Python debugger by adding the following line to a piece of code:

```
import pdb; pdb.set_trace()
```

TIP   It's uncommon in Python to put two lines into one by using a semicolon, but here it's handy so that when you come to delete or comment it out later, you have only one line to comment.

That will cause a breakpoint in the code execution, and Zope will stop processing and open the debugger. This is why you really want to run Plone from a console when developing. This doesn't work with a service or a daemon because there's no console to which to connect. Now if you re-create your problem, you'll be dropped into the Python debugger, and you can debug your product. For example, in my now fixed-up and correctly importing PloneSilverCity, I added the following pdb trace function to the getLanguages method:

```
def getLanguages(self):
    """ Returns the list of languages available """
    import pdb; pdb.set_trace()
    langs = []
    ...
```

Now when you run Plone and connect to the skin (something you'll add a moment), this function will be called, and, sure enough, on the console you started Zope with, you'll see the following:

```
--Return--
> /var/tmp/python2.3-2.3.2-root/usr/lib/python2.3/pdb.py(992)set_trace()->None
-> Pdb().set_trace()
(Pdb)
```

You can type **help** to get a list of help options. The two main choices are n for next and s for steppng into an item. For example:

```
(Pdb) n
> /var/zope.zeo/Products/PloneSilverCity/PloneSilverCity.py(97)getLanguages()
-> langs = []
(Pdb) n
> /var/zope.zeo/Products/PloneSilverCity/PloneSilverCity.py(99)getLanguages()
-> for value, description in list_generators():
(Pdb) langs
[]
```

For more information on the debugger, I recommend the online documentation at the Python Web site (http://python.org/doc/current/lib/module-pdb.html). You have other ways to debug Zope, such as using ZEO to get an interpreter, for example. Chapter 14 covers using ZEO. Integrated developer environments such as Wing (http://wingide.com/wingide) or Komodo (http://www.activestate.com/Products/Komodo) can remotely debug Zope instances and have nice graphical interfaces.

Writing a Custom Tool

Writing a tool is simpler than writing a content type, mostly because there's little to do in terms of registering the product and because the user interface is simple. For an example, I use simple statistics tool on my ZopeZen Web site (http://www.zopezen.org) for giving information about the amount of content, number of users, and so on. This simple tool prints a few numbers that interest me as a manager of the site. Figure 12-2 shows my ZopeZen stats.

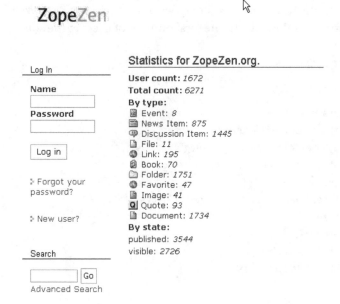

ZopeZen

Statistics for ZopeZen.org.

Log In

Name

Password

Log in

⊰ Forgot your password?

⊰ New user?

Search

Go
Advanced Search

User count: *1672*
Total count: *6271*
By type:
▦ Event: *8*
▣ News Item: *875*
⬤ Discussion Item: *1445*
▢ File: *11*
◉ Link: *195*
▤ Book: *70*
▢ Folder: *1751*
◉ Favorite: *47*
▦ Image: *41*
▣ Quote: *93*
▢ Document: *1734*
By state:
published: *3544*
visible: *2726*

Figure 12-2. PloneStats on ZopeZen

These are Web site statistics—I can get those by parsing the Web logs for my Plone server. Tools—such as Analog, Webalizer, WebTrends, and so on—can happily parse your Plone or Apache Web logs for you. Again, you can find the entire code for this project in the Collective at `http://sf.net/projects/collective` in the PloneStats package.

Starting the Tool

You should place the tool in a product directory the same way you did with the content type—by making a directory inside the instance home product directory. Into that folder add the `refresh.txt`, `install.txt`, `readme.txt`, and `__init__.py` files.

In that directory, the main module is called `stats.py`, which contains all the code for creating the stats. Again, I'll cover how the module looks without any extra Zope code. However, since you're directly plugging into the other Plone tools, running outside of Zope will make little sense.

Listing 12-13 shows the start of the tool. This is a simple version that has two methods: one to return the number of content types by type and by workflow state and the other for users that returns the total number of users in the site.

Listing 12-13. The Basic Stats Object

```
class Stats:
    def getContentTypes(self):
        """ Returns the number of documents by type """
        pc = getToolByName(self, "portal_catalog")
        # call the catalog and loop through the records
        results = pc()
        numbers = {"total":len(results),"bytype":{},"bystate":{}}
        for result in results:
            # set the number for the type
            ctype = str(result.Type)
            num = numbers["bytype"].get(ctype, 0)
            num += 1
            numbers["bytype"][ctype] = num

            # set the number for the state
            state = str(result.review_state)
            num = numbers["bystate"].get(state, 0)
            num += 1
            numbers["bystate"][state] = num
        return numbers

    def getUserCount(self):
        """ The number of users """
        pm = getToolByName(self, "portal_membership")
        count = len(pm.listMemberIds())
        return count
```

Turning the Package into a Tool

To turn the package into a tool, you have to do the same process for the content type. In other words, you have to register the tool in the __init__.py module. Just like in the content type example, make a config.py file that contains all the configurations. The config.py file looks like this:

```
from Products.CMFCore import CMFCorePermissions

view_permission = CMFCorePermissions.ManagePortal

product_name = "PloneStats"
unique_id = "plone_stats"
```

The security for this product is simpler, but that's because the product is quite simple—all it does is interact with other tools and produce some statistics. There's nothing for users to add, edit, delete, or otherwise interact with. This means you have really only one permission, ManagePortal, which is the permission to actually manage Plone's configuration and is usually given only to managers. For this purpose, this means only managers can go into the ZMI and see the information the tool provides. You could quite easily add a nice-looking skin for the Plone control panel or a portlet that displays this information in your site if you wanted.

Returning to __init__.py, add the initialization code for the tool. There's a special initialization script for tools, called ToolInit. In this tool, the __init__.py file looks like this:

```
from Products.CMFCore import utils
from stats import Stats
from config import product_name

tools = (stats.Stats,)

def initialize(context):
    init = utils.ToolInit( product_name,
                    tools = tools,
                    product_name = product_name,
                    icon='tool.gif'
                    )
init.initialize(context)
```

The ToolInit function can take multiple tools; in this case, you have only one tool. If you have multiple tools, you can have only one product name and icon to show in the ZMI. This is all that's needed to register the tool. Now you have to complete the main module to turn it into an actual tool object.

Altering the Tool Code

Next, add the code to the class to turn into a tool. Like the content type, this is just a matter of adding security inheriting from the correct base classes, like so:

```
from Globals import InitializeClass
from OFS.SimpleItem import SimpleItem
from AccessControl import ClassSecurityInfo

from Products.CMFCore.utils import UniqueObject, getToolByName
```

The SimpleItem class is the default base class for a simple (not a folder) object in Zope. Actually, all content types inherit from a class that, somewhere in its class hierarchy, inherits from SimpleItem; it's just that you don't need all the extra attributes those other classes provide. UniqueObject ensures that there will be one and only one instance of this object inside your Plone site and that it can't be renamed or moved around. This means your object will always be available.

Next, you import the variables from the config file as usual. By assigning the ID of your object, you ensure that the tool will have the ID of whatever unique_id is in the config file—in this case, plone_stats. The two base classes for the tool are the UniqueObject and SimpleItem classes, which are the minimum it needs. For example:

```
from config import view_permission, product_name, unique_id

class Stats(UniqueObject, SimpleItem):
    """ Prints out statistics for a Plone site """
    meta_type = product_name
    id = unique_id
```

Next, you need to set up the security, and again you'll use the ClassSecurityInfo class to set explicit permissions on the methods. For example:

```
security = ClassSecurityInfo()
security.declareProtected(view_permission, 'getContentTypes')
def getContentTypes(self):
    ...
```

Adding Some User Interface Elements

The main code is complete, so it'd be nice to show some response to the user when they click the tool in the ZMI, such as giving an example of how to use the product. For this, you'll alter the ZMI so that you can display something.

Specifically, you write a page template that does what you want it to do. In this example, this is a simple page template that hooks into the ZMI. The ZMI is an unsophisticated user interface that just spits back Web pages to the user, so no fancy macros or slots render the page. All you need to do is write a HTML and add the following:

```
<span tal:replace="structure here/manage_tabs" />
```

This one `tal:replace` function gets the management tabs and makes them appear at the top of the page. My ZMI page loops through the two methods of the plone_stats tool and spits out the results for the user, as shown in Listing 12-14.

Listing 12-14. A Page to Show in the Management Interface

```
<html>
<body>
<span tal:replace="structure here/manage_tabs" />

<p>Statistics for this Plone site.</p>

<h3>Content Types</h3>
<span tal:define="numbers here/getContentTypes">
    <p>
        Total count: <i tal:replace="numbers/total" /><br />
        Content types by type:
    </p>

    <span tal:repeat="type python:numbers['bytype'].keys()">
        <ul>
            <li>
              <span tal:replace="type" />:
              <i tal:replace="python: numbers['bytype'][type]" />
            </li>
        </ul>
    </span>
```

```
    <p>Content types by state:</p>
    <span tal:repeat="type python:numbers['bystate'].keys()">
        <ul>
            <li>
                <span tal:replace="type" />:
                <i tal:replace="python: numbers['bystate'][type]" />
            </li>
        </ul>
    </span>
</span>

<h3>Users</h3>
<p>
  User count: <i tal:replace="here/getUserCount" />
</p>

</body>
</html>
```

This is called output.pt and placed inside the www directory. You don't have to use a separate directory, but doing so makes it easier to remember.

The last step is to hook this up into the ZMI for your product. You do this by returning to the Stats class and adding the following (first import a PageTemplateFile class that can handle the template from the file system):

```
from Products.PageTemplates.PageTemplateFile import PageTemplateFile
```

Then you register the page template as a method for the product that can be accessed. In the following, the method outputPage can now be called through the Web, and the matching page template is returned:

```
outputPage = PageTemplateFile('www/output.pt', globals())
security.declareProtected(view_permission, 'outputPage')
```

Finally, the tabs at the top of the ZMI are determined by a tuple called manage_options that maintains a list of all the tabs to be shown on a page. You need to insert the new management page in there, so you do the following:

```
    manage_options = (
        {'label':'output', 'action':'outputPage'},
        ) + SimpleItem.manage_options
```

Testing the Tool

Now that the tool is done, you can test that it works. First, restart your Plone instance so that it'll read the product directory in and register your new tool. Second, access the ZMI and go to the Add drop-down box in the top-right corner. You'll notice that PloneStats is now in the drop-down list, so select this option and click Add. The next form will list the tools available in the PloneStats product; in this case, just one appears, as shown in Figure 12-3.

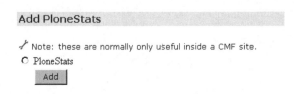

Add PloneStats

Note: these are normally only useful inside a CMF site.
○ PloneStats
  Add

Figure 12-3. Adding the tool

Select the tool, and click Add. To test that the tool works, click it. You should see a series of statistics, as you saw earlier on ZopeZen.

This tool is simple because I'm really not sure what presentation people want; if I make a standard reporting tool, then you can use it as you want. Some ideas that spring to mind are a page in the control panel, a little portlet box, a Portable Document Format (PDF) that contains pretty graphs and is e-mailed to the manager, or an API that's an external reporting tool, such as Crystal Reports could use. At this point, I'll wait and see what happens in the future.

CHAPTER 13

Developing with Archetypes

ARCHETYPES IS A FRAMEWORK for automating the development of products in Plone. Once a description has been written for a content type in Python, Archetypes handles almost everything else, including creating view and edit forms for the developer. This allows you to develop content types quickly and with a minimum amount of code. The less code written means a lower probability of bugs, less code to maintain as Plone changes, a quick development cycle, and generally lower costs.

Because the entire product is based upon this object description, it allows you to use tools to generate that product. For example, ArchGenXML, which I'll cover later, allows you to generate a product in a Unified Modeling Language (UML) tool. You can then take the output of the UML model and pass it through ArchGenXML to have a product instantly appear in Plone; you don't actually have to write any code. If you found that writing the product in Python in Chapter 12 was a little too much like hard work, then this chapter is something you'll appreciate.

This doesn't mean Archetypes is right for every product; sometimes I've found Archetypes to be a little too much. For example, in one case my content type had one field, but about 16 different permutations on the data on that field were presented, which meant little of the existing Archetypes framework was used. That was an extreme case, however. Most of the time you'll find Archetypes is exactly what you need.

Several people complain that Archetypes makes life a little too easy for developers, and of course it's hard to charge people much for work that can take ten minutes. Personally I've never had a problem with this, and Archetypes has gotten me out of many sticky situations when all of a sudden the specification changes from four content types to fourteen.

One anecdote I've heard concerns a Web site development company. When the company visits clients, it takes along a programmer. As the client describes its needs, the programmer furiously types away into Archetypes. Before the meeting is finished, they can demonstrate a quick prototype of the working product to the client.

Overall, most of the Plone development team has adopted Archetypes as the way to develop products, so it has a great deal of mind share and really has become the standard for Plone development. Some of Archetypes' other key features are as follows:

- It automatically creates view and edit pages, so you don't actually have to write any page template code.

- It maintains unique object IDs. Every object you create will have a unique ID that users can't change. This means you can always find an object, even if it has moved.

- It creates references between objects. Each object can have any number of relations to any other objects. For example, you could have any number of link objects attached to a news item.

- It has standard security setup. All the security work is done for you, so if you want the default setup, you don't have to change anything.

- It has alternate storage options, such as storing your data in relational database instead of Zope's standard database.

- It has data transformation capabiliti es, such as changing Microsoft Word in Hypertext Markup Language (HTML), for example.

Archetypes isn't just Plone specific but can also be used in other Zope frameworks such as the Content Management Framework (CMF); however, at the moment it's used mostly by Plone. Eventually, when Plone moves to Zope 3, it's planned that the Archetypes and Zope 3 schemas will converge. So using Archetypes is a good way to future-proof your product so it's compatible with future Plone versions.

In this chapter, then, I run through building new content types with Archetypes. This chapter really pulls together all the information you've learned over the last few chapters and runs quite quickly through some basic concepts. After showing how to install Archetypes, I take you through how to create a basic content type.

Introducing Archetypes

Archetypes comes in the installers and packages for Plone, so chances are you'll already have Archetypes installed in your distribution. If you're unsure if this is the case, you should be able to see Archetypes in the Products part of the ZMI control panel. In these examples, I've tested Plone with Archetypes version 1.2.5-rc4. If you've got Archetypes installed, skip to the "Developing with Archetypes" section.

To install Archetypes, you'll need to go the Web site at http://sf.net/ projects/archetypes, click Files, and get the latest Archetypes release. In my example, this is archetypes-1.2.5-rc4.tgz. You'll need to unzip it, like so:

```
$ tar -zxf archetypes-1.2.5-rc4.tgz
$ cd archetypes-1.2.5-rc4l
```

At this point you'll need to decide what to install. The minimum to install is the Archetypes directory and the generator and validation modules. To install these modules, move them into the Products directory of your instance home. Again, in my case, this is /var/zope, so my command is as follows:

```
$ mv Archetypes /var/zope/Products
$ mv generator /var/zope/Products
$ mv validation /var/zope/Products
```

ArchExample and ArchGenXML are both optional, and you don't need them for Plone to work; however, I cover both of these as examples in this chapter, so you'll probably want to install them.

To install ArchExample, move the ArchExample product into the Products directory of your instance home, like so:

```
$ cd ..
$ mv ArchExample /var/zope/Products
```

If you want to use ArchGenXML, you don't need to install it anywhere in particular, so place it in any directory where you won't forget it. I usually just place it into the Products directory of my instance home along with everything else. It doesn't do any harm there, and I won't forget it. For example:

```
$ mv ArchGenXML /var/zope/Products
```

As stated in the ArchGenXML documentation, ArchGenXML does require PyXML to be installed. Again, if you used an installer such as the Windows or Mac installer, this was already included for you. If not, then go to http://pyxml.sf.net and download the package. In my case, the latest package was 0.8.3, so after downloading, I ran the following:

```
$ tar -xvf PyXML-0.8.3.tar.gz
$ cd PyXML-0.8.3
$ python setup.py install
```

NOTE   Usually, installing in this manner requires root privileges on Unix to install into the Python directories.

Now that you have everything set up and installed, you'll see some of the examples.

Diving Into Archetypes

A whole bunch of great examples are available for Archetypes, so rather than constructing one for the book, I show ArchExample, which comes with the Archetypes installation. This adds a content type called article to give a rough example of the power of Archetypes.

Article.py contains the main product code. You'll see that the code looks quite different from previous examples. It contains *schemas*, *widgets*, and *fields*. This file contains the schema for the article content type. Take a look at the following snippet from that schema:

```
StringField("blurb",
            searchable = 1,
            widget = TextAreaWidget(),
            ),
```

This piece of code denotes that you have an attribute on the content type called blurb, that it's a string, and that it's going to be shown as an HTML text area. I discuss all the options for fields and widgets in a moment. For now, take a look at the content type in Plone. In Figure 13-1, I've added the blurb content type.

With just those four lines of code, you've added a field to your content type. The standard form elements that you'd expect in Plone are present; if you edit something and come back later, the old value is shown, errors are handled gracefully, and so on. As a demonstration of how easy it is to modify, change the label in the form to appear as Article Blurb, and change the field to be required. To do this, make the following changes:

```
StringField("blurb",
            required = 1,
            searchable = 1,
            widget = TextAreaWidget(label="Article Blurb"),
            ),
```

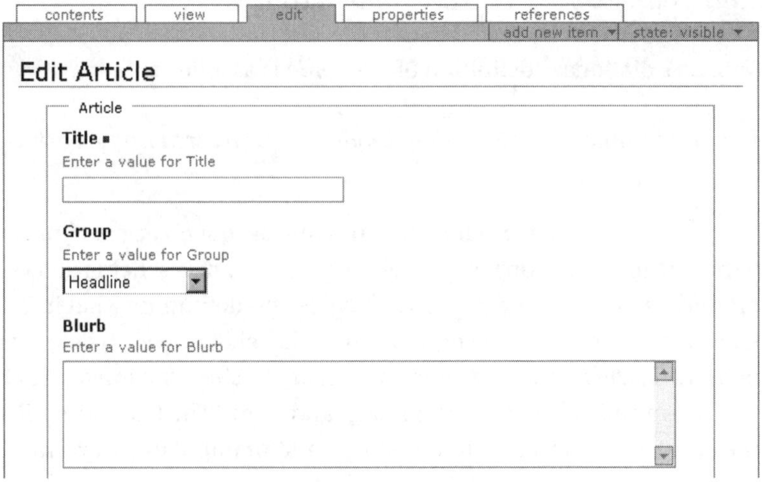

Figure 13-1. The blurb *part of the content type*

Here you've added the required = 1 parameter, which makes this field required, and a label parameter. If you restart Plone and add a new article, the user interface has now changed to reflect the new schema. The field is now called *Article Blurb*, and it has the red required box next to it, as shown in Figure 13-2.

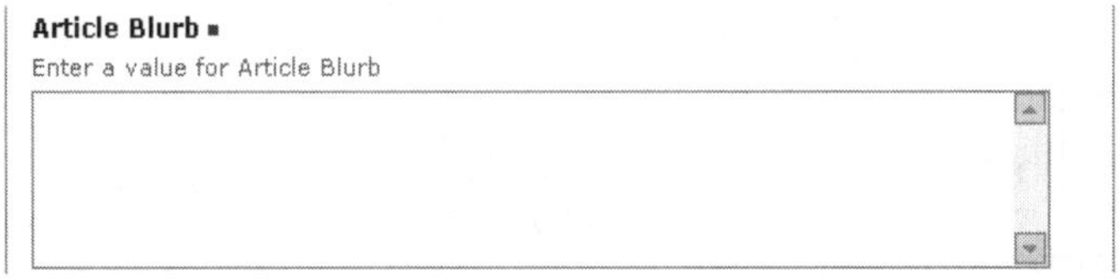

Figure 13-2. The Article Blurb part of the content type

This isn't just a cosmetic change; the change reflects the alteration of the underlying schema, and this is the real power of Archetypes. Just comparing this to writing products in Python, you can see that all the drudgery has been removed from writing a product. It's like this: If you can define a schema, you can throw together an archetype in absolutely no time. Once you've done that, you can edit it easily and have the changes take effect.

If you do make any of these changes to try the following examples, you'll have to restart Plone. Only then will all the new changes be loaded and properly registered. For more information on this, see the "Developing with Archetypes" section later in this chapter.

Explaining Schemas, Fields, and Widgets

Merriam-Webster's dictionary definition of a schema is as follows:

sche·ma: a diagrammatic presentation; broadly; a structured framework or plan

In Archetypes terms, a *schema* defines the structure of your objects; essentially, it specifies what attributes are on your content type. Defining a schema allows you to programmatically examine the content types and determine what information to show a user. The schema contains multiple fields, and each field is an attribute such as title, description, expiration date, or attached document. A field has a type definition such as string, text, integer, and so on. The field primarily describes the type of data and how it'll be stored and manipulated in your content type.

Each field has one widget defined. A *widget* is the visual representation of that field in the user interface. A string field tells you that the data will be in the form of a string; however, it doesn't tell you anything about the field that'll display in the user interface. For example, a string field could display as a textbox, a choice from a drop-down list, or a choice from a list of radio buttons. By defining a widget for a field, you can define exactly how the widget displays. If you don't define a widget for a field, then a default one will be used.

Figure 13-3 shows the relationship between schemas, fields, and widgets.

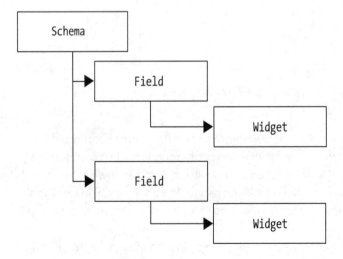

Figure 13-3. The relationship between schemas, fields, and widgets

Schemas and the BaseSchema

To create a schema, pass the fields you'd like in the schema object as a tuple of fields. For example, the article schema has three fields: group, blurb, and body. The following code starts the schema:

```
Schema((
    StringField('group',
        vocabulary=ARTICLE_GROUPS,
        widget=SelectionWidget(),
        ),
    # other fields here
    )
```

It's possible to add schemas together to get a summation of more than one schema. This is exactly what ArchExample actually does: it adds the schema defined in the content type to a schema called BaseSchema.

The BaseSchema contains the two elements every Plone content type should have, a title and an ID. The title is required so that something can display in the user interface, and the ID, or short name, corresponds to the standard Plone conventions for a naming scheme. The two schemas are simply added together to create one bigger schema. In ArchExample, you do this by adding the schema for the content type to the already existing BaseSchema. For example:

```
schema = BaseSchema +  Schema((
    StringField('group',
              vocabulary=ARTICLE_GROUPS,
              widget=SelectionWidget(),
              ),
    ...
```

It's worth noting that the items are returned from queries of the schema in the order they're added to the schema. This means you can rearrange the order that elements appear in the user interface by moving the fields around in the schema. That's also why the BaseSchema is added at the beginning so that the ID and title fields will appear at the top of the view and edit page, rather than at the bottom.

Fields

So far you've seen the StringField field, which is a common field that represents a string on your content type. A number of fields are available in Archetypes, as described in Table 13-1. Over time, more fields are being added, and if you need to, it's possible to create your own.

Each field has a default widget that will be used, unless you specify one. In the blurb example earlier, I specified a TextAreaWidget. (Widgets are covered in the next section.) All these fields are imported from the Archetypes public module; for example:

```
from Products.Archetypes.public import BooleanField
```

All fields are instantiated the same way—by creating a field and passing in the one required parameter for the field: name. You can optionally pass in any number of keyword parameters as needed. For instance:

```
from Products.Archetypes.public import IntegerField
# a simple field for age
age = IntegerField('age')
```

Table 13-1. Fields Available in Archetypes

Name	Type	Default Widget	Description
BooleanField	Boolean values	ComputedWidget	Simple storage of true or false for a field.
DateTimeField	Date and time objects	CalendarWidget	For storing dates and times.
FileField	Files	FileWidget	Storage for large chunks of data such as plain-text files, Microsoft Word documents, and so on.
FixedPointField	Fixed-point numbers	DecimalWidget	For storing numerical data with fixed points.
FloatField	Floats	DecimalWidget	For storing numerical data with floating points.
ImageField	Image	ImageWidget	Stores an image and allows dynamic resizing of the image.
IntegerField	Integer	StringWidget	For storing numerical data as integers.

Table 13-1. Fields Available in Archetypes (Continued)

Name	Type	Default Widget	Description
LinesField	Lists	LinesWidget	A list of data such as keywords.
PhotoField	Image	PhotoWidget	Same as an image field but has more default image sizes.
ReferenceField	Reference	ReferenceWidget	Contains a reference between this object and another.
StringField	String	StringWidget	A string field optimized for smaller strings—say, fewer than 100 words.
TextField	String	TextWidget	A string field optimized for larger strings—say, larger than 100 words. The string can also be transformed into multiple formats.

Each of the fields has attributes you can assign to the field. You've already seen at least two: the name and the widget attributes. The name attribute is the only required parameter to a field and should be unique, lowercase, and without spaces or periods. The name attribute is going to be used internally only, so sticking to this naming rule is important. All the other values are optional. Table 13-2 describes the attributes.

Table 13-2. Field Attributes

Name	Description	Possible Values
accessor	The name of the method to get the value of the field, so you could change how this field is retrieved.	Any method name (for example, specialGetMethod). See the "Overriding Default Methods" section later in this chapter.
default	The default value for the field.	Should be appropriate to the field.
default_method	A string for obtaining a value for the field; one is created for you by default if you don't define one.	Any string (for example, getSpecialDescription). See the "Overriding Default Methods" section later in this chapter.

Table 13-2. Field Attributes (Continued)

Name	Description	Possible Values
edit_accessor	The name of a method to get the raw value of a field.	Any method name (for example, rawGetMethod). See the "Overriding Default Methods" section later in this chapter.
enforceVocabulary	If enabled, you won't accept anything outside the vocabulary.	True or False.
index	If you want this field to be placed in its own catalog index, then specify the type of index here as a string. If you append :schema onto the end of the schema, then this will also be added as a metadata column.	The name of any index, such as KeywordIndex or KeywordIndex:schema.
name	A unique name for this field.	Any string, lowercase conforming to standard Python variable rules (for example, description, user_name, or coffee_bag_6).
mode	The read and write mode of field, as a string; the default is to be read and write.	For read only: r, for write only: w, for read and write: rw.
multiValued	If this field can have multiple values, this is useful for things such as drop-down lists.	True or False.
mutator	The name of the method to alter the value of the field, so you could change how this field is set.	Any method name (for example, specialSetMethod). See "Overriding Default Methods" later in this chapter.
primary	If True on a field, then this will be the field that responds to File Transfer Protocol (FTP) and WebDAV requests. There can be only field that does this; if multiple are defined, the first one in the schema will be used. You normally do this for the main body attribute.	True or False.

Table 13-2. Field Attributes (Continued)

Name	Description	Possible Values
required	Specifies that some value for this field required.	True or False.
schemata	Place the field into the grouping of other fields called *schematas*, where each schemata is defined by its own name. The default schemata is default, and all the standard metadata is placed in a metadata schemata.	Any string. For example, user_information.
searchable	A boolean that specifies if this field will be added to the searchable text and can be used in the searches.	True or False.
validators	The validations that will be performed on the field as a tuple of strings; it starts at first and validates against each validation.	Any validator; see the "Validations of Input" section later.
vocabulary	A list of values that a user can choose from, for example, the values to show in a drop-down list.	List of strings (for example, ["Green", "Red", "Blue"]).
storage	Where to store the value; the default is Attribute Storage, which stores the field as an attribute of the object.	Any valid storage object such as AttributeStorage or SQLStorage. You can find these in the Archetypes Application Programming Interface (API). For more information, see the "Storing Your Content in a SQL Database" section later in this database.
widget	The widget that will be used to display this field.	Any widget object.

Now that I've covered the default fields and attributes, it's time to move onto the actual widgets that are available.

Widgets

A widget contains the information about how the object will be represented
visually. The view of an attribute displayed is often closely related to the type of
the attribute; however, you have options for the display—a string could be selected
in many ways. Given the set of widgets, the widget object can be almost anything.
You can import any of the widgets from the Archetypes public module. For example:

```
from Products.Archetypes.public import BooleanWidget
```

All widgets are instantiated the same way—by creating a widget and passing
in keyword parameters as needed. For example:

```
from Products.Archetypes.public import IntegerField
from Products.Archetypes.public import IntegerWidget
# a simple field for age
age = IntegerField('age',
        widget=IntegerWidget(label="Your age")
        )
```

Widgets can also have extra attributes, depending upon the type of widget.
In most cases, these extra attributes correspond directly to HTML attributes; for
example, on a StringWidget, you can set a size attribute. This will produce the
appropriate HTML widget with the HTML size attribute set. So to have input
that's 20 characters wide, you'd create the following widget:

```
bankAccountNumber = StringField('bank',
    widget=StringWidget(
            label="Bank account number",
            size=20)
        )
```

Table 13-3 describes all the widgets available to you in Archetypes.

Table 13-3. The Available Widgets

Name	Description	Other Attributes
BooleanWidget	Shows two checkboxes for the possible values.	
CalendarWidget	Returns a set of input boxes with a link to a helper pop-up box so that a user can select a date.	
ComputedWidget	Returns the computed value as HTML.	
DecimalWidget	A simple HTML input box for a string.	size.
EpozWidget	An HTML Epoz widget that shows the Epoz rich-text editor for the content.	You can provide format, rows, mode, and cols (for columns).
FileWidget	Displays an HTML file element for users to upload files.	
IdWidget	A simple HTML input box that's used for rendering autogenerated IDs.	
ImageWidget	Shows and allows the editing of images.	You can provide a display_threshold that allows you to set the size of an image; if it's below this size, the image will display in the Web page.
IntegerWidget	A simple HTML input box for a string.	size.
KeywordWidget	This displays a list of keywords from the catalog in a complicated widget, such as the one in the Properties tab on a normal object.	

Table 13-3. The Available Widgets (Continued)

Name	Description	Other Attributes
LabelWidgets	Used to display labels on forms; no values or form elements.	
LinesWidget	Displays a text area that users can enter values.	rows and columns.
MultiSelectionWidget	A selection widget; by default it's an HTML select widget.	format, which can be one of select or checkbox.
PasswordWidget	An HTML password element.	
RichWidget	Allows the input of a file in multiple formats that are then transformed. See "Transforming Data," later in this chapter for more information.	You can provide rows, cols (columns), and format.
ReferenceWidget	Shows an HTML select element of a list of possible references.	
SelectionWidget	Shows a selection widget. If it's flex (the default), then if the number of choices is more than four, a select element is used; otherwise a radio button is used.	format, which can be one of flex, select, or radio.
StringWidget	A simple HTML input box for a string.	size and maxlength.
TextAreaWidget	A text area widget that allows the uploading of the content in multiple formats.	You can provide allowed_content_types, which is a list of string; each string represents a meta_type of the type of content uploaded.

For each of the widgets listed in Table 13-3, Table 13-4 describes all the attributes that are common to all widgets. You've already seen the label attribute, which sets the description on your widget. In conjunction with the extra attributes for each widget, you have a complete set of widget attributes.

Table 13-4. Possible Values for the Widgets

Name	Description	Possible Values
label	The label that will appear in the user interface with this field.	Any string, for example, Start Date for a field start_date.
modes	The modes that this widget will be shown in; by default there are two modes: view and edit.	A list of modes as strings; by default it's ("view", "edit").
populate	If this is enabled, the view and edit fields will be populated. Usually this enabled, but for fields such as a password field, this shouldn't be the case. Usually this is true by default.	True or False
postback	If this is enabled, then when an error is raised, the field is repopulated; for fields such as a password field, this shouldn't be the case. Usually this is true by default.	True or False
visible	If the attribute should be visible in the user interface. This is a dictionary mapping the view mode to a string, describing the visibility. Choices are visible, hidden (shown in an HTML hidden form value), invisible (not shown at all).	For example, {'view': 'visible', 'edit': 'hidden' } means that the view will show, but the edit page will hide the value.

Some Example Field and Widget Combinations

This section contains some useful combinations that seem to be commonly used and that you may find as useful examples. For this example, make a drop-down list of your favorite fruits. You'll define the vocabulary attribute as a list of strings. Each of the values in the list is a string of the fruit type; hence, the field type is a StringField. Because you're defining the widget as a SelectionWidget, it'll show up as a drop-down list, like so:

```
StringField('fruit'
    vocabulary = ["Apple", "Orange", "Mano", "Banana"],
    widget = SelectionWidget(label = "Favourite Fruit")
    )
```

The `ImageField` is a useful one for creating and maintaining images in a Plone site. To have a nice simple field that users can upload images into, use the following:

```
ImageField('portrait',
    widget = ImageWidget(label = "My picture"),
    )
```

The following is quite a complicated content type. Most content types will have one main field that can take data. If you think of the basic document type, you'll notice a body field that you enter and edit. This one body field is the main text of the content type. So for this standard field, you'll have only a few attributes that should be added.

First, you'll want this field to be searchable, so you should set the searchable attribute. Second, you'll want this field to respond to FTP and WebDAV requests, so you must set the `primary` attribute (you can find more information on this in the sidebar "The Primary Field: Marshaling and Responding to FTP and WebDAV"). You'll want multiple content types to be uploaded, so for this reason you set some `allowable_content_types`. Then, of course, you need to know how to show the field, so for that you set the `default_output_type`. This then gives you the following field:

```
TextField('body'
          searchable = 1,
          primary = 1,
          default_output_types = 'text/html',
          allowable_content_types = ('text/plain',
                                     'text/structured',
                                     'text/restructured',
                                     'text/html'),
          widget = RichWidget(label = 'Body'),
          )
```

The Primary Field: Marshaling and Responding to FTP and WebDAV

Plone is an object-oriented system where an object has many attributes and can't simply be represented as a plain file. Unfortunately, most the existing protocols such as FTP and WebDAV treat content in exactly this manner. So there needs to be some way to translate between the two, and the primary field does this. By setting the primary field on an object, this field will become the one that's sent and received by these protocols—rather than the entire object.

This is an imperfect solution to a tricky problem, of course. If you've used FTP or External Editor on a file, you'll know that it tries to solve this by placing a number of lines at the top of the page containing key/value pairs for metadata on the object. This is another attempt to solve the same problem.

To set up primary field marshaling, you need to add the following to your schema: `marshall=some_marshaller()`. Currently, there are only two marshalers: a `PrimaryFieldMarshaller`, which takes the whole content and places into your object, and an `RFC822Marshaller`. This second marshaler handles the content for field name/value pairs as used in e-mail. For this chapter's purposes, I'll use the `PrimaryFieldMarshaller` to handle content with External Editor.

Validations of Input

Although the forms handle the content and some basic errors, such as omitted content, quite well, you'll probably want some more sophisticated error handling. You can make a series of validations to test that the content in your content type is correct. For example, if you have an integer field, you'll probably want to test that the data they've added is what it's meant to be.

To do this, you can add a validation parameter to the field. To test that your `IntegerField` really is an integer, for example, you'd do this:

```
from Products.Archetypes.public import IntegerField
from Products.Archetypes.public import IntegerWidget
# a simple field for age
age = IntegerField('age',
    validators=("isInt"),
    widget=IntegerWidget(label="Your age")
    )
```

Where did isInt come from? Well, isInt is the name of a validator registered in the validation framework. Only a few are in there, but they're quite useful; Table 13-5 describes them. For the exact details of some of these, I recommend reading the code and looking at the regular expressions—you can find these in the validation/validators/__init__.py module in your Products directory:

Table 13-5. Available Validations

Name	Description
isDecimal	This validates that the string is a decimal, including positive and negative, exponentials, and so on.
isInt	This validates that it's an integer.
isPrintable	This validates that this is a letter or a number.
isSSN	This validates that it's nine numbers (the length of a U.S. Social Security number).
isUSPhoneNumber	This validates that it's ten numbers and is optional.
isInternationalPhoneNumber	This validates that it's at least one number and is optional.
isZipCode	This validates that it's five or nine numbers.
isURL	This validates that the input starts with http://, ftp://, or https://.
isEmail	This validates that this conforms to the standard e-mail syntax.

You can also register your own validations. A validator is actually a simple class that implements the ivalidator interface. Two are already done: a RegexValidator that verifies a regular expression and a RangeValidator that verifies a range of values. To register a new validator that checks that a user is between, say, 0 and 150 years old (seems reasonable), you'd add the following to your content type in the Python module, before creating the field:

```
from validation.validators.validator import RangeValidator
from validation import validation

# the RangeValidator takes a name for the validator
# and a start and end value
validAge = RangeValidator("validAge", 0, 150)
validation.register(validAge)
```

Then you can change your validator to the following:

```
validators=("isInt","validAge"),
```

First, the code will check that you have a valid integer; second, it'll check that the integer is within the range of sensible ages. If you wanted to add a totally new validator that did something other than a regular expression or range validation, you'd need to add a new validation system. For this example, make a validation that a date is between two values. In the following example, this is called DateRangeValidator and will return a boolean value if the given date fits between the two given dates. This could be useful to assert that a vacation is within the school holidays.

So, now define a new validator called DateRangeValidator in the validators module. This will allow you to register date ranges to assert that the given date falls in the middle. To do this, you'll use the Zope DateTime object (which is covered in more detail in Appendix A). A validator is simple—it's a class that has a name and will respond to the __call__ method by checking the date. The following is the DateRangeValidator class, which was added to the validators module:

```
from DateTime import DateTime

class DateRangeValidator:
    __implements__ = (ivalidator,)

    def __init__(self, name):
        self.name = name

    def __call__(self, value, *args, **kwargs):
        min, max = args[:2]
        if not isinstance(value, DateTime):
            value = DateTime(value)

    return min < value and value < max
```

After restarting Zope, you can now register a new validation, like so:

```
from validation.validators.validator import DateRangeValidator
from validation import validation
from DateTime import DateTime

christmas = DateRangeValidator("ChristmasHolidays",
    DateTime('12/18/2004'),
    DateTime('01/09/2005'),)
validation.register(christmas)
```

Then you can create a validator in your schema in the following manner:

```
validators=("ChristmasHolidays",)
```

Overriding Views and Actions in the Base Class

Archetypes creates default views and actions for you based on a standard set of requirements that will suit many needs. The actions are view, edit, and properties, of course; references is another action you'll look at it a moment. You won't find any view or edit page templates for the object; those are generated automatically for you by Archetypes. However, you can override them.

I expect that in most cases you'll want to override the view method and provide one of your own; the default is basic and isn't aimed at being a perfect page (of course, being a Plone page, it's better than your average content management system). However, you may have specific needs that relate to the content; perhaps it's a matter of presenting your content in a certain way.

Archetypes actually creates a class for each content type. Much in the same way that you created a class for the source code type in the previous chapter, you can create a base class for your archetype. This base class is called BaseContent and is available in the public module of Archetypes for importing. This BaseContent class defines all the things that Archetypes needs to know. Making this class provides you with an opportunity to override almost anything you want in the class.

As I now show, there are two parts to this. First, you make an action that's to be used by the factory type information; in Archetypes you do this by assigning the actions attribute of the class. For example:

```
from Products.Archetypes.public import BaseContent

class Article(BaseContent):
    # other stuff
    actions = ({ 'id': 'view',
                 'name': 'View',
                 'action': 'string:${object_url}/article_view',
                 'permissions': (CMFCorePermissions.View,)
               },)
```

Second, you need to create a page template for the actual view of the object called article_view. This string defines a page template that the content type will locate in the skin for this product. In this case, you'll find the matching page template on the file system in the skins/archexample directory of ArchExample. You can also find a copy of this page template in Appendix B. This can be as simple or as complicated a page template as you'd like.

You have to restart Plone for the changes to take effect. In this case, you're changing an action that's installed into the portal_types tool whenever the product is installed. For this reason, if you do change this action, you'll need to reinstall the product. To do this in the Plone interface, click *plone setup*, select Add/Remove Products, and reinstall the corresponding product.

All the elements in the factory type information can be overridden by creating an attribute of that name on the object. To override the content_icon setting, you'd make an attribute called content_item. For example:

```
class SomeProduct(BaseContent):
    """ Some product """
    content_icon = "some_icon.gif"
```

Overriding the Default Methods

In Table 13-2, I mentioned the option of overriding some of the default methods that occur on content types, such as accessor and mutator. This is an advanced option that allows you to manipulate the way fields are edited.

Just as with the source code project in the last chapter, you access these attributes or fields using accessors and mutator methods. Some default methods are available for you. If your field name is blurb, then these methods will be getBlurb and setBlurb. The term *get* or *set* is prepended, and the first letter is capitalized.

However, you may want to do something different in the accessor or mutator. Suppose you wanted to filter the value of a field, such as always correcting the spelling of your company name or changing the value of some other fields when a certain field changes. Then you could do so by overriding the default methods. In the following example, you'll make a new method called getSpecialBlurb that takes the blurb someone has entered and manipulates it before returning to the client. In this case, you're replacing the text *Perl* with *Python*. The getSpecialBlurb method is a method of the Article class created in the previous examples. Here's the code:

```
class Article(BaseContent):

    def getSpecialBlurb(self):
        """ The view for an article """
        blurb = self.getField('blurb').get(self)
        blurb = blurb.replace('Perl', 'Python')
        return blurb
```

You'll also need to change your field so that it uses this method:

```
StringField('blurb',
    searchable=1,
    widget=TextAreaWidget(),
    accessor="getSpecialBlurb",
),
```

In this example, anytime the blurb field is accessed in a view or edit page, for example, the value of getSpecialBlurb is returned. Archetypes knows to access that method because the name of the method is defined as a string value passed to the accessor parameter. There's one bit of trickery involved—to access the raw value of the attribute, you need to get the field and then call the get method. This is the rather confusing blurb = self.getField('blurb').get(self) line. The pattern of getting the field and then calling a method on it is actually quite common in Archetypes.

The practical upshot of this is that now, no matter when or how a person types in the word *Perl* into the Blurb field, the value *Python* will always be returned.

Putting Together the Rest of the Content Type

I've now covered all the main elements of the content type. Listing 13-1 shows all the code together. You'll note that the rest of the code is more compact than the Python product because Archetypes does so much work for you.

Listing 13-1. Article.py

```python
from Products.ArchExample.config import ARTICLE_GROUPS
from Products.Archetypes.public import BaseSchema, Schema
from Products.Archetypes.public import StringField, TextField
from Products.Archetypes.public import SelectionWidget, TextAreaWidget
from Products.Archetypes.public import RichWidget
from Products.Archetypes.public import BaseContent, registerType
from Products.Archetypes.Marshall import PrimaryFieldMarshaller
from Products.CMFCore import CMFCorePermissions
from config import PROJECTNAME

schema = BaseSchema +  Schema((
    StringField('group',
                vocabulary=ARTICLE_GROUPS,
                widget=SelectionWidget(),
                ),
    StringField('blurb',
                searchable=1,
                widget=TextAreaWidget(),
                ),
    TextField('body',
              searchable=1,
              required=1,
              primary=1,
              default_output_type='text/html',
              allowable_content_types=('text/plain',
                                       'text/structured',
                                       'text/restructured',
                                       'text/html',
                                       'application/msword'),
              widget=RichWidget(label='Body'),
              ),
          ),
    marshall=PrimaryFieldMarshaller(),
    )

class Article(BaseContent):
    """This is a sample article; it has an overridden view for show,
    but this is purely optional
    """

    schema = schema
```

```
actions = ({
    'id': 'view',
    'name': 'View',
    'action': 'string:${object_url}/article_view',
    'permissions': (CMFCorePermissions.View,)
    },)

registerType(Article, PROJECTNAME)
```

Apart from a bunch of imports at the top and the schema, I've covered all the contents of this code, with one exception: `registerType`. This function registers your object with the product. Each product can have multiple content types, so this function takes the object and the name of the project. In this case, the name of the project is imported from the configuration file, as you saw earlier. The configuration file, `config.py`, contains similar variables for the product configuration, as shown in Listing 13-2.

Listing 13-2. The Configuration File for ArchExample

```
from Products.CMFCore.CMFCorePermissions import AddPortalContent
from Products.Archetypes.public import DisplayList

ADD_CONTENT_PERMISSION = AddPortalContent
PROJECTNAME = "ArchExample"
SKINS_DIR = 'skins'

GLOBALS = globals()

ARTICLE_GROUPS = DisplayList((
    ('headline', 'Headline'),
    ('bulletin', 'Special Bulletin'),
    ('column', 'Weekly Column'),
    ('editorial', 'Editorial'),
    ('release', 'Press Release'),
    ))
```

The variable `ARTICLE_GROUPS` is a tuple of a tuple of strings for use in the group widget. You could just use a simple tuple of strings, but in this case the example is using the `DisplayList` class, which is a chance to show a different value to the user from what will be put in the form. In this case, the HTML for `ArticleGroups` is displayed in an HTML select element, like so:

```
<option value="headline">Headline</option>
<option value="bulletin">Special Bulletin</option>
...
```

One other unusual insight is the use of globals function—this is a Python built-in function that contains all the global symbols. This calculates the path to the skins directory on the file system so that you can make a file system directory view of the skin for the skins tool. The product initialization function, __init__.py, is also much simpler. With one new inclusion, the process and list type functions look like this:

```
from Products.Archetypes.public import process_types, listTypes
content_types, constructors, ftis = process_types(
    listTypes(PROJECTNAME),
    PROJECTNAME)
```

The listTypes function is an Archetypes utility that will return all the types you've previously registered. This is then passed into the process_types function, which in turn returns you all the content types, constructors, and factory type information objects. These are all the same items you registered in the Python product; it's just that this utility function makes it all a little easier.

Finally, you have the installation function in the Extensions install.py. This script is now embarrassingly small because all the work you've done previously is handled by two utility functions, installTypes and install_subskin. The term *subskin* is actually a little misleading—it really means a layer. Listing 13-3 now shows the final install script (again, this is totally generic).

Listing 13-3. Installation Script

```
from Products.Archetypes.public import listTypes
from Products.Archetypes.Extensions.utils import installTypes,
install_subskin
from Products.ArchExample.config import  PROJECTNAME, GLOBALS

from StringIO import StringIO

def install(self):
    out = StringIO()
    installTypes(self, out, listTypes(PROJECTNAME), PROJECTNAME)
    install_subskin(self, out, GLOBALS)
    out.write("Successfully installed %s." % PROJECTNAME)
    return out.getvalue()
```

The full version of ArchExample is available from the Plone Book Web site at `http://plone-book.agmweb.ca`, and you should be able to drop this and run it on your site. As you've seen, this content type is quick and easy to develop and easy to alter, without having to write lots of code.

Developing with Archetypes

This section provides some more in-depth coverage on some of Archetypes' more advanced features. These features will provide some useful tools for the development of your content types. This will include making references, creating new widgets, and transforming content.

For this chapter, it's important to recognize how the changes you'll make can be carried through to Plone. As you've seen in the past, you have different stages in your product setup. When you change your product, it helps to know the steps you need to take.

If you change something in a skin, then just running in debug mode will ensure that the changes are propagated. If you change something that's passed onto the `portal_actions` tool such as actions or icon, then you need to restart Plone and reinstall the product through Add/Remove Products.

If you change a schema, then you just need to restart Plone, and all new instances of your class in Plone will be updated. However, what about all the old instances of the product? Fortunately, Archetypes has provided a dynamic update tool that goes through all the old instances of your product and updates them to the new schema. In the ZMI, click *archetype_tool* and select Update Schema. Here you can select your classes, and then click Update Schema; this will allow you update your schema dynamically from whatever is on the file system in your product.

Using Unique IDs

The concept of unique IDs is simple but something that was missing in Zope. Originally Zope developers assumed using the path to an object would do; unfortunately, this has shown to be inadequate. As a simple example, consider what happens when someone moves the location of a document—your unique reference to that document has been lost. A unique ID is a truly useful tool to have. Archetypes creates a unique ID on every object it creates and saves it for you on the object. It also saves it in a separate catalog for you called `uid_catalog`.

You can see the `uid_catalog` in the ZMI, and it's like the `portal_catalog` object except it's missing a little bit of extra Application Programming Interface (API) wrapping and all the indexes that the former contains. It's pretty simple to get an object now by going through this catalog. All you have to do is search the catalog for your object. For example, the following Script (Python) object can pull any registered object, provided you know its UID:

```
##paramaters=objectId
results = context.uid_catalog(UID=objectId)
return results[0].getObject()
```

But where this really is useful is in references between existing objects. Say you want to reference one or more separate images with your article. These images could be images uploaded by other users at another date, perhaps part of an image database. If those images are Archetypes objects, then you could add a field to your article schema that reads as follows:

```
ReferenceField("images"
    allowed_types=("Archetype Images",),
    multivalued=1,
    ),
```

The user will now get a drop-down box of all the Archetype Image objects and be able to choose them. Behind the scenes it's making a reference of that object's UID through the catalog. You'll find an excellent example on references in a product called ACME in the Archetypes CVS repository at http://sf.net/projects/archetypes.

Altering Widgets

A commonly asked question is, why does this widget do this? Another is, why does this widget look like this? Often the answer is something like, because it does—now go and write your own. Since widgets are what the client sees, these requirements are often client driven.

All the widgets are represented as page template macros on the file system. So it's pretty simple to alter widgets or make your own. If you click *portal_skins*, click *archetypes*, then click *widgets*, you'll see all existing widgets. Unfortunately, the portal_skins tool has one small bug. Because the widgets are a subdirectory, you can't easily modify just one of the objects. You can, however, make a new layer in your skin and then specify that the widget should be represented using a different macro. Each widget has a macro property defining which macro should be used as a path expression to the widget location.

Actually, the term *macro* is misleading since it points to a page template, and that template then contains at least three macros: view, edit, and search. These are the macros used to display your widget in the different situations.

The view macro displays on the view page and is a read-only, user-friendly view of the item. The edit macro is the one shown on the edit page, and it's the macro where a user edits the data. The search macro is called when you're assembling search pages for the code; it sometimes looks like the edit macro, although it may not. A string field may be edited as a string field and viewed as a string, but it's searched using a drop-down box to select from all the options available.

So, in the example product, assume you have a string field that's a person's e-mail address, and you want to show this is a clickable e-mail link. For this you'll make a new macro. In this case, you don't need to actually override the edit and search macros—it's just a string after all. So, make a new a page template called email_widget.pt, as follows, which you'll place in the skin of your product:

```
<html xmlns:tal="http://xml.zope.org/namespaces/tal"
      xmlns:metal="http://xml.zope.org/namespaces/metal"
      i18n:domain="plone">

  <body>
    <div metal:define-macro="edit">
      <div metal:use-macro="here/widgets/string/macros/edit" />
    </div>

    <div metal:define-macro="search">
      <div metal:use-macro="here/widgets/string/macros/search" />
    </div>
```

For the view, you need to make the string show as a mailto link, which is just the following simple adjustment:

```
    <div class="field" metal:define-macro="view">
      <a href="#" tal:attributes="href string:mailto:${accessor}"
        tal:content="accessor">email</a>
    </div>
  </body>
</html>
```

Now that you've defined a page template that contains your code, you can simply reference the name of the template as the macro in your widget. In the following code, you define the e-mail field and a StringWidget as normal. You then change your macro to use your nice new email_template macro, like so:

```
StringField('email',
    validators = ('isEmail',),
    widget = StringWidget(
        label='Email',
        macro='email_template'
    )
)
```

At this point you're just changing the macro of an existing widget. Making an entirely new widget is just a matter of defining a new widget and then registering it. All widgets share the same base class. The following is a new module called EmailWidget.py that's placed inside the ArchExample directory. It creates a new widget and then registers it into the registry. Note that the macro property of the widget (highlighted) is set to the value of the template:

```
from Products.Archetypes.Widget import TypesWidget
from Products.Archetypes.Registry import registerWidget

class EmailWidget(TypesWidget):
    _properties = TypesWidget._properties.copy()
    _properties.update({
        'macro' : "email_template",
        'size' : '30',
        'maxlength' : '255',
        })

registerWidget(EmailWidget,
    title='String',
    description='Renders a clickable email field',
    used_for=('Products.Archetypes.Field.StringField',)
)
```

To include this in your article, you can now directly import the EmailWidget and use it without having to explicitly define the macro, like so:

```
from EmailWidget import EmailWidget

StringField('email',
    validators = ('isEmail',),
    widget = EmailWidget(
        label='Email',
    )
)
```

Developing Folderish Objects

You've already worked with folderish objects a lot in Plone, but you may not have known it. A folderish object is one that exhibits similar characteristics to a folder or directory, namely, that it can contain separate individual objects. There really is nothing special about a folderish object—just that it inherits from a certain base class to provide its properties, and new content can be added to it.

Folderish objects are useful for you to make for several reasons. They provide a simple way to create collections of disparate objects in one location. They also allow users to manage the contents using the standard Plone user interface, without you having to do anything. Generally, it's best to keep the folder quite simple, and the logic should be on your objects and in the objects' workflow. However, some exceptions to that always exist, and a classic example is the family of collectors, CMFCollector and PloneCollector—both of which are quite complicated collector objects that provide logic for a bunch of collector issues.

The easiest way again to make a folderish object is to use Archetypes. You've seen that there's a BaseContent type that handles all the work needed to create a nonfolderish object. Well, there's also a BaseFolder content type that contains everything for creating a folder. Futher, you'll find a special schema for folders, since folderish object also usually have a description. To make a folderish type, just ensure that you change your base classes and your schema. For example, possibly the simplest folder is as follows:

```
from Products.Archetypes.public import BaseFolder, BaseFolderSchema

schema = BaseFolderSchema

class SimpleFolder(BaseFolder):
    """A simple folderish archetype"""
    schema = schema

registerType(SimpleFolder)
```

If you're going to store a huge amount of content in a folder, then a folder tends to become inefficient at about 100 objects. That's a rather arbitrary figure that should be taken with a pinch of salt; normal folderish objects are designed to be fast for small numbers of object. If you wanted, you could use a binary tree folder, which stores the objects internally in a more efficient binary tree, rather than a Python dictionary. To use this, just import BaseBTreeFolder and BaseBTreeFolderSchema and use these in your object instead. As far as developing a product is concerned, they work just the same, but unless you put a lot of data into them, you wouldn't likely notice any difference. I've stored more than 100,000 objects in `BTreeFolder`, and it's always responded well.

Handling Microsoft Office Content

Handling Microsoft Office content such as Word and Excel documents is a bane that all content management systems face at some point. However, this is really the case for every type of content—Microsoft Office, OpenOffice.org, Portable Document Format (PDF), images, and so on. Using these content forms on Web sites usually causes a few problems; this is well known, of course. Editing is clumsy because clicking a document causes you to download it or, even worse, open it in your browser. When you've finished, you have to upload back up to the Web site, which can normally mean clicking around a bit to get back to it. When the content is online, the contents aren't searchable because they aren't in a plain-text format the catalog can understand. Further, you can't view the content online because again it isn't in a Web-friendly format.

You have a couple of solutions for solving the first problem of editing content. If again you assume most of your users are using Windows, then using WebDAV can be tricky for you because Microsoft's Web folder implementation is of questionable quality. Instead, External Editor fulfills this function quite well—if Plone can tell External Editor that this is a Word file, it'll open in Word.

As for the rest, well, Archetypes has a built-in transformation package, called Portal Transforms, that handles the transformation of content types. This can take a file in a certain format and transform it into HTML, which will then be cataloged, and the HTML will display to the user in the user interface. It does this by using an external transformation process to transform the data and read the results. For example, if you're using Windows (on the server), then Portal Transforms will take the uploaded Word document and start a Component Object Model (COM) object that transforms it.

This all happens behind the scenes for you; all you have to worry about is ensuring that any requirements for your transforms are installed and operational. You can do lots of different types of transforms, and there's more than one way to transform the data.

The OpenOffice.org suite provides excellent transformation of Microsoft content, so if you're running on a non-Microsoft platform, this is an excellent way to transform that content. I've also used wvWare (`http://wvware.sourceforge.net/`) quite successfully as another way of transforming content. All these options are available to you; however, they aren't trivial to set up. Once they're set up, of course, people usually report getting higher-quality transformations than when using a Microsoft server.

I recommend thinking first about exactly what you want to transform and then taking a look at the Portal Transforms source code to see if you can find a transformation that will do the job for you.

Setting Up a Content Type

You'll now create a simple content type for handling Microsoft Word documents, probably the most common type of content you'll have to handle. For this example, I did the transformation on Windows. However, if you can set up an alternative system, most of the following worked on Linux. In this case, the easiest thing to do is to use Windows to install your Plone instance. This creates an install with all the Win32 API modules installed and working. I had Microsoft Office installed on the server. Then you need to make a content type to handle the example, called WordExample. Essentially one field in the schema handles the content so that the schema looks like the following:

```
schema = BaseSchema +  Schema((
    TextField('body',
                searchable=1,
                required=1,
                primary=1,
                default_output_type='text/html',
                allowable_content_types=('application/msword',),
                widget=RichWidget(label='Body'),
                ),
    ),
    marshall=PrimaryFieldMarshaller(),
    )
```

The only difference is that you've added a Multipurpose Internet Mail Extensions (MIME) type for the Word document, application/msword. For each of content types to be transformed, add the MIME type into allowable_content_types. For example, if you wanted to handle Word and PDF documents, you'd have the following line:

```
allowable_content_types=('application/msword','application/pdf'),
```

This content type is about as simple as you can get at this point. But you could plug more stuff into this into the content type—such as a description or more properties. If you're doing a lot of work, then it'd conceivably be possible even to pull the metadata information from the Word document and place it as metadata inside Plone.

Setting Up a Transformation on Windows

The transformation should be set up for you automatically inside the portal_transforms tool. There isn't really a lot to look at in the tool; it merely provides a list of the transforms that are available. A transformation has a list of incoming MIME types that it'll transform (such as application/msword) and the output that will be produced (such as text/html). Each transformation is a module on the file system; in this case, you can find it in PortalTransforms/transforms/word_to_html.

For that transformation to work, though, you must run a utility to generate the COM bindings for Python. To do this, select Start ➤ Plone ➤ Pythonwin and then select Tools ➤ COM Makepy Utility. This lists all the COM interfaces available; if you have Office installed, you'll see an entry for Word somewhere in the list. On my particular Windows server, this is called Microsoft Word 9.0 Object Library (8.1). Select that option, and click OK. Pythonwin will now generate the appropriate information. Once you've done this, you'll get a message back regarding "Generating to..".

You can now close Pythonwin and restart Plone.

Testing the Content Type

To test your content type, you'll need to restart Plone, ensure that the product is registered as usual, and install it using the Add/Remove Products screen. To add a new Word document, go to the Plone interface and in the drop-down box select Word Document; it's pretty obvious since you'll also see a little Word logo.

Next, select your file from the file system, and click Save to upload your file. Once this has been done, the file will be uploaded, and you'll be taken to the view page. This may take a little bit longer than you expect—it has to upload the document to the server and then perform the transformation. But you'll be taken to the view page for your content type, and sure enough it'll be shown in HTML, as shown in Figure 13-4.

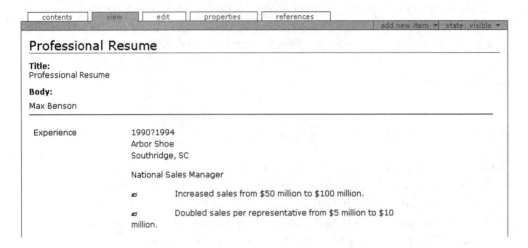

Figure 13-4. The uploaded file

Now that it's uploaded, you'll want to edit it; for this, your best bet is to use External Editor. If you have External Editor installed on your local client, click the pencil icon in the top-right corner, and the file will open in Word, as shown in Figure 13-5. You can now alter and edit your Word document. Each time you save the file, it will be loaded back into Plone and transformed.

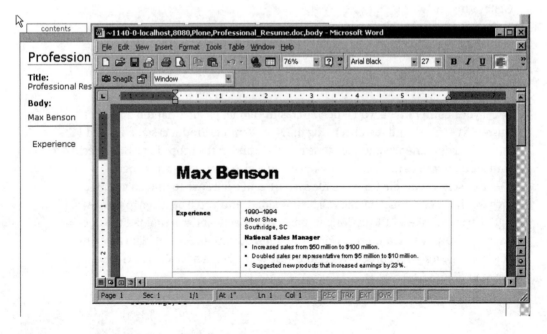

Figure 13-5. The document loaded into Word

TIP You can download Portal Transforms from the Archetypes CVS
repository at `http://sf.net/projects/archetypes`. You'll find some
limited documentation on Portal Transforms in the code, and you'll
find an online version at `http://www.logilab.org/projects/portal-
transforms/documentation`.

Going Further: Writing Content Types in a UML Diagram

So you have a complicated content type and the idea of writing it manually is
boring? Well, never fear, because ArchGenXML is here! This is a neat product that
allows you to write your content in a UML graphical modeling tool and develop a
product straight from that.

Robert Boulanger developed ArchGenXML, and Sidnei da Silva has provided
some excellent documention. With kind permission, I'll reproduce some of those
diagrams here.

The UML modeling tool must support a standard Extensible Markup Language
(XML) generation system called XML Metadata Interchange (XMI). This tool has
been tested with the following programs:

- ObjectDomain (commercial, with a free demo for 30 classes) from
  `http://www.objectdomain.com`

- ArgoUML (free) from `http://argouml.tigris.org`

- Poseidon (commercial, based on ArgoUML) from `http://www.gentleware.com`

- Sybase Powerdesigner (commercial, demo download) from
  `http://www.sybase.com`

There are slightly different export properties for each of these, but if you take
a look in the ArchGenXML samples, you'll see example outputs from the UML
tools. Figure 13-6 shows a class project that shows a few objects: room, person
project, resource, and task. There are relationships between all these objects, and
there's even Python code specified on some of the objects.

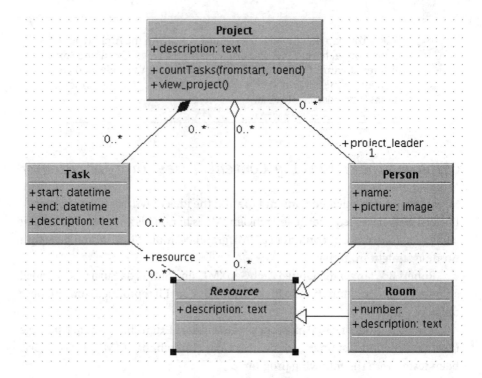

Figure 13-6. A complex ArchGenXML example

The quickest way to test this is to go into the ArchGenXML folder on your file system that you kept around from the original install and then change into the examples folder. In that folder you'll see the mkdemo script. To run it, just type **./mkdemo** on Linux. On Windows, you'd have to run it separately, so the following command would work to build the example from ArgoUML:

```
python ../ArchGenXML.py outline.zargo outline_argo
```

You then need to copy the product folder created (for example, outline_argo) into your Products directory and restart your Zope instance. If you take a peek inside the outline_argo directory, you'll see that everything has been created for you—the entire directory and all the relevant product initialization. Click *plone setup*, select Add/Remove Products, and install the outline_argo product. You can now add an outline object that has all the schema defined in the UML.

That's about as rapid development as you can get, and there are many, many options inside ArchGenXML for defining abstract classes, code fragments, and so on. Furthermore, generating code this way easily allows you to make changes and have great documentation. The only real drawback is a lack of *round-tripping*— which is the ability to make changes in the Python and have them put back into the UML. If you change the object in Python, you'll end up overwriting them the next time you do an update. You can find some documentation about this at http://plone.org/documentation/archetypes/ArchetypesDeveloperGuide/ index_html#archgenxml-generating-archetypes-using-uml.

Storing Your Content in a SQL Database

For almost all of this book, the content you've seen has been stored in the Zope object database. I've shown you how to store content on the file system, but a commonly asked question is, how do you store it in a relational database? Placing it inside a relational database is often a good thing to do if the following are true:

- Your structure is rigid, and the schema doesn't change often (although Archetypes mitigates this aspect).

- You have other applications that can or do access the relational database.

- There are tools or other requirements that are already fulfilled by a relational database.

- You have a large amount of repetitive data that's updated often.

In more a traditional CGI environment, you'd probably write some SQL statements for pulling the content out of a relational database. You can do this if you really want to by using ZSQL methods. These are useful for many situations and are covered in great detail in the Zope Book and several other books, but they can't be used to directly store content. A ZSQL method stores SQL statements and makes queries into your relational database based upon those queries. This is great if you want to make simple queries into relational database, but it doesn't persist Python classes or content types, and it really isn't the Plone way of thinking. You'll find an excellent chapter in the Zope Book on this at http://zope.org/ Documentation/Books/ZopeBook/2_6Edition/RelationalDatabases.stx.

SQLStorage uses the fact that Archetypes provides an extra layer on top of normal objects to allow for special persistence mechanisms. Zope provides many different relational database adapters, and SQLStorage plugs into those. Currently there are two adapters, Postgres and MySQL. However, if the database supports standard SQL, then there's no reason one of these existing SQLStorage formats can't be used. If you find that your database adapter needs to do something different, then it wouldn't be difficult to alter the SQL statements inside SQLStorage so it worked with another database.

Making a Content Type Persist in a Relational Database

To persist the data, you must set up a relational database and make a Zope connection to it. In this case, I'll use Postgres, mainly because I already have a Postgres database for other work available but also because Postgres is good database for all levels of users. To connect Zope to Postgres, psycopg and ZPsycopg are probably to hardest to pronounce but most commonly used and best supported. You'll also find Debian packages and even Windows packages available from http://initd.org/software/psycopg.

Install your database adapter, and make a database connection from your Zope site to your relational database. Again, this is covered in great detail in the Zope Book at http://zope.org/Documentation/Books/ZopeBook/2_6Edition/ RelationalDatabases.stx. But the short answer is go to the ZMI, add the database connection from the drop-down menu, and then enter the configuration to point to your relational database. If you're connecting as a certain user to your relational database, you need to make sure that the user has the privilege ability to create, insert, update, and delete tables. The create and delete privileges will be needed only during the debugging phase as you add and remove schemas and objects. Once your development has settled down or you move to production, this won't be necessary.

Next, in the ZMI click *archetypes_tool* and select Connections. This allows you to map the content type to the database adapter type. The easiest way is to map the default to your database connection. If you wanted, you could of course map specific types to different databases. Now you'll change the schema to use the new storage. For this you need to import the appropriate storage class from SQLStorage (in this case, PostgreSQLStorage).

Then you need to set the storage parameter on the fields you want to store in the relational database. At this point, you'll note that you can put as many or as few fields inside the relational database as you want—you could have all the fields in the database or just some. Either way there will be content stored inside your Plone database, but at the least it'll be an object that has an ID. Anyway, in the example schema, you have two fields: an integer (age) and a string (email), as shown in Listing 13-4.

Listing 13-4. A Content Type Using SQLStorage

```
from Products.Archetypes.public import Schema
from Products.Archetypes.public import IntegerField, StringField
from Products.Archetypes.public import IntegerWidget, StringField
from Products.Archetypes.SQLStorage import PostgreSQLStorage
from config import PROJECTNAME

schema = BaseSchema + Schema((

  IntegerField('age',
      validators=("isInt",),
      storage = SQLStorage(),
      widget=IntegerWidget(label="Your age"),

      ),

  StringField('email',
      validators = ('isEmail',),
      index = "TextIndex",
      storage = SQLStorage(),
      widget = StringWidget(label='Email',)
      ),

  ))

class PersonSQL(BaseContent):
    """Our person object"""
    schema = schema

registerType(PersonSQL, PROJECTNAME)
```

Finally, restart Plone and register your content type in your Plone site. You're now ready to test it. If you create a PersonSQL object, everything should proceed as normal and as expected for the content type. But of course the real test is if you look at your database.

You'll see that in the database you have a new table called personsql, and in that table you'll find four columns: uid, parentuid, age, and email. Using psql you can see this:

```
db=# \d
                    List of relations
  Schema |          Name          |  Type  | Owner
 --------+------------------------+--------+-------
  public | personsql              | table  | www-data
 ...
db=# \d personsql
  Table "public.personsql"
  Column   | Type | Modifiers
-----------+------+-----------
 uid       | text | not null
 parentuid | text |
 age       | int  |
 email     | text |
Indexes: personsql_pkey primary key btree (uid)
```

The column for age has been created as an int, and the column for email has been created as text. These are mappings created inside SQLStorage; you could change these mappings to more appropriate ones if you so desired. The uid column is the unique ID for your object inside Plone. The parentuid is the uid of the parent object. These are all the unique IDs for Archetypes that I've already mentioned. For example:

```
db=# SELECT * FROM personsql;
           uid           | parentuid | age | email
-------------------------+-----------+-----+--------------------
 PersonSQL.2003-07-23.4935 |         | 30  | andy@clearwind.ca
```

That's it—your data is being persisted inside your relational database. No SQL needs to be written, and you can have all the advantages a relational database brings! Joel Burton has written an excellent how-to article on SQLStorage at http://plone.sourceforge.net/archetypes/sqlstorage-howto.html. With kind permission, some parts of this section are based on Joel's document.

CHAPTER 14

Administering and Scaling Plone

THIS CHAPTER COVERS the tasks you have to worry about once you've built your site and are using it. I start by covering the administration of a Plone site, which is actually quite straightforward. Next, I cover what files to back up, including when and how to back them up. I also cover upgrades to Plone.

Then, I cover performance and show techniques for finding the hotspots. Once you've found those spots, I cover common problems. Then I go into the main technique for making your Plone site really fast and scalable: caching. When it comes to performance, you'll definitely need to know how to scale your server outward using multiple processes and how to cope with high-cost requests. For this you'll need Zope Enterprise Objects (ZEO), which is covered at the end of this chapter.

Administering a Plone Site

As it turns out, the administration of a Plone site is quite simple; you need to perform only a few tasks, which are common to all services. The tasks are as follows:

- You should back up the database regularly.

- You should pack the database regularly.

- You should back up and rotate the log files.

You should perform these actions regularly to maintain your site. In enterprises, you'll usually often have standard tools for backing up and rotating logs; these tools are all easy to integrate since Plone data is all contained as files on the file system.

Backing Up Your Plone Site

You should run backups regularly on a Plone site; most people run backups nightly. Your application needs should determine the schedule for backups. If large amounts of data are written into your data, then perhaps more frequent backups are necessary. In the case of a smaller site with less content, a less frequent schedule such as once a week may be more suitable.

In a standard Plone site, only one file needs backing up: the Zope database where all the content for the Plone site resides. You can find this file by accessing the Zope Management Interface (ZMI) control panel, selecting Database Management, and then clicking *main*. This page shows the database size and location. The file is called Data.fs, and you can find it in the var directory of instance home. To perform the backup, copy this file locally; then you can safely copy it to a remote storage such as another hard drive, server, tape drive, or whatever backup system you have. You can even perform this backup while Plone is running.

You can use your own scripts or tools for backing up or use a tool from Zope. As an example of the first option, Listing 14-1 shows a Linux bash script I use to back up a Zope site.

Listing 14-1. Bash Script for Backing Up

```
#!/bin/bash
# script to copy, gzip, and then copy Zope databases
# to remote server
# make up a filename
fn=`uuidgen`.fs
# copy it locally, you'll want to change the
# path
cp /var/zope.test/var/Data.fs /tmp/$fn
# gzip the file up
gzip /tmp/$fn
# scp over to my backup server and then remove
# the temporary file
# change the destination file
scp /tmp/$fn.gz backup@backups.agmweb.ca:~/Zope
rm /tmp/$fn.gz
```

For the second of these choices, a Python script called repozo.py is available in the Zope Object Database (ZODB) for backing up. You can find this script online at http://cvs.zope.org/ZODB3/Tools/repozo.py. It works quite happily on Windows and Linux. This script can do a whole host of things such as full backups, incremental backups, and database restores.

To back up a database with this script, you first need to make a directory to store the backups; in the following examples, this directory is /home/backups. However, this location is up to you. To do a complete backup of a database, run the following:

```
$ python repozo.py -B -F -v -r /home/backups -f /var/zope.test/var/Data.fs
looking for files b/w last full backup and 2003-11-21-18-33-17...
no files found
doing a full backup
writing full backup: 3601549 bytes to /home/backups/2003-11-21-18-33-17.fs
```

To run an incremental backup, just omit the -F (full) flag. The script will compare the current ZODB with the last backup and only back up the differences. If no updates have occurred, then no backup will occur. The following is an example backup after making a change in Plone:

```
$ python repozo.py -B -v -r /home/backups -f /var/zope.test/var/Data.fs
looking for files b/w last full backup and 2003-11-21-18-39-09...
files needed to recover state as of 2003-11-21-18-39-09:
        /home/backups/2003-11-21-18-33-17.fs
repository state: 3601549 bytes, md5: ab9e46bcdf52641ad6f71db62a9da333
current state    : 3624968 bytes, md5: 73c871bbe2528e152342abea9e25ab27
backed up state : 3601549 bytes, md5: ab9e46bcdf52641ad6f71db62a9da333
doing incremental, starting at: 3601549
writing incremental: 23419 bytes to /home/backups/2003-11-21-18-39-11.deltafs
```

At this point, you now have one full backup and one incremental. The same script now can do a recovery of this data. To do this, pass the -R (recovery) option and -o specifying the output file, like so:

```
$ python repozo.py -R -v -r /home/backups -o /var/zope.test/var/Data.fs
looking for files b/w last full backup and 2003-11-21-18-50-21...
files needed to recover state as of 2003-11-21-18-50-21:
 /home/backups/2003-11-21-18-33-17.fs
 /home/backups/2003-11-21-18-39-11.deltafs
Recovering file to /var/zope.test/var/Data.fs
Recovered 3624968 bytes, md5: 73c871bbe2528e152342abea9e25ab27
```

For a full list of options, run repozo.py with the -h command. This prints a full set of instructions.

Logs exist in the log directory of your instance home by default, and there are two log files: an access log file and an event log file. You set the location of these logs in the configuration file that you looked at in Chapter 2. z2.log logs all incoming requests, and event.log logs all errors. These log files should be backed up regularly, along with any proxy server log files such as those that Apache or Internet Information Services (IIS) produces.

You should regularly back up code, templates, and custom products that reside outside the ZODB. Even if you have these in source control, such as Concurrent Versioning System (CVS), backing them up to make a valid snapshot of your installation never hurts.

If you have content, other databases, or other data that doesn't reside in the ZODB, this should form part of the backup plan, depending upon how often it changes. This could include data in relational databases and content on the file system. All of these are created by the site developer and don't exist in a standard "out-of-the-box" Plone site. If you're upgrading Zope or Plone, it may be prudent to make a backup of all the files involved, including Zope and Plone, so that if the upgrade fails for some reason, a full restoration is possible.

Packing the ZODB

The ZODB records every change to every object in the system. Each time an object changes, a new copy is appended to the end of the ZODB file. That file is the Data.fs file I discussed in the previous section. If the database has large pieces of content or has a large number of changes, then this can cause the ZODB to really grow.

A large ZODB isn't a problem—it works just fine, and startup times are similar (unless the index has been removed). Pack times will get longer the larger the database is, and it does make sense to occasionally go and remove those old copies of objects that are no longer used to make the database smaller. It's key to remember that all you're doing when you're packing is cleaning your existing database and throwing out some old copies.

The Old 2GB Limit on Databases

A problem exists with older versions of Python (before Python 2.1 on Unix and before Python 2.2 on Windows), which weren't capable of large file support. When the ZODB reaches 2 gigabytes (GB), the Plone site dies and can't be restarted. To test if you're running a Python version that has large file support, open a file in Python and see if its size is reported as an integer or a long, like so:

```
>>> import os
>>> from stat import ST_SIZE
>>> type(os.stat('/tmp/test.txt')[ST_SIZE])
<type 'long'>
```

This Python has large file support enabled and can support files larger than 2GB. If an integer is reported, then you'll need to upgrade your Python version or recompile with large file support enabled (again, enabled in new version by default). If you try to compile Plone with a version of Zope that doesn't have large file support, you'll get an error, like so:

```
andy@thorin:/tmp/Zope-2.7.0-b3$ ./configure
Configuring Zope installation
...

This Python interpreter does not have have 'large file support' enabled.
```

If this is the case, then you'll need to go and fix your Python installation. You can find more details about this at http://www.python.org/doc/current/lib/posix-large-files.html. If you're happy with just limiting to 2GB, then you can pass the --ignore-largefile option to the configure script. If you're limited to a 2GB database, then you'll need to pack more regularly.

Cleaning up the database is called *packing*, and it removes old revisions of objects. For example, if you change the home page of a Plone site five times, you'll have six copies of that page in the database (the first version, plus the four changes, plus the current). So you've now got all these old copies of your document. These revisions are useful for reviewing who made what change when, but they fill up your database. These revisions are the target of a pack and will be cleaned. A pack will never remove the current version of an object, so nothing current will be deleted.

Packing can be intensive, and when its process is run, it's in a separate thread, so although it will affect a site's speed, it will still be able to respond to requests. To pack sites and keep Plone running at peak performance, see the "Using ZEO" section later in this chapter. To run a pack, access the ZMI control panel, select Database Management, and click *main*. Figure 14-1 shows the pack screen.

Enter the number of days you'd like to keep objects for, and click Pack. For example, setting the number of days at zero (the default) will remove all revisions of objects. Again, it doesn't delete the object itself, just those old copies. A more common setting is something such as seven, which will remove revisions older than one week. By making a setting appropriate with your backup schedule, you can ensure that you'll keep a copy of every object. The pack will take a bit of time and processing power depending upon the size of your ZODB. Plone will still work, albeit slower, so you may want to use ZEO to do this.

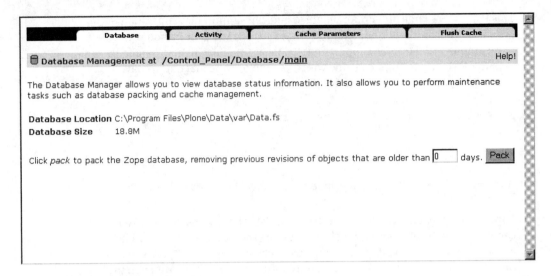

Figure 14-1. Packing a database

Upgrading Plone

Plone is continually being updated and improved, so new versions of Plone come out quite regularly. Before you upgrade to a new version of Plone, though, check that you actually need it. Quite often releases have minor changes or changes that may not be relevant. Each release has a change list, accessible from the download page. It's always worth reviewing this list to see if the upgrade is worthwhile.

After performing your backup, download the upgrade. Probably the easiest way to perform an upgrade is to repeat the same steps you performed on the installation. For example, if you installed using the Windows installer, download the new installer and run the install again. If you installed from source or a Debian package, repeat those steps. The upgrade steps are as follows:

1. Download the relevant upgrade.

2. Stop Plone.

3. Back up (as described previously).

4. Install the upgrade.

5. Start Plone.

At this point I recommend actually starting Plone in debug mode. On Windows, you can do this by selecting Start ➤ Plone ➤ Plone Debug. On Linux you can do this using the runzope script inside the bin directory of your instance home, like so:

```
bin/runzope -X "debug-mode=on"
```

By running this in debug mode, you'll directly see any errors that may have occurred during the upgrade to the new version. If you're happy with this, you can now proceed on to the next step, migration.

For each Plone site you have, access the ZMI and access the portal_migration tool in your Plone site. It will have a bright-red exclamation mark next to it, indicating that the site *isn't* up to date. You'll now need to perform a migration of Plone up to the current version. A migration is necessary because you've upgraded the file system, but your database isn't synchronized with the file system. There could be changes to the content types, the tools, or other parts of your site that need to be made.

The migration will attempt to make those changes for you. Until you run this migration it's possible that your Plone site may be broken. Depending upon what needs to be done in the migration, this may take some time. To perform a migration, follow these steps:

1. From portal_migration, click the Migrate tab.

2. Click the *upgrade* button. This may take some time, especially on large sites or if a large upgrade is necessary.

3. The result of the migration, a rather lengthy message, will display on the screen. If the final message is "End of upgrade path, migration has finished," then the migration was successful. Any error messages will be highlighted in red.

Repeat this process for each Plone site within your Zope instance. If you're then happy with the migrated site, stop running Plone in debug mode. Restart Plone in your usual manner, and carry on using as normal.

Improving Plone Performance

So you've written a wonderful Web site, millions of visitors come to the site, and it just isn't quite performing as fast as you'd like. Well, Plone is designed out of the box to be feature rich, not fast, since speed is greatly dependent on the application in question. But many techniques can make Plone really fast, and you can easily scale Plone. In the following sections, I cover how to figure out the slow parts of your site and then show you methods to improve it.

Benchmarking a Plone Site

Before you try optimizing a site, the key task is to get a numeric value of the performance of the site. Users will often give feedback such as "it's too slow" or "takes too long to load." These comments are next to useless for a developer; you need to be able to quantify the speed so you can know how fast it is now and how fast you need to make it. Only then can you begin to do the optimization.

For getting a benchmark, you can use a tool called ab, or Apache Bench. This is a tool that comes with the Apache server. If you have Apache 1.3 or later installed on Linux, ab is included. On Windows it's included with the Apache 2 release. Running ab is straightforward—just pass the uniform resource locator (URL) you want to test, like so:

```
ab http://localhost/
```

The ab tool will output some information first about the site you tested, like so:

```
Benchmarking localhost (be patient).....done
Server Software:        Zope/(unreleased
Server Hostname:        localhost
Server Port:            80

Document Path:          /
Document Length:        20594 bytes
```

Then it'll output some aggregate statistics, like so:

```
Concurrency Level:      1
Time taken for tests:   0.771151 seconds
Complete requests:      1
Failed requests:        0
Write errors:           0
Total transferred:      20933 bytes
HTML transferred:       20594 bytes
Requests per second:    1.30 [#/sec] (mean)
Time per request:       771.151 [ms] (mean)
Time per request:       771.151 [ms] (mean, across all concurrent requests)
Transfer rate:          25.94 [Kbytes/sec] received
```

This tells you how long the request took, the number of errors, and the time it took to get a request, which is probably the key statistic. The most useful value to reference is usually the Requests per second, which in this example is 1.30 [#/sec]. The ab tool provides some more statistics that give information on how long it took to connect, process, and get a result for each request. For example:

```
Connection Times (ms)
              min  mean[+/-sd] median   max
Connect:        0    0   0.0      0       0
Processing:   770  770   0.0    770     770
Waiting:      766  766   0.0    766     766
Total:        770  770   0.0    770     770
```

This last piece of information is useful and includes the time taken to get a connection. Since my server is on the same computer as the client, this is quite short. This test demonstrates that it took 1.30 seconds to complete a request. Of course, that hasn't really tested the server much at all. When testing, you'll probably want to hit the server with a few concurrent requests to simulate the real world a little more. You can do this by specifying the number of requests and the concurrency by using the -c (concurrent threads) and -n (number of requests) options. For example:

```
ab -n 20 -c 4 http://localhost/
```

This sends a total of 20 requests over four concurrent threads. The end result is a slightly different request per second of 1.78 seconds. For more information on all the options available, please see the Apache Bench manual at http://httpd.apache.org/docs/programs/ab.html.

One advantage of using ab is that you aren't actually assembling the pages on the client; they're just being downloaded and then thrown away. If you have a page that has lots of scripts or features big images, the time it takes for a client to assemble that page into something the user can understand won't be included. A classic example of this is that in the old Netscape browser, a large number of tables can slow down or even crash Netscape. This wouldn't be evident using ab, which gives you a more independent number with which to work.

Lies, Damned Lies, and Benchmark Numbers

At this point, you may be concerned about these numbers. They seem to indicate a very slow site. In these examples, my machine is a Toshiba laptop with 1.8 gigahertz (GHz) Celeron processor, 256 megabytes (MB) of Random Access Memory (RAM), Red Hat Linux 9.0, and a beta version of Plone 2. Furthermore, Plone is running in debug mode at the same time as KDE, OpenOffice.org, Instant Messenger, and several other development tools, including the actual benchmarking tool. This means Plone is nowhere near optimized or running in an ideal environment. A similar test on a faster server yielded results around 20 requests per second.

The key point is that creating an objective number for site performance allows you to measure the success of your optimizations. Developers can perform tweaks and then test again to compare the "before" and "after" numbers. If it's possible, you should run performance tests against a machine as similar to the production server as possible to get sensible numbers. For this chapter it isn't important that a site can produce X requests per second; instead, it's important that a change be able to produce a significant increase in performance.

Also, remember that numbers about how fast a certain part of your site is are pretty meaningless in isolation. You must take into account how often the page is visited, users' expectations at that point, and realistic requirements. Micromeasuring just one part of a site can be useful to track down a certain issue, but it may not make your site much faster. As with most things, you need a sensible approach to optimizations.

Production Mode vs. Debug Mode

One of the biggest speed killers for Plone is to run your site in debug mode. When running in debug mode, each and every template, script, and object in the portal_skins tool is compared against the file system to see if it's up to date. This check happens with each and every request, which is useful for testing but is a huge performance hit. For example, on my test server, turning off debug mode increases the speed per request from 1.30 to 2.41 requests per second, a significant improvement.

To find out if your site is running in debug mode, in the ZMI access the portal_migration object in your Plone site. At the bottom of the page will be a list of information, including Debug Mode status. To change this, alter the configuration file, as discussed in Chapter 2.

Other Reasons for Slow Performance

A server may be running slowly for reasons outside of Plone. If you're running optimization, you should always take a look at these considerations first, since these will provide quick speed improvements for little cost.

Processor Usage

If you're running a great number of applications, or just some intensive ones, then this will limit the amount of processor time available to Plone. Assembling pages in Plone can take a lot of Central Processing Unit (CPU) power. When an application is bound by the amount of processing power it has available, it's called *CPU bound*.

To find out how much load the server is under in Linux, use the top command. In Windows, the Task Manager (accessible by pressing Ctrl+Alt+Del) will give you similar statistics. The recommended speed of your CPU depends upon the size and traffic load your Plone server will be under, but a 2GHz processor is a good starting point.

Amount of Memory

Zope likes to use a great deal of memory as objects are loaded from the ZODB. Of all the key features, giving a Zope server more memory is probably the best thing you can do. When an application is bound by the amount of memory it has available, it's called *memory bound*. Most likely, your server will start to thrash as it swaps a lot with the hard drive, if it reaches this limit.

To find out how much load the server is under in Linux, use the top command. In Windows, the Task Manager (accessible by pressing Ctrl+Alt+Del) will give you similar statistics. The recommended amount of memory depends upon the size and traffic load your Plone server will be under, but a 512MB processor is a good starting point. If you can afford more memory, it's recommended.

You can make a few tweaks to the memory parameters in Plone by increasing the target number of objects in the cache. By default, Plone ships with 400 objects in the cache. For a site, you could increase this to 5,000, as shown in Figure 14-2. Although this increases memory usage, this will *also* increase performance. Since objects are by nature variable in size, it's impossible to predict the increase in memory performance. Probably your best approach is to increase this and then run some requests to see if it's worth the trade-off.

Further, the fewer threads Zope uses, the less potential memory usage will occur. Although Zope is multithreaded, most of the time only one Zope thread will actually be used. Reducing the number of threads to three provides a more memory-efficient server. Instead of trying to run a large number of threads, it's recommended to run ZEO clients to serve more requests. The "Zope Enterprise Objects" section covers this in more detail.

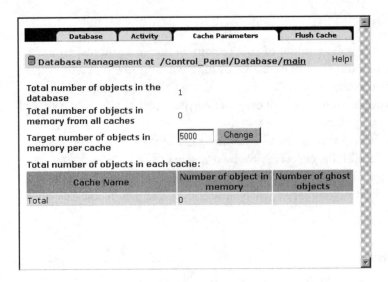

Figure 14-2. Changing the cache parameters in the control panel

Network Connection

The network connection can be critical to the performance of any application—you're only as fast as the slowest connection between you and the client. When you're optimizing a Plone site, take into account the amount of time needed to connect. If it takes two seconds to actually connect, optimizing code is rather pointless.

Here again, the ab tool can help. When running a benchmark of Plone.org from British Columbia (the server is located in Texas), you can see in the following output that the median wait for connections over the network was 125 milliseconds:

```
            Connection Times (ms)
            min   mean[+/-sd] median    max
Connect:     90   133   40.2    125     211
Processing: 511  1103  400.2   1113    1846
Waiting:    202   310  110.3    293     565
Total:      601  1236  411.2   1211    2043
```

The server may also have a limit on the number of connections or on traveling through internal firewalls. When a process is bound by the time it takes to do an Input/Output (I/O) process such as this, it's called *I/O bound*. What you can do with this is limited to your control over the network. If your client is a long way away from your server and the connection is slow, then caches nearer your client or colocation may be an option.

Your Application

It could, of course, be that your application is actually causing the slowdown. The examples from service companies about clients with problems are numerous (and probably exaggerated). Some of better-known examples include the following:

- Copied code from a Web site that had a `sleep` call buried deep in the system, which caused the script to pause for a few seconds. A code review by someone spotted this and removed the offending line.

- Multiple relational database lookups, such as more than a dozen on one page. A more intelligent design combined the lookups and allowed for caching.

- A script that pulled information from the ZODB by waking up every object inside the database. Using the catalog (covered in Chapter 10) made performance much faster.

- A query that gets all the records in a database, but then shows only 100 on a page at a time, discarding the other 99,900. This was solved by writing the SQL statements in more efficient manner.

Before jumping to conclusions about what's causing the problem, it's worth profiling the site to determine where the bottleneck is.

Profiling Plone

Since you can quantify the time taken to produce pages, you can now attempt to optimize. However, the first problem is finding where to optimize. As shown in earlier chapters, the front page is a collection of templates, scripts, and other code that's assembled to create a page. Where should a developer look among that pile of code? To help track down performance bottlenecks, you can use Call Profiler, Page Template Profiler, and Python Profiler. Each of these profilers takes an element of the site and reports how long was spent in producing the page and the time spent on each of these three components.

Please note that if you enable all three of these profiling tools, you'll find that your Plone site really starts to slow down (by a significant magnitude). Each of these profilers exacts a toll on performance for the number of hooks it has to install. You should always uninstall or turn off these profilers after using them to ensure that your site is running at maximum efficiency. Also, if you enable all three of these profilers, you'll start to profile the profilers (and that's when things start to get confusing). I recommend you start with Call Profiler. Then turn on each of the other profilers in turn, turning off the preview profiler, until you have enough information.

Call Profiler

This Zope product takes a request, such as getting a front page, and reports the objects that were used and how long was taken by each. You can find Call Profiler at http://zope.org/Members/richard/CallProfiler. Despite comments on the download page, the product isn't integrated into Zope 2.6. Install the product in the standard way, and then restart your Zope.

To enable Call Profiler, go to the ZMI control panel and select Call Profiler. The product works by installing hooks into an object so that when the object is accessed, the amount of time spent on rendering the object can be measured. This means Call Profiler will be activated only on objects you choose to monitor, as shown in Figure 14-3. For a standard Plone installation, you'll need to monitor Filesystem Script (Python) and Filesystem Page Template. Call Profiler doesn't remember these settings between Zope restarts, which means a simple restart will turn off the hooks and leave you ready to deploy.

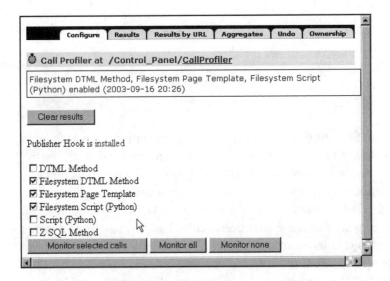

Figure 14-3. Call Profiler with the file system hooks selected

Once the objects to monitor have been selected, access the URL you want to monitor. The easiest way to access the URL to be tested is to run the ab tool mentioned earlier; however, using a Web browser will work just fine. In this case, if you're profiling the home page on localhost, then run the following:

```
ab -n 20 -c 4 http://localhost/
```

This will cause 20 requests to be made to Plone. Once complete, you can access the timing of those requests. Returning to the Call Profiler interface, you'll see three tabs across the top of the Call Profiler tool: Results, Results by URL, and Aggregates. Since multiple requests have been run, select the Aggregates tab, which is the easiest to understand. In the list of pages called will be the URL tested. Click that link to view the results for that URL. You should now see something like Figure 14-4.

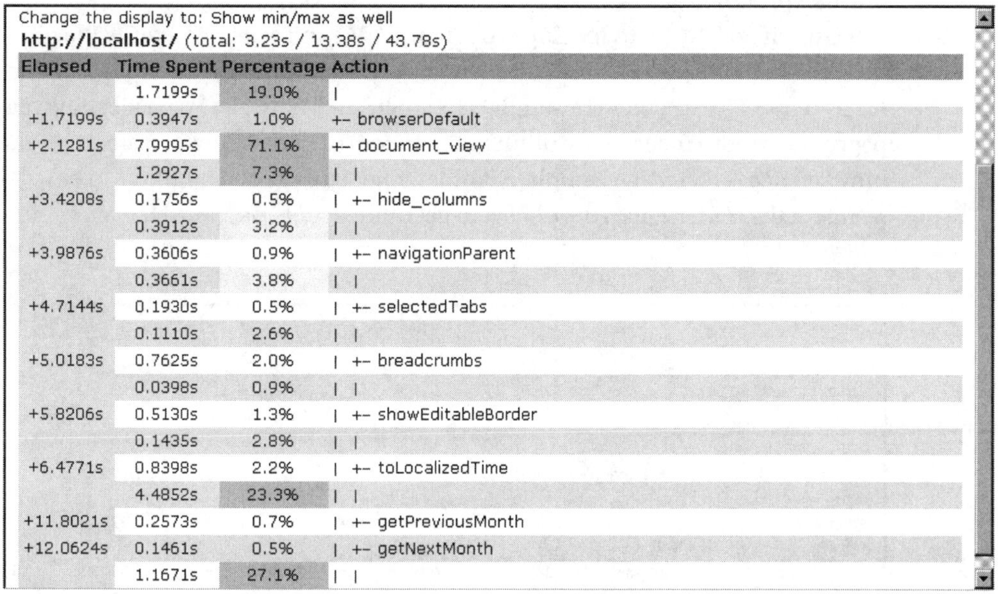

Change the display to: Show min/max as well
http://localhost/ (total: 3.23s / 13.38s / 43.78s)

Elapsed	Time Spent	Percentage	Action
	1.7199s	19.0%	|
+1.7199s	0.3947s	1.0%	+– browserDefault
+2.1281s	7.9995s	71.1%	+– document_view
	1.2927s	7.3%	| |
+3.4208s	0.1756s	0.5%	| +– hide_columns
	0.3912s	3.2%	| |
+3.9876s	0.3606s	0.9%	| +– navigationParent
	0.3661s	3.8%	| |
+4.7144s	0.1930s	0.5%	| +– selectedTabs
	0.1110s	2.6%	| |
+5.0183s	0.7625s	2.0%	| +– breadcrumbs
	0.0398s	0.9%	| |
+5.8206s	0.5130s	1.3%	| +– showEditableBorder
	0.1435s	2.8%	| |
+6.4771s	0.8398s	2.2%	| +– toLocalizedTime
	4.4852s	23.3%	| |
+11.8021s	0.2573s	0.7%	| +– getPreviousMonth
+12.0624s	0.1461s	0.5%	| +– getNextMonth
	1.1671s	27.1%	| |

Figure 14-4. The results of the profile

In this example, you'll see the elements that Call Profiler is able to detect. Unfortunately, the results can be a little complicated to decipher. At first glance, the results add up to more than 100 percent. In this case, document_view takes 71.1 percent of the processing time. However, this is misleading because values below that figure relate to document_view, not the whole page. In this example, for the whole page, everything before browserDefault takes 19.9 percent of the request. Then it moves into document_view, and you see the percentages for that part. So in this case, going from toLocalizedTime to getPreviousMonth takes 23.3 percent of the time taken to render document_view.

Page Template Profiler

Page Template Profiler works only with the Zope Page Templates system. In a similar way to Call Profiler, it reports how long was spent enacting each call inside a page template. Since in the previous example you saw that most of the time is spent in one page template (document_view), you may find it instructive to see how the time is spent in that template.

You can find Page Template Profiler at http://zope.org/Members/guido_w/ PTProfiler. Install the product, and then restart Zope. To deinstall Page Template Profiler, you'll have to remove it from your Products directory when you've finished profiling.

Once installed, go to the Zope root in the ZMI and select PT Profile Viewer from the Add drop-down box. Complete the creation form, giving a unique value for ID (enter **PTProfiler**, for example), and then click Add. Now repeat calling the page you want to measure by running the ab tool or accessing the page in a browser. Access the Page Template Profiler object just added, and you'll see a result for the request just run. Click it to get more details, as shown in Figure 14-5.

Expression	Total time	Number of calls	Time per call
Total rendering time	44.618	23	1.93991
python: path(pathexpr)	18.3256	184	0.0996
path: here/calendar_slot/macros/calendarBox	16.8383	23	0.7321
path: here/global_elements/macros/skin_tabs	3.9568	23	0.17203
python: request.get('news', here.portal_catalog.searchResults (meta_type='News Item' , sort_on='Date' , sort_order='reverse' , review_state='published')[:5])	2.1732	23	0.09449
python: here.portal_actions.listFilteredActionsFor(here)	1.8614	23	0.08093
python: here.breadcrumbs(here)	0.8098	23	0.03521
python: here.toLocalizedTime(here.ModificationDate (),long_format=1)	0.6545	23	0.02846
path: options/slots_mapping|here/prepare_slots|nothing	0.6096	23	0.02651
python: here.showEditableBorder(template_id=template_id , actions=actions)	0.5987	23	0.02603
path: here/navigationLocalRelated	0.5436	23	0.02363
python: here.plone_utils.createNavigationTreeBuilder (portalObject,navBatchStart)	0.5375	23	0.02337

Figure 14-5. Page Template Profiler results

In this case, you can see that on my site that calendarBox is taking 0.7321 seconds to call each time it's being called. Since the entire page is taking 1.9 seconds, you can assume this is an area I could optimize.

Python Profiler

The Python Profiler provides very low-level timing information and is normally used for more complex debugging of underlying code. It gives you a detailed report of the amount of time spent in various areas of Python code. This isn't something you'd normally use while profiling a site; however, for completeness, I'll describe it in this section.

To activate the Python Profiler, you need to add a variable to the configuration file. In the zope.conf file of your etc directory, enable the publisher-profile-file command. To do this, define a file to which it'll write. On Windows this could be c:\zope.output; on Linux it's /tmp/zope.output. Add the following line on Linux:

```
publisher-profile-file /tmp/zope.output
```

Then restart Plone, but it will run very slowly. If you're running a large number of requests and want to examine the results, then the file specified in the environment variable will contain output of the data. As in previous examples, call the page that's being profiled using the ab tool or a Web browser. Then access the control panel through the ZMI, select Debug Info, and then select the Profiling tab; you'll get output from the Python Profiler, as shown in Figure 14-6.

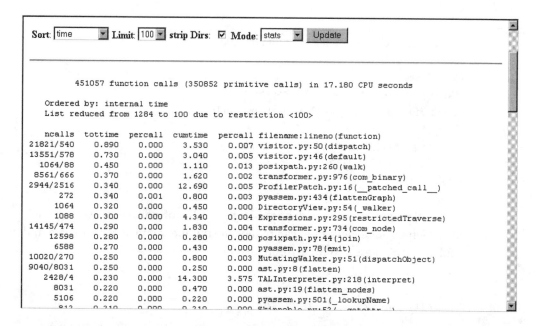

Figure 14-6. Python Profiler results

As you can see in Figure 14-6, the output shows the gory details of what takes time. I've rarely had to use this.

Simple Optimization Tricks

After looking at quite a lot of Plone, the Plone development team has come up with the following optimization tricks.

Limit Name Lookup

Overdoing name lookups is a common mistake; the solution is to define a variable locally. In the following example, Plone has to perform lookup for portal_url on each repetition of the loop:

```
<tal:block
 tal:repeat="result here/portal_catalog">
   <a href=""
      tal:attributes="href here/portal_url/getPortalUrl">Home</a>
   ...
</tal:block>
```

But it'd be faster to use a tal:define, like so:

```
<tal:block
 tal:repeat="result here/portal_catalog"
 tal:define="url here/portal_url/getPortalUrl>
   <a href=""
      tal:attributes="href url">Home</a>
   ...
</tal:block>
```

As already stated, Plone defines a large number of global defines. By using those definitions, a developer can reduce the number of traversals. You can find a full list of all these defines in Appendix A.

Security Checks and Traversal

Whenever an object, an object's attributes, or an object's methods are accessed, a security check is performed. Although each security check isn't that expensive, a large number of security checks can really add up.

This is especially true when you traverse to an object, for example, to here/
folderA/folderB/object. In this case, Zope will be doing security checks on each
of those folders and then on the object. If the information can be accessed without
doing that traversal each time, you'll find a performance gain. Another way to avoid
doing security checks is to write code in Products on the file system. Code in Products
is considered trusted code, is subject to fewer checks, and is hence faster.

The ZCatalog

The ZCatalog is an efficient binary tree of data about objects. You should use it
(in most situations) when getting a list of objects, such as search results, providing
summaries, finding objects, and so on. When the catalog returns a set of results
that accesses a series of lightweight objects (called *brains*), accessing these brains
doesn't mean doing traversal to the object or performing any security checks.

Too Many Features

This may seem obvious, but Plone ships with lots of features you may not necessarily need. For example, both the calendar and navigation portlet take up a large
number of resources yet are generally of limited use. Turning these features off if
not needed will increase performance.

Is Optimization Worth It?

Before you start any optimization, you should perform a simple cost-benefit
analysis to see if the optimization is worth performing.

For example, say you have a page that takes 0.5 seconds to generate. Of that
page, on script takes 10 percent of the time to generate. If you're able to double
the speed of that one script, that will shave only 0.025 seconds off the execution
of that page. In this case, the benefit to performing the optimization is small because
there are some basic costs such as the cost of a developer to do the analysis, the cost
of testing to check it works, and possibly changes to documentation.

Performing this work also creates substantial risk. Changing code can break
or introduce bugs into the application. Given agile programming methodologies,
though, these could be minimized. Further, a programmer may not be able to
complete the speed increase or may make it slower.

You have alternatives to optimizing code; for example, you could install more
memory or hardware if the application is bound by one of these constraints.
Although many programmers think that throwing hardware at a solution is a lazy

option, it can be an extremely cost-effective solution. Introducing new hardware is low risk, can bring a large speed gain, and often costs less than a programmer.

Further, you can really scale your server by caching or adding more computers and separating the load. These techniques form the rest of the chapter.

Caching of Content

So now that you've found the slow parts of your application, you'll turn to the main tool to increase performance: caching. *Caching* is the saving of data to be reused without having to calculate the result again. There are many, many types of caching, and they can be used in different ways.

When talking about caching, I'm talking about two things that can be cached: content and skins. *Content* is the data entered by the user into content types. *Skins* refer to anything in portal_skins and can be templates, scripts, images, or files. These two types are cached differently.

I like to think of caching in terms of the amount of control I'll have over the caching mechanism. In other words, the closer to the client that caching is performed, the faster the response will be but also the less control I will have over that cache. This in fact includes the possibility that there may be no cache at all. Figure 14-7 illustrates caching between a client and a server.

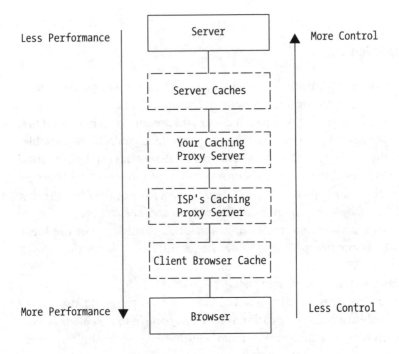

Figure 14-7. Caches between a client and a server

The user's browser cache is the fastest place to cache things, but you have no idea if a user will actually have caching turned on in their browser. Next come the intermediate caches of proxy servers; keep in mind this could be your proxy server (which you should have control over) or an Internet service provider (ISP) proxy. Finally, there are the server caching options.

In the following sections, I'll discuss the following caching mechanisms:

- Caching skin elements using the Accelerated HTTP Cache Manager

- Caching of code using the RAM Cache Manager

- Caching of content added by users via the Caching Policy Manager

I'll then discuss how to use Apache and Squid, two commonly used external servers that provide a whole host of high-performance configuration options.

Caching Skins

Hypertext Transfer Protocol (HTTP) allows you to set HTTP headers for caching. When a response returns with these headers, it's the responsibility of the proxies between the client and the server to cache the object according to these headers. In Figure 14-7, this could be any of the caches from the server cache down. This proxy can be a Web server that you control on the server, such as Apache, or a proxy that the ISP controls. As I'll discuss, this makes a powerful tool when combined with Apache or Squid.

This caching can also include the browser if it's set to use caching (the default for Internet Explorer). However, if a browser does a refresh on a page, the browser sends the Pragma: no-cache header, which forces proxies to also reload their copy.

Caching in this manner applies to the entire response, so it can be risky if you try applying this to a whole page. This is most commonly used with images, style sheets, JavaScript, or pages that don't change a great deal. Images used repeatedly in your pages for making nice elements, such as rounded corners or background images, are ideal for this.

By default, Plone creates an Accelerated HTTP Cache Manager called HTTPCache in the root of your Plone site. Accessing this object through the ZMI will bring up the management options for the cache. The following are all reasonable defaults, and nothing needs to be changed initially:

- **Title:** This is the title of the cache manager and is optional.

- **Interval:** This is the time for the object to be cached, in seconds.

- **Cache anonymous connections only**: This means only cache if the user is anonymous.

- **Notify URLs (via PURGE)**: These are URLs of downstream proxies that need to be purged when the object changes. The "Using Squid" section discusses this in more detail.

To see how the Accelerated HTTP Cache Manager works, the following is an example based on a test object, an image called test.gif. To see what headers are returned, you need to test the headers being returned. For this you can use a simple Python script called header.py. You can find this script in Appendix B. On Linux the wget command also does the same thing if you pass -S, although it will still download the file for you. For example:

```
wget -S http://www.agmweb.ca
```

First, the following are the headers returned for test.gif *before* you added this to the cache manager:

```
[andy@basil scripts]$ ./header.py http://localhost:8080/test.gif GET
Accept-Ranges: bytes
Connection: close
Content-Length: 2541
Content-Type: image/gif
Date: Wed, 03 Sep 2003 23:55:38 GMT
Etag:
Last-Modified: Wed, 03 Sep 2003 23:54:27 GMT
Server: Zope/(unreleased version, python 2.2.2, linux2) ZServer/1.1
```

After adding the image to the cache, you'll recheck the HTTP headers using the script again. You'll find that there are two new headers. For example:

```
[andy@basil scripts]$ ./header.py http://localhost:8080/test.gif GET
...
Cache-Control: max-age=3600
Expires: Thu, 04 Sep 2003 00:56:03 GMT on 2.2.2, linux2) Zserver/1.1
```

NOTE Unfortunately, Zope 2 doesn't conform to the Request for Comments (RFC) regarding HEAD requests. Instead of sending the full set of headers when a HEAD request is sent, the values from the cache manager are missing. When testing, you should always send GET requests.

For more information on the HTTP headers and how they relate to caching, see RFC 2616 at http://www.w3.org/Protocols/rfc2616/rfc2616-sec14.html.

The Accelerated HTTP Cache Manager caches an entire response, which works well for static items. However, the normal Plone page consists of personalized elements, such as the calendar, the personal navigation bar, and so on. In this situation, you need to be able to cache just part of the page, and this is where RAM Cache Manager comes in handy.

RAM Cache Manager will cache the output of an object in RAM so that on the next occurrence of that script, it'll be pulled from the cache. Repeated invocations of that object will cause the output to be pulled from the cache until the cache expires. The point of this manager is that you're really avoiding recomputing complicated or large calculations every time; instead, you're storing the result and reusing. This Cache Manager won't cache images or files. It won't stop users trying to configure the cache to do so, but it has no effect on these objects.

By default, Plone creates a RAM Manager called RAMCache in the root of your Plone site. Accessing this object through the ZMI will open the management options for the cache. The following are all reasonable defaults, and nothing needs to be changed initially:

- **Title**: This is the title of the cache manager and is optional.

- **REQUEST variables**: These are the variables that form the condition for the cache. This is a powerful option that allows the cache to be based upon the user variables. For example, if an item to be cached requires that it should be cached differently for each user, or in different languages, you can enter the REQUEST variables you'd like to cache here.

- **Threshold entries**: This is the maximum number of entries that can be stored in the cache. If the cache is taking up too much RAM, lower this value.

- **Maximum age of a cache entry**: This is the amount of time (in seconds) this object will stay in the cache.

- **Cleanup interval**: This is how often the cache gets cleaned.

Because the requests for the object actually reach Zope, this does nothing to reduce network traffic; it just causes Zope to render the result quicker. Selecting the Statistics tab in the ZMI will report statistics on exactly how many hits were returned by the cache and how many were passed onto the object. If too many hits are being passed on to the object, you may consider altering the cache configuration by having fewer REQUEST variables or increasing the time spent in the cache.

Assigning Caches

To add an object that's on the file system to the cache, simply specify the name of the cache in the .metadata file for that object. (Chapter 7 discussed using .metadata files.) Plone already does this on a large number of images, on CSS, and on JavaScript. For example, plone_skins /plone_images/pdf_icon.gif.metadata reads as follows:

```
[default]
title=Pdf icon
cache=HTTPCache
```

This signifies that the image will be cached using the HTTPCache. Most objects on the file system would be more suitable for adding to the HTTPCache, rather than the RAMCache.

Caching Content Types

Caching content types is a little trickier and requires using the Caching Policy Manager. Plone installs this tool by default, and you can find it in the root of the Plone instance with the ID caching_policy_manager. This policy manager works in a similar way as the Accelerated HTTP Cache Manager in that it adds HTTP headers to objects. As the name suggests, the policy manager contains several policies that users can add and edit. When a page is rendered, each policy from top to bottom is called; when a policy matches a condition, that policy is used.

Before you can cache any content, you must alter the cache settings for templates inside Plone. By default Plone emits headers for content that turns off any caching at all. If you don't do the following, the rest of this section won't work. If you click *portal_skins* and then click *plone_templates*, you'll find the page template global_cache_settings. This is used on every page that uses the main Plone template. The template currently looks like the following:

```
<metal:cacheheaders define-macro="cacheheaders">
    <metal:block tal:define="dummy python:request.RESPONSE.setHeader ➥
'Content-Type', 'text/html;;charset=%s' % charset)" />
    <metal:block tal:define="dummy python:request.RESPONSE.setHeader ➥
('Content-Language', lang)" />
    <metal:block tal:define="dummy python:request.RESPONSE.setHeader ➥
('Expires', 'Sat, 1 Jan 2000 00:00:00 GMT')" />
    <metal:block tal:define="dummy python:request.RESPONSE.setHeader ➥
('Pragma', 'no-cache')" />
</metal:cacheheaders>
```

This will mean that nothing is cached because the HTTP headers
`Pragma: no-cache` and `Expires` have been set. To disable this and make sure you
can cache selectively, customize this template and remove the `Pragma` and `Expires`
directives. Your template should now look like the following:

```
<metal:cacheheaders define-macro="cacheheaders">
    <metal:block tal:define="dummy python:request.RESPONSE.setHeader ➡
'Content-Type', 'text/html;;charset=%s' % charset)" />
    <metal:block tal:define="dummy python:request.RESPONSE.setHeader ➡
('Content-Language', lang)" />
</metal:cacheheaders>
```

Once you've done this, you can continue to cache selectively using the
`caching_policy_manager`. Access the tool via the ZMI, and you'll see the following
options:

- **Policy ID**: This is a unique ID for a policy, used internally only.

- **Predicate**: This is a TALES expression for matching the content. The
  variable `content` contains the object being rendered.

- **Mod. Time**: This is a TALES expression that evaluates and returns a value
  from the object to use for calculating the modification time. The variable
  `content` contains the object being rendered.

- **Max age (secs)**: This is how long to set the cache header for.

- **Vary**: This varies the header to send (you'll learn more about this later in
  the "Using Squid" section).

- **No-cache**: This sends the no-cache HTTP header.

- **No-store**: This sends the no-store HTTP header.

- **Must-revalidate**: This sends the `must-revalidate` HTTP header.

The following is a sample policy that would cache all images on the site:

- **Policy ID**: `Images`

- **Predicate**: `python:content.portal_type=='Image'`

- **Max age (secs)**: 3600

Leave all the other fields blank, and select Add to add this policy. The caching_policy_manager will now looks something like Figure 14-8.

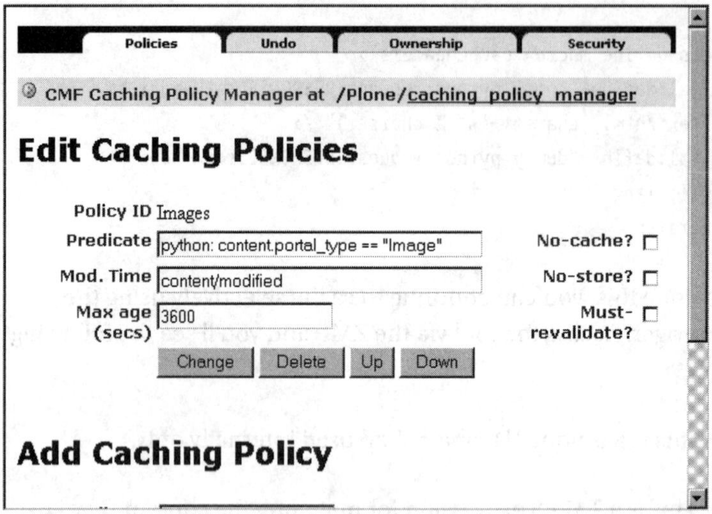

Figure 14-8. The caching_policy_manager *with the Images policy added*

To test this correctly, you'll need to add an image into your site through the Plone interface. Images will get sent with the appropriate headers if you call the view action of the object. I hope later versions of this tool will make the choice of action configurable. You'll test this on test.gif, an image added by a member through the Plone interface, with the following:

```
~/header.py http://localhost/test.gif/view GET
Cache-Control: max-age=3600
Connection: close
Content-Language:
Content-Length: 19810
Content-Type: text/html;charset=utf-8
Date: Fri, 05 Sep 2003 18:42:44 GMT
Etag:
Expires: Fri, 05 Sep 2003 19:42:44 GMT
Last-Modified: Fri, 05 Sep 2003 18:33:41 GMT
Pragma: no-cache
Server: Zope/(unreleased version, python 2.2.2, linux2) ZServer/1.1
```

As expected, the Last-Modified and Expires headers are now being sent. By altering predicates and adding multiple policies, you can build up a rather sophisticated caching system. For complicated rules, you can, of course, pass the handling off to a Script (Python) object if you so desire. For example, if the predicate is as follows:

```
python: here.myCachingRules(content)
```

then add a Script (Python) called myCachingRules to calculate those rules. For example:

```
##parameters=content
# cache all files, images and anything
# thats published
if content.portal_type in ['File', 'Image']:
    return 1
if content.review_state in ['published',]:
    return 1
```

In this script you're caching all files and images, and anything that's in the published state, by setting the HTTP headers through the Caching Policy Manager.

Example: Caching on ZopeZen.org

When developing the site http://www.zopezen.org, there was one major problem. The main page of ZopeZen, which lists the posts and the number of replies, is expensive to generate. In Plone, there's no easy way to efficiently calculate from the catalog the number of discussion replies to an item.

This is an ideal situation for the RAM Cache Manager. Since the traffic that adds news items or posts is quite small, perhaps one or two or day, it seems reasonable that within any 30-minute period, the front page won't change greatly. The function that gets the news and the replies is called getNewsAndReplies, and it performs the task of getting all the data needed for the index_html template.

The index_html template has elements that are specific to the user; for example, the login box on the left shows users what options they have. This means that using the Accelerated HTTP Cache Manager or caching the whole template using the RAM Cache Manager wouldn't work. This would cause users to see others users' options.

Instead, the ZopeZen skin caches the getNewsAndReplies Script (Python) object by adding it to the RAM Cache Manager. Doing so ensures that the majority of the expensive work rendering the page is cached. Since the news items will be same for every user, there's no point in caching based on any REQUEST variables, so AUTHENTICATED_USER was removed from the list of REQUEST variables for the cache. Profiling the front page reveals that without the cache it can produce 1.06 requests per second. With the caching, the site can produce 4.96 requests per second, which is a significant difference for a minor change.

Using Caching Servers

Since you can now send cache headers according to sophisticated rules, you can now use another server to cache requests for Plone. As fast as Zope is, it'll never be faster than Apache, Squid, or IIS for serving out content. These servers can serve static and cached content quickly and simply. Partly it's because these servers are written in C, but it's also because they do less work for each request. There are no security checks, database lookups, or language negotiations to be performed. Also, since you've read Chapter 9, you'll also already have a proxy server installed.

Using Apache

Apache is the standard open-source Web server. The following sections document techniques using Apache 2.0 server on Linux. With only minor syntax modification, most of these tips work on 1.3. For more information on different Apache servers and platforms, please see the excellent Apache documentation at http://www.apache.org.

Deflating Content

The ability to deflate or gzip your pages is useful for saving bandwidth. Before a page is sent by the server, it will be sent down the wire, where the client will decompress the page. This makes pages quicker to download and incurs fewer bandwidth charges for the site's owner since the files are smaller. First, enable the mod_deflate module. This will depend upon your particular setup. For example, on Linux, do the following:

```
LoadModule cache_module modules/mod_deflate
```

Second, just add the following to your server configuration to deflate all Hypertext Markup Language (HTML), Extensible Markup Language (XML), and plain text:

```
AddOutputFilterByType DEFLATE text/html text/xml text/plain
```

Some clients handle the deflation slightly differently, so it's worth reading the mod_deflate documentation for more detailed examples (http://httpd.apache.org/docs-2.0/mod/mod_deflate.html).

Setting Expire Headers

In previous sections you've seen how you can send expiration headers by manipulating tools in Plone. Apache can also send these headers easily using the
ExpiresActive directive; this is an alternative to using the various Plone tools. To
set the expires headers to be 24 hours from now for all images, for example, you
can add the following to your Apache site configuration:

```
ExpiresActive On
ExpiresByType image/gif "access plus 1 day"
ExpiresByType image/png "access plus 1 day"
ExpiresByType image/jpeg "access plus 1 day"
```

You can find more information on mod_expires at http://httpd.apache.org/
docs-2.1/mod/mod_expires.html.

Caching in Apache

Apache comes with several systems that can perform caching for you. The standard
Apache module mod_cache has two caching modes: memory and disk. This will
cache all page requests given a set of parameters for a given amount of time. To
set up a disk cache in the /tmp/apache_cache folder, add the following to the site
configuration:

```
CacheRoot /tmp/apache_cache
CacheEnable disk /
CacheSize 256
CacheDirLevels 5
CacheDirLength 3
```

Unfortunately, proving that Apache is actually caching the content can be a
little hard; perhaps the simplest approach is to test it by watching the z2.log in
Plone and seeing if it's being hit. You can find more information on mod_cache at
http://httpd.apache.org/docs-2.0/mod/mod_cache.html.

Using Squid

Squid is an open-source proxy server that's used commonly with Zope. It enables
you to accelerate Zope by caching content that's produced inside Squid so that
multiple requests are handled by Squid, not Zope. Again, since Squid doesn't
render dynamic content and is written in C, it can respond far more quickly. In
Chapter 10 I covered installing Squid and using it as a proxy. If you're going to use

Squid to accelerate Plone, then please see that chapter for information on setting up Squid as a proxy.

As you've seen earlier in this chapter, you can put almost any information you want in HTTP headers using the Caching Policy Manager and the Accelerated HTTP Cache Manager. Now Squid will act in a similar manner to a browser cache. When a request comes for a page, if those cache headers are present, Squid will cache the page. Repeated hits will cause Squid to return the page, not Plone.

It's relatively simple to tell if a page has been cached. Squid will add an X-Cache header to the response. Using the header.py script, you can see if the page has been successfully cached. A HIT means that a cached copy was found in Squid and returned; if no copy was found in the cache and Plone was queried, a MISS is reported. For example:

```
X-Cache: HIT from www.agmweb.ca
```

Squid shows impressive numbers in testing in the development environment, accelerating the view of a Plone page that's cached from about 2 requests per second to more than 25 requests per second. On fast servers, users have reported speeds of more than 200 requests per second with relative ease.

Cleaning Squid Caches

When a user edits an object, it changes in Plone; however, because this object is cached in an earlier state, the cache contains an old version. Users accessing the site will get the old version rather than the new version. With caches under your control (such as Squid), you can send PURGE commands to the caching server to tell it to remove the objects from the cache.

For the Accelerated HTTP Cache Manager, add the URLs of the caches to the Notify URLs (via PURGE). An example is as follows:

```
http://192.168.1.1:80/example.org
```

In this example, the IP is the address of the cache, and the domain is the site to be purged. For Squid to run the PURGE directive, you must ensure that Squid is configured. If Squid was on localhost, this would be as follows:

```
acl PURGE method purge
http_access allow localhost
http_access allow purge localhost
http_access deny purge
http_access deny all
```

The Caching Policy Manager currently has no PURGE mechanism, although you could add a Script (Python) object to workflow to achieve this. You could save Python code shown in Listing 14-2 as an external method and invoke it in workflow as needed.

Listing 14-2. A Script to Purge the Squid Cache

```python
import urllib
import urlparse
import httplib

URLs = [
    # enter the URLs you would like
    # to purge here
    'http://localhost:8080',
]

def purge(objectURL):
    for url in URLs:
        if not url:
            continue
        assert url[:4] == 'http', "No protocol specified"

        url = urlparse.urljoin(url, objectURL)
        parsed = urlparse.urlparse(url)
        host = parsed[1]
        path = parsed[2]

        h = httplib.HTTP(host)
        h.putrequest('PURGE', path)
        h.endheaders()
        errcode, errmsg, headers = h.getreply()
        h.getfile.read()

if __name__ == '__main__':
    print purge('/')
```

The Collective has a new tool called CMFSquidTool that does this work for you. It watches for changes on content and when that occurs sends a purge to a Squid cache for you. I haven't tried this new tool yet, but it's definitely worth a look if you're using Squid.

Avoiding Having to Clean Squid Caches

The best way to avoid cleaning caches is to be more selective on the caching. Both the Caching Policy Manager and the RAM Cache Manager provide methods for being selective about what to return from a cache.

Vary

Both the Caching Policy Manager and Squid support the Vary tag. If a Vary tag is specified, Squid will extract the headers specified in the Vary tag from the request. Those headers are then checked against the cache—if they match, the page is returned from the cache. If they don't, the request is passed on down the chain to Plone.

As an example, in the Caching Policy Manager the Vary tag has the value of Accept-Language. When a request comes into Squid, the page will be cached according to the Accept-Language setting in that request header. When a user requests a page with a different setting, a new page will be returned. This means you can cache the pages based upon language.

The least aggressive value for Vary is *, which will cache any request that's the same as any other request. Different requests are passed straight on to Plone. Although this is the least aggressive caching system, it does ensure that the user will see only up to date content.

REQUEST Methods

The RAM Cache Manager REQUEST methods are the same concept as Vary except the tool accepts a list of Zope request variables. The result of a cache lookup is then based upon those variables. The default value is AUTHENTICATED_USER, which means that each authenticated users will see their own versions of the cache. Nonregistered users (anonymous) will all see the same content.

Using Zope Enterprise Objects

The final key to scaling and administering Plone is using Zope Enterprise Objects (ZEO). This is a key tool in so many areas of Plone for development and production. Many people think it should be the default setup for Plone, and it may be one day soon. For the moment, however, ZEO comes with Plone on Linux but isn't installed. It also works in Windows but isn't fully supported with services or easy installs.

In a standard Plone installation, there's one instance of Plone talking to one instance of the ZODB. While that one instance of Plone is accessing the ZODB, it's locked and no other process can access it. This limits the scale of the site and creates a single point of failure. In a the world of relational databases, this would be equivalent to only one process being able to access your database.

ZEO breaks this linkage and separates the access of the ZODB (called the *ZEO server*) so that multiple processes may connect to the ZODB (called *ZEO client*), as shown in Figure 14-9. In relational database terms, this is the equivalent of a process making a database connection.

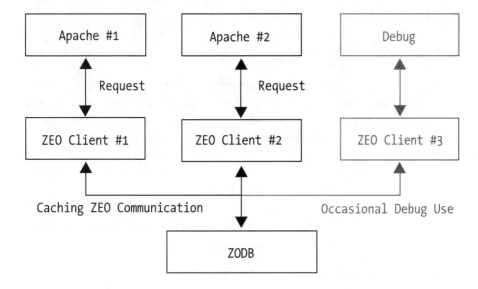

Figure 14-9. A standard ZEO setup

Because multiple processes are able to connect to a ZODB, you're now able to have several copies of Plone. In essence you can now have two or three Plone instances that all share the same content. Not only does this mean you can spread the load of your site over many computers, but you can now connect to your site programmatically and run expensive tasks on other computers or examine your site at the Python level while it's live.

Finally, one minor point is that restart times for a ZEO client are very quick. The cost of having to load up the databases has been removed, which means you can restart Plone sites quickly.

Installing ZEO

ZEO is included with Zope 2.7, the version of Zope supported by this book. In earlier version of Zope, it was distributed separately. At the moment there's no easy way to install ZEO on Windows—the mkzeoinstance script doesn't work. ZEO itself works just fine, but you'll have to read the ZEO source to see how to do this.

Further, zopectl doesn't work on Windows, meaning the following examples don't work.

Linux

To create a ZEO server, use the mkzeoinstance script located in the /opt/Zope-2.7/ bin directory. This assumes that Zope is already installed, as described in Chapter 2. The script takes the following parameters:

- **Directory**: This is the directory in which to create the ZEO server instance.

- **Host and port**: This is the host and port for the server to listen on, in the format host:port. The port will be the port that ZEO clients connect to and should be protected by a firewall, since ZEO provides no security against unauthorized access. These are optional. The default port is 9999.

- **User and password**: This is the default user and password for the server in the format user:password and is optional.

For example, the following will install ZEO at /var/zeo on the default port:

```
cd /opt/Zope-2.7/bin
./mkzeoinstance /var/zeo
```

This has created a new database with all the appropriate configuration. This database is a new location, but this is fine. If you want to move an existing Zope installation to ZEO, then you'll need to stop the running Zope and then move the database from your old installation to the new ZEO directory. In my case, that means moving the Data.fs file from /var/zope/var to /var/zeo/var.

Next you'll need to alter the configuration of your Zope instance. To do this, open the zope.conf in etc and enter the following information:

```
# ZEO client storage:
#
<zodb_db main>
    mount-point /
    <zeoclient>
      server localhost:9999
      storage 1
      name zeostorage
      var $INSTANCE/var
    </zeoclient>
</zodb_db>
```

In the previous code you're setting the port and the server where the ZEO Server can be found. You'll also need to comment out the existing map to the local database. This is should look like the following:

```
#<zodb_db main>
#    # Main FileStorage database
#    <filestorage>
#      path $INSTANCE/var/Data.fs
#    </filestorage>
#    mount-point /
#</zodb_db>
```

To test that this works, first start the ZEO server. This may require more permissions than the user you installed it as:

```
$ cd /var/zeo/bin
$ ./zeoctl start
daemon process started, pid=29316
```

The ZEO daemon has successfully started. Now fire up a Zope client, and try to connect to it, like so:

```
$ cd /var/zope/bin
$ ./zopectl start
daemon process started, pid=29338
```

This means things are good to go, and you can now access your Plone as usual.

Using ZEO Clients

In this configuration, the ZODB is accessed via the ZEO server, and each Zope instance is a ZEO client. Multiple ZEO clients can be connected to the server. There's no need for the client and server to be on the same computer, as long as the client can make a connection to the server. If the clients are on the same computer, each client will need to bind to different HTTP and FTP ports to avoid conflict with each other.

When your client starts, it'll connect to the storage specified in your configuration instead of the standard local storage. One common requirement is to allow a second computer to run intensive tasks, such as updating the catalog, packing the database, or performing complex lookups, without causing the other client's performance to degrade. This is actually easy to do using the zopectl function:

```
$ cd /var/zope/bin
$ ./zopectl debug
Starting debugger (the name "app" is bound to the top-level Zope object)
```

To pack the database, you'd then do the following:

```
>>> app.Control_Panel.Database.manage_pack(days=0)
```

Because you're running on a ZEO client, you have to tell the server that a change has been made and the caches have been updated. To complete the transaction, do this:

```
>>> get_transaction().commit()
>>> app._p_jar.close()
```

This is actually a useful thing to do if you're running a high-performance site and need to pack the database. The site will run a little slower when the transaction is committed, but most of the hard work will happen on the client that's performing the pack. This could be a totally separate machine from your site and is an excellent way to distribute the load.

For debugging, getting to this prompt is extremely useful, as you can now examine the objects inside that app object. You'll find that they match the objects you see in the ZMI. For example:

```
>>> app.objectIds()
['acl_users', 'Control_Panel', 'temp_folder',...
```

What's the API for that app object? You can use the built-in dir function in Python to examine the object and even use the __doc__ method to see the comment strings contained therein, like so:

```
$dir(app)
>>> dir(app)
['COPY', 'COPY__roles__', 'Control_Panel', 'DELETE',...
>>> app.valid_roles.__doc__
'Return list of valid roles'
```

One good example of a ZEO based application is CMFNewsFeed (http://sf.net/projects/collective). This connects to Plone using a ZEO client. That separate client then goes and collects all the news feeds it can find and inserts the data into the site. By doing all the collection and cataloging in a separate process, this ensures that the main site's performance isn't degraded.

ZEO is an indispensable tool for developers. It allows you to interact programmatically with your server while it's running. If at this point you're still confused about Plone and the object database, then for experienced programmers ZEO is normally an eye-opener.

Load Balancing and Failover

Although ZEO provides the ability to run Plone on many servers, it doesn't provide any load balancing for the user. *Load balancing* is the act of sending incoming requests to different servers and spreading out the load of producing pages. Sophisticated tools test to see if the server is up before sending it a request.

You have hardware and software options for load balancing. For example, Squid can perform dynamic failover. Pound is one example load balancer; you can find it at http://www.apsis.ch/pound/index.html.

The Internet Cache Protocol (ICP) is a protocol that Squid can use to check that a Plone site is running prior to forwarding a request to it. In highly dynamic sites, this can be a necessity. You can find more information about ICP and Zope at http://www.zope.org/Members/htrd/icp/intro.

Key Configurations and Some APIs

THIS APPENDIX CONTAINS some of the key development configurations for Zope, Plone, and Python. This appendix provides information for developers of sites, and it also lists some of the most useful Application Programming Interfaces (APIs).

Setting Up Your Environment

The following sections relate to configuring your development or production environment for optimal usage. If you're developing a lot with Plone, I recommend these settings.

Setting Up PYTHONPATH

Setting up PYTHONPATH is extremely useful because it allows you to easily access all the Zope functionality from a Python prompt. You can easily test if you have this set up—you can just attempt to import the PageTemplate module from Products. If this isn't set up, you should see the following:

```
$ python -c "import Products.PageTemplates"
Traceback (most recent call last):
  File "<string>", line 1, in ?
ImportError: No module named Products.PageTemplates
```

Unix, Linux, and Mac OS X

First, find the Products directory of your Zope installation (not the instance home). On the standard installation, this is at /opt/Zope-2.7/lib/python; on Windows it's at c:\Program Files\Plone\Zope\lib\python. When Python starts, it reads an environment variable called PYTHONPATH and puts all those directories in that variable into the search path for new modules. So you need to add your directory to that variable.

You do this using the export command, to see if PYTHONPATH contains anything initially, run the following:

```
$ export | grep PYTHONPATH
declare -x PYTHONPATH="/home/andy/modules"
```

In my case, I already have an environment variable called PYTHONPATH, although chances are your computer won't have this set up. In my case, it contains a path to some internal modules, so you need to add Zope 2 into that path, like so:

```
$ export PYTHONPATH="/opt/Zope-2.7/lib/python:$PYTHONPATH"
```

You can check that this works by repeating the following command and ensuring no error is raised.

```
python -c "import Products.PageTemplates"
```

Windows

The key directory on Windows is at c:\Program Files\Plone\Zope\lib\python. When Python starts, it reads an environment variable called PYTHONPATH and puts all those directories in that variable into the search path for new modules. So you need to add your directory to that variable. On Windows, to add an environment variable, right-click the My Computer icon and select Properties. In the System Properties dialog box, click the Advanced tab and then, underneath System Variables, click New, as shown in Figure A-1.

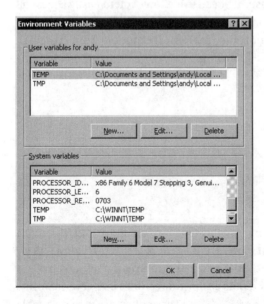

Figure A-1. The Environment Variables dialog box

This will open the System Variable dialog box. To edit a variable, select a variable from the list and edit the value, as shown in Figure A-2. The variable should be PYTHONPATH, and the value should be the place your Plone is located, for example, c:\Program Files\Plone 2\Zope\lib\python.

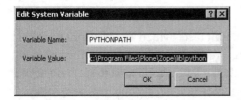

Figure A-2. Adding the variable

Now you should be able to run the import statement as usual. You can do that from the command line or fire up PythonWin and try the import as Figure A-3 demonstrates.

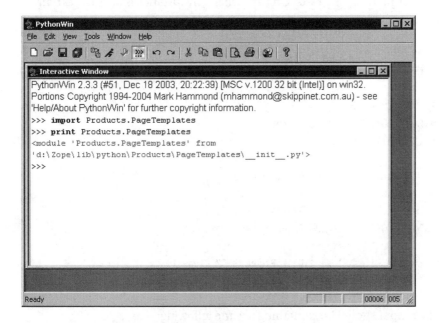

Figure A-3. Importing in PythonWin

Not only can you now import products, but you can also import Zope from the Python command line, which is key for many scripts and tools in the more advanced chapters of the book.

Setting Up to Run Unit Tests

Plone comes with some several hundred unit tests, which are excellent ways of ensuring that your Plone is functioning correctly. You can find Plone unit tests in CMFPlone/tests. If you develop in Plone, then it'd be a good idea to set these up so you can add your own tests. To run these tests, you need ZopeTestCase. In the future, this will probably be packaged with Plone, but for the moment you can download it from http://zope.org/Members/shh/ZopeTestCase.

The installation is a little unusual—you need to untar the package and then place it in lib/python/Testing directory of your Zope software home. On Unix this is usually in /opt/Zope-2.7. On Windows this is c:\Program Files\Plone 2\Zope.

Next you need a script that will run the tests. I usually write a little shell script to do so and place it in the bin directory of my Plone instance. I can then just run the shell script to run the tests. On Unix where my instance is at /var/test, my script looks like the following:

```
export SOFTWARE_HOME=/opt/Zope-2.7/lib/python
export INSTANCE_HOME=/var/test123

echo Testing CMFPlone...
cd $INSTANCE_HOME/Products/CMFPlone/tests
python2.3 runalltests.py
```

On Windows the equivalent is as follows:

```
set SOFTWARE_HOME=c:\Program Files\Plone 2\Zope
set INSTANCE_HOME=c:\Program Files\Plone 2\Data

cd "c:\Program Files\Plone 2\Data\Products\CMFPlone\tests"
"c:\Program Files\Plone 2\Python\python.exe" runalltests.py
```

The output should be something like the following:

```
[root@basil bin]# ./testAll.sh
Testing CMFPlone...
SOFTWARE_HOME: /opt/Zope-2.7/lib/python
INSTANCE_HOME: /opt/Zope-2.7/lib/python/Testing
Loading Zope, please stand by ... done (7.899s)
Installing CMFCore ... done (1.363s)
Installing CMFDefault ... done (1.179s)
Installing CMFCalendar ... done (0.195s)
And so on...
```

The unit testing framework is a great basis for allowing you to unit test your own products. If you do write products or software development in Plone, then ideally you'd write unit tests for them. The unit tests in Plone provide an excellent set of examples for you.

Zope Configuration File

The Zope configuration file is written in a format called ZConfig. You can find more information on ZConfig at http://www.zope.org/Members/fdrake/zconfig/. The configuration file is called zope.conf and is contained in the etc directory of your Zope installation. Some installers also create a plone.conf file that contains Plone-specific information.

The recommended platform for all Plone 2 installations is Zope 2.7. This was the first version of Zope to feature this file; in earlier versions of Zope, parameters were passed to Zope in one command line.

All comments in the file begin with #. In ZConfig you define variables that can then be used later in the configuration file; you do this with a line in the following format:

```
%define variable-name variable-value
```

The following are example definitions in my config file:

```
%define INSTANCE /var/test
%define ZOPE /opt/Zope-2.7
```

You can then reference the variables using a $prefix (for example, $INSTANCE).

Table A-1 shows the full Zope configuration for 2.0.1. The Directive column shows the name of the variable in the configuration file. The Description column details what the directive does, and the Default column tells you what will happen if no value is set. In the Example column, I've detailed some examples to help explain the directive.

Table A-1. Directives in the Zope Configuration File

Directive	Description	Default	Example
instancehome	The path to the data files, local product files, import directory, and Extensions directory. Each instance of Zope should have one of these.	None	/var/zope or the $INSTANCE
client home	The directory in which a running Zope's process identifier files are placed, such as the process ID file, Z2.pid. Not recommended for use; look at pid-filename instead.	INSTANCE/var	$INSTANCE_HOME/var
path	Name of a directory that should be inserted into the beginning of Python's module search path. This directive may be specified as many times as needed to insert additional directories. Since this may be too late, altering the PYTHONPATH, described earlier in this appendix, is preferred.	None	path /home/pythonModules
products	Name of a directory that contains additional Product packages. This directive may be used as many times as needed to add additional collections of products. Each directory identified will be added to the __path__ of the Products package. I don't recommend using this; normally I find using an instance home is enough. Using this has also caused some bug reports with Plone.	None	products /home/chrism/ projects/myproducts

Table A-1. Directives in the Zope Configuration File (Continued)

Directive	Description	Default	Example
environment	A section that can be used to define arbitrary key/value pairs for use as environment variables during Zope's run cycle. It isn't recommended to set system-related environment variables such as PYTHONPATH within this section. Most startup scripts will define system-related environment variables for you, so this isn't recommend for use.	None	`<environment>MY_PRODUCT_ENV VAR foobar</environment>`
debug-mode	A switch that controls several aspects of Zope operation useful for developing under Zope. I recommend running all development servers in this mode. Plone installers may set this to off by default for performance reasons.	On	`debug-mode off`
effective-user	If you intend to run Zope as the root user, you must supply this directive with an effective username or user ID number to which Zope will suid after the server ports are bound. This directive has effect only under Unix and if Zope is started as the root user. This is useful because you can create a user account called zope and set the effective user to zope, ensuring Zope will be run as that user. It'll also let you bind to low-value ports such as 21 or 80.	None	`effective-user zope`

Table A-1. Directives in the Zope Configuration File (Continued)

Directive	Description	Default	Example
enable-product-installation	If this directive is turned on, Zope performs "product installation" (the registration of Python modules in various Products directories) at startup. Turning this off can speed Zope/ZEO startup time, but it can also cause your Control_Panel product list to become desynchronized with the contents of your Products directories.	On	enable-product-installation off
locale	This enables locale (internationalization) support by supplying a locale name to be used. See your operating system documentation for locale information specific to your system.	None	locale fr_FR
port-base	This is the offset applied to the port numbers used for ZServer configurations. For example, if the http-server port is 8080 and the port-base is 1000, the HTTP server will listen on port 9080. This is great if you're running multiple Plones on one box and need to quickly change all the port numbers.	0	1000
datetime-format	This sets this variable either to us or international to force the DateTime module to parse date strings either with month-before-days-before-year (us) or with days-before-month-before-year (international). The default behavior of DateTime (when this setting is left unset) is to parse dates as U.S. dates.	us	datetime-format international

Table A-1. Directives in the Zope Configuration File (Continued)

Directive	Description	Default	Example
zserver-threads	This specifies the number of threads that Zope's ZServer Web server will use to service requests. Setting this high doesn't increase performance on most sites. Instead use ZEO and caching.	4	zserver-threads 10
python-check-interval	This specifies an integer representing the Python interpreter "check interval." This interval determines how often the interpreter checks for periodic things such as thread switches and signal handlers. Setting this high doesn't increase performance on most sites.	500	python-check-interval 1000
zserver-read-only-mode	If this directive is set to on, it'll cause Zope to inhibit the creation of log files and process ID (PID) files. Access and event log files will be presented on standard output.	off	zserver-read-only-mode on
pid-filename	The path to the file in which the Zope PIDs will be written. This defaults to client-home/Z2.pid.	CLIENT_HOME/ Z2.pid	pid-filename /home/chrism/ projects/sessions/var/ Z2.pid
lock-filename	The path to a "lock file," which will be locked by Zope while it's running.	CLIENT_HOME/ Z2.lock	lock-filename /home/chrism/ projects/sessions/var/ Z2.lock
mime-types	This tells Zope about additional mime.types files that should be loaded. The files have the same format as the mime.types file distributed with Apache. The mime-types setting may be given more than once in the configuration file.	None	mime-types $INSTANCE/etc/ mime.types

Table A-1. Directives in the Zope Configuration File (Continued)

Directive	Description	Default	Example
structured-text-header-level	This sets the default starting HTML header level for Structured Text documents. The default is 3, which implies that top-level headers will be created with an <H3> tag. Unfortunately, at the moment, CMF ignores this value, something that'll be fixed one day.	3	structured-text-header-level 1
rest-input-encoding	This specifies the input encoding of re-StructuredText documents (for example, utf-8, iso-8859-15, or any other valid encoding recognized by Python). The default is your Python's default encoding.	The system default	rest-input-encoding iso-8859-15
rest-output-encoding	This specifies the output encoding of re-StructuredText documents (for example, utf-8, iso-8859-15, or any other valid encoding recognized by Python). The default is your Python's default encoding.	The system default	rest-output-encoding iso-8859-15
cgi-environment	A section that allows a user to define arbitrary key/value pairs for use as the initial CGI environment variables.	None	<cgi-environment> HTTPS_SERVER Foobar Server 1.0 HTTPS_PORT 443 </cgi-environment>
dns-server	This specifies the IP address of your Domain Name System (DNS) server to cause resolved hostnames to be written to Zope's access log. If you set this, DNS delays in lookups will slow your site down.	None	dns-server 127.0.0.1

Table A-1. Directives in the Zope Configuration File (Continued)

Directive	Description	Default	Example
ip-address	This is the default IP address on which Zope's various server protocol implementations will listen for requests. If this is unset, Zope will listen on all IP addresses supported by the machine.	None	`ip-address 127.0.0.1`
http-realm	The HTTP Realm header value sent by this Zope instance. This value often shows up in basic authentication dialog boxes.	Zope	`Plone`
automatically-quote-dtml-request-data	Set this directive to `off` to disable the autoquoting of implicitly retrieved REQUEST data by Dynamic HTML (DTML) code, which contains a `<` when used in `<dtml-var>` construction. When this directive is on, all data implicitly retrieved from the REQUEST in DTML (as opposed to addressing REQUEST.somevarname directly) that contains a `<` will be HTML-quoted when interpolated via a `<dtml-var>` or `&dtml-` construct. This mitigates the possibility that DTML programmers will leave their sites open to a client-side Trojan horse attack.	on	`automatically-quote-dtml-request-data on`
trusted-proxy	This defines one or more trusted-proxies directives, each of which is a hostname or an IP address.	None	`trusted-proxy www.example.com`

Table A-1. Directives in the Zope Configuration File (Continued)

Directive	Description	Default	Example
publisher-profile-file	This names a file on the file system that causes Zope's Python profiling capabilities to be enabled. For more information, see the Profiling tab of Zope's control panel via the Zope Management Interface (ZMI). Note that setting this filename will cause Zope code to be executed much more slowly than normal. This shouldn't be enabled in production.	None	publisher-profile-file $INSTANCE/var/profile.dat
security-policy-implementation	The default Zope security machinery is implemented in C. Change this to python to use the Python version of the Zope security machinery. The Python version is slower but provides key information via VerboseSecurity.	C	security-policy-implementation python
skip-authentication-checking	Set this directive to on to cause Zope to skip checks related to authentication for servers that serve only anonymous content.	off	skip-authentication-checking on
skip-ownership-checking	Set this directive to on to cause Zope to ignore ownership checking when attempting to execute "through the Web" code. By default, this directive is on in order to prevent Trojan horse security problems whereby a user with less privilege can cause a user with more privilege to execute dangerous code.	on	skip-ownership-checking off

Table A-1. Directives in the Zope Configuration File (Continued)

Directive	Description	Default	Example
maximum-number-of-session-objects	An integer value representing the number of items to use as a "maximum number of subobjects" value of the /temp_folder/session_data transient object container.	1000	maximum-number-of-session-objects 10000
session-add-notify-script-path	This is an optional Zope path name of a callable object to be set as the "script to call on object addition" of the session_data transient object container created in the /temp_folder folder at startup. For use with sessions.	unset	session-add-notify-script-path /scripts/add_notifier
session-delete-notify-script-path	An optional Zope path name of a callable object to be set as the "script to call on object deletion" of the session_data transient object container created in the /temp_folder folder at startup. For use with sessions.	Unset	session-delete-notify-script-path /scripts/del_notifier
session-timeout-minutes	This is an integer value representing the number of minutes to be used as the "data object timeout" of the /temp_folder/session_data transient object container.	20	session-timeout-minutes 30
suppress-all-access-rules	If this directive is set to on, no access rules in your Zope site will be executed. This is useful if you lock yourself out of a particular part of your site by setting an improper access rule.	off	suppress-all-access-rules on

Table A-1. Directives in the Zope Configuration File (Continued)

Directive	Description	Default	Example
suppress-all-site-roots	If this directive is set to on, no site roots in your Zope site will be effective. This is useful if you lock yourself out of a particular part of your site by setting an improper site root.	off	suppress-all-site-roots on
database-quota-size	Set this directive to an integer in bytes to place a hard limit on the size to which the default FileStorage-backed Zope database can grow. Additions to the database will not be permitted once this file size has been exceeded.	None	database-quota-size 1000000
read-only-database	This causes the main Zope FileStorage-backed ZODB to be opened in read-only mode. Other files, such as log files, will be written.	off	read-only-database on
zeo-client-name	If you want a persistent ZEO client cache that retains cache contents across ClientStorage restarts, you need to define a zeo-client-name. If you use ZEO and you don't set a zeo-client-name, the client cache is stored in temporary files that are removed when the ClientStorage shuts down. The value of zeo-client-name uniquely identifies the local cache files created if this Zope is a ZEO client.	None	zeo-client-name on

Table A-1. Directives in the Zope Configuration File (Continued)

Directive	Description	Default	Example

logger	This area should define one or more logger sections of the names access, event, and trace. The access logger logs Zope server access. The event logger logs Zope event information. The trace logger logs detailed server request information (for debugging purposes only). Each logger section may contain a level name/value pair that indicates the level of logging detail to capture for this logger. The default level is INFO. Level may be CRITICAL, ERROR, WARN, INFO, DEBUG, and ALL. Each logger section may additionally contain one or more handler sections that indicate a type of log handler (file, syslog, NT event log, and so on) to be used for the logger being defined. There are five types of handlers: logfile, syslog, win32-eventlog, http-handler, and email-notifier. Each handler type has its own set of allowable subkeys that define aspects of the handler. All handler sections also allow for the specification of a format (the log message format string), a dateformat (the log message format for date strings), and a level, which has the same semantics of the overall logger level but overrides the logger's level for the handler it's defined upon.	The access log will log to the file log <instancehome>/ log/Z2.log at level INFO, the event log will log to the file log at level INFO, and the trace log won't be written anywhere.	`<eventlog>`
			`  level all`
			`  <logfile>`
			`    path $INSTANCE/log/event.log`
			`    level info`
			`  </logfile>`
			`</eventlog>`
			`<logger access>`
			`  level WARN`
			`  <logfile>`
			`    path $INSTANCE/log/Z2.log`
			`    format %(message)s`
			`  </logfile>`
			`</logger>`

Table A-1. Directives in the Zope Configuration File (Continued)

Directive	Description	Default	Example
warnfilter	A section that allows you to define a warning filter. The following keys are valid within a warnfilter section: action: one of the following strings: error, ignore, always, default, module, and once; message: a string containing a regular expression that the warning message must match (the match is compiled to always be case insensitive); category: a Python dotted-path class name (must be a subclass of warning) of which the warning category must be a subclass in order to match; module: a string containing a regular expression that the module name must match (the match is compiled to be case sensitive); lineno: an integer that the line number where the warning occurred must match, or 0 to match all line numbers.	None	```<warnfilter>
action ignore
category
exceptions.DeprecationWarni
ng
</warnfilter>```
max-listen-sockets	The maximum number of sockets that ZServer will attempt to open in order to service incoming connections.	1000	```max-listen-sockets 500```

Table A-1. Directives in the Zope Configuration File (Continued)

Directive	Description	Default	Example

servers	A set of sections that allow the specification of Zope's various ZServer servers. Seven server types may be defined: http-server, ftp-server, webdav-source-server, persistent-cgi, fast-cgi, monitor-server, and icp-server. If no servers are defined, the default servers are used. Ports may be specified either in simple form (80) or in complex form including hostname 127.0.0.1:80. If the hostname is omitted, the default-ip-address is used as the hostname. Port numbers are offset by the setting of port-base, which defaults to 8000. Your Plone installation may have changed these for you to make it easier for an initial install.	HTTP server on port 8080 and FTP on 8021	\<http-server\>
			# valid keys are "address" and "force-connection-close"
			  address 8080
			# force-connection-close on
			\</http-server\>
			
			\<ftp-server\>
			# valid key is "address"
			  address 8021
			\</ftp-server\>

Table A-1. Directives in the Zope Configuration File (Continued)

Directive	Description	Default	Example

database	A database section allows the definition of custom database and storage types. More than one zodb_db section can be defined. The values inside the storage are set by the values in the particular database client.	See example.	```
			<zodb_db main>
			# Main FileStorage database
			    <filestorage>
			        path $INSTANCE/var/
			Data.fs
			    </filestorage>
			    mount-point /
			</zodb_db>
			<zodb_db temporary>
			# Temporary storage
			database (for sessions)
			    <temporarystorage>
			        name temporary storage
			for sessioning
			    </temporarystorage>
			    mount-point /
			temp_folder
			        container-class Prod-
			ucts.TemporaryFolder.Tempor
			aryContainer
			</zodb_db>
			``

Of all configurations, the last few (database, servers, and loggers) are directives inside a simple Extensible Markup Language (XML) style syntax. Users of the Apache log file will be familiar with this format. You can apply these directives multiple times. For example, one common configuration from the Mac and Windows installer is to create HTTP connections on two ports, port 80 and port 8080. You do this in the following manner:

```
<http-server>
  address 8080
</http-server>

<http-server>
  address 80
</http-server>
```

Text Formatting Rules

Plone has External Editor and Epoz, two excellent tools for editing HTML. However, two formats of plain text are common in Zope and Python: Structured Text and restructured text. Because of the quality of these editors, I don't believe you'll need to use these formats, but if you're going to develop Zope or Plone, then chances are you'll come across these formats.

Both of these formats try to do similar things—they provide a system for marking up plain text in such a manner that it produces HTML. This is aimed at developers who like and are familiar with plain text but who don't want to go to the effort of producing HTML.

Structured Text

The following is the reproduction of an article written previously. For an online example, refer to `http://plone.org/documentation/howto/UsingStructuredText`. In the following article, the indentation of the text in code font is crucial to how the text displays.

Basic Formatting

The basic idea in structured text is a paragraph. The following snippet:

```
This is the first paragraph.

This is the second paragraph.
```

is converted to the following in HTML:

```
<p>This is the first paragraph.</p>
<p>This is the second paragraph.</p>
```

Whitespace matters in structured text. In this case, a blank line between two lines causes a new paragraph. This is an intuitive idea. For instance, in e-mail, paragraphs are separated by whitespace. To introduce emphasis, structured text uses another text convention: asterisks. Note the following snippet:

```
This is the *first* paragraph.

This is the **second** paragraph.
```

In HTML, this snippet introduces the em tag and the strong tag:

```
<p>This is the <em>first</em> paragraph.</p>
<p>This is the <strong>second</strong> paragraph.</p>
```

Again, this is a common pattern in e-mail. Several other common patterns are supported, such as referring to a piece of jargon:

```
When you see 'STX', you know this is shorthand for 'Structured Text'.
```

The HTML output is as follows:

```
<p>When you see <code>STX</code>, you know this is shorthand for
<code>Structured Text</code>.</p>
```

Using Indentation

The preceding section focused on text conventions that convey a semantic meaning. This semantic meaning, when processed by structured text, produces certain HTML tags. In structured text, indentation is also important in conveying semantic meaning. The most basic is the idea of headings in HTML. In the following snippet, indentation conveys an outline-like structure:

```
Using Indentation
    The preceding section focused on text conventions that convey
    a semantic meaning. This semantic meaning, when processed by
    Structured Text, produces certain HTML tags.
```

This produces the following HTML:

```
<h1>Using Indentation</h1>

<p>The preceding section focused on text conventions that convey
a semantic meaning. This semantic meaning, when processed by
Structured Text, produces certain HTML tags.</p>
```

That is, the indentation conveyed a semantic meaning. The paragraph was subordinate to the heading, and the relationship is thus expressed in HTML. In fact, outline relationship can be continued, like so:

```
Using Indentation

    The preceding section focused on text conventions that convey a
    semantic meaning. This semantic meaning, when processed by
    Structured Text, produces certain HTML tags.

    Basics of Indentation

        In this section we will investigate the basics of
        indentation...
```

This produces the following HTML:

```
<h1>Using Indentation</h1>

<p>The preceding section focused on text conventions that convey
a semantic meaning. This semantic meaning, when processed by
Structured Text, produces certain HTML tags.</p>

<h2>Basics of Indentation</h2>

<p>In this section we will investigate the basics of
indentation...</p>

<h2>Hyperlinks</h2>
```

Lists and Items

Lists are also supported in structured text, including unordered, ordered, and descriptive lists. The convention unordered lists is a common pattern in text-based communication. HTML has three kinds of lists:

- Unordered lists

- Ordered lists

- Descriptive lists

Structured text allows you to use the symbols *, o, and - to connote list items. The previous example produces this HTML:

```
<p>HTML has three kinds of lists:</p>
<ul>
<li><p>Unordered lists</p></li>
<li><p>Ordered lists</p></li>
<li><p>Descriptive lists</p></li>
</ul>
```

The structured text conventions for ordered lists is as follows:

```
HTML has three kinds of lists:
1. Unordered lists

2. Ordered lists

3. Descriptive lists
```

This produces the following:

```
<p>HTML has three kinds of lists:</p>
<ol>
<li><p>Unordered lists</p></li>
<li><p>Ordered lists</p></li>
<li><p>Descriptive lists</p></li>
</ol>
```

Descriptive lists are also easily accommodated using double dashes, like so:

```
Ordered Lists -- HTML viewers convert the list items into a numbered series.

Descriptive Lists -- Usually used for definitional lists such as glossaries.
```

This becomes the following HTML:

```
<dl>
<dt> Ordered Lists</dt><dd><p>HTML viewers convert the list
items into a numbered series.</p>
</dd>
<dt> Descriptive Lists</dt><dd><p>Usually used for definitional
lists such as glossaries.</p>
</dd>
</dl>
```

Example Code

As mentioned, structured text authors can use an easy convention to get the monotype semantics of the code tag from HTML. For instance, the following code:

```
When you see the dialog box, hit the 'OK' button.
```

is rendered into the following HTML:

```
<p>When you see the dialog box, hit the <code>Ok</code> button.</p>
```

However, sometimes you want long passages of code. For instance, what if you wanted to document a Python function in the middle of an article discussing Python? You can indicate a code block by ending a paragraph with two colons (::) and indenting the following paragraph(s). For instance, this structured text snippet:

```
In our next Python example, we convert human years to dog years:def
dog_years(age):
    """Convert an age to dog years"""
    return age*7
```

would be converted to the following HTML:

```
<p>In our next Python example, we convert human years to dog
years:</p>

<pre>
def dog_years(age):
    """Convert an age to dog years"""
    return age*7
</pre>
```

The convention of combining :: at the end of a paragraph-ending sentence and indenting a block does more than apply code semantics. It also *escapes* the indented block. That is how the structured text and HTML snippets in this article are left alone, rather than being rendered. For example, the less than, greater than, and ampersand symbols in this code block are escaped:

```
Here's an HTML example:
<html>
  <p>This is a page about dogs & cats.</p>
</html>
```

to produce this HTML:

```
<p>Here's an HTML example:</p>

<pre>
  <html>
    <p>This is a page about dogs & cats.</p>
  </html>
</pre>
```

Hyperlinks

The previous sections focused on ways to get certain presentation semantics in HTML by using common text conventions. But the Web isn't just HTML. Linking words and phrases to other information and including images are equally important. Fortunately, structured text supports conventions for hyperlinks and image tags.

For instance, I'll start with a simple hyperlink. If you have a structured text paragraph discussing Python, like so:

```
For more information on Python, please visit the
"Python website":http://www.python.org/.
```

It becomes the following:

```
<p>For more information on Python, please visit the <a
href="http://www.python.org/">Python website</a>.
```

The convention is fairly simple:

• The text of the reference is enclosed in quotes.

• The second quotation mark is followed by a colon and a URL.

• The URL can be followed by punctuation.

This basic convention has a number of variations. For instance, relative URLs are possible, as are `mailto` URLs and images.

reStructured Text

reStructured Text is a new variation on the Structured Text to avoid some of the issues people have encountered with the older version. Not only does Structured Text fail in internationalization cases, but it produces nonvalid markup. Further, the syntax can be a little hard to follow.

The new reStructured Text has now become one of the standards of Python for documenting code and is used in the Docutils project. The online documentation is so good that I fully recommend reading it at `http://docutils.sourceforge.net/rst.html`.

The following is a reproduction of the material by Richard Jones.

Introduction

The most basic pattern recognized is a paragraph. This is a chunk of text that's separated by blank lines (one is enough). Paragraphs must have the same indentation—that is, they must line up at their left edge. Paragraphs that start indented will result in indented quote paragraphs. For example, the following code:

```
This is a paragraph.  It's quite short

    This paragraph will result in an indented block of
    text, typically used for quoting other text.

This is another one.
```

results in this:

```
<blockquote>
<p>This is a paragraph.  It's quite short.</p>
<blockquote>
This paragraph will result in an indented block of
text, typically used for quoting other text.</blockquote>
<p>This is another one.</p>
</blockquote>
```

Text Styles

Inside paragraphs and other bodies of text, you can additionally mark text for *italics* with `*italics*` or **bold** with `**bold**`.

If you want something to appear as a fixed-space literal, use double backquotes: `` `` ``. Note that no further fiddling happens inside the double back-quotes—so asterisks and whatnot are left alone.

If you find that you want to use one of the "special" characters in text, you'll generally be OK—reStructuredText is pretty smart. For example, the asterisk is handled just fine. If you actually want text surrounded by asterisks to *not* be italicized, then you need to indicate that the asterisk isn't special. You do this by placing a backslash just before it, like so:

```
\*
```

Or you enclose it in double backquotes (inline literals), like so:

```
``\*``
```

Lists

Lists of items come in three main flavors: enumerated, bulleted, and definitions. In all list cases, you may have as many paragraphs, sublists, and so on, as you want, as long as the left side of the paragraph aligns with the first line of text in the list item.

Lists must always start a new paragraph—that is, they must appear after a blank line. Start a line with a number or letter followed by a period (.), surrounded by a right bracket ()), or surrounded by brackets (( ))—whatever you're comfortable with. All the forms in Listing A-1 are recognized.

Listing A-1. Example Points

```
1. numbers

A. upper-case letters
   and it goes over many lines

   with two paragraphs and all!

a. lower-case letters

   3. with a sub-list starting at a different number
   4. make sure the numbers are in the correct sequence though!

I. upper-case roman numerals

i. lower-case roman numerals

(1) numbers again

1) and again
```

Listing A-2 shows the results (note that the different enumerated list styles aren't always supported by every Web browser, so you may not get the full effect here).

Listing A-2. Example List

```
<ol class="arabic simple">
<li>numbers</li>
</ol>
<ol class="upperalpha">
<li><p class="first">upper-case letters
and it goes over many lines</p>
<p>with two paragraphs and all!</p>
</li>
</ol>
<ol class="loweralpha simple">
<li>lower-case letters<ol class="arabic" start="3">
<li>with a sub-list starting at a different number</li>
<li>make sure the numbers are in the correct sequence though!</li>
```

```
</ol>
</li>
</ol>
<ol class="upperroman simple">
<li>upper-case roman numerals</li>
</ol>
<ol class="lowerroman simple">
<li>lower-case roman numerals</li>
</ol>
<ol class="arabic simple">
<li>numbers again</li>
</ol>
<ol class="last arabic simple">
<li>and again</li>
</ol>
```

Just like enumerated lists, start the line with a bullet point character, either -, +, or *, like so:

```
* a bullet point using "*"

  - a sub-list using "-"

    + yet another sub-list

  - another item
```

That code results in the following:

```
<ul class="last simple">
<li>a bullet point using &quot;*&quot;<ul>
<li>a sub-list using &quot;-&quot;<ul>
<li>yet another sub-list</li>
</ul>
</li>
<li>another item</li>
</ul>
</li>
</ul>
```

Unlike the other two, the definition lists consist of a term and the definition of that term. The format of a definition list is as follows:

```
what
    Definition lists associate a term with a definition.

*how*
    The term is a one-line phrase, and the definition is one or more
    paragraphs or body elements, indented relative to the term.
    Blank lines are not allowed between term and definition.
```

That code results in the following:

```
<ul class="last simple">
<li>a bullet point using &quot;*&quot;<ul>
<li>a sub-list using &quot;-&quot;<ul>
<li>yet another sub-list</li>
</ul>
</li>
<li>another item</li>
</ul>
</li>
</ul>
```

Preformatting (Code Samples)

To just include a chunk of preformatted, never-to-be-fiddled-with text, finish the prior paragraph with : :. The preformatted block is finished when the text falls back to the same indentation level as a paragraph prior to the preformatted block. For example:

```
An example::

        Whitespace, newlines, blank lines, and all kinds of markup
            (like *this* or \this) is preserved by literal blocks.
    Lookie here, I've dropped an indentation level
    (but not far enough)

  no more example
```

That code results in the following:

```
<blockquote>
<p>An example:</p>
<pre class="literal-block">
  Whitespace, newlines, blank lines, and all kinds of markup
    (like *this* or \this) is preserved by literal blocks.
Lookie here, I've dropped an indentation level
(but not far enough)
</pre>
<p>no more example</p>
</blockquote>
```

Note that if a paragraph consists only of : :, then it's removed from the output, like so:

```
::

    This is preformatted text, and the
    last "::" paragraph is removed
```

That code results in the following:

```
<pre class="literal-block">This is preformatted text, and thelast "::" paragraph
is removed</pre>
```

Sections

To break longer text up into sections, you use section headers. These are a single line of text (one or more words) with adornment: an underline alone, or an underline and an overline together, in dashes -----, equals ======, tildes ~~~~~~, or any of the nonalphanumeric characters that you feel comfortable with:

```
= - ` : ' " ~ ^ _ * + # < >
```

An underline-only adornment is distinct from an overline-and-underline adornment using the same character. The underline/overline must be at least as long as the title text. Be consistent, since all sections marked with the same adornment style are deemed to be at the same level, like so:

```
Chapter 1 Title
===============


Section 1.1 Title
-----------------


Subsection 1.1.1 Title
~~~~~~~~~~~~~~~~~~~~~~~


Section 1.2 Title
-----------------


Chapter 2 Title
===============
```

This results in the following structure, illustrated by simplified pseudo-XML:

```
<section>
    <title>
        Chapter 1 Title
    <section>
        <title>
            Section 1.1 Title
        <section>
            <title>
                Subsection 1.1.1 Title
    <section>
        <title>
            Section 1.2 Title
<section>
    <title>
        Chapter 2 Title
```

Pseudo-XML uses indentation for nesting and has no end tags. It's not possible to show actual processed output, as in the other examples, because sections can't exist inside block quotes. For a concrete example, compare the section structure of this document's source text at http://docutils.sourceforge.net/docs/rst/quickstart.html to the processed output.

Note that section headers are available as link targets, just using their name. To link to the Lists_ heading, you write Lists_ . If the heading has a space in it such as text styles_, you need to quote the heading like so: `text styles`_.

To indicate the document title, use a unique adornment style at the beginning of the document. To indicate the document subtitle, use another unique adornment style immediately after the document title. For example:

```
================
Document Title
================

----------

Subtitle

----------


Section Title
=============


...
```

Note that Document Title and Section Title both use equals signs but are distinct and unrelated styles. The text of overline-and-underlined titles (but not underlined-only) may be inset for aesthetics.

Images

To include an image in your document, you use the ``image`` directive, like so: For example, the following code:

```
.. image:: images/biohazard.png
```

results in this:

```
.. image:: images/biohazard.png
```

The images/biohazard.png part indicates the filename of the image you want to appear in the document. There's no restriction placed on the image (format, size, and so on). If the image is to appear in HTML and you want to supply additional information, you may do the following:

```
.. image:: images/biohazard.png
   :height: 100
   :width: 200
   :scale: 50
   :alt: alternate text
```

Miscellaneous

The following are some tips that may be useful to Plone developers.

All the Global Defines in the Main Template

Table A-2 lists the global defines in the main template, the code that defines them, and a description. As ever, this list is flexible and may change, so I recommend looking at the source. This is taken from `CMFPlone/skins/main_template/global_defines.pt`.

These definitions are used mostly in page templates and are useful shortcuts. For example:

```
<a href="" tal:attributes="portal_url">Url to the portal</a>
```

Table A-2. Global Defines in the Main Template

Name	Code	Description
utool	nocall:here/portal_url;	The portal_url tool
portal	utool/getPortalObject;	The actual portal object
portal_object	nocall:portal;	Another name for portal
portal_url	utool;	Another name of the portal_url tool
mtool	nocall:portal/portal_membership;	The portal membership tool
gtool	nocall:portal/portal_groups | nothing;	The portal groups tool, if present
dtool	nocall:portal/portal_groupdata | nothing;	The portal groups data tool, if present
atool	nocall:portal/portal_actions;	The portal actions tool
aitool	nocall:portal/portal_actionicons | nothing;	The portal action icons tool
putils	nocall:portal/plone_utils;	The portal utils tool
wtool	nocall:portal/portal_workflow;	The portal workflow tool
ifacetool	nocall:portal/plone_interface | nothing;	The portal interface tool, if present
portal_title	portal_object/Title;	The title of the portal

Table A-2. Global Defines in the Main Template (Continued)

Name	Code	Description
object_title	here/Title;	The title of the current object
member	mtool/getAuthenticatedMember;	The current member
checkPermission	nocall:mtool/checkPermission;	The check permission function of the membership tool
membersfolder	mtool/getMembersFolder;	The Members folder the current member, if present
isAnon	mtool/isAnonymousUser;	Boolean if the user is anonymous
actions	python: portal.portal_actions.listFilteredActionsFor(here);	The actions for the current location
keyed_actions	python: portal.keyFilteredActions (actions);	The list of all actions that have IDs
user_actions	actions/user;	Actions for the user
workflow_actions	actions/workflow;	Workflow actions
folder_actions	actions/folder;	Folder actions
global_actions	actions/global;	Global actions
portal_tabs	actions/portal_tabs|nothing;	Portal tabs actions
wf_state	python:wtool.getInfoFor(here,'review_state',None);	The workflow state of the current object
portal_properties	portal/portal_properties;	The portal properties object
site_properties	portal_properties/ site_properties;	The site properties object
ztu	modules/ZTUtils;	The ZTUtils module, a useful module with some utilities
actions	options/actions|actions;	The actions passed through to the template explicitly
wf_actions	workflow_actions;	Another name for workflow actions
isFolder	python:here.getTypeInfo(). getId() in site_properties. use_folder_tabs;	Boolean if the context is a folder
template_id	options/template_id | template/ getId | nothing;	The ID of the current template

Table A-2. Global Defines in the Main Template (Continued)

Name	Code	Description
slots_mapping	options/slots_mapping|here/ prepare_slots|nothing;	The slots mapping
Iterator	python:modules['Products. CMFPlone'].IndexIterator;	An iterator, for use in templates
tabindex	python:Iterator(pos=30000);	The tabindex iterator for forms
here_url	here/absolute_url;	Current absolute_url
sl	slots_mapping/left;	Left slots mapping
sr	slots_mapping/right;	Right slots mapping
default_language	site_properties/ default_language|nothing;	The default language from site properties
allowed_types	here/getAllowedTypes;	Allowed content types into this folder
is_editable	python:here.showEditableBor- der(template_id=template_id, allowed_types=allowed_types, actions=actions);	If the current object is editable and should have the green border

DateTime API

I've used DateTime objects throughout the book and haven't explained their API. These objects are used a great deal in Plone. Some common operations include searching on dates or displaying dates.

To create a DateTime, pass a string that can be interpreted as a date:

```
>>> from DateTime import DateTime
>>> d = DateTime('2004/12/01')
>>> d.month()
12
```

You can then perform operations on the dates. For example, to subtract two dates, you use the following:

```
>>> x = DateTime('2004/11/02')
>>> z = DateTime('2004/11/30')
>>> z - x
28.0
```

This section contains an abbreviated API; you can find the full notes in the DateTime directory in your Zope installation.

DateTime objects represent instances in time and provide interfaces for controlling its representation without affecting the absolute value of the object.

You can create DateTime objects from a wide variety of string or numeric data, or you can compute them from other DateTime objects. DateTimes support the ability to convert their representations to many major time zones, as well as to create a DateTime object in the context of a given time zone.

DateTime objects provide partial numerical behavior:

- Two DateTime objects can be subtracted to obtain a time, in days between the two.

- A date DateTime object and a positive or negative number may be added to obtain a new DateTime object that's the given number of days later than the input DateTime object.

- A positive or negative number and a DateTime object may be added to obtain a new DateTime object that's the given number of days later than the input DateTime object.

- A positive or negative number may be subtracted from a DateTime object to obtain a new DateTime object that's the given number of days earlier than the input DateTime object.

You can convert DateTime objects to integer, long, or float numbers of days since January 1, 1901, using the standard int, long, and float functions. (Note that int, long, and float return the number of days since 1901 in Greenwich mean time rather than local machine time zone.) DateTime objects also provide access to their value in a float format usable with the Python time module, provided that the value of the object falls in the range of the epoch-based time module.

A DateTime object should be considered immutable; all conversion and numeric operations return a new DateTime object rather than modify the current object.

To create a DateTime object, pass in a string that's recognizable as a valid date. If you create a DateTime object, the current time will be used. A DateTime object always maintains its value as an absolute UTC time and is represented in the context of some time zone based on the arguments used to create the object. A DateTime object's methods return values based on the time zone context.

Table A-3 describes all the methods that can be called on a DateTime object.

Table A-3. Available Methods on a DateTime *Object*

Method	Description
aMonth()	Returns the abbreviated month name.
pCommon()	Returns a string representing the object's value in the format Mar. 1, 1997 1:45 pm.
minute()	Returns the minute.
isLeapYear()	Returns true if the current year (in the context of the object's time zone) is a leap year.
pMonth()	Returns the abreviated (with period) month name.
DayOfWeek()	Compatibility: see Day().
Day_()	Compatibility: see pDay().
isCurrentDay()	Returns true if this object represents a date/time that falls within the current day, in the context of this object's time zone representation.
Mon()	Compatibility: see aMonth().
hour()	Returns the 24-hour clock representation of the hour.
Date()	Returns the date string for the object.
aCommonZ()	Returns a string representing the object's value in the format Mar 1, 1997 1:45 pm US/Eastern.
fCommonZ()	Returns a string representing the object's value in the format March 1, 1997 1:45 pm US/Eastern.
isCurrentYear()	Returns true if this object represents a date/time that falls within the current year, in the context of this object's time zone representation.
AMPMMinutes()	Returns the time string for an object not showing seconds.
dd()	Returns day as a two-digit string.
TimeMinutes()	Returns the time string for an object not showing seconds.
h_24()	Returns the 24-hour clock representation of the hour.
isPast()	Returns true if this object represents a date/time earlier than the time of the call.
dow()	Returns the integer day of the week, where Sunday is 0.
isFuture()	Returns true if this object represents a date/time later than the time of the call.

Table A-3. Available Methods on a DateTime *Object (Continued)*

Method	Description
pCommonZ()	Returns a string representing the object's value in the format Mar. 1, 1997 1:45 pm US/Eastern.
timezone()	Returns the time zone in which the object is represented.
h_12()	Returns the 12-hour clock representation of the hour.
PreciseTime()	Returns the time string for the object.
isCurrentMinute()	Returns true if this object represents a date/time that falls within the current minute, in the context of this object's timezone representation.
rfc822()	Returns the date in RFC 822 format.
equalTo(t)	Compares this DateTime object to another DateTime object or a floating-point number such as that's returned by the Python time module. Returns true if the object represents a date/time equal to the specified DateTime or time module-style time.
yy()	Returns calendar year as a two-digit string.
mm()	Returns month as a two-digit string.
Mon_()	Compatibility: see pMonth().
toZone(z)	Returns a DateTime with the value as the current object, represented in the indicated time zone.
earliestTime()	Returns a new DateTime object that represents the earliest possible time (in whole seconds) that still falls within the current object's day in the object's time zone context.
aDay()	Returns the abbreviated name of the day of the week.
dayOfYear()	Returns the day of the year, in context of the time zone representation of the object.
latestTime()	Returns a new DateTime object that represents the latest possible time (in whole seconds) that still falls within the current object's day in the object's time zone context.
notEqualTo(t)	Compares this DateTime object to another DateTime object or a floating-point number such as that's returned by the Python time module. Returns true if the object represents a date/time not equal to the specified DateTime or time module-style time.
PreciseAMPM()	Returns the time string for the object.

Table A-3. Available Methods on a DateTime *Object (Continued)*

Method	Description
day()	Returns the integer day.
timeTime()	Returns the date/time as a floating-point number in UTC, in the format used by the Python time module. Note that it's possible to create date /time values with DateTime that have no meaningful value to the time module, and in such cases a DateTimeError is raised. A DateTime object's value must generally be between Jan 1, 1970 (or your local machine epoch) and Jan 2038 to produce a valid time.time() style value.
ampm()	Returns the appropriate time modifier (a.m. or p.m.).
greaterThan(t)	Compares this DateTime object to another DateTime object or a floating-point number such as that's returned by the Python time module. Returns true if the object represents a date/time greater than the specified DateTime or time module-style time.
month()	Returns the month of the object as an integer.
AMPM()	Returns the time string for an object to the nearest second.
second()	Returns the second.
parts()	Returns a tuple containing the calendar year, month, day, hour, minute, second, and time zone of the object.
greaterThanEqualTo(t)	Compare this DateTime object to another DateTime object or a floating-point number such as that's returned by the Python time module. Returns true if the object represents a date/time greater than or equal to the specified DateTime or time module-style time.
lessThanEqualTo(t)	Compares this DateTime object to another DateTime object or a floating-point number such as that's returned by the Python time module. Returns true if the object represents a date/time less than or equal to the specified DateTime or time module-style time.
isCurrentHour()	Returns true if this object represents a date/time that falls within the current hour, in the context of this object's time zone representation.
aCommon()	Returns a string representing the object's value in the format Mar 1, 1997 1:45 pm.
dow_1()	Returns the integer day of the week, where Sunday is 1, as opposed to the dow method.
Day()	Returns the full name of the day of the week.

Table A-3. Available Methods on a DateTime *Object (Continued)*

Method	Description
fCommon()	Returns a string representing the object's value in the format March 1, 1997 1:45 pm.
Month()	Returns the full month name.
isCurrentMonth()	Returns true if this object represents a date/time that falls within the current month, in the context of this object's time zone representation.
year()	Returns the calendar year of the object.
lessThan(t)	Compares this DateTime object to another DateTime object or a floating-point number such as that's returned by the Python time module. Returns true if the object represents a date/time less than the specified DateTime or time module-style time.
Time()	Returns the time string for an object to the nearest second.
pDay()	Returns the abbreviated (with period) name of the day of the week.

Table A-4 describes all the built-in methods that DateTime supports.

Table A-4. Python Built-In Methods for DateTime *Objects*

Method	Description
`aDateTime`	Converts a DateTime to a string that looks like a Python expression
str(aDateTime)	Converts a DateTime to a string
cmp(aDateTime, other)	Compares a DateTime with another DateTime object or a float such as those returned by time.time()
hash(aDateTime)	Computes a hash value for a DateTime object

Table A-5 describes the generic services that DateTime supports.

Table A-5. Generic DateTime *Functions*

Method	Description
aDateTime + other	A DateTime may be added to a number, and a number may be added to a DateTime; two DateTime objects can't be added.
aDateTime - other	Either a DateTime or a number may be subtracted from a DateTime; however, a DateTime may not be subtracted from a number.
other + aDateTime	Add aDateTime to other. A DateTime may be added to a number, and a number may be added to a DateTime; two DateTimes can't be added.
int(aDateTime)	Converts to an integer number of days since Jan. 1, 1901 (GMT).
long(aDateTime)	Converts to a long int number of days since Jan. 1, 1901 (GMT).
float(aDateTime)	Converts to floating-point number of days since Jan. 1, 1901 (GMT).

Writing Workflows in Python

This section covers the API for writing a workflow in Python so that you don't need to develop through the Web. The following sections contain an abbreviated list of the methods you'll need to create a workflow. For an exhaustive list, you'll need to read the source, available in the Products/DCWorkflow directory of your Plone instance.

Writing a workflow stars by creating a definition. This is importable from here:

```
from Products.DCWorkflow.DCWorkflow import DCWorkflowDefinition
```

Create a new instance of this definition and give it an ID:

```
wf = DCWorkflowDefinition(id)
```

You now have a workflow you can start manipulating. In the following, wf is the workflow definition I just created.

States

The following are the methods for states:

- **addState(Id)**: This adds a state of a given ID. You must add states prior to being able to manipulate them.

- **setInitialState(Id)**: This sets the initial state for this workflow.

- **setProperties([key=value,...])**: This is a series of key/value pairs that map to properties for a state. For example, to set the transitions to be new and reject, use setProperties(transitions=('publish', 'reject')).

- **setPermission(permission name, acquire, (role, [role...]))**: This is the permission name, if acquire is enabled or not (a boolean value) and then a tuple of all the roles to which this applies.

To access these methods, use the states object inside the workflow object. For example, use wf.states.addState('new').

Transitions

The following are the methods for transitions:

- **addTransition(id)**: This adds a state of a given ID. You must add transitions prior to being able to manipulate them.

- **setProperties([key=value,...])**: This is a series of key/value pairs that map to properties for a state.

To access these methods, use the transitions object inside the workflow object. For example, use wf.transitions.addTransition('reject').

Variables

The following are the methods for variables:

- **addVariable(id)**: This adds a variable of a given ID. You must add variables prior to being able to manipulate them.

- **setStateVar(id)**: This sets the state variable name, which is usually `review_state`.

- **setProperties([key=value,...])**: This is a series of key/value pairs that map to properties for a variable.

To access these methods, use the variables object inside the workflow object. For example, use `wf.transitions.addVariable('action')`.

Others

Worklists perform in the same manner as the transitions, variables, and states. To add a worklist, call `addWorklist`. One other useful method is to add permissions to the list of managed permissions for the workflow. The `addManagedPermission(permission name)` method achieves this.

APPENDIX B

Code Listings

THIS APPENDIX LISTS the code used in the rest of the book. Some of these scripts that are run externally require that you have the Zope/lib/python directory in your Python path, as described in Appendix A. All these scripts are described in detail in the book.

Chapter 5

The following are the code listings for Chapter 5.

Page Template: test_context

Listing B-1 shows all the variables that are available in page templates. It's useful to show information for debugging.

Listing B-1. test_context

```html
<html>
  <head />
  <body>
    <h1>Debug information</h1>
  <h2>CONTEXTS</h2>
  <ul>
    <tal:block
        tal:repeat="item CONTEXTS">
    <li
        tal:condition="python: item != 'request'"
        tal:define="context CONTEXTS;">
            <b tal:content="item" />
            <span tal:replace="python: context[item]" />
    </li>
    </tal:block>
  </ul>
  <h2>REQUEST</h2>
  <p tal:replace="structure request" />
  </body>
</html>
```

Page Template: user_info (1)

user_info (1) is a crude page template that isn't in the Plone style and that shows user information, as shown in Listing B-2. To user this template, you'll have to pass the user ID you want to examine in the query string. For example, use user_info?userName=andy.

Listing B-2. user_info (1)

```
<html>

<body>
<div
  tal:omit-tag=""
  tal:define="
    userName request/userName|nothing;
    userObj python: here.portal_membership.getMemberById(userName);
    getPortrait nocall: here/portal_membership/getPersonalPortrait;
    getFolder nocall: here/portal_membership/getHomeFolder
  ">
    <p tal:condition="not: userName">
       No username selected.
    </p>
    <p tal:condition="not: userObj">
      That username does not exist.
    </p>

    <table tal:condition="userObj">
      <tr>
        <td>
          <img src=""
            tal:replace="structure python: getPortrait(userName)" />
        </td>
        <td>
          <ul>
          <li>
            <i>Username:</i>
            <span tal:replace="userName" />
          </li>
          <li>
            <i>Full name:</i>
            <span tal:replace="userObj/fullname" />
          </li>
```

```
    <li
      tal:define="home python: getFolder(userName)"
      tal:condition="home">
      <i>Home folder:</i>
      <a href=""
        tal:attributes="href home/absolute_url"
        tal:content="home/absolute_url">Folder</a>
    </li>
    <li>
      <i>Email:</i>
      <a href=""
        tal:define="email userObj/email"
        tal:attributes="href string:mailto:$email"
        tal:content="email">Email</a>
    </li>
    <li>
      <i>Last login time:</i>
      <span tal:replace="userObj/last_login_time" />
    </li>
  </ul>
 </td>
</tr>
</table>

</div>
</body>
</html>
```

Chapter 6

The following are the code listings for Chapter 6.

Page Template: user_info (2)

Listing B-3 shows a refined version of the user info page template from Chapter 5. You don't need to pass the userName because it's just going to loop through every member in the site for you.

Listing B-3. user_info (1)

```
<html xmlns="http://www.w3.org/1999/xhtml" xml:lang="en-US"
      lang="en-US"
      i18n:domain="plone"
      metal:use-macro="here/main_template/macros/master">

<body>
<div metal:fill-slot="main">
  <tal:block
    tal:define="
      getPortrait nocall: here/portal_membership/getPersonalPortrait;
      getFolder nocall: here/portal_membership/getHomeFolder
      ">
    <table>
     <tal:block
      tal:repeat="userObj here/portal_membership/listMembers">
       <metal:block
         metal:use-macro="here/user_section/macros/userSection" />
     </tal:block>
    </table>
  </tal:block>
</div>
</body>
</html>
```

Page Template: user_section

Listing B-4 shows a page template macro that accompanies the user_info page template previously and shows the individual users information for each invocation.

Listing B-4. user_section

```
<div metal:define-macro="userSection"
 tal:define="userName userObj/getUserName">
 <tr>
   <td>
     <img src=""
       tal:replace="structure python: getPortrait(userName)" />
   </td>
```

```
    <td tal:define="prop nocall: userObj/getProperty">
      <ul>
        <li>
          <i>Username:</i>
          <span tal:replace="userName" />
        </li>
        <li>
          <i>Full name:</i>
          <span tal:replace="python: prop('fullname')" />
        </li>
        <li
          tal:define="home python: getFolder(userName)"
          tal:condition="home">
          <a href=""
          tal:attributes="href home/absolute_url">Home Folder</a>
        </li>
        <li>
          <i>Email:</i>
          <a href=""
            tal:define="email python: prop('email')"
            tal:attributes="href string:mailto:$email"
            tal:content="email">Email</a>
        </li>
        <li>
          <i>Last login time:</i>
            <span tal:replace="python: prop('last_login_time')" />
        </li>
      </ul>
    </td>
  </tr>
</div>
```

Script (Python): google_ad_portlet

Listing B-5 shows a page template that provides Google ads in a slot.

Listing B-5. google_ad_portlet

```
<div metal:define-macro="portlet">
    <div class="portlet">
<script type="text/javascript"><!--
google_ad_client = "yourUniqueValue";
google_ad_width = 120;
google_ad_height = 600;
google_ad_format = "120x600_as";
//--></script>
<script type="text/javascript"
  src="http://pagead2.googlesyndication.com/pagead/show_ads.js">
</script>
    </div>
</div>
```

Script (Python): recentlyChanged

Listing B-6 shows a script that examines all objects passed to the script and then finds out what's new. The objects need to be passed in using the object's parameter.

Listing B-6. google_ad_portlet

```
##title=recentlyChanged
##parameters=objects
from DateTime import DateTime

now = DateTime()
difference = 5 # as in 5 days
result = []

for object in objects:
  diff = now - object.bobobase_modification_time()
  if diff < difference:
    dct = {"object":object,"diff":int(diff)}
    result.append(dct)

return result
```

External Method: readFile

Listing B-7 shows a sample external method that reads a file.

Listing B-7. `readFile`

```python
def readFile(self):
    fh = open(r'c:\Program Files\Plone\Data\Extensions\README.txt', 'rb')
    data = fh.read()
    return data
```

Python Script: zpt.py

Listing B-8 shows a script totally external to and independent of Plone that will syntax check a page template. This is useful for when you're debugging page templates written outside of Plone.

Listing B-8. `zpt.py`

```python
#!/usr/bin/python
from Products.PageTemplates.PageTemplate import PageTemplate
import sys

def test(file):
    raw_data = open(file, 'r').read()
    pt = PageTemplate()
    pt.write(raw_data)
    if pt._v_errors:
        print "*** Error in:", file
        for error in pt._v_errors[1:]:
            print error

if __name__=='__main__':
    if len(sys.argv) < 2:
        print "python check.py file [files...]"
        sys.exit(1)
    else:
        for arg in sys.argv[1:]:
            test(arg)
```

Page Template: feedbackForm

Listing B-9 shows the form for users to enter feedback.

Listing B-9. feedbackForm

```
<html xmlns="http://www.w3.org/1999/xhtml" xml:lang="en-US"
lang="en-US" i18n:domain="plone"
metal:use-macro="here/main_template/macros/master">
  <body>
    <div metal:fill-slot="main"
    tal:define="errors options/state/getErrors;">
      <p>Please send us any feedback you might have about the
      site.</p>
      <form method="post" tal:attributes="action template/id;">
        <fieldset>
          <legend class="legend"
          i18n:translate="legend_feedback_form">Website
          Feedback</legend>
          <div class="field"
      tal:define="error_email_address errors/email_address|nothing;"
          tal:attributes="class python:test(error_email_address,
          'field error',
          'field')">

            <label i18n:translate="label_email_address">Your email
            address</label>
            <span class="fieldRequired" title="Required"
            i18n:attributes="title"
            i18n:translate="label_required">(Required)</span>
            <div class="formHelp"
            i18n:translate="label_email_address_help">Enter your
            email address.</div>
            <div tal:condition="error_email_address">
              <tal:block i18n:translate=""
              content="error_email_address">Error</tal:block>
            </div>
            <input type="text" name="email_address"
            tal:attributes="tabindex tabindex/next;
            value request/email_address|nothing" />
          </div>
```

```
        <div class="field">
          <label i18n:translate="label_feedback_comments">
          Comments</label>
          <div class="formHelp" id="label_feedback_comments_help"
          i18n:translate="label_feedback_comments_help">Enter the
          comments you have about the site.</div>
          <textarea name="comments" rows="10"
          tal:content="request/comments|nothing"
          tal:attributes="tabindex tabindex/next;" />
        </div>
        <div class="formControls">
          <input class="context" type="submit" tabindex=""
          name="form.button.Submit" value="Submit"
          i18n:attributes="value"
          tal:attributes="tabindex tabindex/next;" />
        </div>
      </fieldset>
      <input type="hidden" name="form.submitted" value="1" />
    </form>
  </div>
 </body>
</html>
```

Controller Python Script: sendEmail

Listing B-10 shows the controlled script to actually send the e-mail to the user.

Listing B-10. sendEmail

```
mhost = context.MailHost
emailAddress = context.REQUEST.get('email_address')
administratorEmailAddress = context.email_from_address
comments = context.REQUEST.get('comments')

# the message format, %s will be filled in from data
message = """
From: %s
To: %s
Subject: Website Feedback
```

```
%s

URL: %s
"""

# format the message
message = message % (
    emailAddress,
    administratorEmailAddress,
    comments,
    context.absolute_url())

mhost.send(message)

screenMsg = "Comments sent, thank you."
state.setKwargs( {'portal_status_message':screenMsg} )
return state
```

Controller Python Script: validEmail

Listing B-11 shows the script to validate the e-mail.

Listing B-11. validEmail

```
email = context.REQUEST.get('email_address', None)

if not email:
    state.setError("email_address',
    'An email address is required',
    new_status='failure')

if state.getErrors():
    state.set(portal_status_message='Please correct the errors shown.')

return state
```

Chapter 7

The following are the code listings for Chapter 7.

Script (Python): setSkin

If assigned as an access rule in your Plone site, the script in Listing B-12 will change all requests to internal.somesite.org to use the skin Plone Default. If not, the Custom Chrome skin will be used.

Listing B-12. setSkin

```
##title=Skin changing script
##parameters=
req = context.REQUEST
if req['SERVER_URL'].find('internal.somesite.org') > -1:
    context.changeSkin("Plone Default")
context.changeSkin("Custom Chrome")
```

CSS: ploneCustom.css

Listing B-13 shows the Cascading Style Sheet that powers the NASA Mars site.

Listing B-13. ploneCustom.css

```
body {
    background: #343434;
}

#visual-portal-wrapper {
    width: 680px;
    margin: 1em auto 0 auto;
}

#portal-top {
    background: url("http://mars.telascience.org/header.jpg") ➡
transparent no-repeat;
    padding: 162px 0 0 0;
    position: relative;
}
```

```
#portal-logo {
    background: transparent;
    background-image: none;
    margin: 0;
    position: absolute;
    top: 130px;
    left: 5px;
    z-index: 20;
}

#portal-logo a {
    padding-top: 25px;
    height /**/: 25px;
    width: 375px;
}

#portal-globalnav {
   background: url("http://mars.telascience.org/listspacer.gif") ➥
transparent;
    padding: 0;
    height: 21px;
    border: 0;
    margin: 0 0 1px 6px;
    clear: both;
}

#portal-globalnav li {
    display: block;
    float: left;
    height: 21px;
    background: url("http://mars.telascience.org/liststart.gif") ➥
transparent no-repeat;
    padding: 0 0 0 33px;
    margin: 0 0.5em 0 0;
}

#portal-globalnav li a {
    display: block;
    float: left;
    height: 21px;
    background: url("http://mars.telascience.org/listitem.gif") ➥
```

```
transparent right top;
    padding: 0 33px 0 0;
    border: 0;
    line-height: 2em;
    color: black;
    font-size: 90%;
    margin: 0;
}

#portal-globalnav li a:hover,
#portal-globalnav li.selected a {
    background-color: transparent;
    border: 0;
    color: #444;
}

#portal-personaltools {
    clear: both;
    margin-left: 6px;
    border-top-color: #776a44;
    border-top-style: solid;
    border-top-width: 1px;
}

#portal-breadcrumbs {
    clear: both;
}

#portal-breadcrumbs,
#portal-columns,
.documentContent {
    background: white;
    margin-left: 6px;
}

.documentContent {
    margin: 0;
    font-size: 100%;
}

.screenshotThumb {
  float:right;
}
```

```
#portal-footer {
    margin: -1px 0 0 6px;
    padding: 0.8em 0;
    border: 1px solid #ddd;
    border-style: solid none none none;
    background: white;
    color: #666;
    font-size: 90%;
}

#portal-footer a {
    color: #333;
    text-decoration: underline;
}

dt {
    color: #ECA200;
}

.documentDescription {
    font-size: 110%;
}

#portal-breadcrumbs img {
    display: none;
}

li.reqlist {
    margin-top: 0;
    margin-bottom: 0;
}
```

Chapter 8

The following are the code listings for Chapter 8.

Script (Python): mail.py

Listing B-14 shows a script to send mail to users whenever the object changes in the workflow.

Listing B-14. `mail.py`

```
##parameters=state_change
# the objects we need
object = state_change.object
mship = context.portal_membership
mhost = context.MailHost

# the message format, %s will be filled in from data
message = """
From: noreply@yourwebsite.com
To: %s
Subject: New item submitted for approval - %s

%s

URL: %s
"""
for user in mship.listMembers():
    if "Reviewer" in mship.getMemberById(user.id).getRoles():
        if user.email:
            msg = message % (
                user.email,
                object.TitleOrId(),
                object.Description(),
                object.absolute_url()
                )
            mhost.send(msg)
```

Chapter 9

The following are the code listings for Chapter 9.

External Method: importUsers

Listing B-15 shows an external method to import users from a `.csv` file on the file system.

Listing B-15. importUsers

```
# An external method to import user
import csv

# the full path to your csv file
fileName = "/var/zope.zeo/Extensions/test.csv"

def importUsers(self):
    reader = csv.reader(open(fileName, "r"))
    pr = self.portal_registration
    pg = self.portal_groups
    out = []

    # if your csv file contains a header line that
    # explains the contents of each column
    ignoreLine = 1
    for row in reader:
        if ignoreLine:
            ignoreLine = 0
            continue

        # check we have exactly 4 items
        assert len(row) == 4
        id, name, email, groups = row
        groups = groups.split(',')

        # make a password
        password = pr.generatePassword()
        try:
            # add in member
            pr.addMember(id = id,
                password = password,
                roles = ["Member",],
                properties = {
                    'fullname': name,
                    'username': id,
                    'email': email,
                    }
                )
```

```
        # groups are separated by commas
        for groupId in :
            group = pg.getGroupById(groupId)
            group.addMember(id)

        out.append("Added user %s" % id)

    except ValueError, msg:
        # if we skipped this user for a reason, tell the person
        out.append("Skipped %s, reason: %s" % (id, msg))


# return something
return "\n".join(out)
```

External Method: fixUsers

Listing B-16 shows a script that sets the properties for all users to Epoz.

Listing B-16. fixUsers

```
def fixUsers(self):
    pm = self.portal_membership
    members = pm.listMemberIds()

    out = []
    for member in members:
        # now get the actual member
        m = pm.getMemberById(member)
        # get the editor property for that member
        p = m.getProperty('wysiwyg_editor', None)

        out.append("%s %s" % (p, member))
        if p is not None and p != 'Epoz':
            m.setMemberProperties({'wysiwyg_editor', 'Epoz',})
            out.append("Changed property for %s" % member)
    return "\n".join(out)
```

External Method: getGroups

Listing B-17 shows a script that first gets the creator of the object. Then it gets all the users in same group as that creator.

Listing B-17. getGroups

```
##parameters=object=None
# object is the object to find all the members of the same group for
users = []
# get the creator
userName = object.Creator()
user = context.portal_membership.getMemberById(userName)
pg = context.portal_groups

# loop through the groups the user is in
for group in user.getGroups():
  group = getGroupById(group)

  # loop through the users in each of those groups
  for user in group.getGroupUsers():
    if user not in users and user != userName:
      users.append(user)

return users
```

Chapter 11

The following are the code listings for Chapter 11.

Script (Python): scriptObjectCreation

Listing B-18 shows a script to create a folder and then a document inside it.

Listing B-18. scriptObjectCreation

```
##title=Create
##parameters=
# create with a random id
newId = context.generateUniqueId('Folder')

# create a object of type Folder
context.invokeFactory(id=newId, type_name='Folder')
newFolder = getattr(context, newId)

# create a new Document type
newFolder.invokeFactory(id='index.html', type_name='Document')
```

```
# get the new page
newPage = getattr(newFolder, 'index.html')
newPage.edit('html', '<p>This is the default page.</p>')

# return something back to the calling script
return "Done"
```

Page Template: *getCatalogResults*

Listing B-19 shows a sample catalog query that takes the REQUEST parameters and runs a query on them.

Listing B-19. getCatalogResults

```
##title=Get Catalog Results
##parameters=
return context.portal_catalog.searchResults(REQUEST=context.REQUEST)
```

Page Template: *testResults*

Listing B-20 shows a sample results from a catalog query.

Listing B-20. testResults

```
<html xmlns="http://www.w3.org/1999/xhtml" xml:lang="en-US"
      lang="en-US"
      metal:use-macro="here/main_template/macros/master"
      i18n:domain="plone">
<body>
<div metal:fill-slot="main">
<ul tal:define="results here/getCatalogResults">
    <li tal:repeat="result results">
        <a href=""
           tal:attributes="href result/getURL"
           tal:content="result/Title" />
        <span tal:replace="result/Description" />
    </li>
</ul>
</div>
</body>
</html>
```

Page Template: testForm

Listing B-21 shows a sample form to call the testResults page with a drop-down list based on a catalog query.

Listing B-21. testForm

```
<html xmlns="http://www.w3.org/1999/xhtml" xml:lang="en-US"
      lang="en-US"
      metal:use-macro="here/main_template/macros/master"
      i18n:domain="plone">
<body>
<div metal:fill-slot="main">
    <p>Select a content type to search for</p>
    <form method="post" action="testResults">
        <select name="Type">
            <option
  tal:repeat="value python:here.portal_catalog.uniqueValuesFor('Type')"
  tal:content="value" />
        </select>
        <br />
        <input type="submit" class="context">
    </form>
</div>
</body>
</html>
```

Chapter 12

The following relate to Chapter 12.

Example Product: PloneSilverCity

You can find this product in the Collective at http://sf.net/projects/collective.
You can also download this product from the Plone book Web site at
http://plone-book.agmweb.ca.

Example Product: PloneStats

You can find this product in the Collective at http://sf.net/projects/collective. You can also download this product from the Plone book Web site at http://plone-book.agmweb.ca.

Chapter 13

The following relate to Chapter 13.

Example Product: ArchExample

This product is in the Archetypes release, and you can download a copy from the Plone book Web site at http://plone-book.agmweb.ca.

Page Template: email_widget.py

Listing B-22 shows an example custom widget for Archetypes.

Listing B-22. email_widget.py

```
<html xmlns:tal="http://xml.zope.org/namespaces/tal"
      xmlns:metal="http://xml.zope.org/namespaces/metal"
      i18n:domain="plone">

  <body>
    <div metal:define-macro="edit">
      <div metal:use-macro="here/widgets/string/macros/edit" />
    </div>

    <div metal:define-macro="search">
      <div metal:use-macro="here/widgets/string/macros/search" />
    </div>

     <div class="field" metal:define-macro="view">
     <a href="#" tal:attributes="href string:mailto:${accessor}"
        tal:content="accessor">email</a>
     </div>

  </body>
</html>
```

Example Product: WordExample

You can download the product listing for WordExample from the Plone book Web site at http://plone-book.agmweb.ca.

Python Module: PersonSQL.py

Listing B-23 shows an Archetypes content type for a person who stores the data in a relational database.

Listing B-23. PersonSQL.py

```
from Products.Archetypes.public import Schema
from Products.Archetypes.public import IntegerField, StringField
from Products.Archetypes.public import IntegerWidget, StringField
from Products.Archetypes.SQLStorage import PostgreSQLStorage
from config import PROJECTNAME

schema = BaseSchema + Schema((

  IntegerField('age',
      validators=("isInt",),
      storage = SQLStorage(),
      widget=IntegerWidget(label="Your age"),

      ),

  StringField('email',
      validators = ('isEmail',),
      index = "TextIndex",
      storage = SQLStorage(),
      widget = StringWidget(label='Email',)
      ),

  ))

class PersonSQL(BaseContent):
    """Our person object"""
    schema = schema

registerType(PersonSQL, PROJECTNAME)
```

Chapter 14

The following are the code listings for Chapter 14.

Python Module: header.py

Listing B-24 shows a script that'll print the headers for a URL.

Listing B-24. header.py

```python
#!/usr/bin/python
import sys

from httplib import HTTP
from urlparse import urlparse

def getHeaders(url, method):
    p = list(urlparse(url))
    if not p[0]:
        url = 'http://' + url
        p = list(urlparse(url))

    h = HTTP(p[1])

    h.putrequest(method, p[2])
    h.putheader('Accept-Encoding', 'gzip, deflate')
    h.endheaders()

    reply = h.getreply()
    print "Status:", reply[0]
    print "Status message:", reply[1]
    hdrs = reply[2].headers
    hdrs.sort()
    for header in hdrs:
        print header[:-1]

def usage():
    print """Usage: headers.py URL [method]

URL - the URL to get headers for, http:// default
method - GET default
"""
    sys.exit()
```

```
if __name__=='__main__':
    if len(sys.argv) < 2: usage()
    method = 'GET'
    if len(sys.argv) > 2:
        method = sys.argv[2]
    getHeaders(sys.argv[1], method)
```

Script (Python): myCachingRules

Listing B-25 provides a custom caching rule for a policy manager, just to give you more options.

Listing B-25. myCachingRules

```
##parameters=content
# cache all files, images and anything
# that is published
if content.portal_type in ['File', 'Image']:
    return 1
if content.review_state == ['published',]:
    return 1
```

External Method: Purge Cache

Listing B-26 shows an example script to purge a cache.

Listing B-26. Purge Cache

```
import urllib
import urlparse
import httplib

URLs = [
    # enter the URLs you would like
    # to purge here
    'http://localhost:8080',
]
```

```
def purge(objectURL):
    for url in URLs:
        if not url:
            continue
        assert url[:4] == 'http', "No protocol specified"

        url = urlparse.urljoin(url, objectURL)
        parsed = urlparse.urlparse(url)
        host = parsed[1]
        path = parsed[2]

        h = httplib.HTTP(host)
        h.putrequest('PURGE', path)
        h.endheaders()
        errcode, errmsg, headers = h.getreply()
        h.getfile.read()

if __name__ == '__main__':
    print purge('/')
```

APPENDIX C

Glossary and Tools

THIS APPENDIX DESCRIBES all the default tools, objects that are created in a Plone site, and references to their location in the book. The glossary provides a list of all the terms used in this book and Plone.

Tools

Table C-1 describes the default tools that Plone creates.

Table C-1. Plone Tools

Tool Name	Description
caching_policy_manager	Handles caching for content; see Chapter 14.
content_type_registry	Provides different ways of processing new content; see Chapter 11.
plone_utils	General utility functions that aren't usually accessed.
portal_actionicons	Associates an image to an action.
portal_actions	The core action provider.
portal_calendar	Provides the calendar slot and isn't used beyond that; see Chapter 4 for information about the calendar slot.
portal_catalog	Catalog tool for providing indexes content; see Chapter 11.
portal_controlpanel	Provides an interface to the actions visible in Plone control panels.
portal_discussion	Handles discussions of content; see Chapter 4.
portal_factory	Ensures the default creation of content doesn't leave partially created objects in the database; see Chapter 12.

Table C-1. Plone Tools (Continued)

Tool Name	Description
`portal_form`	Deprecated, maintained for backward compatability.
`portal_form_controller`	Provides form handling services; see Chapter 7.
`portal_groupdata`	Stores information about the groups; see Chapter 9.
`portal_groups`	Handles group creation; see Chapter 9.
`portal_interface`	This provides an Application Programming Interface (API) for developers to examine object interfaces.
`portal_memberdata`	Stores information about the users; see Chapter 9.
`portal_membership`	Handles user membership options; see Chapter 10.
`portal_metadata`	Metadata about portal content types. This isn't used much.
`portal_migration`	Handles the migration to new versions of Plone; see Chapter 14.
`portal_navigation`	Deprecated but is maintained for backward compatibility.
`portal_properties`	Properties and values for the site; see Chapter 4.
`portal_quickinstaller`	A utility for quickly installing products; see Chapter 10.
`portal_registration`	Handles options for registering users; see Chapter 9.
`portal_skins`	Provides skinning services and contains all the skins; see Chapters 4–7 for more information.
`portal_syndication`	Access to RSS feeds for Plone content. (RSS stands for Rich Site Summary or Really Simply Syndication.)
`portal_types`	Main tool for handling content types within a portal; see Chapters 11–13.
`portal_undo`	Provides access to Plone's undo mechanisms.
`portal_url`	Access to useful APIs for determining Uniform Resource Locators (URLs).
`portal_workflow`	Handles and provides workflow capabilities; see Chapter 7.

Default Objects

Table C-2 describes the default objects that Plone creates inside a Plone site.

Table C-2. Plone Objects

Object	Description
HTTPCache	Provides HTTP headers for skins; see Chapter 14.
MailHost	Simple Mail Transfer Protocol (SMTP) server access for sending e-mail.
Members	A large folder where site members folders are created; see Chapter 9.
RAMCache	Provides Random Access Memory (RAM) caching for skins; see Chapter 14.
acl_users	The main user folde; see Chapter 9.
cookie_authentication	Provides authentication of users via cookies; see Chapter 9.
error_log	The log of errors that have occurred in the system; see Chapter 4.
index_html	The default index_html that appears in the site; see Chapter 6.

Glossary

Table C-3 defines all the useful terms in the Plone world.

Table C-3. Plone Definitions

Object	Description
Action	In Plone terminology, *actions* are a configurable way of providing navigational elements in a site. Some examples are view, edit, and members. See Chapter 5 for more details.
Acquisition	*Acquisition* is a Zope mechanism for inheriting object properties. Zope object hierarchy is built using acquisition and makes heavy use of it.

Table C-3. Plone Definitions (Continued)

Object	Description
Anonymous role	This is a standard role in the Zope security architecture. The anonymous role is assigned to site visitors until they log in using their Zope ID/password.
Archetypes	This is a framework for the development of new content types in Zope/CMF/Plone; see Chapter 13.
Authenticated user	An authenticated user is a user who is logged into the Zope system. If no user is currently logged in, anonymous users are considered the authenticated user.
Authentication	This is the identification process used by Zope.
Base class	A *base class*, or *top class*, is a class that passes its methods, properties, and so on, to its subclasses. The subclasses inherit the properties and methods of their base class.
Calendar	The portal_calendar allows for a mechanism to administer what content is shown in calendar.
Catalog	The *catalog* is an internal index of the content inside Plone so that it can be searched. The catalog object is accessible through the ZMI as the portal_catalog object; see Chapter 11.
CSS	*Cascading Style Sheets* are a system in Hypertext Markup Language (HTML) to allow styles to be specified for elements. Plone uses a great deal of CSS; for some examples, see Chapter 7.
Class	A *class* is the mold from which objects are stamped out. Objects are instances of a class. You can think of a class as a blueprint for an object.
Class constructor method	A *constructor method* for a class is a method that allows execution of certain actions as soon as a class instance is created and before it's started to be used. For example, setting the standard attributes would be done in a constructor method.
CMF	The *Content Management Framework* (CMF) is a Zope addition to provide services that a content management system needs.
CMFTypes	This is the old name for Archetypes.
CMS	A *Content Management System* (CMS) is a system to, well, manage content.

Table C-3. Plone Definitions (Continued)

Object	Description
Content	In the CMF worldview, everything is *content*. This applies to traditional things such as Hypertext Markup Language (HTML) pages. But it also applies to dynamic information such as posts in a threaded discussion or calendar events. It also means that images, downloadable executables, logic in scripts, and so on, are also content.
Content Type	*Content type* is the type of content allowed in a CMF/Plone instance. Plone comes with stock content types, but you can create your own content types specific to your needs and plug them into your Plone instance.
Cookie authentication	`cookie_authentication` (also known as `CookieCrumbler`) allows form-based login; see Chapter 9.
DTML	*Document Template Markup Language* (DTML) is a server-side templating language used to produce dynamic pieces of content. It's primarily used in conjunction with HTML. It's hardly used in Plone and generally is considered deprecated; see page templates.
Discussions	The `portal_discussion` tool holds the policy regarding how the discussions work in a Plone system.
ECMAscript	This is essentially JavaScript.
External method	*External methods* are essentially Python modules sitting on the file systems linked into Zope via the external method object that you can create from the drop-down list. External methods are more powerful than Script (Python) objects because they aren't subjected to the Zope security architecture as rigorously as the Script (Python) objects may be.
Factory	A *factory* is a tool for creating other objects.
Folderish object	A *folderish* object in Zope is an object that can contain other objects. The `Folder` and Plone `Folder` objects are examples of folderish objects.
Factory Type Information (FTI)	*Factory type information* contains the information to be loaded into the `portal_types` tool.
GPL	This includes the terms under which Plone is licensed.
Globbing (ZCatalog)	*Globbing* allows you to search the ZCatalog using wildcards (*). Globbing also enables partial word searches in that ZCatalog.

Table C-3. *Plone Definitions (Continued)*

Object	Description
HTML	*Hypertext Markup Language* is the basic mark up language for the Web. This book assumes you know what HTML is.
Instance	Objects are also called *instances*. An instance or object is an instance of a given class.
i18n	*Internationalization* is preparing a program so that it can be used in multiple languages without further altering the source. The term *i18n* is formed by the first and last letter of the word and the number of letters in between.
JavaScript	This is the language that's shipped with Web browsers that allow them to make Web pages dynamic. A good example of JavaScript is in the green drop-down menu for adding items.
Keywords	In the Properties tab of content, you can assign *keywords* (also known as *subject* in metadata terminology). This is a mechanism that allows you to relate content to each other. Keywords can be predefined in the `portal_metadata` tool.
Layer	A *skin* in Plone is an enumerated collection of *layers*. Layers aren't currently circumscribed in what they can do. They can change visual aspects of a Plone site, they can surface new content types in a more or less presentation-neutral way, or they can change/override the behavior specified in other skins.
Local role	*Local roles* are assigned to a particular Zope user with respect to a given Zope object. A local role determines that users' permissions for that object. A local role may be used to restrict a users' permissions for a given object. You can also use a local role to give users—who may have limited global rights—expanded rights for a small subsets of objects.
Login	This is the process you go through when you enter your username and password on the login screen. This is the same as authentication.
l10n	*Localization* is the actual preparing of data for a particular language. For example, Plone is i18n aware and has localization for several languages. The term *l10n* is formed by the first and last letter of the word and the number of letters in between.
Manager	This is a standard role in Zope.

Table C-3. Plone Definitions (Continued)

Object	Description
Metatype	This is a unique string for each Zope product in the Available Objects menu in the Zope Management Interface (ZMI). Product instances are created using this metatype. Each product has a unique metatype.
Metadata	Information about content, see http://www.dublincore.org.
METAL	Macro Expansion Template Attribute Language.
Memberdata	In Plone, portal_memberdata stores the attributes of users.
Migration	*Migration* is the mostly automated process through which you upgrade your Plone instance to a new release level.
Namespace	A *namespace* contains the names of all valid variables of a given class instance (an object) in a specific scope.
Nonfolderish objects	These are objects that can't contain other Zope or Plone objects. For example, these can be documents or files.
Object	An *object* is an instance of a class.
Object DataBase (ODB)	This is a system that stores a heirarchy of instances. The ZODB is an example of an object database. You can't query object databases like you can their relational counterparts.
Owner role	This is the owner standard Zope role.
Ownership (of objects)	Users who create objects in Zope are given *ownerships* of those objects. Every object in Zope has an owner except perhaps the ones created by the Zope Install process.
OOTB	Plone is an example of an *out-of-the-box* (OOTB) Web application.
Permissions	*Permissions* tell you what actions a user can take while in Zope. Permissions can be applied only to roles. You *can't* give permissions directly to individual users.
Portal actions	*Portal actions* affect the whole site, as opposed to the content types actions, which are more localized.
Properties	Essentially these are the attributes of any given object. You can see a Zope object's properties by clicking the Properties tab in the ZMI when you're viewing that particular object. Properties are also used on objects in the Plone interface to describe properties an object may have, such as keywords.
Plone	"If you don't know by now...."

Table C-3. Plone Definitions (Continued)

Object	Description
Portal type	*Portal type* is a unique string for each content type in Plone. In Plone each content type will have a unique string to identify it (although they may be based on the same metatype).
Portlets	*Portlets* are the little sections on a Plone site that manifest themselves as little boxes on the left and right side of a Plone instance.
Python	*Python* is an object-oriented high-level scripting language. Zope is written in Python.
QuantumLeap	When viewing large result sets in Plone, you'll notice they're presented in pages. You can leap to any of these pages, and the navigation will display nearby pages. This mechanism is affectionately known as *QuantumLeap(ing)*.
Registration	More specifically, portal_registration controls the sitewide policy for how users register with the system.
Request	Each page view by a client generates a request to Plone. This incoming request is encapsulated in a request object in Zope, usually called REQUEST or *request*.
Response	For each request a response is generated. This outgoing request from Zope is encapsulated in a response object, usually called RESPONSE or *response*.
Repurposing	Content types can be based on another content types' FTI, which is called *repurposing*. You can then specify unique metadata attributes for new content type such as id, title, and description.
Services	The goal of the CMF is to unify the management of content and apply a suite of services. These services include cataloging, workflow, and syndication. CMF and Plone provide many services to your site. There are publicly available services such as search and discussion and management services such as workflow.
Skin	Think of *skins* as the look and feel of a Plone experience. A skin contains the HTML, CSS, JavaScript, images, and all the interactions between the user and the Plone. You can apply different skins to the same content, meaning a content can be viewed in many different ways. Some skins provide extra features and pages.

Table C-3. Plone Definitions (Continued)

Object	Description
Syndication	*Syndication* is the process by which a site is able to share information with other sites. Content syndication in the CMF allows you to make content available to other sites. The syndication tool allows site managers to control sitewide syndication of content. Syndicated content is made available in RSS format for folders where syndication has been enabled.
TAL	*Tag Attribute Language* (TAL) is a method for dynamically marking up HTML.
TALES	*TAL Expression Syntax* (TALES) is a syntax for extending TAL.
Tool	A *tool* is an instance of a class inside the Plone site. However, unlike other objects, there can only ever be one instance of a particular tool inside a Plone site at any one time. Some tools, such as portal_catalog, give administration options for the site manager.
UI (User Interface)	The *User Interface* (UI) consists of the screens and way in which you interact with a software program.
View	A presentation *view* displays information in a predefined structure. The actions in portal_types, for instance, are views.
Workflow	This is a method for encapsulating business logic in a separate module; see Chapter 8.
XML	*Extensible Markup Language* (XML) is a standard for data interchange.
Zope	*Zope* is an open-source Web application server written in Python. Plone uses Zope.
ZMI	The *Zope Management Interface* (ZMI) generally refers to the Web interface used for Zope Management and Administration. (When you log in using http://your.zope.site:8080/manage, note the manage at the end.)
ZPT	*Zope Page Templates* (ZPT) is the system for creating dynamic pages using TAL.
ZPL	The *Zope Public License* (ZPL) includes the terms under which Zope is licensed.

Index

T

U

V

forums.apress.com

FOR PROFESSIONALS BY PROFESSIONALS™

JOIN THE APRESS FORUMS AND BE PART OF OUR COMMUNITY. You'll find discussions that cover topics of interest to IT professionals, programmers, and enthusiasts just like you. If you post a query to one of our forums, you can expect that some of the best minds in the business—especially Apress authors, who all write with *The Expert's Voice*™—will chime in to help you. Why not aim to become one of our most valuable participants (MVPs) and win cool stuff? Here's a sampling of what you'll find:

DATABASES

Data drives everything.

Share information, exchange ideas, and discuss any database programming or administration issues.

INTERNET TECHNOLOGIES AND NETWORKING

Try living without plumbing (and eventually IPv6).

Talk about networking topics including protocols, design, administration, wireless, wired, storage, backup, certifications, trends, and new technologies.

JAVA

We've come a long way from the old Oak tree.

Hang out and discuss Java in whatever flavor you choose: J2SE, J2EE, J2ME, Jakarta, and so on.

MAC OS X

All about the Zen of OS X.

OS X is both the present and the future for Mac apps. Make suggestions, offer up ideas, or boast about your new hardware.

OPEN SOURCE

Source code is good; understanding (open) source is better.

Discuss open source technologies and related topics such as PHP, MySQL, Linux, Perl, Apache, Python, and more.

PROGRAMMING/BUSINESS

Unfortunately, it is.

Talk about the Apress line of books that cover software methodology, best practices, and how programmers interact with the "suits."

WEB DEVELOPMENT/DESIGN

Ugly doesn't cut it anymore, and CGI is absurd.

Help is in sight for your site. Find design solutions for your projects and get ideas for building an interactive Web site.

SECURITY

Lots of bad guys out there—the good guys need help.

Discuss computer and network security issues here. Just don't let anyone else know the answers!

TECHNOLOGY IN ACTION

Cool things. Fun things.

It's after hours. It's time to play. Whether you're into LEGO® MINDSTORMS™ or turning an old PC into a DVR, this is where technology turns into fun.

WINDOWS

No defenestration here.

Ask questions about all aspects of Windows programming, get help on Microsoft technologies covered in Apress books, or provide feedback on any Apress Windows book.

HOW TO PARTICIPATE:

Go to the Apress Forums site at **http://forums.apress.com/**.

Click the New User link.